# Neither Lady nor Slave

EDITED BY SUSANNA DELFINO & MICHELE GILLESPIE

# Neither *Lady* nor *Slave*

## Working Women of the Old South

THE UNIVERSITY OF NORTH CAROLINA PRESS

Chapel Hill and London

© 2002 The University of North Carolina Press
All rights reserved. Manufactured in the United States of America

Designed by Heidi Perov
Set in Garamond MT and Linotype Zapfino by Keystone Typesetting, Inc.

The paper in this book meets the guidelines for permanence and durability of the Committee
on Production Guidelines for Book Longevity of the Council on Library Resources.

• • •

LIBRARY OF CONGRESS CATALOGING-IN-PUBLICATION DATA

Neither lady nor slave : working women of the Old South /
edited by Susanna Delfino and Michele Gillespie.

p. cm.

Includes bibliographical references and index.

ISBN 0-8078-2735-5 (cloth : alk. paper)—ISBN 0-8078-5410-7 (pbk.: alk. paper)

1. Women—Southern States—History—19th century.

2. Women—Employment—Southern States—History—19th century.

3. Women employees—Southern States—History—19th century.

4. Working class women—Southern States—History—19th century.

I. Delfino, Susanna, 1949–  II. Gillespie, Michele.

HQ1438.S63 N445 2002

305.4'0975'09034—dc21

2002003436

cloth    06 05 04 03 02    5 4 3 2 1
paper    06 05 04 03 02    5 4 3 2 1

Sarah H. Hill, "Made by the Hands of Indians: Cherokee Women and Trade,"
was originally published in slightly different form in Sarah H. Hill, *Weaving New Worlds:
Southeastern Cherokee Women and Their Basketry* (Chapel Hill, N.C.: University of
North Carolina Press, 1997). Used by permission of the publisher.

Stephanie McCurry, "Producing Dependence: Women, Work, and Yeoman Households
in Low-Country South Carolina," was originally published in slightly different form in
Stephanie McCurry, *Masters of Small Worlds: Yeoman Households, Gender Relations, and the
Political Culture of the Antebellum South Carolina Low Country* (New York: Oxford
University Press, 1995). Used by permission of the publisher.

For Catherine Clinton

*Noi non potemo aver perfetta vita senza amici*

# Contents

# Tables

· · · · · · · · · · · · · · · · · · · · · · · · · · · · · · · · · ·

# Neither Lady nor Slave

# Introduction

We know too little about the lives of ordinary women in the Old South. We know even less about their working lives. Although the past two decades have witnessed an explosion of scholarship on southern women in the nineteenth century, much of this work has focused on the world of the plantation, where mistresses and slaves carried out an uneasy alliance under the eyes of the master. Women's historians began their inquiry into southern women's history by digging deeply into slaveholding women's lives, highlighting their subordination to husbands, fathers, and white men in general, even as they exposed the important benefits these women reaped by virtue of their class and race. More recently, equally exciting work has begun to appear on slave women. Much of this new research identifies the multiple hardships and tragedies slave women faced, even as it stresses the myriad ways these women established themselves as important historical actors.

Informed by these major developments in scholarship, *Neither Lady nor Slave*, a collection of thirteen essays, eleven of them original, two of them excerpted from award-winning books, pushes southern women's history in significant new directions by exploring ordinary women's working lives. The volume invites readers to rethink the conventional and limiting definition of worker as paid laborer (presumably in a factory). Although several of the essays examine women in these circumstances, many others deal with women whose work was unpaid even as they contributed substantially to their families' incomes. Thus, their work was unacknowledged, owing to prevailing cultural attitudes about women's proper public image in relation to class and race as well as to the developing social construction of man as breadwinner that accompanied the market revolution. The invisibility of some types of female work in relation to existing social norms constitutes another central theme of this collection. In this regard, the essays present an amazingly wide set of combinations of paid versus unpaid and officially visible versus invisible women's work. These complexities illuminate key considerations about class, race, and ethnicity, which shaped ideas and standards of social acceptability about which women could perform what jobs in the Old South. The essays also highlight the centrality of women's roles in developing strategies toward achieving a balance between personal independence—as represented by their involvement in the market economy—and the preservation of traditional spheres of authority—which only could be retained through service to their families and social respectability.

A sizable number of southern women performed jobs that were both paid and officially acknowledged. Their occupations, which ranged from those developing out of the gendered relegation of household duties (such as housekeeping, nursing, sewing, washing, and the like), to seamstressing for hire, to millwork, were traditionally deemed socially acceptable because of their cultural rooting in the pre-industrial economy. For this reason, they were not perceived as a threat to the existing male-dominated social order. However, women's agency again becomes apparent in these realms too. As this volume suggests, working women's actions in the slave South, as Victoria Bynum's fine work has amply demonstrated, produced multiple patterns of resistance and rebellion; the most mature and articulate expressions of which in our volume are probably offered by the textile mill workers.[1]

Thus this book encourages historians to broaden their view of southern women's history, a field that, with its emphasis on gender and race, now sits squarely at the center of antebellum southern studies. Unfortunately, however, southern women's history in the antebellum era currently reveals very little about the vast majority of southern women who resided beyond the plantation. By putting working women in all their diversity into the picture, as this book does, we can begin to show where and how class fits in relation to race and gender in the southern past. Building on work by such well-known scholars as Catherine Clinton, Elizabeth Fox-Genovese, and Suzanne Lebsock, this collection demonstrates that many women in the antebellum South—from free black nuns, to urban prostitutes, to Cherokee basket weavers, to female iron makers—participated in the developing marketplace in an impressive variety of ways, as wage earners and as entrepreneurs, regardless of traditional social expectations about gender and race.[2]

In this respect, the collection challenges those historians who have portrayed the Old South as a static, prebourgeois agricultural society inhabited by planters, slaves, and poor whites. This inadequate portrayal has stood in sharp contrast to the traditional depiction of the rest of the country as caught in the throes of capitalist transformation and the subsequent restructuring of class and gender. While scholars have lavished unparalleled attention on the movement of young, rural women to New England factories in the first half of the nineteenth century, the experiences and circumstances that shaped female work in southern factories have been largely neglected. However, recent historiography on American—and southern—industrialization has opened up new, significant venues for a reappraisal of southern economic and labor history as well.

Meanwhile, southern women's historians have performed an especially noteworthy service by exposing white men's construction of a sexual double standard that allowed them to depict slave women as highly sensual and therefore objects of their lust while simultaneously praising "southern ladies" for their gentility, piety, and virtue. But the danger of this body of work has been that it discouraged a closer analysis of southern women's lives. This collection makes clear that women's experiences in the Old South were profoundly circumscribed by labor—reproductive and productive, paid and unpaid—across age, class, race, place, and time.

Despite the southern lady ideal, which precluded manual work in all its forms, very few plantation mistresses escaped lives of duty, drudgery, and weighty responsibility. The ordinary planter's wife led a very demanding life, for she provided food, clothing, and care for an extended household comprised of family members and slaves. As pioneering southern women's scholar Anne Firor Scott has written, under these circumstances "there was nothing which was not her work."[3] Fox-Genovese's *Within the Plantation Household* presses this analysis further by recognizing the centrality of household production and its inherently gendered nature in shaping all southern social relations as well as economic ones that extended beyond the plantation to cities, commerce, law, and race relations.

If the world of the mistress was not necessarily one of ease and pleasure, and certainly had powerful consequences for the ordering of southern society as Fox-Genovese has argued, consider the slave woman's world on the opposite side of the social spectrum. Historians until relatively recently have assumed that slave women's lives were so profoundly shaped by backbreaking daily toil that closer scrutiny was unnecessary. Fortunately, the work of scholars like Jacqueline Jones, Deborah White, and Brenda Stevenson illustrates both the variety and the uniqueness of slave women's experiences as bonded laborers.[4]

Sandwiched between the tangled worlds of mistresses and slaves lived hundreds of thousands of women in the Old South. These women, white and black, have been largely left out of the historical record. The world in which these (ordinary) women lived—a world of white male supremacy—valued them almost exclusively in relation to their men. They were the wives and daughters of yeoman farmers, shopkeepers, and artisans, poor whites and professionals, slaveholders and nonslaveholders, and as such they inhabited a shadowy corner virtually invisible to the historian's eye.

This book moves these very same women into the spotlight. Although a handful of historians previously attempted to unveil the working lives of these women, their isolated efforts have been largely viewed as marginal and therefore insignificant. Only one such effort, Julia Cherry Spruill's *Women's Life and Work in the Southern Colonies* (1938), stands out, but it addresses the early history of the South, not the antebellum period, when capitalist transformation offered southern women new kinds of opportunities and new forms of independence. Another notable work covering the antebellum decades, Eleanor Boatwright's *Status of Women in Georgia, 1783–1860*, unfortunately refers to a single state.[5]

Over the course of the first half of the nineteenth century, slavery had begun to harden into a seemingly impenetrable institution even as the market revolution was reshaping the South's economic, political, and social life. The inevitable clash of slavery and industrial capitalism, which ultimately manifested itself in the shape of the Civil War, has occupied historians' attention for most of the twentieth century. What these same historians have overlooked is the degree to which ordinary women who entered the marketplace were often the harbingers of this incredible struggle. Scholars tracing capitalist transformation have focused their attention largely on the Northeast, where the growth of the market economy engendered a new entrepreneurial spirit even as it created a wage-earning working class. Production was moved out of the household and into the factory, forever altering the family economy and familial relationships. Women workers were at the forefront of this transformation.

Women's historians have been quick to point out the critical role women played in these developments. Laurel Thatcher Ulrich observed that Martha Ballard, the midwife of Hallowell, Maine, moved from spinning by herself, to hiring servant girls not only to spin but to weave cloth, and then to marketing her wares to the neighborhood in the space of a decade.[6] Like Ballard, myriad numbers of women embraced the new opportunities proffered by early changes in production from 1790 to 1820, despite the fact that such efforts almost always demanded double duty, for household work and household manufacturing were almost never linked. By the 1820s, increased demand for manufactured goods and advances in mechanization led to the creation of factories, making the short-lived putting-out system obsolete. The decline of household manufacturing had enormous implications for the evolution of women's work. Factories flooded markets with cheap goods previously the preserve of domestic industry so that women's role in the household economy became devalued and over time unseen and virtually ignored. Meanwhile, rural industries came to rely on female labor whose wage work was increasingly construed as a dependent and hence an inferior form of employment. Manhood by contrast was increasingly associated with economic independence and agency. Jeanne Boydston has argued that gender relationships in the household were transformed by the new gendered meanings attached to this radically altered work world.[7] The devaluation of women's work, whether paid or unpaid, continued unabated throughout the antebellum era. While women's visibility in the capitalist economy was increasing, their contributions to America's economic growth and development were undervalued, if not outright ignored. The triumph of the bourgeois ideal reinforced these realities as society assigned women the responsibility for raising morally upright children and protecting the family from the vicissitudes of the amoral capitalist world.

These conclusions about the impact of industrialization on women in antebellum America were based almost exclusively on case studies in the Northeast. At the same time, a number of scholars posed new questions about industrialization in the South and unearthed a considerable manufacturing sector in the antebellum period. This body of work, when viewed as a whole, establishes the existence of a viable industrial revolution under way in the Old South. The period was characterized by an entrepreneurial spirit in which individuals sought multiple avenues to the market revolution and in doing so set in motion a powerful upsurge in production that was the key to capitalist transformation. The wage work of southerners, and of southern women, was instrumental in that process.

This volume seeks to demonstrate southern women's critical role in the developing market economy as well as the multiple social and cultural changes produced by their participation. It is women's involvement in this evolution both as an economic concept and as a physical meeting place for exchange that stands as the cornerstone of this collection. On one hand, this book refrains from assuming any predetermined stage of economic development, thereby allowing the investigation of women's work in a variety of contexts and places, replete with their respective social and economic peculiarities. The essays take the reader from the urban realities of the Upper South, which was reminiscent of the urban North, to those unique realities of the Deep South, from the rural industrial settings of western North Carolina to the rural agricultural existence of the South Carolina yeomanry, from the cosmopolitan trade center that was New Orleans to the market exchange economy of the trans-Appalachian South. While these essays do not cover every single corner of the region, they do stand

as pioneering case studies that invite further scholarship in other places and
contexts in the region. Moreover, the authors in this volume have deliberately
chosen to emphasize the notion of "the market" to allow for the investigation of
women's participation in *all* kinds of economic activities. Throughout the antebellum South, white, black, and native women struggled and in many cases
succeeded in controlling the exchange and marketing of their own work, often-
times coming into contact with each other and creating new patterns of mutual
understanding and solidarity in the process.

Many of the essays in this volume speak to this interaction and in some cases
the new bonds that crossed the color line despite the white establishment's
insistence on the separation of the races. The pieces show that the introduction
of industrialization often literally blurred the color line, and thereby challenged,
if only implicitly, the construction of racial difference. These changing color
lines could both enhance and diminish white and black women's roles depending on the context. Thus the essays delve into the implications of women's work
for challenging and reshaping social expectations about race, class, and gender
relations in general and thereby underline the frequently overlooked rich mosaic
that comprised the social world of the antebellum South. Because the volume
pays attention to gender, status, age, nativity, skills, race, and class, as well as
shifting patterns of employment across the antebellum period, it offers a dynamic portrait of a labor market shaped by changing economic variables and
cultural attitudes.

The first section of the collection examines some of the ways in which the
coming of the market economy affected rural women. Stephanie McCurry
shows how women in yeoman households not only performed the kinds of field
labor associated with slaves but were relegated by their husbands and fathers to
a dependent status within a set of social hierarchies that included slavery. Yeomen kept their wives and daughters on the margins of the market economy and
thereby restricted their freedom and experiences in significant ways. Two essays
on Native American women remind readers not only about the increasing
intrusiveness of market forces but about the multi-ethnic nature of women's
work in the antebellum South as well. James Taylor Carson demonstrates Native
American women's gradual but increasingly critical involvement in the market
economy throughout the Southeast. He documents the skillful way Cherokee,
Choctaw, Chickasaw, and Creek women took advantage of new market opportunities without yielding to the allure of profit making, constantly reasserting
their established prerogatives within the bounds of their traditional cultures.
Sarah H. Hill looks at the history of Cherokee women's basket weaving and

more specifically at how these women adapted this craft tradition to the commercial economy that had begun to intrude upon their world by the early nineteenth century. She, too, documents the balanced approach that women weavers adopted in an effort to preserve their values despite the market's press to unravel them.

The second section of the book examines cases of wage-earning women in the urban South. Timothy J. Lockley opens the section by arguing that despite the very real social confines women experienced in the Old South, informal exchanges of goods and services offered ordinary women in Savannah, whether white or black, slave or free, ways to secure personal and financial independence from both men and masters. Both Lockley and Stephanie Cole, in her essay on hiring practices of nannies and governesses, have found that indifference to color preferences for nurses and governesses in the deep South in Savannah and in border state cities gave way to a real preference for hiring white women as nurses. This development suggests the permeability of southern culture to new, bourgeois theories about child-rearing as well as white southern women's incipient assumptions about the superiority of the middle class and the white race. Two other essayists build important new bridges in southern history by pressing us to pay attention to the border states to better view the impact of the market revolution on women in places with a more diversified economy than the Deep South. In her essay, Barbara J. Howe uncovers the amazing variety of wage work women performed in western Virginia towns and cities, while E. Susan Barber, in her piece on prostitutes in Richmond, indicates that factors such as age and skill, rather than race or nativity, may have been more important in determining some women's occupations. These findings hint at the possibility for mutual understanding between races and classes. Regardless, these admittedly very different kinds of women wage earners secured an important measure of independence and self-determination from their identity as workers. The examples described by Howe and Barber represent two extremes in women's work realities: the former being socially and officially acceptable, the latter publicly known but deemed unworthy of official recognition.

In sharp contrast to the opportunities urban women experienced in the changing market economy of the South, the essays in the third section of the book examine the constraints placed on middle-class southern women and how they fought them. Emily Bingham and Penny Richards, for example, investigate social expectations surrounding the Mordecai women's roles as educators and how they managed to carve out a modicum of independence and identity for themselves despite social expectations about their sex and class. Their essay

demonstrates yet another important theme in this volume, the surprising reach
of the market.

Even women belonging to religious orders in the South were not immune to
the demands of the encroaching market, which could be both beneficial and
dangerous to them depending on their circumstances. The two other intriguing
essays in this section highlight the inventive approaches that urban nuns, black
and white, in Baltimore and New Orleans, were forced to pursue in order to
support themselves and their church in the antebellum era. Diane Batts Morrow
uncovers the disciplined economic philosophy of the free black Oblate Sisters
in Baltimore and ties this philosophy to their faith and their race. These black
Catholic women found themselves limited both in their attainment of personal
economic security and the means to achieve it according to the Catholic Church
and its stance on gender, race, and slavery. Emily Clark shows the difficult road
the New Orleans Ursulines traveled to support themselves and their community, including their ambivalence about relying on slave labor. Whether under
the French, Spanish, or Anglo-American government, these white Catholic
nuns were able to exploit accepted economic practices and transactions to give a
practical underpinning to their own moral imperatives about race and slavery.
The peculiar position of these women religious, as well as the scope of their
agency, seem to hint at one intriguing facet of their place within southern society
in that their noninvolvement in typical sex and gender relations did not require
strict definition of their social role and behavior.

The final section of the volume examines women's emergence as an important component of the free labor force in the antebellum South. Scholars of
American industrialization have long pointed to women's critical role as a pro-
tolabor force in northern manufactories. On one hand, the essays in this volume
clearly show that women's participation in southern businesses and industries in
many respects paralleled developments in the North. On the other hand, they
make it exceptionally clear that race, region, the rural, staple-producing economy, and the distinctive culture and ideology of the Old South gave female
labor-force participation in this region a series of unique twists. Two of these
essays focus on the early textile industry and suggest that the theft of wage-
earning women's gendered identity and the emergence of a tradition of strong
female resistance occurred long before the twentieth century. Well-known
southern labor historian Bess Beatty examines women textile workers' experiences and responses throughout the antebellum South, including their efforts at
resistance and protest. She challenges the widespread contention that cotton

mill workers were mainly destitute women. On the contrary, she suggests, many of the women who entered the factory were unencumbered by subsistence worries, thereby challenging the traditional assumption that manual work was viewed as degrading in the Old South. In contrast, Michele Gillespie looks at the defeminization of white women who were hired by the fledgling textile industry in Georgia and put to work alongside slave women. Her work also offers important insights on interracial relations in the factory setting. Finally, Susanna Delfino traces the shadowy presence of women workers in the Upper South's iron and mining industries. Her work indicates the extreme adaptability of female labor in industries generally viewed as male-only enclaves, once more demonstrating the impact of social judgment on the official visibility of women's occupations.

While the subject matter and approach differ widely in these essays, each of the thirteen contributors is committed to the development of working women in the antebellum South as a significant field of historical inquiry. To this end, *Neither Lady nor Slave* marks an important starting point for a true recovery of southern women's work experiences, especially as wage-earning workers and entrepreneurs, in all their variety. The subjects of all of these essays are fascinating women who have been largely left out of the historical record. The methodologies the authors employ to examine these women's lives are consistently innovative and in some cases pathbreaking. In fact, most of the essays in this collection strongly suggest that southern working women before the Civil War, across all their differences, resisted and in some cases rebelled against their unique social, cultural, and economic situations. In different circumstances, these more subtle challenges might have given rise to new forms of organization and labor, as was happening in the North.

This volume marks only the beginning of a serious attempt to reconstruct female participation in the workforce in the Old South. Achieving this end will be no mean feat as each of the authors points to a daunting dearth of sources and the need for thoughtful, imaginative readings enlarged by context, given the few sources that remain extant. While ordinary women in all their diversity served as critical actors in the South's transformation to a capitalist economy, their presence was taken for granted and in many cases deemed unworthy of description or quantification. It is this reality that will continue to haunt as well as challenge investigators as they begin seriously to pursue women's role in the market revolution in the South. These difficulties notwithstanding, we hope that this volume raises as many questions as it answers. We invite scholars to continue to closely analyze the complicated relationship between culture and political economy and how that relationship shaped women workers' perceptions about themselves and their society. We hope future scholars will continue to ask how race, class, age, ethnicity, and nativity, along with political culture and economic opportunity, shaped the motives and perspectives of individual women workers over place and time, just as we hope scholars will examine more closely the relationship between women's reproductive and productive lives and ask how family fits into these newly emergent work relations. And there are many other new paths to pursue as well. How was women's morality affected by the transition to a capitalist economy? How and under what circumstances did women resist oppressive working conditions? And how does racial identity and the institution of slavery reflect all these realities? Most of all, we hope that future historians will not only respect but contribute to the multiplicity of working women's voices and experiences in the antebellum South and the history of the South as a whole. In this way we can begin to uncover the origins of the southern working class in all its variety.

Putting this essay collection together has been a labor of love despite the considerable distance between the editors (an entire ocean) and the unanticipated length of time it has taken to complete. We think our book is better for these two key realities, however, and we certainly know our fondness for each other, as well as our respect for each other's ideas, has only grown over the course of our collaboration. We are also especially appreciative of our contributors, each of whom is an impressive scholar in his or her right, and a consummate professional. We could not have asked for a better set of colleagues to work with, and we are grateful for their commitment to this project. The idea for this volume grew out of an exciting conversation between Catherine Clinton, Stephanie Cole, and Susanna Delfino at the Southern Historical Association meeting in 1996. We will always be grateful to Catherine and Stephanie for their initial enthusiastic imaginings about this project. Catherine deserves special kudos for bringing us together as coeditors, conceiving the title, offering critical suggestions and supporting us in so many integral ways throughout the process, and for being our dear friend, hence the dedication of this book. Neither of us knows what we would do without her.

We are especially grateful for the impressive support we have received from the fine staff at the University of North Carolina Press. Charles Grench not only was enthusiastic about this project from the time it first arrived on his desk but paid close attention to its development right up to its actual publication. Assistant editors Ruth Homrighaus and Amanda McMillan were consummate professionals as well as champions of the volume. We also thank Mary Caviness for her outstanding copyediting. This book has been a truly collaborative effort in all the best senses of the word.

Michele Gillespie and Susanna Delfino

. . .

I would also like to thank the many people in my life that gave so generously of their time and energy to complete this project. At Agnes Scott College, Amy Whitworth was an unfailingly wonderful assistant in all respects. Cynthia Hall, student researcher, never lost her zeal or sense of humor throughout her work. At Wake Forest University, Janice Walker and Linda Dunlap typed essays quickly and expertly at zero hour and gave fine advice along the way. As editors, Susanna and I depended enormously on their talents. My husband, Kevin, and sons, Michael Thomas and Matthew Colin (who arrived in the middle of this project), have grown accustomed to "mommy's work" and the way it overshadows so much of our lives together. They are always unstinting with their love and affection nonetheless and deserve much love and many thanks in return.

Michele Gillespie

. . .

I wish to express unending gratitude to my wonderful family. My husband, Bruno, my mother, Eleonora, and my sisters, Patrizia and Daniela, never failed me their loving understanding and unfaltering support even during the hardest time for us all, which occurred at a critical moment in the preparation of this volume. My father, Rinaldo, would have been proud to see it completed. To his memory I also ideally dedicate this work, as a daughter and a woman.

Susanna Delfino

### NOTES

1. Victoria Bynum, *Unruly Women: The Politics of Social and Sexual Control in the Old South* (Chapel Hill: University of North Carolina Press, 1992).

2. Catherine Clinton, *The Plantation Mistress: Woman's World in the Old South* (New York: Pantheon Books, 1982); Suzanne Lebsock, *The Free Women of Petersburg: Status and Culture in a Southern Town, 1784–1860* (New York: W. W. Norton, 1984); Elizabeth Fox-Genovese,

*Within the Plantation Household: Black and White Women of the Old South* (Chapel Hill: University of North Carolina Press, 1988).

3. Anne Firor Scott, *The Southern Lady: From Pedestal to Politics, 1830–1930* (Chicago: University of Chicago Press, 1970).

4. Jacqueline Jones, *Labor of Love, Labor of Sorrow: Black Women, Work, and the Family from Slavery to the Present* (New York: Basic Books, 1985); Deborah Gray White, *Ar'n't I a Woman? Female Slaves in the Plantation South* (New York: W. W. Norton, 1985); Brenda E. Stevenson, *Life in Black and White: Family and Community in the Slave South* (New York: Oxford University Press, 1996).

5. Julia Cherry Spruill, *Women's Life and Work in the Southern Colonies* (Chapel Hill: University of North Carolina Press, 1938); Eleanor Miot Boatwright, *Status of Women in Georgia, 1783–1860* (New York: Carlson Publishers, 1994).

6. Laurel Thatcher Ulrich, *A Midwife's Tale: The Life of Martha Ballard, 1785–1812* (New York: Knopf, 1990).

7. Jeanne Boydston, *Home and Work: Housework, Wages, and the Ideology of Labor in the Early Republic* (New York: Oxford University Press, 1990).

. . . . . . . . . . . . . . . . . . . . . . . . . . . . . . . . . . . . . . .

# Part One

# The Rural World and the Coming
# of the Market Economy

# Chapter One

# Dollars Never Fail to Melt Their Hearts:
# Native Women and the Market Revolution

JAMES TAYLOR CARSON

In the spring and summer of 1797, Louis-Phillipe, Duke of Orleans and heir to the French throne, fled the violence of the French Revolution for the hustle and bustle of the New Republic. During his tour of the United States, he and his fellow exiles visited the big cities of the Northeast, the small towns of the West, and, most remarkably of all, the Cherokees of East Tennessee. The duke wrote down much of what he saw, and among the several things that struck him as either odd or novel about Cherokee culture was the allegedly amorous proclivities of the women. He compared their sureness in matters of the flesh to the women of his homeland, but the apparent commonplaceness of prostitution in the Cherokee towns shocked his otherwise open mind. "[A]ll Cherokee women," Louis-Phillipe reported, "are public women in the full meaning of the phrase: dollars never fail to melt their hearts."[1]

The love of the dollar that the duke noted was linked to the particular sexual and hospitality mores of Cherokee women that predated contact with Europeans as well as to the inroads that new forms of economic production and exchange were making among the towns and households of the native South in the late eighteenth and early nineteenth centuries. For the most part, native women lived and worked beyond the gaze of the settlers, the officials, and the missionaries who created the historical record ethnohistorians use to study the past. They also left very few documents of their own. But when native women appear in diaries, letters, and papers, it is clear that the market revolution challenged older modes of production and exchange and introduced new demands, new forms of exchange, and new forms of household production.

Scholars who have studied native women and the market revolution generally have characterized the changes that resulted in their lives as deleterious and degrading. The switch from household subsistence production to production for sale in a money economy not only subjugated native women to an alien economic order, some have argued, but also eroded their self-sufficiency, influence, and power within their own societies.[2] To be sure, the economic changes that accompanied the market revolution of the early nineteenth century impinged upon women's self-sufficiency and power. Creeping capitalism also introduced to native people the style and substance of the class system that structured southern settler society. Before the federal government removed the southern First Nations in the 1830s, such economic inroads introduced to native people notions of consumerism and class but failed to overturn wholly older forms of inherited and earned status. As long as native women maintained control over their homes and families, the means of production, buying, selling, and trading, they were able to retain the cultural, social, and political rights and responsibilities that had defined them as women long before Europeans had set foot in North America. Finding a balance between material innovation and cultural conservation constituted the central theme of their working lives.

The basic patterns of native women's working lives had been set several centuries before contact. By 1000 B.C., women in some parts of the South had domesticated a variety of wild plants, which they added to the nuts, berries, roots, and fruits that they gathered to complement the meat procured by the men who hunted.[3] The introduction of corn to the South between A.D. 700 and 900 enabled women to assume an even more important role in the economy. They raised the large quantities of food that fueled the formation of the great Mississippian societies that covered the region on the eve of contact. With the development of horticulture, women replaced the old hunting and gathering subsistence economy with a form of production that met the societies' subsistence needs while also providing a surplus that could be stored for future use.[4]

Stories told by the descendants of the Mississippians and other early peoples placed women, corn, and farming at the center of their lives. According to the Cherokees, corn came from their ancestral mother, Selu, and was passed on to them through the shedding of her blood. Choctaw elders told children the story of a crow that flew up from the south and dropped a small grain at the feet of a little girl. "What is this?" the girl asked. "Corn," replied the mother. The Creeks believed that corn came to them in the guise of an old woman, and that "if it is not treated well it will become angry."[5]

It is not altogether clear how men and women in Mississippian societies partitioned economic and political power. Because of their association with warfare and diplomacy, men controlled relations with outsiders and dominated political offices. Vested with the official power to make decisions on behalf of the communities that they represented, men held what scholars have defined as "authority." Women lacked access to such formal expressions of power, but through the institutions of the clans and the households, women were able to enjoy the "influence" that came with the control of land, property, and children.[6] There were, nevertheless, important exceptions that suggest women's exercise of power was more complex than notions of either authority or influence allow. Early reports of Spanish explorers, for example, make clear that women governed some Mississippian chiefdoms. The Lady of Cofitechequi attempted to enlist Hernando de Soto as a military ally in 1540. Some years later, Juan Pardo met the female chief of Guatari in the piedmont of present-day North Carolina. Female leadership may not have been common in the Mississippian South, but it is reasonable to conclude that women could exercise considerable authority as well as influence.[7]

European colonization of the South introduced to Mississippians many things that shaped the way native women lived and worked. First and foremost were lethal Old World diseases like smallpox, measles, and influenza that decimated the region's population and brought a quick end to the Mississippian societies. In the aftermath of the demographic collapse, remnant groups clustered into new social groupings that shared certain Mississippian cultural features but that held identities wholly distinct from the earlier societies. In the Lower Mississippi River valley, remnants coalesced into groups that French and English traders called the Choctaws, who, in 1700, numbered approximately twenty-one thousand, and the Chickasaws, who had a population of nearly five thousand. In present-day Georgia and Alabama, the same process produced the roughly nine thousand Creeks. Future infusions of other remnant groups augmented the Creek population throughout the eighteenth century. In the Appalachians, new groups infiltrated the fertile valleys, merged with the people who had survived contact, and formed the original sixteen or so thousand Cherokees.[8]

Equally important to the changing world in which native women lived were new flora, like peach trees and cotton plants, and new fauna, like poultry, cattle, and horses, that the Europeans had brought with them. When women adopted new plants and animals, they enhanced their ability to feed their families and their towns and to trade with the newcomers. Without forsaking the cultivation of aboriginal crops like corn, squash, and beans, the manufacture of pottery, and the weaving of cloth spun from plant fibers, women began in the 1730s to raise chickens and hogs, to use brass kettles and glass bottles, to sew clothing from European strouds, and to trade their produce to the skin traders who frequented their towns in order to cover the cost of the goods they purchased. By the late 1700s, women had become thoroughly enmeshed in the frontier exchange economy, a trade in foodstuffs, household items, and personal services that linked native people and colonists in economic relationships beyond the oversight of the imperial governments.[9]

Over time a new interest in profit challenged ancient traditions of hospitality and reciprocity that had previously conditioned women's behavior toward outsiders who came into their towns and homes. Cherokee women, for example, sought to make the English garrison at Fort Loudon dependent on them for supplies of corn and other fruits and vegetables. One woman in particular, Nancy Butler, worked for the soldiers as a purchasing agent.[10] Choctaw women as well provisioned military men stationed in their midst. "We began our Traffic for Provisions," one soldier reported, "with the Women, who for Paint and Beads gave us Fowls, Eggs, [and] Indian Corn."[11] Another visitor to the Choctaws remarked that the women carried on a lively trade in pigs and chickens and that they "carried the spirit of husbandry so far as to cultivate leeks, garlic, cabbage and some other garden plants, of which they make no use, in order to make profit of them to the traders."[12]

The frontier exchange economy created a tension between the traditional ethic of reciprocity by which native women had welcomed visitors with gifts of food and shelter and the novel idea of profit. Market possibilities that grew out of hospitality triggered women's departure from a subsistence-surplus economy toward a market economy. For the transition from a subsistence-surplus economy to a market economy to occur, economic activity had to be separated from the cultural moorings that tie production to gender roles and other cultural imperatives, and it had to begin to be replaced by alien ideas like price and profit. Southern native women never completed the transformation before their removal in the 1830s. Instead, they created what one historian has called a marketplace economy, an economy where cash, credit, and surplus production coexisted with the particular cultural conventions of the indigenous precontact economy.[13] By the middle of the eighteenth century, native women had begun to value market-oriented production and exchange, but they still looked to their cultures instead of to their markets for their identities as women, mothers, daughters, and farmers.

What changed was their power as women relative to the power of their sons and husbands in the postcontact South. The ambiguous mixture of authority and influence enjoyed by native women in Mississippian times survived well into the eighteenth century but diminished in the face of the deerskin trade and colonial warfare. Among the Creeks, "Beloved Women," who belonged to the most prestigious clans, weighed in on discussions of government and diplomacy.[14] The Cherokees, too, had "Beloved Women."[15] Captain Henry Timberlake likened them to "Amazons," and trader James Adair marveled at what he described as their "petticoat government."[16] The extent of Cherokee women's power is, however, a subject of some debate. Anthropologist Raymond Fogelson has characterized their power as one of indirect influence on brothers, sons, and clan members. In contrast, historian Theda Perdue has attributed to Cherokee women a much more direct role in government and diplomacy. From deciding the fate of war captives, to exchanging wampum belts with Seneca women, to adjudicating infractions of certain cultural rules, it is clear, Perdue argues, that Cherokee women exerted an important influence in the home as well as in the council house.[17] Choctaw women, like their Cherokee counterparts, also made decisions regarding war captives, and their oral tradition attributed a great deal of importance to a female chief named Ohoyao Minko.[18] By the latter decades of the 1700s, however, women's power seems to have diminished, becoming, in the words of one historian, "almost negligible."[19] The deerskin trade and the colonial system of client warfare had put more and more economic and political authority into the hands of male hunters and warriors, which may have circumvented traditional avenues of female power and transformed it from fact to rumor. "I never heard of, or knew of," naturalist William Bartram wrote in the 1770s, "any late instances of the female sex bearing rule or presiding either in council or the field, but according to report, the Cherokees & Cricks [*sic*] can boast of their Semiramis's [*sic*], Zenobeas, & Cleopatra's [*sic*]."[20]

Although their power may have decreased over the seventeenth and eighteenth centuries, the early nineteenth century was a world where farming replaced deer hunting and warring as the economic mainstays of the South's First Nations. Women stood at the forefront of the new economy, and as they adopted new agricultural products and livestock and new technologies, they reinvigorated traditional gender roles and responsibilities. Nowhere is this more clear than in their relationship to livestock because men, not women, had always shared a deeply spiritual relationship with animals. But because chickens, pigs, cattle, and horses were animals associated with farming and domestication as well as the forest and hunting, women incorporated them into their household economies.[21] The profusion of European animals on native farms struck visitors to the South. During a trip among the Cherokee towns, federal agent Benjamin Hawkins passed two women on horseback who were driving their cattle to market. Among the Creeks, economic innovation may have been tied to political power, for the "Queen of Tuckabatche" possessed a "fine stock of cattle." Creek and Cherokee women also began to supplement their daily diet with milk, cheese, and butter.[22] The Chickasaws raised "plenty of hogs and cattle." Beef and pork, wrote their federal agent, were two of their most important "articles for exportation."[23] Choctaw parents gave daughters and sons and nieces and nephews a cow and calf, a sow and piglet, and a mare and colt, so that as the children grew older they would, upon marriage, have a sizable herd.[24] "These people," one observer remarked, "have stocks of horses, cattle, hogs, etc. some of them have *large* stocks, and appear to live plentifully."[25]

Raising and selling livestock were important to women, but horticulture still occupied the bulk of female labor in the early nineteenth century. Female farmers adopted the profit motive that had come with colonization. Disappointed by the lack of hospitality he witnessed during his tour of the South, Englishman Adam Hodgson remarked of Creek women, "A desire of gain, caught from the whites, has chilled their liberality."[26] While staying overnight at an inn in the Creek nation, Hodgson noted several women who sold chickens and corn to travelers. Judging from the amount of silver jewelry they wore, business must have been brisk.[27] Benjamin Henry Latrobe likewise deplored the dearth of free food and accommodation in native towns. "Hospitality exists everywhere food cannot be bought or sold," he wrote of his trip through the Choctaw towns along the Natchez Trace, "[but] a good market in the neighbourhood always puts an end to it."[28] "[A]lmost every Indian we passed had something to sell," remembered the Reverend Jacob Young of his trip down the trace, "especially corn at two dollars per bushel, corn blades at a bit, [and] pumpkins for a quarter."[29] Cherokee women provisioned travelers as well, but unlike their counterparts in the other nations, they also exported their crop surpluses. Wagons laden with corn bound for American settlements were common sights. One chief believed that because market prices for Cherokee produce were so high the women were reluctant to devote energy to anything else.[30]

Despite the success of some native women in the marketplace economy, the federal government believed that they were impoverished and doomed to extinction. In order to save them from such a fate, federal officials crafted a plan to introduce settler ways of life to native men and women. First, federal agents would be sent among the various tribes to teach men how to farm and to own private property and to take women out of the fields and to put them in the home. Second, if native families could be confined to small private farms, policymakers reasoned that they would cede their surplus land to the federal government for sale to settlers. Assimilation, the ultimate goal of the "civilization" policy, proved illusive, but the federal government acquired native land through a number of treaties negotiated between the government and the southern First Nations in the 1810s and 1820s.[31]

Native men and women worked out their own compromises to the civilization policy. Among the Creeks, Cherokees, Choctaws, and Chickasaws men began to farm, but they relied on slaves to labor for them in the fields so that they did not violate their cultures' proscriptions that forbade them from farming.[32] Cherokee men and women struck a deal whereby men plowed fields with horse-drawn ploughs and helped the women to sow seed, but women continued to tend and harvest the crops.[33] Choctaw women, however, resisted attempts to transform their gender roles. When the wife of an American trader urged a woman she had hired to weed her garden to put her son to work as well, the woman replied, "Would you have me make a woman of my son? He is to be a man and a warrior & he is not going to work like a woman!"[34] As long as little boys grew up to be warriors, the Choctaw woman knew, women could remain farmers.

Federal agents enjoyed little success in completely overturning native gender roles in horticulture, but they made substantial gains introducing to women other ways to make a living. Benjamin Hawkins was by far the most influential of the various men appointed to oversee the implementation of the "civilization" policy in the South. Stationed among the Creeks, Hawkins distributed cotton seed and handed out cotton cards, spinning wheels, and looms. More important, he and a weaver he had hired taught women how to spin cotton fibers into thread, which could be woven into cloth.[35] Creek men resented the agent's plan. "[T]hey are," Hawkins wrote, "apprehensive that the women by being able to clothe themselves will become independent and compell [*sic*] the men to help them in their labour."[36] The women were nevertheless overjoyed at the spinning and weaving skills Hawkins had taught them. In 1798, two of the weaver's pupils provided Hawkins with fifty yards of fine cloth. Private individuals soon took advantage of the women's new skills. One Scottish planter set up a shop in which eleven women worked five wheels and one loom, and an Irishman established a business that employed slaves and Creek women to turn out yards of cloth. In a demonstration of just how far they had moved from the imperatives of a subsistence-surplus economy to a marketplace one, some Creek women reinvested their profits, buying hogs and cattle with the money they earned from cloth sales.[37] Indeed, the desire for more cards, wheels, and looms led several women to pressure the male chiefs to demand more supplies from the federal government. "Our women have told us to come to you," explained the chiefs of Coosa and seven other towns to Hawkins, "and beg you to give them some wheels and cards and they will give us clothes."[38] Similar pressures may have been behind the chiefs' demand for one thousand spinning wheels in exchange for giving the federal government permission to build a road through the nation.[39] Cherokee women had heard Hawkins's implicit message of economic independence, and they promised him that "they were willing to labour if they could be directed how to profit by it."[40] The cloth economy took off rapidly with the help of missionaries from the Boston-based American Board of Commissioners for Foreign Missions, which set up schools to teach young girls how to spin and weave. Between 1810 and 1826, Cherokee women increased the number of looms and spinning wheels in their homes from 467 to 762 and from 1,600 to 2,488, respectively.[41] According to the missionaries, by the 1820s, women's capacity to provide clothing for their families equaled or bettered settler women's.[42] The plan introduced by Hawkins and overseen by the American Board missionaries and by Cherokee agent Silas Dinsmoor had worked. As one Cherokee chief recollected, "When Mr. Dinsmoor . . . spoke to us on the subject, about fifteen years ago, many of us thought it was only some refined scheme calculated to gain an influence over us. . . . He then addressed our women, and presented them with cotton seeds for planting. . . . They acquired the use of them with great facility, and now most of the clothes we wear are of their manufacture."[43]

Cotton cultivation and weaving made similar inroads among the Choctaws. In December 1801, a prominent chief requested that the federal government send weavers to the Choctaw towns to teach women how to spin thread and weave cloth. One year later, twelve families had begun to produce homespun cloth, and, thanks to the efforts of agents like John McKee and regular requests by chiefs for weeding hoes, cotton cards, and other necessary tools, the cotton economy took off.[44] In 1820, one federal investigator reported that women had spun and woven ten thousand yards of cloth.[45] According to Stephen Ward, the federal subagent, they produced such surpluses that they sold cloth regularly to travelers on the Natchez Trace.[46]

Chickasaw women were equally avid weavers but less committed to market-place economics than either Creek, Cherokee, or Choctaw women. In 1800, a chief requested Agent Samuel Mitchell to hire a weaver to teach women how to make clothing. By the 1810s, chiefs complained to the federal government that the supply of cotton cards and spinning wheels was insufficient to keep up with production. By 1830, most Chickasaw females knew how to make cloth, and families proudly wore their finest homemade clothes to council meetings and when they went shopping in the American settlements.[47] As sellers, however, Chickasaw women seem to have lacked the acquisitive drive that motivated Choctaw, Creek, and Cherokee women. Preferring to conserve the subsistence-surplus values of their culture, as soon as Chickasaw women earned enough money from weaving to satisfy their needs, "they converted their wheels," their agent reported, "into *play things for their children* and their looms into hen roosts."[48]

For women unable or unwilling to learn how to grow, spin, or weave cotton, other opportunities existed in the American plantation economy that surrounded their towns. In fact, picking cotton on plantations enabled hundreds if not thousands of women to move with their husbands during the hunting season and to preserve to a degree the seasonal lifestyle that had characterized life before contact. Planters near the Creek and Choctaw towns were quick to hire women to augment their slave forces. One man paid Creek women a half pint of salt or some beads for every bushel basket they filled with cotton. For two baskets, women could earn a bottle of tafia, rum diluted with water. On average, the women picked two to three baskets a day. Other landowners paid cash wages, and although few believed Creek and Choctaw women worked as well as slave women, without them, one planter's wife remarked, they would not have been able to harvest the large volume of crops that they planted year after year.[49]

Some Creek or Choctaw women worked alongside slaves, but other native women owned them. Outside of the home, slaves were important markers of status. Theda Perdue has shown that chattel slavery initiated among the Cherokees the formation of social classes akin to those that characterized southern settler society and that coexisted in uneasy tension with traditional social divisions. Although the vast majority of Creeks did not own slaves, Kathryn Holland Braund and Claudio Saunt have argued as well that a small slaveholding elite emerged and imbibed the racist and classist notions that characterized settler society. It is reasonable to suspect the same also could be said for the Chickasaws, but among the Choctaws, social divisions that predated contact, like kin and clan, remained at least as influential as newer ideas of class and status.[50]

Prestige goods, like slaves, had long been indicators of status among the native inhabitants of the South. Mississippian chiefs wore copper breastplates and exotic shells, and chiefs in the colonial era brandished silver gorgets, military coats, flags, and swords as emblems of their economic power and chiefly authority. Women wore other markers like beads, jewelry, and cloth. The profits they earned in the marketplace economy enabled them to perpetuate older social categories as well as to generate newer class sensibilities. The women associated with Creek chief William McIntosh represented the fullest elaboration of the female prestige-goods system in both its indigenous and its settler forms. Susanah McIntosh, one of William McIntosh's wives, owned more jewelry than any poultry vendor Adam Hodgson had ever seen—fifteen pairs of silver earrings, two pairs of gold earrings, and twenty-four silver breastplates. She was equally conspicuous in terms of settler fashion given her predilection for silk and cashmere shawls and fine china. Her wealth, however, was not a function of dependence on her husband. She earned it from her considerable farm that was home to fifty-seven hogs, eleven cows and calves, and five steers. Louisa McIntosh was even wealthier. At one time she owned twenty pairs of silver earrings, thirty silver broaches, three spinning wheels, tools, a farm, forty chickens, thirty acres of corn, one hundred head of cattle, one hundred thirty hogs, four horses, and eight slaves. The wealth that such women could command was formidable and engendered serious resistance among Creeks who resented some women's ability to adapt and prosper in the marketplace economy.[51]

As far as can be seen, native women conducted marketplace transactions in cash as well as in kind. Only rarely were women able to obtain credit for their own purchasing power or for their own profit. One of the first of the South's native female entrepreneurs was Sophia Durant, the eldest sister of Creek chief Alexander McGillivray. While her slaves worked for themselves on her ramshackle plantation, she brokered trade between Creeks and Panton, Leslie and Company, a trading firm based in Spanish Pensacola. When Agent Hawkins met her in 1796, her business was apparently dwindling because she had exhausted her credit.[52] A Choctaw named Molly McDonald also made a go at credit purchasing. In the 1820s, she bought a male slave from some traders and made regular payments amounting to seven-eighths of the original purchase price. Because her creditors had specified no particular time for the total repayment, McDonald was shocked one morning to find the men on her doorstep demanding the final installment. Unable to pay and lacking any documentary proof of the purchase, Molly watched the men repossess the slave without returning any of her hard-earned savings. Her son James was furious, and in a letter to Secretary of War John C. Calhoun he asked, "How is a Choctaw to obtain redress, when he is debarred, by the statutes of Mississippi from giving his testimony in a court of justice?"[53] Lack of basic legal protections for native people in all of the southern states made any credit arrangements precarious.

One Cherokee woman, Elizabeth Pack, was thoroughly enmeshed in the paper economy. In 1826, John McGowan purchased on credit from Pack a slave woman and child. Lacking any legal standing in the United States, she entrusted McGowan with a set of notes worth $2,680 and asked him to redeem them for her. When Pack refused to share the proceeds of the notes with McGowan, he absconded with the slaves and eight of her cattle to Georgia, where he mortgaged the slaves to a man named Cunningham. When Cunningham pressed McGowan for payment, McGowan took the slaves and the purloined cattle back into the Cherokee nation beyond the reach of the Georgia courts. It was a bad move on McGowan's part because in the Cherokee nation Pack had legal standing and a well-established claim to the slaves and to the cattle, so she called the Lighthorse, the Cherokee national police force, to apprehend McGowan and to confiscate her property. With the tables turned against him, McGowan turned to the federal agent Hugh Montgomery, who found in his favor. Unable to compel Elizabeth Pack to pay him his proceeds from the redeemed notes, he demanded that Montgomery compensate him.[54] How many other women were engaged in such complicated financial transactions is difficult to say, but the credit nexus of the market revolution was not wholly out of the reach of native women.

Regardless of the variety of strategies native women undertook to make a living in the antebellum South, one thing linked the wealthiest slave mistress to the poorest potter woman; they continued to own their property separately from men, and most native men and federal agents recognized their property rights. Benjamin Hawkins, for example, warned settler men who were anxious to marry Creek women that the women were "in the habit of assuming and exercising absolute rule" over their children and their property.[55] Similarly, the Cherokee national council stipulated that if a woman married a settler, "the property of the woman so married shall not be subject to the disposal of her husband, contrary to her consent."[56] The Chickasaws as well continued to respect the long-standing rule.[57] Such arrangements assured native women that they could continue to control the production and the sale of their products in the market revolution in spite of the "civilization" program and without being trodden underfoot by their settler husbands, by their chiefs, and by agents of the federal government.

The ability of Chickasaw, Choctaw, Creek, and Cherokee women to prosper and to participate so fully in the market revolution without losing their responsibilities for production and their rights to property was, nevertheless, conditioned by their historically ambivalent relationship to the kinds of formal political authority like treaty councils that Europeans had taken to be the seats of native sovereignty. The formal circumscription of women's power in the aftermath of colonization was most systemic in the Cherokee republic founded in 1827. The planters and chiefs who sat on the national council passed a series of laws intended to abrogate matrilineal clan responsibilities and to shift inheritance from the mother's line to the father's line. The government also reserved political offices and seats on the national bench for men.[58] The first constitutional Choctaw government likewise sought to replace the judicial functions of the matrilineal clans with a national court system, brought inheritance rules into conformity with settler norms, and required Choctaw women who wanted to marry settler men to get permission from their chief before marrying, as one chief wrote, "cordin [*sic*] to white Laws."[59]

Whatever setbacks women might have encountered in the circles of their national governments paled in comparison to the complete disregard the federal and state governments held in political matters for the descendants of the Lady of Cofitachequi and the Chief of Guatari. In the mid-1820s the southern state governments called increasingly for the removal of the southern First Nations and for the sale of their land. President Andrew Jackson and his supporters pushed through Congress a removal bill that empowered the federal government to negotiate exchanges of native land in the South for tracts of land west of the Mississippi River.[60] The Choctaws signed the first such removal treaty, and although government documents make no mention of women's presence at the meeting, a former slave passed along his account of seven women who made a striking presence at the treaty talks. On the morning of 22 September 1830, federal treaty commissioners John Eaton and John Coffee sat themselves on a log before a small group of women and a broad semicircle of men between the forks of Dancing Rabbit Creek. The first man to speak, Killihota, urged that "the Choctaws ought to sell everything they owned, land, cattle, horses, and hogs, and all in a body emigrate west." Land, however, lay outside his and the other men's authority, and the seven women who sat between the men and the commissioners made this clear. "Killihota," snapped one of the women, "I could cut you open with this knife. You have two hearts." Although he survived the encounter, each subsequent speaker rebuked Killihota's advice and seconded the women's refusal to cede any land. The women had exercised authority and, for the time being, succeeded in defending their land. After the negotiations ended, most of the men and women returned to their homes, but a rump council consisting solely of men signed away their homeland.[61]

Among the Chickasaws, women played no visible role in either the 1832 Treaty of Pontotoc Creek negotiations or in the 1834 Treaty of Washington, which amended the first document. Nevertheless, they influenced the chiefs' interpretation of the two accords. What concerned women most was a provision for reserves of land in Mississippi for heads of households that could be either sold for profit or lived upon after removal. The treaty made no mention of the gender of heads of households, but the federal government presumed that only men would qualify for the reserves. A group of Chickasaw women pressed their chiefs to make clear their claims to the reserves. After explaining in elaborate detail to President Jackson the Chickasaw customs of female control of the household and separate ownership of property, the chiefs concluded, "It is an ancient and universal law . . . that the wife had a separate estate in all her property whether derived from her relations or acquired by her. . . . The home of each [wife] is regarded as her own, and is generally so known and distinguished by the community."[62] Having had their wishes put to the president, it is unclear whether or not the women got what they wanted, but they had drawn on their long-standing and important place in Chickasaw society to influence diplomatic affairs and to seek redress for what they felt was wrong.

Of all the southern First Nations, Cherokee women had been by far the most active in what settlers understood as formal politics.[63] The restrictions placed on them by their national government notwithstanding, they continued through the early nineteenth century to impress upon men their concerns and their wishes, and when they could not influence affairs to their satisfaction, they took matters into their own hands. In 1816, prior to the selection of delegates to represent the Cherokees in negotiations for a land cession, several women held a dance in which they chose their partners. In one instant, remarked an observer, "a grave, aged Chief, is seized upon, and snatched from among his Brother Counsellors by these merry Dames."[64] If the possible choices for the delegation were seated in the council house to watch the dance, then it is reasonable to suspect that the women used the occasion to demonstrate their support for certain leaders and their views. Women also petitioned the national council to resist further cessions. At the urging of the "Beloved Woman" Nancy Ward, the petition read, "Your mothers, your sisters ask and beg of you not to part with any more of our land."[65] A year later, they turned up the pressure by invoking the sacred relationship between women, farming, and land. "The land was given to us by the Great Spirit above as our common right," the women asserted, "to raise our children upon, & to make support for our rising generations. We, therefore, humbly petition our beloved children . . . to hold out to the last in support of our common rights . . . we, therefore, claim the right of the soil."[66]

Unable to stop the land cessions of 1817 and 1819, women turned to securing the reserves to which the removal treaties entitled heads of households. Sally Lowry received such a reserve, but she was unable to occupy it because squatters had already made it their home. The Cherokee agent passed on to the secretary of war her desire for a new reserve.[67] Other women in a similar situation gave their powers of attorney to John Walker Jr. to press their claims to land in state and federal courts.[68] Walker's Cherokee wife, Elizabeth Walker, however, did not need her husband's services. She worked a "small Plantation" separate from her husband and claimed a reserve of 640 acres. Unable to gain clear recognition of her title, she pressed a congressman to forward her claim in the House of Representatives.[69] Some years later, when confronted with a squatter on her land, she filed suit and won her case before the Cherokee Supreme Court.[70] In spite of such gains, however, Cherokee women were unable to forestall the signing of the 1835 Treaty of New Echota, which set them on the Trail of Tears that the Choctaws, Creeks, and Chickasaws had also traveled.

By keeping the scope of economic innovations within the boundaries of their traditionally accepted gender roles as farmers, southern native women adapted but did not abandon the cultures that gave their lives meaning. Regardless of the persistence of their culture or of the power that they held, they still could not resist the expansion of the United States. But contact was as much a phenomenon of interaction between individuals as it was between nations, and so long as the conflicts and accommodations that characterized native women's entry into the market revolution remained on the level of buyer and seller, producer and consumer, they could defend what had been theirs all along. In a sense, Louis-Phillipe had been right. Dollars did melt their hearts because many native women had acquired the skills and the motivations that were necessary to compete in the economy of nineteenth-century America. But the future king of France also missed the point. The desire for profits and for prestige goods was never so pervasive that it uprooted women from the ancient cultural traditions that had structured their working lives and that had defined them as women long before Europeans had ever arrived in the Americas.

## NOTES

1. Louis-Phillipe, *Diary of My Travels in America*, trans. Stephen Becker (New York: Delacorte Press, 1977), 72.

2. Mary C. Wright, "Economic Development and Native American Women in the Early Nineteenth Century," *American Quarterly* 33 (1981): 525–36; Regina Smith Oboler, *Women, Power, and Economic Change* (Stanford: Stanford University Press, 1985); Theresa Amott and Julie Matthaei, *Race, Gender, and Work* (Boston: South End Press, 1991); Eirlys M. Barker, "Princesses, Wives, and Wenches: White Perceptions of Southeastern Indian Women to 1770," in *Women and Freedom in Early America*, ed. Larry D. Eldridge (New York: New York University Press, 1997), 44–61.

3. Jefferson Chapman, *Tellico Archaeology* (Knoxville: University of Tennessee Press, 1985), 33–46; John H. Blitz, *Ancient Chiefdoms of the Tombigbee* (Tuscaloosa: University of Alabama Press, 1993), 33–39; John A. Walthall, *Prehistoric Indians of the Southeast* (Tuscaloosa: University of Alabama Press, 1980), chs. 3 and 4; Patty Jo Watson and Mary C. Kennedy, "The Development of Horticulture in the Eastern Woodlands of North America: Women's Role," in *Engendering Archaeology*, ed. Joan M. Gero and Margaret W. Conkey (Oxford, U.K.: Basil Blackwell Ltd., 1991), 255–75.

4. R. Douglas Hurt, *Indian Agriculture in America* (Lawrence: University Press of Kansas, 1987), 6–11; Roy Dickens, *Cherokee Prehistory* (Knoxville: University of Tennessee Press, 1976), 13, 94, 209; James B. Griffin, "Comments on the Late Prehistoric Societies in the Southeast," in *Towns and Temples along the Mississippi*, ed. David H. Dye and Cheryl A. Cox (Tuscaloosa: University of Alabama Press, 1990), 6–9; Chapman, *Tellico*, 56–77.

5. Theda Perdue, *Cherokee Women: Gender and Culture Change, 1700–1835* (Lincoln: University of Nebraska Press, 1998), 13–15; Choctaw corn myth, folder 42, microfilm reel 2, Henry S. Halbert Papers, Mississippi Department of Archives and History, Jackson, Miss.; "The Origin of Maize (Creek)," in *Native American Legends*, comp. and ed. George E. Lankford (Little Rock, Ark.: August House, 1987), 155.

6. Daniel Maltz and JoAllyn Archambault, "Gender and Power in Native North America," in *Women and Power in Native North America*, ed. Laura F. Klein and Lillian A. Ackerman (Norman: University of Oklahoma Press, 1995), 234.

7. Charles Hudson, *The Juan Pardo Expeditions* (Washington, D.C.: Smithsonian Institution Press, 1990), 66–67; Charles Hudson, *Knights of Spain, Warriors of the Sun* (Athens: University of Georgia Press, 1997), 174–84.

8. Alfred W. Crosby, "Virgin Soil Epidemics as a Factor in the Aboriginal Depopulation in America," *William and Mary Quarterly*, 3d ser., 33 (April 1976): 289–99; Marvin T. Smith, *Archaeology of Aboriginal Culture Change in the Interior Southeast* (Gainesville: University Press of Florida, 1987); Vernon James Knight Jr., "The Formation of the Creeks," in *The Forgotten Centuries*, ed. Charles Hudson and Carmen Chaves Tesser (Athens: University of Georgia Press, 1994), 373–92; Patricia Galloway, "Confederacy as a Solution to Chiefdom Dissolution: Historical Evidence in the Choctaw Case," in ibid., 393–420; Peter H. Wood, "The Changing Population of the Colonial South: An Overview by Race and Region, 1685–

1790," in *Powhatan's Mantle*, ed. Peter H. Wood, Gregory A. Waselkov, and M. Thomas Hatley (Lincoln: University of Nebraska Press, 1989), 38–39, 56–72.

9. James Adair, *Adair's History of the American Indians*, ed. Samuel Cole Williams (Johnson City, Tenn.: Watauga Press, 1930), 241, 436–38, 453–55; William Bartram, *William Bartram on the Southeastern Indians*, ed. and annot. Gregory A. Waselkov and Kathryn E. Holland Braund (Lincoln: University of Nebraska Press, 1995), 127; Lt. Dumont de Montigny, *Memoires Historiques sur la Louisiane* (Paris: C. J. B. Bauche, 1753), 1:154; Kathryn E. Holland Braund, *Deerskins and Duffels: The Creek Indian Trade with Anglo-America, 1685–1815* (Lincoln: University of Nebraska Press, 1993), 67–68, 131; Daniel H. Usner Jr., *Indians, Settlers, and Slaves in a Frontier Exchange Economy* (Chapel Hill: University of North Carolina Press, 1992).

10. Intelligence from Indian Nancy to Captain Rayd. Demere, 12 December 1756, *Colonial Records of South Carolina: Documents Relating to Indian Affairs, 1754–1765*, ed. William L. McDowell Jr. (Columbia: University of South Carolina Press, 1970), 2:269; Intelligence from Nancy Butler to Captain Rayd. Demere, 20 December 1756, ibid., 2:275.

11. Edward Mease narrative, 1770–71, "Peter Chester, Third Governor of the Province of West Florida under British Dominion, 1770–1781," ed. Eron Opha Rowland, *Publications of the Mississippi Historical Society, Centenary Series* 5 (1925): 84.

12. Bernard Romans, *A Concise Natural History of East and West Florida* (Gainesville: University of Florida Press, 1962), 84.

13. Usner, *Indians, Settlers, and Slaves*, 211; Winifred Barr Rothenberg, *From Market-Place to a Market Economy* (Chicago: University of Chicago Press, 1992), 5–23; Karl Polyani, *The Great Transformation* (New York: Farrar & Rinehart, Inc., 1944), 43–71.

14. Braund, *Deerskins*, 22–23.

15. Raymond D. Fogelson, "On the Petticoat Government of the Eighteenth-Century Cherokee," in *Personality and the Cultural Construction of Society: Papers in Honor of Melvin E. Spiro*, ed. David K. Jordan and Marc J. Swartz (Tuscaloosa: University of Alabama Press, 1990), 168.

16. James Mooney, *History, Myths, and Sacred Formulas of the Cherokees* (Asheville, N.C.: Bright Mountain Books, 1992), 501; Adair, *History*, 152–53.

17. Fogelson, "Petticoat Government," 167; Raymond D. Fogelson, "Cherokee Notions of Power," in *The Anthropology of Power*, ed. Raymond D. Fogelson and Richard N. Adams (New York: Academic Press, 1977), 192; Perdue, *Cherokee Women*, 54–58.

18. "Discussion of Choctaw History by Nathaniel Folsom," Peter Perkins Pitchlynn Papers, Thomas Gilcrease Institute of American History and Art, Tulsa, Okla.; Gideon Lincecum, "History of the Chahta Nation," microfilm copy, 317, The Center for American History, University of Texas at Austin.

19. William G. McLoughlin, "Cherokee Anomie, 1794–1810," in *The Cherokee Ghost Dance*, ed. William G. McLoughlin (Macon, Ga.: Mercer University Press, 1984), 16.

20. Bartram, *William Bartram*, 153.

21. Perdue, *Cherokee Women*, 116; Claudio Saunt, " 'Domestick . . . Quiet Being Broke': Gender Conflict among Creek Indians in the Eighteenth Century," in *Contact Points: Ameri-*

can *Frontiers from the Mohawk Valley to the Mississippi, 1750–1830*, ed. Andrew R. L. Cayton and Frederika J. Teute (Chapel Hill: University of North Carolina Press, 1998), 157–63.

22. 26 November 1796 journal entry, in Benjamin Hawkins, *Letters, Journals, and Writings of Benjamin Hawkins*, 2 vols., ed. C. L. Grant (Savannah: Beehive Press, 1980), 1:2; Benjamin Hawkins to Elizabeth House Trist, 25 November 1797, ibid., 1:163; Benjamin Hawkins to Silas Dinsmoor, 7 June 1798, ibid., 1:199.

23. Jesse D. Jennings, ed., "Nutt's Trip to the Chickasaw Country," *Journal of Mississippi History* 9 (January 1947): 41; John Allen, "Report of the Chickasaws," 7 February 1830, reel 136, M234, Correspondence of the Office of Indian Affairs and Related Records, Records of the Bureau of Indian Affairs, National Archives Record Group 75, Washington, D.C. (hereafter Correspondence).

24. *Missionary Herald* 17 (April 1821): 110.

25. *Niles' Weekly Register* 38 (5 July 1830): 345.

26. Adam Hodgson, *Letters from North America* (London: Hurst, Robinson & Co., 1824), 1:131.

27. Ibid., 1:117, 132–33.

28. Benjamin Henry Latrobe, *The Journal of Latrobe* (New York: Burt Franklin, 1971), 249.

29. Jacob Young, *Autobiography of a Pioneer* (Cincinnati: L. Swormstedt & A. Poe, 1857), 213–14.

30. *Missionary Herald* 26 (December 1830): 382; Jedidiah Morse, *A Report to the Secretary of War of the United States* (New Haven, Conn.: S. Converse, 1822), 167–68.

31. Henry Knox to George Washington, 7 July 1789, *American State Papers. Class II. Indian Affairs*, 2 vols., ed. Walter Lowrie and Matthew St. Clair Clarke (Washington, D.C.: Gales and Seaton, 1832, 1834), 1:53; Francis Paul Prucha, *The Great Father*, unabridged (Lincoln: University of Nebraska Press, 1984), ch. 1; Bernard Sheehan, *Seeds of Extinction* (Chapel Hill: University of North Carolina Press, 1973.

32. Allen, "Report of the Chickasaws."

33. Perdue, *Cherokee Women*, 127–29.

34. "Papers of George S. Gaines, Copied from the Original Now on File in the Mississippi State Department of Archives and History in a Collection Once Owned by J. F. H. Claiborne," 1, typescript, Indian Archives, Oklahoma Historical Society, Oklahoma City, Okla.

35. See, for example, Benjamin Hawkins to Henry Dearborn, 15 June 1807, in Hawkins, *Letters*, 2:518, which discusses Hawkins's work among the Uchees.

36. Benjamin Hawkins to Silas Dinsmoor, 7 June 1798, ibid., 1:199.

37. E. Price to Daniel Man, 20 January 1797, reel 1, M4, Records of the Creek Trading House, 1795–1816, Records of the Superintendent of Indian Trade, National Archives Record Group 75, Washington, D.C.; Benjamin Hawkins to James McHenry, 23 February 1798, in Hawkins, *Letters*, 1:177; Hawkins to McHenry, 9 January 1799, ibid., 1:238; "A Sketch of the Present State of the Objects under the Charge of the Principle Agent for Indian Affairs South of the Ohio," 1 March 1801, ibid., 1:353.

38. Benjamin Hawkins to William Eustis, 24 February 1811, ibid., 2:583.

39. Benjamin Hawkins to John Armstrong, 26 April 1812, ibid., 2:634.

40. 30 November 1796 journal entry, ibid, 1:5, and 1 December 1796 journal entry, ibid., 1:6.

41. *Panoplist, and Missionary Magazine United* 2 (March 1810): 474–75; *Missionary Herald* 23 (April 1827): 116.

42. *Panoplist and Missionary Herald* 16 (March 1820): 133; *Missionary Herald* 25 (February 1829): 59; ibid., 26 (May 1830): 154; ibid., 27 (March 1831): 81.

43. Carl F. Klinck and James J. Talmer, eds., *The Journal of Major John Norton, 1816* (Toronto: Champlain Society, 1970), 36.

44. Minutes of the Fort Adams Treaty, 12 December 1801, reel 1, T494, Documents Relating to the Negotiation of Ratified and Unratified Treaties with Various Indian Tribes, 1801–69, Records Relating to Indian Treaties, National Archives Record Group 75, Washington, D.C.; James Wilkinson, Andrew Pickens, and Benjamin Hawkins to Henry Dearborn, 18 December 1802, reel 1, M271, Letters Received by the Secretary of War Relating to Indian Affairs, 1800–1823, Office of the Secretary of War, ibid.; "Memorandum of Goods for Mushulatubbee's Dist. 1826," reel 169, M234, and "Abstract of Articles Delivered to Chactaw Indians as a Part of Their Annuity for the Year 1828," ibid.

45. Morse, *Report*, 182.

46. *Niles' Weekly Register* 38 (3 July 1830): 345.

47. Samuel Mitchell to David Haley, 23 January 1800, Henley Papers, Special Collections, William R. Perkins Library, Duke University, Durham, N.C.; Benjamin Hawkins to Henry Dearborn, 28 October 1801, in Hawkins, *Letters*, 1:387; Chinabu King et al. to Secretary of War, 10 February 1817, reel 2, M271, Correspondence; Allen, "Report of the Chickasaws."

48. Benjamin Smith to Thomas L. McKenney, 6 October 1825, reel 135, Correspondence.

49. 10 December 1796 journal entry, in Hawkins, *Letters*, 1:14; Frederick Law Olmsted, *A Journey in the Back Country* (New York: Schocken Books, 1970), 174; James R. Creecy, *Scenes in the South* (Washington, D.C.: Thomas McGill, 1860), 121; H. G. Hawkins, "History of Port Gibson," *Publications of the Mississippi Historical Society* 10 (1909): 283; Fortescue Cuming, *Sketches of a Tour to the Western Country* (Pittsburgh: Cramer, Spear & Eichbaum, 1810), 322.

50. Theda Perdue, *Slavery and the Evolution of Cherokee Society, 1540–1866* (Knoxville: University of Tennessee Press, 1979); Gregory Evans Dowd, "North American Indian Slaveholding and the Colonization of Gender: The Southeast before Removal," *Critical Matrix* 3 (Fall 1987): 152–53; Kathryn E. Holland Braund, "The Creek Indians, Blacks, and Slavery," *Journal of Southern History* 57 (November 1991): 601–36; Claudio Saunt, *A New Order of Things: Property, Power, and the Transformation of the Creek Indians, 1733–1816* (Cambridge: Cambridge University Press, 1999), 139–232; James Taylor Carson, *Searching for the Bright Path: The Mississippi Choctaws from Prehistory to Removal* (Lincoln: University of Nebraska Press, 1999), 70–85.

51. "Claims of the friendly Creek Indians for losses sustained by them in their civil war," 22 April 1826, reel 220, M234, Correspondence; "A list of property belonging to Susanah

McIntosh taken or destroyed on the 30th April 1825 by the hostile Indians," Claimants Accounts, Book H, 1826, ibid.; "A List of Property belonging to Louisa McIntosh taken or destroyed by the Hostile Creek Indians April 30th 1825," ibid.; Saunt, "Domestick," 163–74.

52. 20 December 1796 journal entry, in Hawkins, *Letters*, 1:24; Saunt, *New Order*, 120–21.

53. James McDonald to John C. Calhoun, 9 November 1824, reel 169, M234, Correspondence.

54. Deposition of Abidah Bings, 18 December 1826, reel 72, M234, ibid.; Hugh Montgomery to Charles Hicks, 23 October 1826, reel 72, ibid; John McGowan to Hampton Williams, 23 September 1829, reel 73, ibid.; Montgomery to John Eaton, 19 January 1830, reel 74, ibid.; Montgomery to Eaton, 12 April 1831, reel 74, ibid.; McGowan to James Standefer, 8 January 1830, reel 74, ibid.

55. 16 February 1797 journal entry, in Hawkins, *Letters*, 1:47.

56. Morse, *Report*, 176.

57. John Allen to Thomas L. McKenney, 16 October 1829, reel 135, M234, Correspondence.

58. Perdue, *Cherokee Women*, 139–57.

59. Allene Smith, *Greenwood LeFlore and the Choctaw Indians of the Mississippi Valley* (Memphis: C. A. Davis Printing Co., 1951), 50–53; *Missionary Herald* 19 (January 1823): 10; ibid., 25 (May 1829): 153; Greenwood LeFlore to Thomas L. McKenney, 3 May 1828, reel 169, M234, Correspondence.

60. James Taylor Carson, "State Rights and Indian Removal in Mississippi: 1817–1835," *Journal of Mississippi History* 57 (February 1995): 32–37; Mary Young, "The Exercise of Sovereignty in Cherokee Georgia," *Journal of the Early Republic* 10 (Spring 1990): 43–64; Michael D. Green, *The Politics of Indian Removal: Creek Government and Society in Crisis* (Lincoln: University of Nebraska Press, 1982), 145–47.

61. Henry S. Halbert, "The Story of the Treaty of Dancing Rabbit Creek," *Publications of the Mississippi Historical Society* 6 (1902): 374–77.

62. Ishtahotopa, Martin Colbert, Pistalutubbee, et al. to Andrew Jackson, 1835, reel 136, M234, Correspondence.

63. Perdue, *Cherokee Women*, 47.

64. Klinck and Talmer, eds., *John Norton*, 56.

65. Perdue, *Cherokee Women*, 156–57; Petition, 2 May 1817, *The Cherokee Removal*, ed. Theda Perdue and Michael D. Green (Boston: Bedford Books of St. Martin's Press, 1995), 124.

66. Petition, 20 June 1818, Perdue and Green, eds., *Cherokee Removal*, 125.

67. Hugh Montgomery to James Barbour, 25 April 1826, reel 72, M234, Correspondence; Samuel B. Mead to Unknown, 19 October 1828, ibid.

68. Return J. Meigs to James Barbour, 31 December 1826, ibid.

69. Hugh Montgomery to James Barbour, 28 April 1826, and Gideon Morgan to James Barbour, 22 May 1826, ibid.

70. Elizabeth Walker to Elbert Herring, 7 November 1833, reel 75, ibid.

*Chapter Two*

. . . . . . . . . . . . . . . . . . . . . . . . . . . . . . . . . . . . . . . .

# Made by the Hands of Indians:
# Cherokee Women and Trade

. . . . . . . . . . . . . . . . . . . . . . . . . . . . . . . . . . . . . . . .

SARAH H. HILL

Cherokee women's eighteenth-century autonomy was born of social and economic security. Through most of the century, marriage customs, residence patterns, and social structures protected women and children and enhanced their rights.

After marriage, a woman usually remained in her home village and continued to live in the family compound. Her household might contain her mother, sisters, and aunts, along with her new husband. She owned her house and garden and, through the matrilineage, controlled clan fields as well. Whereas men moved away from their homes and villages after marriage, women remained in their households and towns of origin. Close to their families and fields, they retained access to economic and social resources. "The wives generally have separate property," explained British lieutenant Henry Timberlake, "that no inconveniency may arise from death or separation."[1]

Economically secure through the matrilineage, women participated independently in nearly every kind of trade. Throughout the century, they followed trails to neighboring houses or tribes, to European settlements or garrisons, carrying slaves, food, and crafted goods such as baskets and beadwork to obtain items they wanted or needed. From "Indian Peggy's" 1715 Charles Town exchange of one French captive for a gun and some strouds, to the midcentury bartering of "eatables" that gave Ft. Loudon "the appearance of a market," women's trade was varied and opportunistic.[2] Women used what they had to make what they needed, and took what they made to get what they wanted.

## THE BASKETRY OF CHEROKEE WOMEN

For more than a thousand years, Cherokee women wove an astonishing array of baskets and mats for scores of uses. They made them for exchange with friends, neighbors, and strangers, for food gathering, processing, serving, and storage, and to utilize in ceremonies and rituals. They kept ceremonial objects and medicinal goods in woven baskets and covered ceremonial grounds, seats, floors, and walls with woven mats. They concealed and protected household items and community valuables in baskets. Basketry was central to women's activities and to Cherokee society.

Early European writers consistently identified basketry with women, "the chief, if not the only manufacturers."[3] As the primary users of woven goods, women were also the customary weavers. The association of women with basketry is one of the most enduring aspects of Cherokee culture. Woven goods— baskets and mats—document what women did, when, and how. They illuminate the work of women who transformed the environments that produced materials for basketry. They point to women's roles in ceremonial, subsistence, and exchange systems. As objects created and utilized by women, baskets and mats conserved and conveyed their concepts, ideas, experience, and expertise. They asserted women's cultural identity and reflected their values.

. . .

While ceremonial baskets connect women to ritual power and utilitarian containers point to their varied subsistence activities, trade basketry illuminates the little-known world in which women made and marketed their work. Expressing both individual concepts and shared customs, trade baskets directly linked makers to buyers from different places. They extended women's social, political, and economic relationships beyond their own communities, transcending boundaries of race, gender, geography, and class. Enjoying an unparalleled reputation for weaving, women developed trade networks that reached to the shores of the colonies. As a result, even those who did not know them knew something of their work.

Although the records of women's work are meager, they point to active trade networks. When licensed British trader Theophilus Hastings left the Cherokee settlements in 1715 he loaded his packhorses with "Indian baskets." Ten years later, Carolina governor Francis Nicholson returned to England with two Cherokee baskets among his private possessions; and even at midcentury, when relations between the Cherokees and the crown were strained, British captain Paul Demere wrote Governor Lyttleton that he was sending him "a Nest of Indian Basketts" from his garrison in the Cherokee nation. Charles Town colonists paid with gold for Cherokee baskets, which were renowned "for their domestic usefulness, beauty, and skilful variety."[4] By the early 1700s, baskets had become women's best-known trade item.

While their work is poorly recorded, women's baskets and references to them document technological skill and inherited wisdom. They express women's customs, behaviors, and beliefs, and connect them with subsistence, ceremony, and trade. Baskets inscribe a text that is essentially Cherokee and specifically female. As trade goods made and sold by women, they provide insight into the Cherokee world.

## WOMEN'S WORLDS IN THE 1700S

The world made for and by Cherokees in the 1700s was a land of abundant resources where women worked long and hard to gather and process foods, fashion clothing, and make household goods. It was an arena where women might act as healers and warriors as well as wives and mothers, where they acknowledged kinship with brothers and children more than with husbands. In this realm, women took charge of food, clothing, and households, as well as special dances, certain kinds of exchange, and clan hospitality. They moved freely beyond their towns and villages with pelts or baskets or chestnuts loaded on their backs and walked to European or other native settlements to engage in trade. Neither regarded nor behaving as inferior to men, they also fought in battle, tortured captives, and commanded the deaths of prisoners. On behalf of their clans and families they required vengeance for slain relatives. They called for peace, healed the injured, and adopted outsiders into their clan families.

Most important, they taught young girls how to be Cherokee women. Training took place in homes where girls watched female relatives make meals, baskets, pottery, beadwork, and clothing. Teaching by example, showing girls how to be mothers and sisters, daughters and wives, storytellers and traders, was part of every female relationship. Teaching occurred in household gardens and clan fields where young girls gradually learned about plants and crops, seeds and seasons, formulas and weather. Becoming a Cherokee woman meant weaving together knowledge from and of the past with experiences and resources of the present. With every decade of the 1700s came a change in knowledge, experiences, and resources. With every decade, women transformed and were transformed, continuously weaving new worlds from old.

## NEW CHEROKEES, NEW AMERICANS

The era of the American Revolution brought significant change to the Cherokee world. The American population increased by 35 percent between 1775 and 1800, and competition for land intensified greatly. Lacking money, the Continental Congress and individual states awarded land to Revolutionary veterans. As a result, many who had fought against Cherokees in the Revolution found themselves afterward in possession of their lands. The Piedmont woods of the Carolinas were cleared as restless settlers pressed toward the receding borders of the Cherokee nation. By 1800, more than 300,000 whites had moved into the states of Kentucky and Tennessee, which recently had been carved out of Cherokee land cessions.[5]

Moreover, by the 1790s, the Cherokee nation included a substantial number of offspring of mixed parentage, particularly of Cherokee women and white men. Many soldiers and virtually every trader entered alliances with Cherokee women, leaving English-speaking descendants who occupied the broad middle ground between two distinct cultures. Assimilation proponents usually referred to them as "half Cherokees," "half-breeds," and "half" or "quarter-bloods" and relied on them for everything from interpreting sermons to negotiating boundary disputes. The matrilineage, however, identified them as Cherokees, though they might bear names like Timberlake and Adair, or Scott, Ward, Ross, and Vann. Living in two worlds conceptually if not physically, such women and men bridged the divide between Cherokee and white. From 1791 until the expulsion of Indians from the Southeast, descendants of mixed marriages increasingly assumed positions of leadership and influence and contributed to the brilliant effort to avert removal.

By 1825, nearly 3,000 Cherokees of mixed ancestry lived in the Southeast, 60 with African forbears.[6] Intermarriage with European or African men produced children whose sources of authority increasingly lay beyond the clan system. Intermarriage with European or African women produced children with no clan identity at all. Cherokees of mixed ancestry were well represented on the Cherokee National Council, which was established in 1827 and explicitly modeled on the American form of government. Those with white parentage also comprised the majority of students educated in missionary schools, a high percentage of converts to Christianity, and virtually all the members of the emerging economic upper class.[7] Such Cherokees diverged from clan systems by race, language, and residence, and increasingly by education, wealth, and subsistence. To accommodate a changing population, the Cherokee Nation adopted specific aspects of the American legal system. In the first quarter of the nineteenth century, Cherokees formulated and codified laws comparable to those of whites who were neighbors, supporters, converters, or even detractors. Laws served as written signs of civilization and the abandonment of Cherokee traditions. "The decrees and laws of their council," wrote missionary Abraham Steiner to Rev. John Heckewelder, "conform more and more to the customs and laws of the United States."[8]

Proponents of the federal government's so-called civilization program considered clan revenge "savage and barbarous" and urged its abolition. During the 1700s, horrified colonists had watched the Cherokee retributive system of justice punish innocent white settlers for crimes committed by their neighbors. While American law punished perpetrators, Cherokee clan law required vengeance, punishing anyone who represented the offender. To Cherokees, clan revenge assured everyone of restitution and assigned collective responsibility for individual behavior. Believing that a clan—like a village, a house, and even a basket—was only as strong as its weakest member, each person attended closely to the behavior of clan kin. However, no compromise existed between white and Cherokee interpretations of justice. In 1810, leaders of the seven clans officially ended the custom of clan revenge.[9] Words rather than blood formed the basis of the new Cherokee legal order.

The abolition of clan revenge struck at the heart of social systems by removing from the matrilineage its responsibility for regulating behavior. By 1820, Cherokees had established a new form of government, appointed a Lighthorse Guard, codified laws, and created a court system. Their government conformed to that of America while it devised for the Cherokees a single institution to negotiate with the federal government about land cessions, road building, mission development, river access, and pressures for removal. Whether as sincere converts or as skeptical participants determined to avoid removal, Cherokees who embraced the government's civilization program decried old vengeance customs as "vestiges of ignorance and barbarism."[10]

Although responsibility for the maintenance of order was formally removed from the matrilineage, inheritance had remained centered in the mother's clan. In 1806, however, President Thomas Jefferson encouraged a delegation of Cherokee chiefs to devise new laws of inheritance as well. "When a man has enclosed and improved his farm, builds a good house on it and raised plentiful stocks of animals," Jefferson declared, "he will wish when he dies that these things shall go to his wife and children, whom he loves more than he does his other relations." Private property formed the cornerstone of American liberty, and its inheritance promoted individual wealth. The president instructed the chiefs how best to express their regard for their wives and children. "You will," he asserted, "find it necessary to establish laws for this."[11]

Two years later, the first law passed by the Cherokee National Council gave "protection to children as heirs of their *father's* property."[12] The blow struck directly at the matrilineage and instantly enhanced the rights of clanless men— whites who married Cherokee women. Now children could inherit farms or fields, horses or hogs, ferries or inns, slaves or mills from white fathers who made alliances in the Cherokee Nation. In November of 1825, the council passed a law acknowledging the rights of children of Cherokee fathers and white mothers "as equal to" those of children descended from Cherokee mothers.[13] Since children of white mothers inherited no clan identity, the new laws severed economic inheritance from clan membership.

Like other changes occurring across the Cherokee Nation, the new laws were more complex than they appear. Did they signal a partial or complete break from Cherokee custom, or did they signify partial or complete accommodation to white standards in order to protect Cherokee rights? No single or simple interpretation can encompass the minds and hearts of approximately 14,000 Cherokees living from the Tennessee River in northern Alabama to Deep Creek in the mountains of western North Carolina. Laws directly affecting women, however, reveal some interesting continuities.

The Cherokee National Council left intact the inheritance rights of women, and leader John Ridge pointed out that "property belonging to the wife is not exclusively at the control and disposal of the husband." While hoping to convince his readers that Cherokees were becoming as civilized as whites, Ridge acknowledged that women all over the Nation retained "exclusive and distinct control" of their own property. "The law is in favor of females in this respect," he admitted, regardless of education, affluence, or kin.[14] The Cherokee custom of protecting married women's property rights differed entirely from English and American law, which accorded all property rights to husbands.

Polygyny, which facilitated clan management of land and other resources, also remained "very much in vogue." Ridge acknowledged that the National Council failed in its initial attempt to abolish the custom since "nearly all of our legislature" would be affected. In the 1820s, it was "very common for a man to marry a mother and her daughter at the same time and raise a numerous family from both of them." Missionaries from the Georgia line to the North Carolina Valley Towns besieged supervisors for advice about men with multiple wives and a conflicting interest in Christian conversion.[15] The council finally banned polygamy in 1825. But it established no penalty for infractions and ignored existing polygynous alliances.

Similarly, the council never prohibited adultery. Major John Norton reported that Creeks beat adulterers senseless and cut off their ears, but "the Cherokees have no such punishment for adultery." Husbands scarcely took notice of their wives' infidelity, he claimed in 1809, though they might seek another wife.[16] So doing, of course, was also consistent with polygyny.

Women's independence regarding marriage partners persisted as well. Wives continued to separate from their husbands with such ease and frequency that Moravian missionaries like the Gambolds began to refer to Cherokee women by their family names. "Many an Indian woman," they wrote in 1810, "because of the frequent changing of husbands, would get together a really long catalogue of names." One complication of such alliances was that "the same name could easily be common to a whole string of women." The Gambolds chose to go along with "the customs of the country," calling women by their original names.[17]

However, the importance of clans as regulators of marriage sanctions apparently waned in the decade before removal. In 1783, the prohibition against intraclan marriage had been the one social law Brother Martin Schneider could discover among Cherokees. He confessed that "of their family Order, I could only learn so much, that children of one Family dare not marry each other."[18] As late as 1810, missionary Gambold claimed that intraclan marriages "would be something unheard of." Less than a decade later, however, the *Missionary Herald* reported that the prohibition "is invaded with impunity."[19] The authoritative role of matrilineal clans in society, as in law, seemed to be diminishing.

Although women retained control of their own property, occasionally entered polygynous marriages, and were never punished for adultery, their domestic authority declined as European patriarchal traditions spread. In contrast to her predecessor's reputed position of power, a midcentury woman was likely to find that her husband "treats his wife as an equal." According to William Fyffe's 1760s view, no woman "pretended to lord it over the husband who is absolute in his own family." Tacit acknowledgment of the husband's authority, he claimed, prevented "civil wars."[20] Following his 1775 visit, naturalist William Bartram declared that he "never saw nor heard of an instance of an Indian beating his wife." In return, wives were "discrete, modest, loving, faithful, and affectionate to their husbands." Great distance separates Longe's 1725 assertion that irate wives might "beat their husbands to that height that they kill them outright" and Bartram's judgment a half century later that husbands refrained from abusing their wives.[21] Bartram's description of Cherokee marriage perfectly inverts Longe's, marking a shift in domestic authority.

### NEW ECONOMIES OF TRADE

Changes in Cherokee social structures influenced women's economies in terms of what and where they marketed. In 1795, as part of its Indian trading policy, the federal government established a factory in the old Cherokee town of Tellico. The purpose of government factories was to drive independent traders out of business and gain control of Indian lands through debt. In 1803, President Jefferson wrote to Governor William Henry Harrison "an unofficial and private" letter describing the "extensive policy respecting the Indians." In order to promote a "disposition" to cede their lands, he wrote, "we shall push our trading uses, and be glad to see the good and influential individuals among them run into debt." As their debts mounted, "they become willing to lop them off by a cession of land."[22]

In 1798, the duke of Orleans, Louis-Philippe, found the Tellico store "always well stocked" with a supply of game, eggs, and fruits. When he visited in early May, women were bringing in strawberries to sell at "ninepence the gallon." The following winter, missionaries Steiner and de Schweinitz recorded that "Cherokees supply the local garrison [at Tellico] with butter, eggs, and fruit, chiefly apples." These goods were the province of women, documenting that they continued to trade but were including new kinds of foods in their economy.[23]

As in the early 1700s, women still left their towns and farms to seek markets, but the government's elimination of local traders made it necessary for them to travel greater distances. At the Cherokee town of Pine Log in 1796, Benjamin Hawkins met a woman who had just returned from "the settlements" in Augusta to sell "a bushel and a half of chestnuts" she had carried "on her back," doubtless in a pack basket. The trip took seventeen days. And near the old town of Stecoah, he passed two women on horseback "driving ten very fat cattle to the station for a market."[24] Their destination was likely the Charleston trade centers. If the government store at Tellico could not accommodate native exchange, either in terms of stocked shelves or purchasing power, women took their business elsewhere.

Restricting trade to the Tellico factory also enhanced women's private exchange. Since every neighbor and every visitor represented a potential market, women often kept food or crafted goods in their households to sell. Making his rounds through the Nation, Hawkins more than once stopped to buy "some corn of the women" or "provisions of the road" before proceeding on his travels.[25] Pine Log women showed the agent some items that gave them particular pride: "a sample of their ingenuity in the manufacture of baskets and sifter, out of cane." Hawkins acknowledged the skill of the weavers: "The dies of the splints were good, and workmanship not surpassed in the United States by white people."[26] It was the highest compliment he could offer.

In the early 1800s, the Moravian Springplace Mission became a locus of private exchange between the missionaries and Cherokee converts. Cherokees often came by the mission not for religious instruction but "when they have something to sell." Meticulous mission records reveal how extensive the networks became. "The beads, binding, pocket mirrors, some scarves, some sewing needles and some thread," wrote Brother Gambold, "have been given to the Indians in exchange for meat, some baskets, etc., instead of money."[27] Beads and binding, needles and thread, perhaps even scarves and mirrors, were goods utilized by women who came with trade baskets to the Springplace Mission.

By 1810, a wealthy Cherokee woman who lived near Springplace had become one of the mission's most faithful supporters and a reliable source of trade baskets. Peggy Scott represents many of the crosscurrents that existed in Cherokee society in the early nineteenth century. Born 20 August 1783 to a Cherokee mother and Scottish father, Scott became the third wife of James Vann, a chief who was also of mixed parentage. One of Vann's other wives, who no longer lived with him, was Scott's sister.[28] Following her conversion to Christianity in the summer of 1810, Scott began sending baskets to friends of the Gambolds in Salem, North Carolina, and Nazareth, Pennsylvania. In September, she forwarded to a child in Salem "a little basket constructed more or less like Moses' little 'ark' on the Nile River" as a "remembrance." The next month, she sent six baskets in one "large black package." Around the edges of three of them, she had sewn strips of cloth containing pieces of paper. Each paper requested that the baskets "may be accepted." The three remaining baskets, according to Gambold, Scott had "secured by trading beads of coral." The same mail carried yet another "little basket" holding a pipe and a collection of seeds. "The only thing remarkable about the pipe and the baskets," Gambold concluded, "is that they were made by the hands of the Indians."[29]

Four Springplace baskets have survived to the present.[30] Two of them, one rectangular and one square, indicate the persistence of the oldest Cherokee basketry customs—the use of rivercane material and the complex doubleweave technique—in addition to a traditional selection of dyes, forms, and linear patterns. The other two are completely different in material, form, technique, and function.

The rectangular basket has traditional dark brown dye that enhances its patterns. The form is long and narrow, like customary storage containers made for personal valuables. Its doubleweave is comparable to baskets made throughout the 1700s and traded to prominent and wealthy patrons. Demonstrating an extraordinary continuity of design, its square and cross pattern also appears on an eighteenth-century basket and on several containers made just prior to removal. Similarly, the triangular pattern occurs on one of the baskets Governor Nicholson carried to London in 1725. Across a century of dislocation, epidemics, war, and a 75 percent reduction in land, women had retained the knowledge and skill that produced the same forms, techniques, colors, and designs. The rectangular basket records the preservation of technological expertise and of symbols meaningful to generations of women.

The cubicle basket is dyed red and black, hues similar to those obtained from traditional sources of walnut and bloodroot. Its fabric strap handles also characterize early basketry. But the distinctive patterns on the lid and base tell yet another story. Elaborately woven inside and out on a continuous field of cane, these intricate designs do not appear on any other known Cherokee baskets. They are unique to the Springplace cane basket and lid. Such unfamiliar designs raise questions about personal ownership of patterns and of knowledge. Some designs may have been widely known and shared. Others may have belonged to a particular weaver, family, clan, or settlement, or signified certain customs, concepts, events, stories, or status. As worlds changed in the 1700s, certain patterns on baskets like these must have disappeared, vanishing as well from families, customs, communities, and landscapes.

As some basket conventions faded, however, others emerged in the minds and hands of women. The two remaining Springplace baskets resemble each other but differ entirely in material, form, and function from all other Cherokee baskets of the period. The material is a smooth and round vine that has aged to a light tan. Such slight material would produce an untraditional basket form. In contrast to the rectangular bases found on rivercane baskets, the vine containers have round bases and bodies. Rather than the usual twill or plaited weave associated with rivercane, the vine baskets are like wicker, with flexible splits laced around sturdy frames. No color ornaments these unusual containers. Interlaced vines rather than fabric straps form their handles. Unlike traditional Cherokee containers, these two baskets are light, delicate, and fragile. They could neither protect valuables nor process foods. They could not carry anything heavy, bulky, hot, or damp. Whereas rivercane baskets were extraordinarily resilient, these containers would disintegrate in water and incinerate in fire. They appear to be fanciful items of exchange, made for decoration more than for labor or storage. The two little vine containers represent changing customs, new trading partners, and different concepts about how baskets should look and what they should do.

The four Springplace baskets were presentations, much like the food or dances or baskets offered by earlier women to visiting Europeans. "Made by the hands of Indians," each container initiated relationships. They established alliances between women, cultures, belief systems, and nations. Collectively, they bore more than messages from one Moravian community to another. They contained the intention and wishes of their makers to signify their culture, in all its dimensions of change and continuity, to those living beyond the boundaries of their world. As a collection of disparate baskets, they capture a moment and an era of complexity, when past and present interwove. They represent not one but two civilizations—the Cherokee and the European—joined in a reciprocating relationship.

Like their basketry, women's agricultural goods diversified as the century ended. Following the 1791 inauguration of the civilization program, Cherokee women expanded their farming economy to raise cotton, their first crop that produced neither food nor medicine nor dye. In his 1796 trip through the Nation, Benjamin Hawkins was gratified that the women of Pine Log "had made some cotton, and would make more and follow the instructions of the agent and advise [*sic*] of the President." By 1805, Agent Return J. Meigs believed that "raising cotton, spinning and weaving is carried on in almost every part of the nation." Wherever cotton production occurred, "it is done totally by the females."[31]

Other visitors also reported favorably on women's progress with "civilized" crops. In the broad river valleys of the Oostanaula and Tennessee, Major John Norton discovered over and over "women who were busily employed in spinning cotton on the large wheel." The "great industry of Cherokee women enabled them to make cloth, not only in sufficient quantities for their own families, but to trade with the Creeks or Muscogui in exchange for cattle."[32] Like food, medicines, and baskets, cotton became a part of women's economy, good for trade as well as home use.

Such changes among women point beyond their resourcefulness or their embrace of new federal programs. Differences in crops, husbandry, and even baskets represent more than new tastes, varied resources, diverse skills, and changing bloodlines. They grew out of and were part of larger transformations. Each kind of change forged new systems of living as Cherokees faced their greatest challenge, their expulsion from the Southeast along the Trail of Tears.

## TRADE AFTER REMOVAL:
### NEW SETTLEMENTS AND NEW NEIGHBORS

Following removal in 1838, approximately 1,000 Cherokees remained in North Carolina along the Oconaluftee, Tuckasegee, Valley, Nantahala, and Cheoah Rivers. Surrounded by whites and restricted to mountain farming, women actively transformed old customs and created new ones. Trade was essential to the changes they made.

Whites who moved into the Cheoah Valley traded labor and goods with Cherokee neighbors. From household to household, baskets were among the items commonly exchanged. In the 1840s, one of the earliest white settlers of the valley received two baskets from Cherokee women. They were small rivercane storage baskets, doublewoven in twill and dyed with bloodroot and walnut, testifying to the persistence of cane basketry as an expression of women's culture and a survivor of the most profound shock of Cherokee history. The trade baskets also demonstrate how rapidly women established new exchange networks after removal armies disappeared.

Custom married change among weavers of baskets. They continued to make baskets for their own domestic use and to sell or barter. However, the manufacture of baskets for ceremonies disappeared. Of the three functions of baskets seen prior to removal—utilitarian, trade, and ceremonial—only two remained visible after 1838, testifying eloquently to deep levels of cultural dislocation.

As portable items made of local materials and useful in every household, trade baskets became increasingly important to Cherokee economies. Near Knoxville in the winter of 1842, Drury Armstrong encountered along the Tennessee River "an encampment of Cherokee Indians, in number ten. Found them making cane baskets." The diarist leaves little information about the group, but it seems likely that they were family members working together. Did they live nearby in a Tennessee enclave hidden from removal soldiers? Or did they load up their wares from North Carolina settlements and walk across the mountains on the trails to Tennessee? Little is certain other than the reason they were there. Armstrong remarks that they "had on hand and up for sale perhaps 100 baskets."[33] His diary entry marks the first documentation of collective basket production among the Cherokees. Basketry had become a cottage industry that, for the first time, included men as well as women. And basket trade took place between households and settlements more than between weavers and traders.

About the same time Armstrong discovered the encampment of basket weavers, Tennessean Sophia Moody Pack purchased from a Cherokee neighbor a large rivercane doubleweave clothes hamper. The cane, doubleweave technique, and walnut dyes, and the hamper's shape, form, and geometric patterns characterize traditional Cherokee basketry. Like the Cheoah Valley baskets, the hamper documents values that women continued to share through the removal period. It testifies to the transmission of certain kinds of knowledge across place and time. These cane trade baskets tie weavers of the past to those of the present and future.

## STORES AS CENTERS OF EXCHANGE

Regardless of their widespread use as currency, baskets seldom appear in surviving store records or inventories. Although not centers of basket exchange, stores served multiple other purposes. William Thomas's Ft. Montgomery store and post office became a meeting ground for the three cultures of Cheoah Valley. Account books from the 1850s reveal the kinds of interactions that gradually recast the societies of those who lived there. William Thomas and Samuel Sherrill's black slaves bought and sold merchandise on their owners' accounts. Whites like smithy William Adams, miller John Hyde, and Reverend R. Deaver were among more than one hundred whites purchasing everything from wool hats and tin plates to cows and coffee pots. In 1852, nearly one hundred Cherokees also kept active accounts.[34] Men came to the store more often than women, and Cherokee women came more frequently than white or black women. All three races shopped in every season and for similar items. The transactions indicate a degree of trust, at least rudimentary common language, and comparable needs and interests.

Women who kept accounts apparently made clothing for their entire families. Over the course of a single year they purchased, usually on credit, hundreds of yards of shirting, stripes, checks, prints, and muslins. Some bought vesting, and others purchased velvet. Their sewing baskets held much from the store—a pair of scissors, a paper of needles, "thimbols," buttons, pins, ribbon, patterns, hooks and eyes, and spools and skeins of thread. Women like *Charlotta* and *Cut-clo-clena* purchased silk and cotton handkerchiefs several times a year, usually two at a time. In December, they took home dress shawls and hats, and *Charlotta* included marbles, a brass bucket, and a "looking glass."[35]

Blankets from the store in green, red, or "blew" warmed many Cheoah Cherokees in the winter of 1852. Sam Owl's wife *Woleyohah* purchased a brass candle stand to brighten their cabin. Some Cherokees may have lacked housewares, but over a period of four years, records indicate that women bought numerous kitchen utensils such as frying pans, skillets, salt cellars, tin cups, coffee pots, pitchers, "tea kittles," plates, knives and forks, and "boles."[36] Such accounts indicate a continuing decline of pottery making, once an important task of women. At the same time, the records suggest the persistence of conventional men's work—the cutting and carving and whittling of furniture. No one, white or Cherokee, purchased furniture of any kind. And no records indicate that anyone, white, black, or Cherokee, bought or sold baskets at the store.

The variety of tools women and men purchased traces an outline of how they lived. Axes, saws, and knives of every sort and size transformed wood into cabins and whatever furnishings they contained, including beds and baskets. Spades, shovels, and hoes turned the earth for planting or extracting roots. Gunlocks, powder, flints, lead, and fishhooks confirm the continuing importance of game. Whites sometimes paid on their accounts with apples, but no Cherokees did. The almost complete absence of foods on store accounts indicates a successful subsistence based on farming, gardening, gathering, and trade—activities that encouraged basket production.[37]

## CHANGES IN SOCIAL SYSTEMS

Indian removal had affected virtually every aspect of women's worlds and diminished their positions of authority and autonomy. Repeated land cessions and the relocation of families eroded town and clan structures. Populations were drastically reduced and townships were small. The land base was restricted, and its ownership often uncertain. As families of origin moved apart, women no longer held clan fields in common and no longer assumed responsibility for clan production of agriculture.

Similarly, matrilocal residence no longer bound Cherokees to one another in an orderly pattern. Once an intrinsic part of matrilineal inheritance and clan agriculture, matrilocal residence diminished in importance after removal. Wives and husbands established their own households apart from the women's family of origin.

As clan members dispersed and couples moved into nuclear households, polygyny also disappeared. Although *Walliz*, Little *Suaga*, and *Yonaguska* each had two wives, postremoval census rolls generally do not indicate the presence of multiple wives. In 1843, Cherokees "passed an ordinance prohibiting polygamy." In addition, they "required those having a plurality of wives to confine themselves to one."[38] When wives shared landownership and farm responsibilities with marriage partners rather than clan relatives, polygyny became ineffective.

Traditions of matrilineal land inheritance also declined. During the years that William Thomas purchased property for Cherokees and retained the titles in his own name, matrilineality effectively ceased. . . . Like their white and black neighbors, North Carolina Cherokees increasingly lived in nuclear households on small farms passed down from fathers, as well as mothers, to their children. . . . Women's trade supported the farming economy of their immediate families.

## THE CIVIL WAR'S IMPACT ON THE CHEROKEE WORLD

The Civil War brought a new wave of misery to the Cherokees. Hundreds of men enrolled under Thomas to serve in a home guard, and western North Carolina became the site of skirmishes and raids that depleted the countryside of natural and cultivated resources. Farm, store, tanyard, mill, and odd jobs vanished, and few could purchase the blackberries and chestnuts, peaches and corn, deerskins and ginseng Cherokees customarily bartered even from those fortunate enough to acquire them.

Battles were fought in Charleston adjacent to Bird Town, on Deep Creek where many Cherokees lived before and after removal, and in Murphy at the junction of the Valley and Hiwassee Rivers. Skirmishes and raids crossed the gap at Soco and pocked the long valley. Disease rolled through encampments, and Cherokee soldiers died of mumps and measles as often as battle wounds. "Today I am not well," one soldier wrote home to *Ino-li*, "but I am alive." Many of his comrades were not so fortunate. Five died shortly after they encamped at Strawberry Plains, and others were "very sick." Sickness also afflicted those at home, for *Tse-ghisini* wrote to ask "how those quite a few sick at home are getting along."[39]

When crops failed in 1863, the counties of western North Carolina were reduced to a "suffering and bleeding country." Even "the best of our citizens," wrote Margaret Love of Quallatown to Governor Vance, "are not able to get provisions." Clergymen cautioned their mourning congregations that they could offer no help. In the spring of 1864, Cherokee women and children were living "on weed and the bark of trees." To feed their children, Love wrote, many women "have gone to the South in search of bread."[40] Those who remained at home planted their crops with hoes made of gun barrels.[41]

Women's trade, once a sign of their social and economic security, had become a matter of necessity. Rather than expressing women's autonomy, it was now a response to their poverty. In their own settlements and those of neighboring whites, women walked from house to house to exchange baskets for a bit of pork, an old dress, or some household necessity.

· · ·

From the time of earliest contact with Europeans in the late 1600s until removal's 1838 destruction of the southeastern Cherokee Nation, women developed informal trade relations with other Cherokees, other Native Americans, and European Americans. Long-established systems of matrilineal inheritance, polygyny, and matrilocal residence ensured their economic and social autonomy. Traveling to private and public markets in colonial settlements and Indian villages, women traded everything from baskets and human captives to corn and medicinal herbs.

Increasingly, however, Cherokees found it expedient to establish social, legal, and political institutions that closely mimicked those of the dominant European American culture. Even though the systems that had once supported them were formally circumscribed, there is written and woven evidence that women continued to establish trading partners.

After completion of Indian removal in 1840, Cherokees remaining in North Carolina struggled to succeed on limited land with diminished resources. Women continued to barter with neighbors, contributing to the subsistence of their nuclear families. By the time the Civil War brought increased poverty and disease to the Cherokees, women's trade had become an essential aspect of survival, a pattern that continued well into the twentieth century. Over time, baskets continued to be their most enduring trade goods. Although records of women's work scarcely exist, surviving trade baskets offer powerful testimony to the skill of Cherokee women in establishing markets wherever and however they lived.

NOTES

1. Samuel Cole Williams, *The Memoirs of Lieut. Henry Timberlake, 1756–1765* (1765; reprint, Marietta, Ga.: Continental Book Co., 1948), 92.

2. William C. McDowell Jr., ed. *Colonial Records of South Carolina: Journals of the Commissioners of the Indian Trade, September 20, 1710–August 29, 1718* (Columbia: University of South Carolina Press, 1955), 16 and 24 November 1716; Raymond Demere to William Henry Lyttleton, 13 October 1756, in McDowell, *Colonial Records of South Carolina: Documents Relating to Indian Affairs, 1754–1765* (Columbia: University of South Carolina Press, 1970).

3. Samuel Cole Williams, ed. *Adair's History of the American Indians* (1775; reprint, New York: Promontory Press, 1930), 454.

4. McDowell, *Colonial Records of S.C.: Journals*, 23 November 1716, 23 January and 5 February 1717; Sarah H. Hill, *Weaving New Worlds: Southeastern Cherokee Women and Their Basketry* (Chapel Hill: University of North Carolina Press, 1997), 336 n. 48; Paul Demere to Lyttleton, 2 May 1759, in McDowell, *Colonial Records of S.C.: Documents*; Williams, *Adair's History*, 454.

5. Kentucky gained independence from Virginia and was admitted to statehood in 1792. Tennessee became a state in 1796, when its population exceeded 60,000 (D. W. Meinig, *The Shaping of America* [New Haven: Yale University Press, 1986], 348–49, 351).

6. William G. McLoughlin and Walter H. Conser, "The Cherokees in Transition: A Statistical Analysis of the Federal Cherokee Census of 1838," *Journal of American History* 64, no. 3 (December 1977), 681, 693–94. The Cherokee census of 1825 enumerated 13,583 Cherokees, 147 white men married to Cherokees, 73 white women married to Cherokees, 1,277 African slaves, and 400 North Carolina Cherokees "not included in the census and who have since merged among us" (John Ridge to Albert Gallatin, 27 February 1826, John Howard Payne MSS, 9:103, Ayer Collection, Newberry Library, Chicago (hereafter AC).

7. See Theda Perdue, *Slavery and the Evolution of Cherokee Society, 1540–1866* (Knoxville: University of Tennessee Press, 1979), 50–69, and "Cherokee Planters: The Development of Plantation Slavery before Removal," in *The Cherokee Indian Nation: A Troubled History*, ed. Duane King (Knoxville: University of Tennessee Press, 1979), 110–28; and William G. McLoughlin and Walter H. Conser, "The Cherokee Censuses of 1808, 1825, and 1835," in *The Cherokee Ghost Dance*, by William G. McLoughlin (Macon, Ga.: Mercer University Press, 1984), 215–50. With the establishment of a national and centralized government, the Cherokee nation became officially known as the Cherokee Nation.

8. Steiner to Heckewelder, 6 March 1820, Vaux Papers, Historical Society of Pennsylvania, Philadelphia.

9. *Missionary Herald* 25, no. 4 (April 1829): 132, AC; Rennard Strickland, *Fire and the Spirits: Cherokee Law from Clan to Court* (Norman: University of Oklahoma Press, 1975); Laws of the Cherokee Nation, Resolutions 3, 4, 11–12, ibid. Codification of laws was an aspect of change among Cherokees. It is difficult to assess its effect on those who lived in the nation's hinterlands.

10. *Missionary Herald* 24, no. 4 (April 1829): 132, AC; Strickland, *Fire and the Spirits*, esp. 81–102; Laws of the Cherokee Nation, Resolutions 1, 2, 11, 20, ibid.; Hawkins to James McHenry, 4 May 1797, in Benjamin Hawkins, *A Sketch of the Creek Country in the Years 1798 and 1799 and, Letters of Benjamin Hawkins, 1796–1806* (Spartanburg, S.C.: The Reprint Co., 1974). The Lighthorse was established in 1808, clan revenge abolished in 1810, and courts and judges appointed in 1820. Hawkins claimed Cherokees asked to abandon blood revenge in cases of accidental deaths.

11. Thomas Jefferson, *Writings* (New York: Library of America, 1984), 561.

12. Strickland, *Fire and the Spirits*, 98. Emphasis by the author.

13. Laws of the Cherokee Nation, Resolution 57, ibid., 217–18. The Cherokee National Council and courts arbitrated numerous inheritance disputes. See John Howard Payne MSS, 7:57–61, AC; and Gambolds to Rev. John Herbst, 10 November 1810, Moravian Archives, Salem, N.C. (hereafter MAS).

14. Ridge to Gallatin, 27 February 1826, John Howard Payne MSS, 9:109, AC; see also Springplace and Oothcaloga Mission Diaries and Letters, 22 May 1809, MAS. Ridge's letter is reproduced in Theda Perdue and Michael D. Green, eds., *The Cherokee Removal: A Brief History with Documents* (Boston: Bedford Books of St. Martin's Press, 1995), 34–45. John Ridge, son of Chief Major Ridge and his "mixed-blood" wife, Susie Wickett, attended the Brainerd Mission School, then went on to Cornwall Academy in Connecticut. After marrying the white daughter of a local innkeeper, he returned to the Cherokee Nation and assumed a position of leadership. By 1832, he was leading a group of dissidents known as the Ridge or Treaty Party, who conspired to accept the federal government's terms of Cherokee removal. In 1835, John Ridge violated the Cherokee law prohibiting land sales and signed the Treaty of New Echota ceding all remaining southeastern Cherokee land. Following removal, John Ridge and two other leaders of the Treaty Party were executed by the Cherokees.

15. Ridge to Gallatin, 27 February 1826, John Howard Payne MSS, 9:111, AC; Raymond D. Fogelson, "On the Petticoat Government of the Eighteenth-Century Cherokee," in *Personality and the Cultural Construction of Society: Papers in Honor of Melvin E. Spiro*, ed. David K. Jordan and Marc J. Swartz (Tuscaloosa: University of Alabama Press, 1990), 171; Evan Jones to Dr. Bolles, 20 January 1830, Papers of the American Board of Commissioners for Foreign Missions, 18.3.1, vol. 2, Shorter College, Rome, Ga.; William G. McLoughlin, *Cherokees and Missionaries, 1789–1839* (New Haven: Yale University Press, 1984), 204–5, 217.

16. Carl F. Klinck and James J. Talmer, eds., *The Journal of Major John Norton, 1816* (Toronto:

Champlain Society, 1970), 77–78. For examples of other marriage laws, see Laws of the Cherokee Nation, Resolutions 38 and 57, in Strickland, *Fire and the Spirits*.

17. The Gambolds to Rev. Charles Gottlieb Reichel, 15 September 1810, 3, M412, Folder 1, MAS.

18. "Brother Martin Schneider's Report of His Journey to the Upper Cherokee Towns (1783–1784)," in *Early Travels in the Tennessee Country, 1540–1800*, ed. Samuel Cole Williams (Johnson City, Tenn.: The Watauga Press, 1928), 262; William Harlan Gilbert Jr., "Eastern Cherokees," *Bureau of American Ethnology Bulletin* 133 (1943), 318–21.

19. Gambold to the Rev. John Herbst, 10 November 1810, 2, MAS; *Missionary Herald* 24, no. 4 (April 1829): 132, AC.

20. William Fyffe, "Letter to Brother John, Feb. 1, 1761," 19, Thomas Gilcrease Institute of American History and Art, Tulsa, Oklahoma.

21. "William Bartram's Observations on the Creek and Cherokee Indians," in *William Bartram on the Southeastern Indians*, ed. Gregory A. Waselkov and Kathryn E. Holland Braund (Lincoln: University of Nebraska Press, 1995), 152; Alexander Longe, "A Small Postscript of the ways and maners of the Indians called Charikees," copy of (lost) MSS, Box 5536, Great Britain Society of the Propagation of the Gospel in Foreign Parts, South Carolina, 1715–1851, Library of Congress, 22; M. Thomas Hatley (*The Dividing Paths: Cherokees and South Carolinians through the Era of Revolution* [New York: Oxford University Press, 1993]) examines changing European attitudes toward native women in the eighteenth century. Fogelson relates changes in women's status to "local ecology, economics, social structure, and political organization" ("On the Petticoat Government," 170).

22. Jefferson, *Writings*, 1117–18.

23. Louis-Philippe, *Diary of My Travels in America*, trans. Stephen Becker (New York: Delacorte Press, 1977), 75, 81–83; "Report of the Journey of the Brethren Abraham Steiner and Frederick C. de Schweinitz to the Cherokee and the Cumberland Settlements (1799)," in Williams, ed., *Early Travels in the Tennessee Country*, 464; "Francois Andre Michaux's Travels West of Alleghany Mountains, 1802," in *Early Western Travels, 1748–1846*, vol. 3, ed. Reuben Gold Thwaites (Cleveland: The Arthur H. Clark Co., 1904), 264. See also Ora Brooks Peake, *A History of the United States Indian Factory System, 1795–1822* (Denver: Sage Books, 1954), 13. See in particular 28 November, 2 and 3 December 1796, and 26 January 1797.

24. Hawkins, *Sketch and Letters*, 28 November 1796.

25. Ibid., 28 November, 2 and 3 December 1796, 26 January 1797.

26. Ibid., 30 November 1796.

27. Jacob Wohlfarht to Rev. Charles Gotthold Reichel, 13 February 1803, 15, M411, Folder 3, MAS; John Gambold to Rev. Christian Lewis Benzien, 7 December 1806, 24, M411, Folder 5, MAS. For Moravian work among the Cherokees, see Adelaide L. Fries, *Records of the Moravians in North Carolina*, vol. 5 (1784–92) (Raleigh: State Dept. of Archives and History, 1968); Robert S. Walker, *Torchlight to the Cherokees* (New York: Macmillan, 1931); Henry W. Malone, *American Indians and Christian Missions* (Chicago: University of

Chicago Press, 1981); McLoughlin, *Cherokees and Missionaries*; and Rowena McClinton Ruff, "To Ascertain the Mind and Circumstances of the Cherokee Nation, Springplace, Georgia, 1805–1821" (master's thesis, Western Carolina University, 1992).

28. According to the Meigs 1809 Cherokee census (in MAS), Vann was one of the wealthiest Cherokees in the Cherokee Nation and one of the richest men in the Southeast. By the time of his death in 1809, he owned a ferry on the Chattahoochee River, 115 black slaves, 250 horses, 1,000 cattle, 150 hogs, and 9 sheep.

29. Gambolds to Reichel, 15 September 1810, M412, Folder 1, MAS; John Gambold to a friend in Salem, 14 November 1810, 1, M420:b1, MAS.

30. In 1955, the director of the Moravian Historical Society in Bethlehem, Pennsylvania, donated the baskets to the Peabody Museum of Natural History at Yale University and identified them as having come from Springplace Mission (William Sturtevant, personal communication, 1991).

31. Hawkins, *Sketch and Letters*, 30 November and 1 December 1796; Return J. Meigs, "Journal of Occurrences," 13 February 1805, Records of Cherokee Indian Agency in Tenn., 1801–35, RG75, M208, Roll 6, U.S. Federal Record Center, East Point, Ga.; William G. McLoughlin, "Cherokee Anomie, 1794–1809," in *Uprooted Americans: Essays to Honor Oscar Handlin*, ed. Richard Bushman, Neil Harris, David Rothman, Barbara Miller, Solomon Thernstrom, and Stephen Thernstrom (Boston: Little, Brown, and Co., 1979), 138–39.

32. Norton, *Norton's Journal*, 71, 125, 132.

33. Drury P. Armstrong, *Diary: 1842–1848*, TVA Archaeology Bibliography Note, Museum of the Cherokee Indian, Cherokee, N.C. Original in the McClung Historical Collection, Lawson McGhee Library, Knoxville, Tennessee.

34. Among many examples of slave purchases, see Day Book, Ft. Montgomery, 1852–54, 13, 18, 39, 54, 57, 70, 99 116, and 126, William Holland Thomas Collection, Special Collections Library, Duke University; for a record of the purchases of Adams, Hyde, and Deaver, see ibid., 8, 12, 13, 30, 41, 44, 50, 60, and 61.

35. Ibid. Among the numerous examples, see 8, 23, 27, 39, 42, 44, 45, 46, and 47.

36. Ibid., 13, 23, 52, 58, 64, 65, 79, 92, 99, 100, and 178. Purchases in 1852 also reflect the federal disbursement of approximately fifty dollars to each Cherokee.

37. Ibid., 18, 22, 27, 32, 102, 110, 130, and 131.

38. William Sloane to Richard Simpson, 28 December 1843, MS 87–52, Museum of the Cherokee Indian, Cherokee, N.C.

39. *Tse-ghisini* to *Ino-li*, 8 and 20 July 1862, in Jack Frederick Kilpatrick and Anna Gritts Kilpatrick, *Shadow of Sequoyah: Social Documents of the Cherokees, 1862–1964* (Norman: University of Oklahoma Press, 1965), 6, 7.

40. Margaret E. Love to Governor Vance, 10 May 1864, Governor's Papers 177, North Carolina Department of Archives and History, Raleigh, N.C.; see also William Holland Thomas to Vance, 13 May 1864, ibid.; John Finger, *The Eastern Band of Cherokees* (Knoxville: University of Tennessee Press, 1990), 82–100; Vernon Crow, *Storm in the Mountains: Thomas' Confederate Legion of Cherokee Indians and Mountaineers* (Cherokee, N.C.: Museum of the

Cherokee Indian, 1982); Kilpatrick and Kilpatrick, *Shadow of Sequoyah*, 3–15; and E. Stanley Godbold Jr. and Mattie U. Russell, *The Life of William Holland Thomas, Confederate Colonel and Cherokee Chief* (Knoxville: University of Tennessee Press, 1990), 90–128.

41. Jack Frederick Kilpatrick and Anna Gritts Kilpatrick, "Record of a North Carolina Cherokee Township Trial (1862)," *Southern Indian Studies* 16 (1964): 22–23.

# Chapter Three

# Producing Dependence:
# Women, Work, and Yeoman Households
# in Low-Country South Carolina

STEPHANIE MCCURRY

"Self-working farmer." That was the face low-country yeomen turned to the world beyond the fence. But it was only one profile of yeoman household economy, inseparable from the other, domestic, one. Infinitely more difficult to see, the domestic face turned into the household, where the daily work of producing independence was conducted. But Abner Ginn and his neighbors were not really "self-working farmers." On the contrary, the very term expressed their successful appropriation of the labor of others: the women, children, and, sometimes, slaves who peopled their households and tilled their fields. The vitality of male independence that characterized the public sphere of marketplace and ballot box was tied intimately to the legal and customary dependencies of the household.[1] Dependence was the stuff of which independence—and manhood—was made.

In yeoman households, familial and productive relations were virtually indistinguishable and both were defined by a series of dependencies that subordinated all members to the male head. Any number of factors shaped the particular configuration of labor, including the total number of household members, their sex and age, the stage in the family life cycle, and the presence of slaves, whether hired or owned, and their sex and age. But in yeoman households, the work done by wives, sons, and daughters was, by definition, crucial to the calculus of production. Even the ownership of slaves did not change the predominantly familial character of household economy. Thus, while relations between masters and slaves were part of the social dynamics of a substantial minority of yeoman households, the relations of domination and subordination characteristic of every household were, in fact, those between the sexes. Gender was thus a primary axis of power in yeoman households. It undergirded the material production of independence and framed its political meanings as well.

Abner Ginn's story hints at the importance of women's work and at its unorthodox sphere in yeoman households. With no slaves and only one adolescent son, Ginn had little choice but to rely on his wife and two adult daughters to help him run the three plows he regularly employed on his Beaufort farm. Travelers underlined the point about white women's field work in their shock at the discomfort and apparent disorder of yeoman homes and in their disapproval of a gender division of labor that seemed to weigh unnaturally on women. The bourgeois assumptions embedded in, for example, Frederick Law Olmsted's perspective reveal a great deal more about him than his yeoman subjects, but they do serve the purpose of dramatizing sectional difference, historicizing women's work, and cautioning against acceptance of the still powerful universal claims of bourgeois gender ideology or domesticity. They also provide a sharp reminder of the relevance of class to the workings of gender politics in the slave South.

The literary traveler Frederick Law Olmsted had more than sufficient opportunity to observe the domestic arrangements of yeoman households. Lacking letters of introduction to planter families, he was forced not infrequently to seek plain folk's hospitality. He was a miserable guest. Neither yeoman homes nor their inhabitants conformed to his standards of decency and comfort. He complained incessantly about filthy, vermin-infested cabins, "mere square pens of logs roofed over" with a "shed of boards before the door." He longed for the comforts of home: a private room with a "clean sweet bed" in which to sleep "alone and undisturbed"; hot water in the morning with which to wash; a parlor, curtained, carpeted, and "glowing softly with the light of sperm candles or a shaded lamp"; an armchair; a "fragrant cup of tea" with refined sugar and wheat bread; and the soothing sound of a woman playing classical music or reading aloud from Shakespeare or Dickens. Instead, when he was forced into yeoman homes by the approach of nightfall, "nine times out of ten" he had to sleep in "a room with others, in a bed that stank, supplied with but one sheet if any," and to make his morning ablutions in a common washbasin that doubled as a bread bowl. He found no garden, no flowers, no fruit, no tea, no cream, sugar, or bread, no curtains, no lifting windows, no couch and no carpets, not to mention Shakespeare or sheet music.[2]

At a purely descriptive level, Olmsted's depiction was not inaccurate. Yeoman men and women did live mostly in crude, unchinked double log cabins with porches in front and kitchens behind and with chimneys of sticks and clay and unglazed windows. One former slave from a yeoman neighborhood in Marion District pointed out that there was little difference between her "one room pole house that wad daubed wid dirt" and the one "my white folks live in [which was] a pole house daubed wid dirt too."³ Inventories of yeomen's household goods, moreover, confirm that they were few and basic: wood and pewter dishes, cast-iron pots, more homemade stools than "seting chares," and more "shuck mattresses" than the prized feather beds that, where they existed, were typically the most valuable household goods yeomen owned. Luxury items such as clocks, books, and mahogany furniture were rare even in yeoman slaveholders' households. Upholstered armchairs, pianos, couches, and carpets were nowhere to be found.⁴

Olmsted's tone of moral indignation suggests, however, that something more basic than his sense of comfort was assaulted in yeoman homes. Indeed, his was the vision of the capitalist vanguard. As he saw it, slavery had corrupted all it touched, including the "natural" relations of men and women. Unlike the newly privatized middle-class homes of the urban Northeast (Olmsted's point of reference), from which so-called productive labor had been largely expelled by the 1850s, yeoman households remained the locus of production as well as of reproduction and consumption.⁵ They had not developed the familiar and superior spatial, material, or moral arrangements of bourgeois "homes" associated with separate spheres and domesticity. Instead, house spilled out into yard and yard into house in total disregard of privacy and hygiene, as basic notions of order and morality would suggest. There was no parlor, never mind a womanly parlor culture, and the kitchen, far from representing the emotional center of domestic life, was usually an outbuilding physically separate from the dwelling house.⁶ There was, of course, a customary gender division of labor in yeoman households and distinct ideas about what constituted appropriate work for men and women. But the customary arrangement of work and space that prevailed did not, as Olmsted was acutely aware, conform to bourgeois beliefs about the gender division of labor, space, and spheres of influence. Indeed, it confounded them. Deeply invested in the universalist claims of bourgeois gender ideology, committed to the notion that gender difference was literally written on the body, Olmsted could not confront a different gender division of labor without confronting its discomfiting implications. Olmsted may have written off the yeomanry as backward and uncivilized, but his outrage implies that the challenge to his own universalist assumptions was not so easily dismissed.⁷

If Olmsted's main point was that bourgeois distinctions between public and private, work and home, men and women's spheres had no meaning in yeoman households, then his fruitless search for the "cult of domesticity" made one other point abundantly clear. Southern society was fashioned as distinct not simply by the external relations of households—say those between yeomen and planters—but, perhaps more fundamentally, by the relations that prevailed within them. In yeoman households, gender relations were the key to the organization of production. Independence was achieved by a gender division of labor in which women's work in the fields and in the provision of subsistence and market goods was a central, although still largely invisible and unacknowledged, part.

Women's labor of all sorts has historically been obscured by the public representation of the household in the person of its male head and by definitions of work that focus on the value of market exchange.[8] Such a resolutely ungendered approach cannot even begin to explain how, for example, self-sufficiency was achieved on yeoman farms. Yeoman farmers were fully aware that they could aspire to self-sufficiency in large measure because, in addition to grain, virtually everything else their families ate was grown or raised, preserved, and cooked by women, and virtually everything they wore was spun and woven, dyed and sewed by women. What little milk and butter yeomen had their wives or daughters produced. "Milk cow!" a slave man said incredulously, "I nebber bid to sich a ting in my life. Dat 'oman work."[9] A farm household without a farm wife was a disadvantaged one indeed. Even planters sought married overseers to acquire women's labor in the dairy and poultry house and in the making of cloth and clothing.[10]

The value of women's work was clear. By their industry, wives and daughters ensured that nothing was purchased that could be produced at home, whatever the cost in labor and sweat. In antebellum yeoman households women contributed more than the services and skills that continue to represent the unpaid labor of wives and mothers; they contributed as well the production of goods for household consumption that had elsewhere passed into the realm of the market. "I have been down at York today," the up-country farm wife Mary Davis Brown noted in her diary, and "I did not by much of enything."[11] In the broadest sense, the women's "domestic" production played a critical role in limiting the extent of the home market in consumer goods in the antebellum South. Indeed, the continued high levels of household production throughout the antebellum period point to one local manifestation of the systematic difference between farm women's work North and South. If yeoman farmers escaped relations of debt and dependency with local merchants and planters, they knew that the accomplishment was as much their wives' as their own.

Women's contribution to subsistence notwithstanding, the gender division of labor in yeoman households did not conform to distinctions between domestic and market production. The reason is simple. All economy was "domestic economy," at least in comparative terms; none of the products of yeoman households was definitively a subsistence or a market crop. Even cotton, although it could not be eaten, could be marketed in the raw for cash or goods or, by virtue of women's traditional craft skills, be turned into cloth for use at home or for sale. Yeoman families kept their account balances with local merchants within manageable limits not just with the annual influx of credit from the sale of two or three bales of cotton or a few bushels of surplus corn but also with the steady trickle of "country produce" that testified to women's ability to turn household production to market exchange. Intended chiefly for use in the household, the products of women's labor regularly appeared on the credit side of the ledger in store accounts and in petty trade with local planters; presumably, they figured as well in the informal exchanges, virtually impossible to document, between yeoman households. Eggs, chickens, feathers, butter, tallow, and homespun cloth were sufficiently important to local trade to figure prominently in the advertisements of village and crossroads merchants. "I feel like eating chicken and eggs, please bring me some," one enterprising rural Orangeburg merchant bantered in an illustrated advertisement, promising in another that those who called at "Uncle Tom's Corner . . . will be certain to get as much for [their] money, eggs, chickens, rags, and Raw Hides as [they] can almost anywhere else."[12] The value of such transactions usually did not approach that of the annual sale of the cotton crop, but the $23.50 that Mary Davis Brown was paid for the "web of janes cloth" she sold in 1858 must have been a significant contribution to a typical perennially cash-poor household.[13] At least one household of women, a widowed Barnwell farm wife and her daughters, managed to eke out a living by making cloth for sale, and another low-country woman told federal officials that she had purchased her farm with the proceeds of her "weaving." From this perspective, women's work provides one of the best demonstrations that in the antebellum South, yeoman households did not exist outside the market or fully within its grasp but moved along a continuum of self-sufficiency, interdependence, and market engagement.[14]

The significance of women's work in the production of independence was not lost on contemporary politicians. In periodic prescriptions for economic reform, politicians encouraged the products of women's labor to sustain self-sufficiency at the level of the household and independence at the sectional level. Domestic economy was a proslavery strategy. "True independence is to be found in your own farms," John Belton O'Neall, a prominent jurist and agricultural reformer, exhorted suffering cotton producers in 1844. "Raise my countrymen your own hogs, sheep, cattle horses, and mules, clothe your own household by domestic wheel and loom . . . supply your own tables with flour, potatoes, butter, and cheese of your own crops . . . and you can bid defiance to all the tariffs in the world." The centrality of women's work in such admittedly ill-fated strategies was evident. In the midst of the nullification crisis, the Pendleton Farmers' Society had initiated an antitariff campaign by obliging their members to appear at the next meeting "dressed *entirely in the Homespun of the district.*" This gratifying acknowledgment of the yeomanry's true republican style (they usually wore homespun—planters did not) was, like O'Neall's invocation of the republican producer ideal, a tribute to women's traditional craft skills. But the society went further, voting to cancel the annual prizes for stock and grain in the belief that "the encouragement of our household industry [is] the only means within our reach to avert in some measure the inferior effects of the . . . act." Prizes were awarded only for cuts of plain and twilled homespun of cotton or wool, for linen diapers, coverlets, and imitation gingham cloth, for wool and cotton stockings, and for butter and cheese. Women thus received all of the premiums that year in acknowledgment of their work in the production of independence. And if yeoman women's work acquired added value in political crisis, it was not entirely neglected in quieter times.[15] In their romantic dreams of southern independence, politicians elevated to a sectional strategy the gendered practices that constituted the yeomanry's usual bid for independence.

There was, however, one aspect of women's work that contemporary southerners were entirely unwilling to acknowledge. That was their labor, and especially wives' labor, in the fields. It is an interesting historical omission, especially in light of the inordinate attention such field work drew from northern and European travelers. Frederick Law Olmsted, for one, insisted that he had "in fact, seen more white native American women at work in the hottest sunshine in a single month, and that near mid-summer, than in all my life in the free states." It was, he added, "not on account of an emergency, as in harvesting, either, but in the regular cultivation of cotton and of corn [but] chiefly of cotton." His almost anthropological interest in the subject reflected passionately held but newly constructed truths about women's physiology and the "natural" gender divisions of spheres and labor that existed among the ascendant American and European bourgeoisie. Olmsted revealed as much when he admitted that confronted with the spectacle of slave women plowing, he had "watched with some interest to see if there was any indication that their sex unfitted them for the occupation." Southerners would never have held such essentialist views of gender as to separate it so completely from slave, and thus from class and racial, status. To outsiders, however, the transgressions against white womanhood witnessed in the yeomanry's fields served to confirm the superiority of free-labor society. Frances Trollope's harsh judgment of yeomen and sympathy for their wives, those "slaves of the soil," as she put it, was thus a foreigner's gross misunderstanding of gender, race, and class relations in the slave South.[16] But it captured an important truth.

Perhaps because they, too, remain influenced by bourgeois ideas about separate spheres and the gender division of labor, most historians have assumed that field work was men's work, and, of course, slaves'. In taking this position, they have inadvertently deepened a contemporary southern silence on the subject that derived from very different sensibilities about the gender conventions of slave society.[17] Contemporaries of all classes were aware that the labor yeoman farmers commanded in the field included that of their wives and daughters; most yeomen simply did not own enough slaves to free female family members from field work. In the safe confines of the Black Oak Agricultural Society, an association of largely planter citizens of St. Stephen's Parish in rural Charleston District, Samuel DuBose openly attributed the local yeomanry's success at short-staple cotton cultivation to the fact that it was "a labor in which wives and daughters may conveniently and safely share with the husband and father. While he traces the furrow, they, protected by their sun bonnets, eradicate the weeds with a light hoe." Few public men showed such poor political judgment as did DuBose in acknowledging white women's labor in the fields.[18]

The gender relations of yeoman households embodied a dangerous class divide within low-country society—one that race could not close. The Colleton planter David Gavin jabbed the danger spot when he noted that his neighbor William Salsberry "used to work [his older girls] in the fields like negroes." Everybody knew yeoman women and girls worked in the fields. But the yeomanry's customary gender relations had to be forced into at least ideological conformity with those of the planters lest critics of slavery attempt to open up that class distinction, as, for example, Hinton Rowan Helper did in his famous *Impending Crisis of the South*.[19] In the South as in the North, gender ideology was anything but descriptive, and it functioned, in part, to occlude the centrality of white women's work. The issue for yeoman men and women was less the work women actually performed in the household than the representation of it to the community at large. Yeoman wives and daughters might work in the fields from Monday to Saturday, for example, but they would not appear at church on Sunday without a proper dress and shoes.[20] Ellander Horton embodied the convention in her violation of it. She was ostracized by the respectable community of yeomen in the Coosawhatchie Swamp (Abner Ginn's settlement) not because, as her daughter explained, "[m]e and sister worked together with the colored women in the field ['We had no men servants'] and made the crop," but rather because her mother sustained unorthodox relations with local free blacks, and purportedly had engaged in a love affair with a mulatto man, the father of her four daughters. Likewise, although less dramatically, Gavin's neighbor William Salsberry had violated community conventions not by working his daughters in the fields—all yeomen did that—but by working them "like negroes." The offense, as it turns out, was that he had disinherited his eldest daughters even though they had worked at his side to "make some of this property." Both in his lifetime and afterward Salsberry apparently had denied his three older daughters their rightful place in the community of respectable yeomen and had, as a result, invited community disapprobation of his domestic affairs.[21]

Women's work in the fields, although customary, was customarily ignored and even denied. A collusive silence surrounded one of the labor practices that most clearly distinguished yeoman farms from plantations, that set yeoman wives and daughters apart from their planter counterparts, that dangerously eroded the social distinctions between free women and slaves, and that cut deeply into the pride of men raised in a culture of honor. It was indeed the necessity of denying class difference between white southern women that rendered yeoman women's field labor all but invisible. Out of respect for yeoman masters and particularly for their votes, planter politicians refrained from noticing it.

The gender division of labor in yeoman households had political meaning that inhered in the production of material independence and went well beyond it, supporting the construction and reproduction of the identity of "free man" and master in the head of the household of the female dependents, including the wife. Yet historians have found it difficult to know with any certainty how yeoman farmers deployed their families' labor, especially in the fields, and have been able only to speculate about how it shaped relations with household dependents—with the slaves whose labor they owned or hired and with other subordinates, including women, in their households and Black Belt communities. But one very rare treasure, a yeoman farmer's journal, permits the historian to cross the threshold of the household and take a look inside. It confirms some of the labor patterns discernible in the more intransigent public records, and, more important, it suggests how they supported the manly public identity of its author.

James F. Sloan was not a low-country farmer. He lived in the up-country district of Spartanburg. But notwithstanding the differences in household economy above and below the fall line, Sloan's journals for his farm operation, one identical in size to Abner Ginn's, provide a tantalizing glance into the late-antebellum world of yeoman farmers. For Sloan assiduously recorded the tasks performed by each member of his household on the sixty improved acres that he cultivated. In 1854, when his journal begins, Sloan's household consisted of himself, a thirty-four-year-old native-born South Carolinian, his second wife, Dorcas Lee Sloan, three children from his first marriage (a son, Seth, who was fifteen or sixteen years old, and two daughters, Sarah-Jane and Barbara, who were about thirteen and fourteen years old, respectively), and at least two other children (James Haddon and an unnamed baby girl) from his marriage with Dorcas Lee. For only one year, 1859, did that household include a slave, an adolescent girl named Manda whom Sloan hired for four dollars per month.[22]

If there was ever any doubt about the strategies by which yeoman farmers produced independence in the absence of significant numbers of slaves, Sloan's journal puts it to rest, along with any lingering notions that field labor marked an absolute class and racial divide between southern women, slave and free. Sloan put his "wimmin" to work in the fields regularly throughout the year, from at least late spring to the end of picking season in December. In June 1856, for example, while he and his eldest son, Seth, harrowed the cotton and corn fields, "the wimmin commenced hoeing cotton in the lot field." Prior to that, since May, the "children" had been thinning out the cotton, and in June they were joined by "the wimmin," who hoed first the corn and then the cotton fields. By 5 July, Sloan noted, the "girls had finished the cotton," and by 15 July, his crop was laid by. The children went to school briefly in August, but by 15 September, the cotton was "right smartly open" and picking season began. Sloan did not note the length of the picking season in 1856, but in 1858, it started on 8 September and continued until 30 November, during which time the "children" and the "balance of the family" picked cotton while he and Seth periodically attended to other tasks.[23]

Each year the tempo of work differed slightly. In June 1857, in one tragic interruption of the seasonal cycle, Dorcas Lee Sloan took "very bad" and later that day gave birth to "a still born babe"; she stayed out of the fields for a time after that. A little more than a year later, she was again absent from the fields, but this time the reason was a joyous one. "Mrs Sloan sent out and presented me with a very fine girl child," Sloan recorded with evident pride on 7 July.[24] What Dorcas Lee Sloan thought we can only imagine. But given the toll on her own health of repeated pregnancies and the recent memory of having lost a baby, Mrs. Sloan no doubt shared something of the sentiment of another new up-country mother, Mary Davis Brown, who wrote after the birth of her tenth child, Fanny: "Oh how thankful i should be fore all things to doo so well a living chile and living mother."[25]

Mrs. Sloan did not work in the fields for some time after the baby was born; in fact, it is entirely possible that her husband hired the slave girl to compensate for the field labor lost as a consequence. But yeoman women like Mrs. Sloan made a fundamental contribution to the household economy at great cost to their own health. For household independence required above all else the reproduction of the labor force. Well might yeomen boast, then, as another up-country man did, of the recent "edition to our family," declaring himself "well satisfied" with his riches: "a fine garden . . . a nice little crop . . . a pretty little stock of hogs and Cattle . . . the Best neighbour," and children who were growing "powerful fast and Bids fare to be a smart help to me soon should they be sparrd."[26] Children were precious assets in the relentless struggle to keep the farm.

The particular allocation of labor and tasks changed along with the family life cycle and with the presence of other dependent laborers. Yet every year, Sloan's family, including his teenage daughters and, although with less regularity, his wife, worked in the fields steadily from May until December, enabling them to produce sufficient subsistence and market crops to maintain their status as a respectable yeoman family. And if, unlike some other farmers' daughters, Sloan's girls were spared the indignity of driving a plow, the farm task perhaps most clearly demarcated as masculine, it was, at least in 1859, because another young woman assumed that burden: the slave Manda, who joined Seth Sloan in the fields and matched him task for task the year round.[27] Manda's presence did not, needless to say, relieve the Sloan women of the burden of field work, never mind the housework.

It did, however, change the gender division of labor, although the point is not that the ownership of slaves relieved yeoman women of domestic drudgery but that it relieved wives of the necessity of combining it with regular field labor. Mrs. Sloan escaped the fields (if temporarily); her daughters did not. They continued to work the land with Manda and Seth. In this respect, the Sloan case suggests that the deployment of female family members' labor constituted a significant difference between those yeoman households with slaves and those without. The point is confirmed by comparison with small planters' operations. The most striking distinction between the Sloan household, with its one hired slave, and that of David Golightly Harris (another up-country man), who had eleven slaves of his own and access to more belonging to his planter father, was that unlike Sloan's, Harris's wife and children never worked in the fields, and his children attended school the year round.[28] This comparison is a more stark one, admittedly. But the pattern is clear. The presence of even one slave, even if hired and even if a young woman, changed the gender division of labor among family members in yeoman households; rarely, if ever, however, did it entirely relieve women family members of field labor.

It is startling how easily Sloan appeared to manage the adjustment to master-hood, however temporary, of a slave. With the exception of Mrs. Sloan's withdrawal from the fields, Manda was introduced to his established labor system with little apparent disruption, extending it but not transforming it. On the first day that Sloan put Manda to work, he simply noted, "Seth and Manda hauled wood and rails," and thereafter she worked alongside Seth. Sloan's was an adjustment facilitated, no doubt, by years of commanding the labor of his other dependents, the "wimmin," "girls," "boys," and "children" who peopled his journal and cultivated the fields.[29]

The gender division of labor on Sloan's farm evinced a great deal more flexibility than the relations of power that underlay it. Not all dependents were equally subordinated to the head, and not only because one was a slave. Manda did occupy a position of particular dependence within Sloan's household, but his wife and daughters did as well. Because sons could eventually reproduce their fathers' role as heads of independent households (a chief goal of the yeomanry's strategy, after all), the patriarch's control and discipline of women's labor and the assumptions of natural authority that accompanied it had profoundly different public meaning. It sustained the vaunted independence of the male yeomanry and yeomen's claim to equality in the slave republic. Indeed, the distinct trajectories of the coming-of-age of Sloan's eldest son and his eldest daughter suggest the generational reproduction of gendered relations of power and their implications for the assumptions yeomen brought to public political culture. For those yeomen who were slaveowners, masterhood assumed its characteristic southern form. But for those who were not or who acquired that status only in advanced age, other domestic relations nurtured many of its prerogatives. In all households, complex social structures and relations lay within and gave definition to public postures.

There can be no doubt that Seth labored under his father's authority throughout the 1850s, finding himself "sent" to do specific tasks on and off the farm. But there can also be no doubt that he was being prepared to assume his father's role. Not only was Seth increasingly assigned independent jobs on the farm; he was gradually introduced to the community of independent men and that of their sons and heirs in the surrounding neighborhood. With increasing regularity, Seth Sloan took his father's place in labor exchanges with neighbors and kinsmen and on trips to the gristmill and cotton screw, county store and tavern. These were the sites of male sociability, some of which also provided the social location of electoral politics and rituals of manhood within which they were enacted. In such places, yeoman sons like Seth Sloan were initiated into the culture of freemen.

Although Seth still worked under his father, he gradually came to stand beside him as well, a coming-of-age perhaps ritually marked in Sloan's journal by the entry of 6 April 1859, when for the first time Seth accompanied him to court day at Spartanburg. It was almost certainly a moment of ritualistic significance when father and son first worked together cultivating cotton in the field called "Seth's patch" in April 1860. Finally, Seth became his father's surrogate in the household, commanding dependents in his absence. Thus, while Seth's own path to independence was surely a long one, he had plenty of opportunity to practice the arts and affectations of masterhood, in immediate supervision over Manda's labor and presumably over that of his sisters as well. The economic and political foundations of his own claim to independence—and masterhood—had been laid.[30]

By contrast, the only coming-of-age ritual Sloan recorded for his daughter, Barbara, was a brief note of her marriage, a ritual that we can be sure conferred authority but of a different and far more circumscribed kind. Yeoman daughters did not enjoy a long apprenticeship in the culture of freemen. Instead, their entry into adulthood was most commonly marked by evangelical conversion— the struggle to submit to God's will, representing, perhaps, proper prologue to the submission required of Christian wives. Daughters came of age into their mothers' world, the world inside the enclosure, ushered in with a brief ceremony, commemorated with "sider" and perhaps a few "wedding trimens," and characterized by a model of female excellence that made the submission of self the apotheosis of womanhood.[31]

Assumptions about gender, race, and power were reproduced within yeoman households in inevitable conjunction with the material basis of independence. Some women, like Barbara Sloan and, in profoundly different ways, Manda, retained the identity of dependents permanently. They represented the foundations of masterhood for those, like Seth, who reproduced the paternal claim to independence and to the public recognition and privileged political position that accompanied it in the slave South.

## NOTES

1. For one study that explores the relationship between domestic hierarchies and public, political ones, see Allen Tullos, *Habits of Industry: White Culture and the Transformation of the Carolina Piedmont* (Chapel Hill: University of North Carolina Press, 1989).

2. Frederick Law Olmsted, *The Cotton Kingdom*, ed. Arthur Schlesinger (New York: Random House, 1984), 160–63; Frederick Law Olmsted, *A Journey in the Back Country* (Williamstown, Mass.: Corner House, 1972), 393–96; Charles E. Beveridge and Charles Capen McLaughlin, eds., *The Papers of Frederick Law Olmsted*, vol. 2 (Baltimore: Johns Hopkins University Press, 1981), 291–311.

3. George Rawick, ed., *The American Slave: A Composite Autobiography, South Carolina Narratives*, supplement, series 2, part 1 (Westport, Conn.: Greenwood Press, 1979), 187–95. Yeoman cabins described by Harriet Martineau and others as "log dwelling[s], composed of two rooms, with an open passage between" bear strong resemblance to those Henry Glassie has characterized as the typical folk-houses of the eastern seaboard. See Harriet Martineau, *Society in America* (1837; reprint, Garden City, N.Y.: Anchor Books, 1962), 150, and Henry Glassie, *Patterns in the Material Folk Culture of the Eastern United States* (Philadelphia: University of Pennsylvania Press, 1968).

4. No probate records have survived for coastal districts, but judging from the inventories of yeoman estates in the Barnwell and Darlington districts, the personal property (and household goods) of nonslaveholding and slaveholding yeomen was roughly comparable in value once the value of slave property was subtracted. For the inventories of yeoman estates used in this study, see Barnwell District, Court of Probate, Inventories, Appraisements and Sales Book, 1789–1840, South Carolina Department of Archives and History, Columbia, S.C.; and Darlington District, Court of Probate, Inventories, Appraisements and Sales Book, 1853–59, ibid.

5. Such distinctions as "productive" and "unproductive" or "domestic" work were as much ideological as anything else. As Jeanne Boydston and others have demonstrated, the notion of "productive" work underwent a process of redefinition in free-labor states in precisely this period. As capitalist relations extended their grip, work was increasingly defined as that labor exchanged in the market for a wage. See Jeanne Boydston, *Home and Work: Housework, Wages, and the Ideology of Labor in the Early Republic* (New York: Oxford University Press, 1990), and Nancy Folbre, "The Unproductive Housewife: Her Evolution in Nineteenth-Century Economic Thought," *Signs* 16, no. 3 (Spring 1991): 463–84. This line of analysis, pioneered by feminist historians concerned about the consequences for women's labor in the Northeast, would be deepened by a greater attention to definitions of work and value in the household economy of the slave states.

6. The literature on bourgeois homes, domesticity, and separate spheres is now enormous, but for a few key contributions, see Barbara Welter, "The Cult of True Womanhood, 1820–1860," *American Quarterly* 18 (Summer 1966): 151–74; Kathryn Kish Sklar, *Catharine Beecher: A Study in American Domesticity* (New Haven: Yale University Press, 1973); Nancy Cott, *The Bonds of Womanhood: Women's Sphere in New England, 1780–1835* (New Haven: Yale University Press, 1977); Mary Ryan, *Cradle of the Middle Class*; and Christine Stansell, *City of Women: Sex and Class in New York, 1789–1860* (New York: Knopf, 1986). An overdue interrogation of the spatial conception of gendered spheres has been urged by Linda Kerber, "Separate Spheres, Female Worlds, Woman's Place: The Rhetoric of Women's History," *Journal of American History* 75, no. 1 ( June 1988): 9–39.

7. On the emergence of modern beliefs in the physiological grounding of gender difference, see Thomas Lacquer, *Making Sex: Body and Gender from the Greeks to Freud* (Cambridge, Mass.: Harvard University Press, 1990), esp. 149–92. For evidence that Olmsted's refrain was a common one among bourgeois travelers in other "backward" parts of the nineteenth-century world, see Mary Louise Pratt, *Imperial Eyes: Travel Writing and Transculturation* (New York: Routledge, 1992).

8. For an interesting discussion of the history of census categories and their effect on assessments of women's work, see Folbre, "Unproductive Housewife," and Boydston, *Home and Work*. The slave South presents an intriguing point of contrast to Folbre's argument about the gendering of use value as female in the antebellum North.

9. *The Old Pine Farm, or the Southern Side* (Nashville: Southwestern Publishing House, 1860), 93.

10. When C. C. Pinckney hired an unmarried overseer, he provided him with a "Boy and a Woman to wait on him, cook and wash, and another Woman to take care of the Dairy, his Garden, and Poultry." The terms of the overseer's contract make clear the value of women's labor and the gender division of labor customarily observed (contract of C. C. Pinckney and William Winningham, January 20, 1855, Charles Cotesworth Pinckney and Family Papers, Series III, Library of Congress, Washington, D.C.).

11. Mary Davis Brown Diary, 13 January, 29 July 1857, 25 April, 7, 31 August 1858, and throughout, South Caroliniana Library, University of South Carolina, Columbia, S.C. (hereafter SCL). On the value of women's (and girls') work, see also Elizabeth Finisher to Nancy H. Cowen, 23 August 1846, and Eleibers Cowen and Martha Cowen to John Cowen, February 1846, Nancy H. Cowan Papers, Manuscript Division, Perkins Library, Duke University, Durham, N.C. (hereafter Cowen Papers).

12. *Orangeburg Southron*, 11 June, 21 May 1856. On the sale of butter to planters, see the receipts of 2 July, 4 December 1841, and 17 November 1842, in Lawton Family Papers, SCL. On store accounts, see Account of Rebecca Robertson, 18 April–21 November 1821, Account of Elsey Edwards, 7 March 1821, and Account of Jane Oram, 30 May–28 August 1821, in Anonymous, Account Book, Camden and Hanging Rock, Kershaw District, SCL; Samuel K. Carrigan, Sales Book, 1859–60, SCL; and Lewis Eldon Atherton, *The Southern Country Store, 1800–1860* (Baton Rouge: Louisiana State University Press, 1949), 48–54, 87–91.

13. Mary Davis Brown Diary, 9 October 1858, SCL.

14. John H. Cornish Diary, 9 January 1847, Southern Historical Collection, University of North Carolina, Chapel Hill (hereafter SHC); Claim of Ellender Horton, Beaufort, RG 217, File #8006, Southern Claims Commission Records, National Archives and Records Administration, Washington, D.C. (hereafter SCCR). This complex relation to the market was not peculiar to South Carolina but was a characteristic of rural women's work before the emergence of capitalism in the countryside and thereafter on farms that continued to rely primarily on family labor. For the comparative case, see Laurel Thatcher Ulrich, "Housewife and Gadder: Themes of Self-Sufficiency and Community in Eighteenth-Century New England," in Carol Groneman and Mary Beth Norton, eds., *"To Toil the Livelong Day": America's Women at Work, 1780–1980* (Ithaca, N.Y.: Cornell University Press 1987), 21–34; Laurel Thatcher Ulrich, *Good Wives: Image and Reality in the Lives of Women in Northern New England, 1650–1750* (New York: Oxford University Press, 1982), 13–14, 34–39; Nancy Grey Osterud, " 'She Helped Me Hay It as Good as a Man': Relations among Women and Men in an Agricultural Community," in Groneman and Norton, eds., *"To Toil the Livelong Day"*, 89–97; John Mack Faragher, *Sugar Creek: Life on the Illinois Prairie* (New Haven: Yale University Press, 1987), 101–5; Margaret J. Hagood, *Mothers of the South: Portraiture of the White Tenant Farm Woman* (Chapel Hill: University of North Carolina Press, 1939), 77; and David Levine, *Family Formation in the Age of Nascent Capitalism* (New York: Academic Press, 1977), 12.

15. O'Neall quoted in Lacy K. Ford Jr., *Origins of Southern Radicalism: The South Carolina Upcountry, 1800–1860* (New York: Oxford University Press, 1988), 453; Pendleton Farmers' Society Records, Minutes, 12 October 1827, 9 October 1828, 13 August 1829, SCL; Black Oak Agricultural Society, Constitution and Proceedings, 16 November 1847, SCL. On homespun as a powerful symbol of southern resistance invoked in local political meetings, see *Charleston Mercury*, 25 June, 9, 16 July 1828. I would like to thank John Campbell for bringing the Pendleton Farmers' Society to my attention.

16. Olmsted, *Journey in the Back Country*, 298; Frances Trollope, *Domestic Manners of the Americans* (1832; reprint, Gloucester, Mass.: Peter Smith, 1968), 117, 243.

17. Many southern historians would admit that yeoman women worked in the fields during harvest. But they typically treat that activity as an exception to an otherwise clear gender division of labor, as if harvesting were a crisis or an emergency rather than a regular seasonal activity. In none of the studies cited below, however, did women's field work figure in the analysis of self-sufficiency or yeoman household economy. See Gavin Wright, *The Political Economy of the Cotton South: Households, Markets, and Wealth in the Nineteenth Century* (New York: W. W. Norton, 1978), 82–83; Steven Hahn, *The Roots of Southern Populism: Yeoman Farmers and the Transformation of the Georgia Upcountry* (New York: Oxford University Press, 1983), 30; and Ford, *Origins of Southern Radicalism*, 78–81. It would be interesting to know when this (mis)representation of the gender division of labor among free whites emerged in the South. Certainly no one bothered to deny that white female indentured servants worked the fields in the early colonial period, but by the antebellum period few would have publicly acknowledged such a fact. The representation of a complete racial

divide between slave and free women of all classes thus appears to have emerged as part of a larger ideology of slavery.

18. Samuel DuBose, *Address Delivered at the Seventeenth Anniversary of the Black Oak Agricultural Society* (Charleston, S.C.: A. E. Miller, 1858), 21.

19. David Gavin Diary, 1 September 1856, SHC. Hinton Rowan Helper offered an antislavery platform grounded in a version of an industrial South and pitched it to yeoman farmers in gendered terms as one designed to relieve poor white men of the humiliation of watching their women toil in the fields. That postemancipation South, he insisted, would "see no more plowing, or hoeing, or raking or grain-binding by white women in the southern states; employment in cotton mills and other factories would be far more profitable and congenial to them, and this they shall have within a short period after slavery shall have been abolished." Helper probably miscalculated. Instead of opening up the class divide between white southern men, his vision could well have had the opposite effect, reminding yeomen that in slave society their wives and daughters at least worked for them and were not, as they would be in cotton mills, subject to the authority of other men. See Helper, *The Impending Crisis of the South: How to Meet It* (1851; reprint, Cambridge, Mass.: Harvard University Press, 1968), 300.

20. Of one such woman Sister Martha Shurley said, "She has neither shoes nor bonnet is the reason she has not attended [church]," and the church resolved to "purchase shoes and bonnet for her provided that she cannot obtain them by her husband" (Gum Branch Baptist Church, Darlington District, Minutes, 19 August 1842, SCL).

21. Claim of Ellender Horton, Beaufort, RG 217, File #8006, SCCR; Gavin Diary, 1 September 1856, SHC.

22. James F. Sloan Journals, 24 June 1854 to 27 March 1861, SCL. I would like to thank Lacy Ford for bringing these journals to my attention. Sloan's property holdings are outlined in Ford, *Origins of Southern Radicalism*, 78–80.

23. Sloan Journals, 21 June, 5 July, 15 September 1856, and 8 September 1856 to 30 November 1858, SCL.

24. Ibid., 4 June 1857 and 7 July 1858, SCL.

25. Mary Davis Brown Diary, 14 October 1859, SCL. Although the tenth child, this was the first of Mrs. Brown's births attended by a doctor. Men typically reported news of births differently from their wives. For example, see William P. Benson to Mr. John Cowan, 1846, and William P. Benson to Mrs. John Cowan, 12 October 1830, Cowan Papers. Compare the heartbreaking correspondence between Elizabeth Finisher and her sister Nancy Cowan about her illness during and after pregnancy, her pain at losing two children, and her husband's neglect: Elizabeth Finisher to Nancy H. Cowan, 23 August 1846, Elizabeth Finisher to "Dearest Sister" [Nancy H. Cowan], 11 February 1849, ibid.

26. William P. Benson to Mr. John Cowan, 1846, William Benson to Mr. John Cowan, 13 August 1841, and Elizabeth Finisher to Nancy H. Cowan, 23 August 1846, Cowan Papers.

27. On the global identification of plowing as primarily a male task, see Esther Bosrup, *Women's Role in Economic Development* (London: George Allen and Universal Ltd., 1970), 19–34. The idea has persisted among historians that women, even slave women, did not plow.

But there is considerable evidence that slave women plowed on many plantations and that, on yeoman farms where grown sons were in short supply, wives and daughters took their turn driving the plow. On slave women, see the list of field hands, by task, in James Henry Hammond, Plantation Records, 7 August 1850, James Henry Hammond Papers, in Kenneth Stampp, ed., *Records of Antebellum Southern Plantations*, ser. A, pt. 1, reel 3 (Frederick, Md.: University Pulbications of America, 1986).

28. Philip N. Racine, ed., *Piedmont Farmer: The Journal of David Golightly Harris, 1855–1870* (Knoxville: University of Tennessee Press, 1990), 29–169.

29. Sloan Journals, 14 October and 8 March 1859, SCL.

30. Sloan Journals, 6 April 1859, 13 April 1860, SCL.

31. Ibid., 9 August 1860; and Mary Davis Brown Diary, 14 July 1859, 25 April 1858, 11 August 1859, all SCL.

# Part Two

. . . . . . . . . . . . . . . . . . . . . . . . . . . . . . . . . . .

## Wage-Earning Women in the Urban South

. . . . . . . . . . . . . . . . . . . . . . . . . . . . .

# Chapter Four

# A White Woman, of Middle Age,
# Would Be Preferred:
## Children's Nurses in the Old South

. . . . . . . . . . . . . . . . . . . . . . . . . . . . . .

STEPHANIE COLE

Like so many other parents who agonize over child care, the employer who advertised for a nurse for "an infant and four small children" in Washington in 1833 wanted to clarify how high the family's standards were. The right nurse would undoubtedly have to be "honest and attentive" to receive the "liberal wages" offered. But employers sought trustworthiness in more than personality traits. "A white woman, of middle age, would be preferred," this advertiser apprised potential applicants. In contrast, a housemaid sought at the same time needed only to be "good" to qualify.[1] In sentiments both more and less explicit, over the course of the antebellum period, southern elites increasingly betrayed a heightened anxiety about who should be minding their children. While most white southerners ignored the emerging view that only mothers were suited for the job, they—like the employer above—came to question the appropriateness of two familiar categories of workers that had traditionally filled the position: slaves and youthful workers, enslaved or free. For working white women of the Old South, the new sensibilities about the proper characteristics of children's mistresses brought opportunities for employment but also a special set of dilemmas.

The debate that emerged from the "reification of moral motherhood" challenged the practice of employing slave nurses without actually upending notions about the rightness of slavery, as the first part of this essay suggests.[2] Though mature white women more frequently found employment as a result of the tensions between the politics of domesticity and the politics of slavery, their ability to do so was hardly uniform even in urban border settings, where conditions most favored their presence. The second part of this essay investigates advertisements and personal correspondence in several border cities—Washington, Baltimore, Richmond, Louisville, and Cincinnati—to show how these tensions commonly worked themselves out. A growing sense of the importance of a woman's role as mother, accompanied by shifts within urban labor markets, created less room for African American women and girls in the occupation of children's nurse, and made more room for those who, superficially at least, more closely resembled the white women who employed them. An examination of this occupation reveals how important elite attitudes about gender, race, and class were in determining working women's job choices. Moreover, it illustrates the crucial role the market revolution played in shaping those attitudes, particularly as it redefined "women's work," rendering less visible women's paid and unpaid labor within the household.

The extent to which more white women entered elites' nurseries speaks to the currency of the ideals of domesticity in a region supposedly devoted to patriarchal rule. "Northern" concepts apparently had an impact on "southern" culture and, in the realm of the household, on the heart of southern politics and society. The presence of white nurses also reflected increasingly complex labor pools in southern cities and implies growing overlap between categories of employees assumed to be distinct: nurses were servants, but white. Moreover, white women competed for jobs not only with slaves but also with free African Americans, some of whom achieved their status by emancipation, others by running away. Not incidentally, for African American women, successfully escaping slavery depended in part upon elite whites' assumptions that black and female meant "servant" and their resulting (ostensibly unwitting) decisions to hire runaways as domestics. Confusions within and between ideological lines and social categories were part and parcel of the intersection of slave and market economies in antebellum America. Examining the decisions of employers of children's nurses, particularly of those who lived in cities where the lines between "bond" and "free" were most blurred, gives us entry into the complexities of that world.

The cultural messages about motherhood and slavery that southerners received are a good place to start to uncover why some sought to hire white nurses and others resisted such trends. By the 1840s, most literate southerners would have been well acquainted with proscriptive writers who urged them to believe that no one could make up for a mother's care in the development of a healthy child. In two chapters on the management of infants and children in *A Treatise on Domestic Economy*, Catharine Beecher, the most famous such advice giver, scarcely mentioned the possibility that anyone other than mothers would deal with these malleable beings. Nurses were helpful in assisting with the tedious and menial care of infants, she asserted, but women needed to be prepared to do even that work on their own, and, should they be lucky enough to find a nurse in their employ, needed to watch carefully any of her administrations. Mothers were essential in the rearing of well-disciplined adults. Only a mother had the "natural" kindness and good temper that suited her to be the most important person in a child's life; and only the natural mother had the qualities necessary to raise a child correctly. Servants were apt to neglect children in their care, and sometimes subjected them to physical abuse. Moreover, domestics could not provide essential guidance, generally proving too strict, too lenient, or too quick to use harmful scare tactics to mold young minds properly.[3]

Beecher came from a family famous for its opposition to slavery, and her treatise was certainly oriented toward a nonslaveholding audience, though it invoked slaves as servants without comment in a few examples. Nonetheless, some southerners apparently shared her viewpoint, including the editors of several southern newspapers and magazines. In 1825, the *Hillsborough [North Carolina] Recorder* protested against the custom of "delivering a child over in the hand of a nurse . . . where it may first learn to lisp vulgarity and obscenity, and from whom it inevitably acquires a pronunciation and accent, such as may never be fully corrected." Ultimately, the caution went, "parents are ashamed to introduce their children into society and well may they," for the child is often "unfit for society."[4] In other publications, the possible outcomes were understood as more serious than the child being shunned socially. "A Hint to Mothers," reprinted in Washington, D.C.'s *National Intelligencer*, warned readers of the dangers of leaving a child with a nurse; one careless mother who had done so nearly lost a child to an overdose of paregoric and opium.[5] In "A Whisper to a Newly-Married Pair," another author admonished a young bride inclined to "abandon her children during the greater part of the day to hirelings" to rethink her decision; "*maternal care . . . supersedes all other duties*," he concluded."[6] By the 1840s and 1850s, a clear opposition voice emerged in southern periodicals, challenging the ideal of the fragile southern lady, dependent on servants. The "fashion-pampered women" were "worthless" in the eyes of one commentator. "They dress nobody, bless nobody, and save nobody. . . . If they rear children, servants and nurses do all." This occurred with grave consequences; when grown, the children "amount to . . . weaker scions of the stock," never achieving the status of "our great and good men and women."[7] As "Phil" exhorted his North

Carolina readership to believe, "One of the greatest evils now in existence is that of trusting our children to wicked and ignorant nurses."[8] Women who read the *Ladies' Repository*, published in the border city of Cincinnati, Ohio, heard a consistent message decrying the "decidedly injurious" practice of placing children in the care of servants.[9]

Warnings against the use of children's nurses struck many southerners as difficult to comply with at least, and contradictory, even treacherous, at most. Slaveholders committed to a traditional worldview could not embrace such a radical position against the efficacy of the service of slaves. In their view, slaves, though perhaps childlike or ignorant, were integral parts of the households of white masters and mistresses, and their presence served both economic and social ends. Assigning juvenile slaves, both male and female, to assist with caring for white children helped to make the capital investment in human labor profitable as early, and for as long, as possible.[10] Watching after their owner's children required just the right attributes of young slaves too weak and inexperienced to work elsewhere—minimal strength and maximum energy. In addition, and perhaps more important, was the role enslaved nurses played in socializing white children. Although few urban housekeepers had plantations or large slaveholdings that gave them an economic commitment to maximizing slave value, many did subscribe to the belief that slaves had a "natural" place in white nurseries.[11]

The words of those who kept slaves as nurses illustrate how slaveholders could ignore the idea that mothers alone had the most important part to play in children's lives. In essence they saw in enslaved caregivers familial ties and a qualified deference that were essential.[12] Enslaved nurses not only attended the physical needs of their master's children, they developed affection and devotion for them on par with family members themselves. Those who advertised young slave girls for sale described them as "very fond of" children, "kind," "attentive," or "faithful." Whites' investment in the closeness of these bonds was exemplified in two Richmond women's comments. Mary McGuire believed the slave who cared for her son was a family intimate, describing her as a "faithful and devoted nurse to little Edward." Susan Daniel commented that her nurse had shown "fondness and forbearance to all children" and was especially "devoted to Lizzy."[13]

Attachment to children was not seen as exclusively a characteristic of enslaved caregivers, it should be noted. White child-servants inspired similar feelings on the part of southern mistresses, probably for similar reasons. An indentured girl from Richmond was said to have formed "a violent attachment" to her charge, and Washingtonian Maria Steiger's young servant, Elizabeth, was "very fond of the children, indeed is almost like a mother to them." In each of these cases, the nurse's age and de facto or even de jure dependence on her employer replicated after a fashion the situation of household slaves.[14] But there was a difference in how mistresses understood the role of young white nurses and that of slaves. Women who hired or bound white girls seemed to see the servant's principal task as simply caring for the infant, and might even assign the girl duties in areas separate from the nursery, as did Mrs. Steiger for Elizabeth. In contrast, slaveholders tended to describe their children's attendants as "little maids," who by implication both watched and waited on their charges.[15] As a Louisiana diarist noted, some slaveowning families instituted the practice of giving children a slave to attend them who was generally close in age and perhaps a playmate from infancy. During Frederick Douglass's earliest years in Baltimore he watched over and played with his young white master in just this capacity.[16] Slave nurses then served a dual function: their status presented an opportunity for white children to learn to command the labor of others, and their race taught children (black and white) early on to associate power with whiteness. Though all domestic servants had a part in socializing children, the enslaved nurses' part was particularly crucial.[17]

Familiarity with both points of view—that slaves were harmful, or that they played an essential role—caused southern mothers not a little grief. Ellen Green, who lived in Kentucky, received considerable advice on this topic from her mother in Philadelphia. As her mother saw it, the lesson of white power was actually a lesson in tyranny. She begged her daughter "not [to] permit [your children] to be much with your slaves." Not only would it "spoil there tempers," she warned, but "it is also calculated to make tirents [*sic*] of them."[18] Such child-rearing advice resembled the criticism abolitionists often made about the corruption inherent in slave-master relations. In reading these objections as they applied to her own decisions about slave nurses, Green was witness to the impact domestic ideals could have on southern society.

The cult of domesticity's celebration of a privatized home and family could create problems for slave-employing southerners that went beyond the occasional harangue from a Philadelphian mother. Inasmuch as this ideology helped to create a "domesticated" institution of slavery, it encouraged whites to see and accept slaves as permanently childlike and often frustratingly incompetent.[19] Urban slaveholders offered a litany of complaints about their nurses and betrayed an inconsistent desire for childlike devotion in their slaves but the skill of adults. William Wirt blamed the "silly or rather mischievous girl that nurse[d]" his daughter with feeding her green grapes and making her ill. When concerning a more serious infraction, these kinds of complaints revealed just how shallow whites' faith in "kind and faithful" slaves could be. In what seemed to have been a common practice of worried whites repeating bad news about tragedies caused by slaves, Louisvillian George Anderson reported to his mother an episode in which a child was severely burned when the "servant was absent from the room." Mary Henderson, a planter's wife, actually took this perspective to extreme, constantly questioning in her diary her decision to leave her firstborn (and now dead) daughter with a "selfish and lazy" slave nurse.[20] Because masters and mistresses believed slaves were as attached to the "family, white and black," as whites were, they failed to see these actions as a kind of resistance, although on a few occasions those actions may well have been. Instead, whites interpreted "accidents" as indications of slaves' essential inferiority, which could manifest itself as poor moral fiber.

If, over time, the rhetoric of domesticity could diminish some whites' opinions of slave nurses, it led others to identify maternal qualities in them. The advice Agnes Cabell gave her son when he asked her who to employ as his daughter Sarah's nurse suggests that this Virginian accommodated a growing sense of the importance of motherhood and childhood without undermining her acceptance of slavery. Sometime in the early 1850s, Henry Cabell of Richmond followed the traditional practice of giving a slave child to his daughter and assigned one of the family's young slave girls to attend Sarah as nurse. His mother insisted that the young nurse, Little Eliza, was not adequate and that, for her granddaughter's sake, Henry needed to use the slave's mother, Big Eliza, instead. Big Eliza "is more trustworthy in many respects and her age will make her more suitable to go about with Sarah," she began. Moreover, though Sarah apparently preferred Little Eliza, her grandmother attributed this preference to "finding a playmate in her." "This will soon be lost sight of when [Sarah] has playmates in her little cousins," Agnes predicted. She then demonstrated a broad awareness of the ideology of domesticity's demands on children's nurses. It was simply "more safe and respectable that such a woman as Big Eliza should have charge of her"; Little Eliza was "too young and heedless" to allow her to take the child for a walk. And even though she was "subservient to the other servants, that is not the main thing to be aimed at in the choice of little Sarah's maid." Rather, "a steady sensible woman on whose principles you can depend is the person to be chosen."[21]

Agnes Cabell's emphasis on Big Eliza's principles, respectability, and sensibility rather than her abilities as a maid reflected the currency domestic ideals held by certain slaveholders.[22] Nevertheless, even as she illustrated a preference for character and age, she and her son confined their discussion to slaves. They clearly did not accept the more extreme position of Ellen Green's mother that regardless of the greater expectations whites placed upon slave nurses, the whole caste corrupted children. The Cabells, like many other slaveholders of the era, held that certain slaves, if raised properly within a trusted family, could retain the basic qualities and skills necessary to care for white children.[23]

Such private conversations about the unsuitability of some slaves for responsibilities bestowed upon them, like the more fervently repeated rumors of slave nurses' misconduct, amounted to expressions of uncertainties about the system itself. In the tense climate of the late-antebellum period, however, they never were acknowledged as such. Indeed, for those southerners to whom comments like those from Green's northern mother represented a serious assault on slavery, a new rationalization emerged. Rather than question publicly inconsistencies within their claims for the "natural" deference of slaves, they re-invented the story. As ad hoc comments from northerners coalesced into a prolonged and organized assault on the peculiar institution in the 1850s, apologists forgot their own and neighbors' objections to slave nurses and instead idealized slaves' docility and kindness. They built a legend around the older slave women (like Big Eliza) who nursed the planters' young and called them "mammies." In creating an image for these figures, planters married the theory of the "cultural uplift" of slavery to the "cult of domesticity," as Deborah Gray White has argued. This characterization was an antidote to the disjuncture felt with the assault of the cult of domesticity on the morality of the "peculiar institution." Mammies were benign, devoted slaves and maternal, religious domestic women. After the war and into the 1920s, this stereotypical image became even more important. Supporters of the Lost Cause and makers of the ideology of white supremacy made mammies into a bedrock of the romanticized vision of the Old South.[24]

It is important to keep in mind that this vision of mature, maternal slave women emerged after the ideals of domesticity and assaults on slavery made it necessary. Older women did take care of white children throughout the antebellum period, but they did not carry the moral freight they did later. Mary Henderson, who identified her neglectful nurse as "selfish and lazy," also characterized her as "old and experienced."[25] Moreover, the view that older slave women could be skilled nurses became popular only in the 1850s, and even then it was not widely shared. In 1831, Susan Daniel remarked in a letter to her husband that "my old nurse is a treasure to me."[26] But her description stands out as a single comment sentimentalizing slave nurses in reams of correspondence between women in the border region before 1850, suggesting that her reflection was a personal one, not widely shared by her peers. And the brevity of Daniel's assessment did not match the elaborate sentimentality of later descriptions of mammies. In 1859, for example, Sarah Bonetta Valentine wrote a letter to her brother eulogizing their recently deceased mammy, which could have been a template for the icon-makers of the early-twentieth-century South. "How she loved you and me, her 'two children' as she called us," Sarah gushed. After recalling her mammy's anecdotes of them, her "loving smile and warmth of manner," and her piety, Sarah intoned, "If we but act our parts aright, how joyous is the meeting [with her] that awaits us in the field of flowers above!"[27]

The impact of domesticity on slavery could not have been predicted; the collision could theoretically lead to either more or less reliance on slave women as nurses. The gender, race, and legal status of slave women clearly made employing them as nurses problematic for white elites.[28] On one hand, assumptions about race could lead parents to fear blacks' presence as caregivers. On the other, in the context of the need to defend slavery, ideas about slave devotion and maternal instincts could as likely encourage elites to champion slave women in that same capacity.

• • •

To discover how such dilemmas played out generally, we must move away from prescriptive literature and correspondence anecdotes to a slightly more systematic investigation of who southern elites engaged to care for their children. The right "laboratory" is essential to a successful examination. Given the centrality of gender, race, and status to the confusion, an environment that held many individuals within these categories in differing combinations seems important. Cities along the North-South border suit the bill: slaves, free African Americans, quasi-free slaves for hire, bound whites, and immigrants all competed for work to a varying extent. A number of demographic and social shifts were notable in border cities. The proportion of slave to free workers declined over the antebellum period, and many of the slaves who remained found themselves hired out to employers who did not own them. Moreover, a new category of slaves emerged, particularly in Baltimore and Washington; these "term slaves" served for a set number of years in return for a promise of freedom. Most important within the border region, the decline of slavery (or sometimes, the fear of the decline of slavery) necessitated machinations in support of the system, and these discussions and maneuvers reveal what sorts of ideas and practices gave slaveholders the most difficulty. In such environments, race and legal status were complicated categories, made more complex by the presence of those who existed on the boundaries: African Americans who were not firmly within chattel slavery and working whites whose freedom was compromised by indenture agreements or association with domestic wage labor.[29]

Choosing household workers was central to urban southerners' attempts to exercise some control over what they saw as a dangerously chaotic society. As a result of demographic shifts, the creation of black codes meant to restrict the behavior of free African Americans, long-standing laws that limited the free choices of wage workers, and a variety of other changes, male and female workers in border cities found their true status on a spectrum from slave to free.[30] Within this spectrum there were further differences: workers were young, middle-aged, or older; they were white or black. Those who made up the labor pool of domestic workers were part of a diverse group, indeed much more diverse than indicated by the traditional assumption among historians that southern domestics were enslaved women. By distinguishing between them—that is deciding whether to buy a young mulatto girl or hire a middle-aged white woman for a child's nurse—employers revealed what qualities they associated with slavery, youth, whiteness, and femininity, as well as their own perceptions of who best matched the demands of various tasks.[31] This method of attaching certain characteristics to race, legal status, gender, and age, which happened over and over again in individual households, made those households primary sites for drawing the lines that were the basis of the Old South. Residents of these cities had a more complex set of circumstances to deal with, but the process they followed was simply a magnified version of what elites did throughout the South in justifying a place for patriarchal power and slavery in a world increasingly committed to different values.

Help wanted advertisements of local newspapers most clearly and consistently reveal employers' preferences regarding domestic workers. Newspapers offer an invaluable firsthand look at the dimensions of the labor pool and employers' attitudes about it. Thousands of employers resorted to newspapers to buy, sell, and hire domestics. My sample of advertisements in five border cities, Washington, Baltimore, Richmond, Louisville, and Cincinnati, between 1800 and 1850 provides a glimpse of over 1,600 buyers, sellers, employers, and employees.[32] Of course, determining who read these ads or how representative advertisements were of the domestic servant workforce as a whole, is virtually impossible. But such a source offers a way to compare the workforce that it does capture, however incomplete, across several cities; whatever the disadvantages, they existed consistently across the urban border region. No other source,

TABLE 4.1. Defining Features of Cooks, House Servants, and
Children's Nurses in Advertisements for All Border Cities, 1800–1850

| Features | Cook (%)<br>N=419 | House Servant (%)<br>N=396 | Children's Nurse (%)<br>N=212 |
|---|---|---|---|
| Black | 84.3 | 85.3 | 53.0 |
| White | 15.7 | 14.7 | 47.0 |
| Slave | 72.8 | 75.1 | 31.8 |
| Free | 27.2 | 24.9 | 68.2 |
| Male | 3.3 | 17.8 | — |
| Female | 97.7 | 82.2 | 100 |
| Average age | 25.7 | 16.1 | 22.3 |

Sources: *Baltimore American and Commercial Advertiser*, 1810–35; *Baltimore American and Mercury Daily Advertiser*, 1802–4; *Baltimore Evening Post*, 1805–11; *Cincinnati Advertiser*, 1823–29; *Cincinnati Daily Gazette*, 1829–50; *Cincinnati Liberty Hall and Gazette*, 1808–21; *Cincinnati Inquisitor*, 1818–20; *Cincinnati Inquisitor and Advertiser*, 1820; *Liberty Hall & Cincinnati Mercury*, 1808–15; *Louisville Correspondent*, 1814–15; *Louisville Daily Journal*, 1830–50; *Louisville Public Advertiser*, 1821–26; *National Intelligencer* (Washington), 1800–1850; *Richmond Enquirer*, 1804–50; *The Sun* (Baltimore), 1840–50.
*Note*: These statistics do not include missing values for each variable. See the text for a discussion of imprecise language in certain advertisements. The percentage of missing values is as follows: missing race—for cooks, 25.3%; for house servants, 12.6%; for children's nurses, 44.8%; missing status—for cooks, 20.0%; for house servants, 7.8%; for children's nurses 27.4%; missing sex—for cooks, 0%; for house servants, 7.6%; for children's nurses, 0.5%.

especially when looked at systematically over five decades and five cities, offers so extensive and multifaceted a window into the private world of household workers.

My analysis of the sample of advertisements suggests that complaints about slavery, shifts in the labor pool, and the call for a more central role for mothers had a decided impact on hiring practices for children's nurses in border cities. Though some ads reveal more about potential employees than others, they illustrate enough differences between occupations such as nurse, cook, and "general house servant" to show that employers' preconceptions about race, gender, status, and age as well as demographic and ideological shifts played a part in employers' decisions about who would serve in what capacity. As they linked specific household tasks to particular categories of workers, employers created order for themselves and their peers.[33] As Tables 4.1 and 4.2 suggest, in the aggregate, advertisements for nurses (and a few by nurses looking for situa-

TABLE 4.2. Ages of Cooks, House Servants, and Children's Nurses in Advertisements by Status and with Standard Deviation for All Border Cities, 1800–1850

| Occupation | Average Age (N) | Standard Deviation | Average Age of Slaves (N) | Average Age of Free Workers (N) |
|---|---|---|---|---|
| Cook | 25.7 (89) | 9.8 | 27.1 (67) | 21.4 (21) |
| House servant | 16.1 (225) | 4.8 | 15.8 (162) | 16.0 (51) |
| Children's nurse | 22.3 (114) | 11.8 | 15.9 (35) | 25.8 (55) |

*Sources*: See Table 4.1.

*Note*: The proportion of advertisements that did not specify age were as follows: for cooks, 78.8%; for house servants, 43.2%; for children's nurses, 46.2%.

tions) were more likely to concern females than those for either cooks or general servants, and the advertisements suggest that nurses, more than other skilled workers, were more often free and showed the greatest diversity in age.

Understanding what was unique about nurses requires looking at the demands of and labor supply for other occupations. According to this sample of advertisements, cooks were, by and large, African American, enslaved, and female.[34] Their importance to most households forced housekeepers to remain flexible in who they hired, however. Border families were so desperate to secure good cooks that they would make significant concessions, sometimes showing flexibility in requirements of character, sometimes by stepping outside the assumptions about gender and race that so often shaped their choices. The William Wirt family was once desperate enough to knowingly hire a slave cook with the worst of qualities. "We are told that she drinks," the new mistress admitted.[35] Families interested in prestige sometimes pursued male cooks known for their training in "fancy" cooking. However, one advertiser requested, in a fit of pique and "wearied by a succession of Female Kitchen Servants," that she or he was "desirous to employ a male cook," because a man "neither dreads the fire, nor has an aversion to bringing water or other labor."[36] Over time, employers accommodated the demographic shift away from heavy concentrations of slaves in border cities, and about 20 percent of the ads requested (or offered the services of) white cooks. But, though there were a few exceptions, in the aggregate, these advertisements never betrayed an assumption that white cooks were better than black ones, or that free cooks were better than slave. In the years after 1830, employers were increasingly likely to write advertisements that suggested remarkable flexibility (see Table 4.3). Most notably, a few employers

TABLE 4.3. Distribution of Advertisements by
Race and Status of Cooks for All Border Cities, 1800–1850

| Status or Race | 1800–15 | 1816–29 | 1830–50 | Total |
|---|---|---|---|---|
| Slave ads[a] | 52  (94.5%) | 33 (91.7%) | 159 (65.2%) | 244 (72.8%) |
| Free ads | 3   (5.5) | 3  (8.3) | 85 (34.8) | 91 (27.2) |
| Black ads[b] | 52 (100.0) | 31 (96.9) | 182 (79.1) | 265 (84.3) |
| White ads | 0   (0.0) | 1  (3.1) | 48 (20.9) | 49 (15.7) |

*Sources*: See Table 4.1.
[a]N=335   $\chi^2$=26.8   P <.0000   $\lambda$=.0000
[b]N=314   $\chi^2$=18.0   P <.0000   $\lambda$=.0000

began to leave race and status open by not claiming to prefer slave more than free workers. But they also used wording that left their meaning ambiguous to a present-day reader, and did so much more often than in advertisements for other skilled occupations.[37]

Baltimore housekeeper Ann Mackenzie Cushing's account book offers some insight into why advertisers apparently remained flexible in the qualifications they required of their prospective cooks—or at least provides a good example of how and perhaps why a housekeeper might try alternate courses. Ann Cushing's accounts also reveal that working white women took advantage of increasing employment options by quitting their employ or by testing the limits of their mistresses' authority. In 1839, Ann Cushing fired her African American cook, Mary Ann Tyson, giving as her explanation her desire "to change for a *white* servant." Presumably, racism motivated this decision. Unfortunately for Mrs. Cushing, neither of the next two cooks, both of whom were white, stayed for more than a few weeks. Bridget Halpenny was "crazy of love" and Johanna Coughlin "refused to do the washing." With Johanna's departure, however, Mrs. Cushing returned to an African American worker when a hired slave, Rachel, came to work for her. Rachel proved satisfying, her employers' prejudices not-withstanding. She stayed eleven months before she "ran off to Canada"; over the next year and a half, none of the white women who succeeded her stayed more than three months. Two left on their own accord because they did not like their mistress's demands; the others were dismissed for a variety of infractions from "too slow by half" to "not true."[38] Though antiblack feelings led Cushing to try white servants, and the market accommodated such an exploration, nei-ther her experiences nor the prejudices she shared with other Baltimore elites kept her committed to a single course. Alterations in the labor pool called into

TABLE 4.4. Distribution of Advertisements by Race
and Status of House Servants for All Border Cities, 1800–1850

| Status or Race | 1800–15 | 1816–29 | 1830–50 | Total |
|---|---|---|---|---|
| Slave ads[a] | 55 (100.0%) | 43 (91.5%) | 176 (66.9%) | 274 (75.1%) |
| Free ads | 0 (0.0) | 4 (8.5) | 87 (33.1) | 91 (24.9) |
| Black ads[b] | 55 (100.0) | 46 (97.9) | 195 (79.6) | 296 (85.3) |
| White ads | 0 (0.0) | 1 (2.1) | 50 (20.4) | 51 (14.7) |

*Sources*: See Table 4.1.
[a]$N=365$   $\chi^2=34.6$   $P<.0000$   $\lambda=.0000$
[b]$N=347$   $\chi^2=21.8$   $P<.0002$   $\lambda=.0000$

question the once virtually fixed assumptions about enslaved women as cooks, but that group remained closely associated with the occupation through 1850.[39]

The occupation of general household servant, in contrast, remained more closely and consistently associated with slaves. As Table 4.4 illustrates, throughout the first half of the nineteenth century, advertisements for workers to do general household duties—referred to as "housework," "house servant," or "the work of a small family"—remained relatively consistent and clear in terms of who the advertisers sought to fill these positions. For the most part, employers thought African Americans, slaves, and females best served in this capacity. In this way, house servants and cooks were very similar, though men were more likely to find employment in the former occupation than the latter.[40] After 1830, more free workers entered general household service, but their entrance did not precipitate or accompany any particular open-mindedness about who best served in this capacity, as had the entrance of free and white workers into the occupation of cooking. Instead, ambiguously worded or unclear advertisements comprised about the same proportion throughout the entire period.[41]

What distinguished house servants from other kinds of workers was their age, or, more specifically, their youth. This was an "entry level" job whose occupants were only fifteen or sixteen years old on average, with little variation.[42] General household servants were assigned unskilled or low-skilled tasks in order to make young slaves, both male and female, profitable. A significant minority of employers assigned these tasks to orphaned or otherwise destitute white girls in exchange for their upkeep.[43] While bound workers may have had little choice in what their first jobs would be, from the perspective of employers they were a good option because a social benefit accompanied the economic benefit of hiring them. Young people marked as subordinate by race or class would learn early the habits of deference. More important, given that the majority were young slaves, the rest of society associated blackness and youth with the lowest level of service to white households.

With the analysis of these occupations in mind, the peculiarities of children's nurses are clearer. Other than showing that children's nurses were mostly female, the aggregate profile of these advertisements offers few clues about what border residents believed to be true about child care workers.[44] On average, the workers in this occupation were quite young, as were the workers in household service. But unlike the age requirements indicated in advertisements for general servants, the ages specified in advertisements for nurses varied substantially.[45] More important, the nature of advertisements about nurses changed significantly over the first half of the nineteenth century, again without the same sort of "white or colored" open-endedness that appeared in the ads for cooks. Even after the labor pool diversified after 1830, advertisers remained committed to particular visions of who should be watching their children.

An emphasis on including age in advertisements underscores that employers were not complacent about who they hired as nurses. The information included in these ads indicates that employers of nurses were not willing to leave the age of these domestics open to chance. More than when they were seeking cooks or house servants, advertisers were inclined to specify a particular age, or at least list a preference for "middleaged" or "older."[46] There were, obviously, key differences in these occupations. More than cooks, who worked for the most part away from the house in a kitchen, or house servants, who moved about the house but generally cleaned or served, nurses occupied a place near to employers both in location and affections. They spent a good deal of time in bed chambers or nurseries, and they stayed with their employers' children. Like employers elsewhere in the country, border residents had strong ideas about who should care for their children, though they did not always agree with one another. A given age and/or race in an advertisement for a nurse signaled to potential workers where the employer stood on this issue.

Better than any other source, advertisements disclose the spectrum of attitudes about nurses and demonstrate how urban employers' perceptions of race and status changed. The nature of nursing made it particularly well-suited to reveal the effect of blurred lines between slave and free on border residents' ideas—or how they reacted to unraveling associations between black and slave and free and white. This reaction took place in a context of conflicting messages about a woman's role in the family, household, and society. Employers chose

TABLE 4.5. Distribution of Advertisements by Race
and Status of Children's Nurses for All Border Cities, 1800–1850

| Status or Race | 1800–15 | 1816–29 | 1830–50 | Total |
|---|---|---|---|---|
| Slave ads[a] | 14  (73.7%) | 6 (46.2%) | 29 (23.8%) | 49 (31.8%) |
| Free ads | 5   (26.3) | 7 (53.8) | 93 (76.2) | 105 (68.2) |
| Black ads[b] | 14 (100.0) | 6 (85.7) | 42 (43.8) | 62 (53.0) |
| White ads | 0    (0.0) | 1 (14.3) | 54 (56.3) | 55 (47.0) |

*Sources*: See Table 4.1.
[a]$N=152$  $\chi^2=20.2$  $P<.0000$  $\lambda=.18367$
[b]$N=117$  $\chi^2=18.0$  $P<.0000$  $\lambda=.21818$

nurses based on their interpretation of those messages, as well as on more practical matters. In contrast to the more matter-of-fact business of hiring a general house servant, where employers simply accepted the person they assumed was most compliant at the least cost, hiring a nurse involved reconciling the demands of domesticity and reified motherhood with a declining institution of slavery in the urban border region. Whereas they more often accepted traditional notions determining who they ought to hire for less freighted occupations, when they went to hire nurses, they found themselves rethinking issues of race, age, slavery, and freedom.

By 1830, advertisers had begun to search for free servants who were older, and often white. (See Table 4.5.) As one advertiser put it, the family needed a "middleaged white woman who understands the management of a small children." In contrast to slave nurses who appeared in advertisements, white nurses were older—by ten years, on average—and thus more likely to be closer in years to the mother than the child.[47] Whereas employers of white nurses sought workers who were "experienced," those who hired slave nurses simply wanted those who were "suitable."[48] Middle-aged nurses had acquired knowledge that would aid them in influencing children correctly. Rather than teaching their charges the power of their place in life, white nurses more closely replicated the role of the children's own mother, watching over them and guiding them from a position of moderate authority.

Most important, over time, demand (and supply, as measured in situation-wanted ads) for middle-aged white women displaced that for slaves. Almost three-quarters of all advertisements for nurses before 1816 concerned slaves; between 1830 and 1850 that proportion had reversed, and one-quarter wanted slave nurses and three-quarters wanted free servants. The numbers are equally convincing concerning race. Every advertisement in the early years (1800–1815) mentioned African Americans; less than half did so in the later years (1830–50). Moreover, the move to free and white nurses outpaced the gradual movement overall for either of these categories in other domestic occupations.[49]

A precise explanation for this statistical shift is elusive. In part, it was a natural occurrence related to the influx of nonsoutherners into cosmopolitan cities, such as Baltimore. A request for a German nurse, which appeared in the *Sun* in 1845, testified to the diverse demand and supply created by the changing demographics in the city.[50] But the change also reflects the pressures longtime residents felt as they were influenced by contradictory messages. Susan Grigsby, a Kentucky slaveholder who believed her slave Sarah "too harum scarum" to be a trustworthy nurse, hired for a time a "Mrs. Anderson," who by her title signaled her status as free and probably white.[51] When a Baltimore housekeeper asked for "a young American woman as nurse with a good moral character" in the same ad in which she requested "a colored woman as cook," she suggested that while a hired slave was acceptable on her domestic staff, such a person was not tolerable as her children's caretaker.[52]

An advertiser's dictum that "a white woman, of middle age, would be preferred" revealed the mutability of notions of domesticity that had originated in the market economies of the North.[53] Southerners who expressed such sentiments acknowledged the importance of mothers, and a sense that somehow mothers' work was not truly "work." But they did so in a way that incorporated a regard for the ability and efficacy of servants. Older white workers could temporarily fill a mother's place.[54] Without disregarding the traditional assumptions about the ways in which servants were devoted members of the household, they accommodated ideas that children needed special care. Residents of border cities came to value older white women over young slave girls.[55]

Moreover, by distinguishing between the abilities of older white women and those of slaves, these employers used the assignment of domestic roles to help solidify a color line that seemed to be rapidly eroding. African Americans were changing the social order, and elite whites sought to impose that old order in new forms. White women workers were the unintended benefactors of the struggle. As more free African Americans entered their cities, and contributed to a diminishing authority owners held over their chattel, elites sought to underscore dichotomies that had for so long been transparently meaningful to them. Whereas blackness barred few slaves from finding work as cooks or general servants, it did limit their access to positions as nurses. The actions of these black women—leaving a child alone by a fire or alternately inspiring confidence in their mistresses—conspired to complicate further elites' notion that they knew what character qualities accompanied race, gender, and legal status.

The result was that there was never a consensus among border residents about who best served as children's nurses. While a growing majority of employers felt pressed to hire nurses who were older and white, others remained certain of the suitability of slave girls to infant and childcare. In the second quarter of the nineteenth century, for every three advertisers who wanted middle-aged white women or some other free workers, at least one slaveowner looked to sell, buy, or hire slaves, such as the seller of a nine-year-old "likely girl" who was "very fond of children."[56]

\* \* \*

The complexity of a world that was ostensibly ordered around racial slavery but that increasingly relied on other social relations to replicate that order made for some uncomfortable adjustments to changing circumstances. Race, status, and class appeared in new alignments in elite households. The presence of older white women workers prompted a number of troubling questions. Their age marked them as lifetime wage workers, not apprentices temporarily learning the "art of housewifery." Their race and legal status permitted a relationship between nurses and their employers, with which the latter were unfamiliar. White women could leave employers' households when they wanted and did; as a result, they were not likely to be seen as unambiguous members of the "family." Likewise their class also marked them as outsiders and potentially troublesome commodities.[57]

For example, though white women were not generally perceived as sexual beings in antebellum society—whereas African American women were—white female servants could confuse employers accustomed to all-black household staffs. To what extent did their lower-class position suggest increased proclivity toward sex?[58] Charles Howard carefully assured his wife that she should not see the white women who worked in their home as romantic rivals. While walking about the house he had recently mistaken servant Jane for a stranger. He highlighted the incident in a letter to his wife, asserting, "So you see what little notice I take of your white women in the house, and I do not think you need be very jealous of them."[59] Undoubtedly, Mrs. Howard was hopeful that the adverb "very" was an affectation of speech rather than an indicator that *some* jealously might be in order.

Given that slave women were more commonly depicted as arousing there masters' sexual interest, the dynamics in the Howard family seem unusual. But the story suggests that some elites were not certain of the implications of white subordinates. Slaveholders were used to believing that house servants were available sexually, and may have stumbled over the notion that those servants' blackness, rather than their subordinate positions, was solely responsible for that availability. In addition, because whites believed that enslaved women were so entirely different from themselves, they would not speak of the possibility of sexual relationships between masters and slaves, whether or not a liaison existed. Not a single employer of black servants reassured his wife of his innocence with their black women, even though the preponderance of evidence from other sources suggest there were many relationships of which to be suspicious.[60] Such a possibility was unmentionable, because it was technically unthinkable. With white domestics, however, the dynamics of intimacy changed. Men like Charles Howard felt compelled to verbalize their lack of interest in white subordinates in a way that was not necessary (or possible, really) for African American servants.

Perhaps more common than wealthy white women's fears of white servants' sexuality was their irritation that so many did not know their place—as their slaves supposedly had. This annoyance probably emerged because they were uncertain about what exactly that place was. Ann Cushing had certainly found evidence of "airs" in one of her white cooks who, as she put it, was "too pretty to carry a kettle."[61] In Baltimore in 1833, the Wirt sisters discussed just this problem as it pertained to nurses. Catherine Wirt sought to help Elizabeth find an adequate nurse, both wet and dry, for her new baby. A friend proposed to hire out a slave she owned who was honest and faithful, and Catherine advised her sister to take advantage of the offer. In general, the slave would be more compliant, and the other candidate for the job, "Mrs. A. or any other white woman[,] . . . might be apt to assume airs and be troublesome." More than race, this overt class issue troubled Catherine. Those who had cast aspersions about having an African American wet nurse did not bother her. Two of their sisters and perhaps Catherine herself had been "suckled by a black woman" without consequence, she noted.[62] Despite Catherine's assurances, Elizabeth decided to follow a more recent family tradition of using white women as children's nurses, though slaves served in all other household positions. Mrs. Armstrong remained in her employ for several more months.[63]

Susan Grigsby, new to the employment of free workers, was equally troubled by intraracial class issues. Because she had come to rely on Mrs. Anderson, her free nurse, she was devastated when the woman chose to leave her to take a better job "in a free state." The vaunted system of free labor was overrated from

Mistress Grigsby's vantage point. Indeed, she believed it somewhat perverse that a "cruel" woman who promised her services could revoke them simply because something better came along. Mrs. Anderson's departure left Susan in a quandary. She resolved to move into the nursery herself and (in the manner of northern "moral mothers") commence "teaching and amusing the children" on her own. Of course, slave Jennie would nurse the baby and wash and dress the older children.[64]

That this arrangement apparently did not work either testifies to how much the presence of white women complicated an already complex issue for mothers like Susan Grigsby. Over the years, Grigsby analyzed the performance of various nurses; she delighted in Jennie's performance, Biddie's attentions, and even "harum-scarum" Sarah's strong efforts to be helpful. But her pleasure was never sustained. At one point, confused about who she should pursue next to help care for her children, Susan wrote with exasperation, "I would give anything in the world for a good and faithful nurse."[65] Though other southern women were more confident or consistent in their decisions to employ middle-aged white women or slave girls, Grigsby was not alone in her despair. Changing ideals and practices in domesticity, household relations, and slavery disrupted old assumptions and necessitated new action to shore up old lines, without creating a clear image of a "faithful nurse" matched with a sufficient number of willing workers who would please employers.

Certainly alterations in the border region's workforce compounded the problems of its residents in coordinating their worldview with the recalcitrant workers in their everyday lives. There were larger numbers of free African Americans and a declining proportion of slaves in these cities (as compared to cities in the Deep South). But the peculiarities of the border cities were more a matter of degree, rather than nature. There were many Souths, and no single city or area within the region could legitimately stand in for another. Nevertheless, virtually everywhere in the South small assaults on the institution of slavery took place. The more noticeable changes in the border cities—where elites openly registered tensions created by prior dependence upon enslaved women workers in a society slowly converting to "the free market"—simply highlight one set of reactions.[66]

Cultural messages about race and gender, and in particular the notion that African American women were ordained to serve whites, had structured southerners' understandings of domestic roles for a long time. As the literature on the Old South makes clear, white southerners accepted stereotypical perceptions of black women; they consistently portrayed older female slaves as devoted members of white families, thereby ignoring the possibility that poor treatment might have created resentment in enslaved women. To a certain extent, their construction of what it meant to be black and female persisted in governing domestic service. In the 1850s, most southern elites still saw enslaved servants as acceptable, even natural, caretakers of their homes and families. But new circumstances warranted new measures, most of which employers embarked upon unconsciously. While elites might maintain their equation of young black slave with general house servant, or entertain some flexibility in hiring someone to cook as long as she was skilled, they would not accept either the status quo or flexibility in their views of children's nurses. For that occupation there were firm opinions. When changes in the border region workforce accompanied a growing sense of the importance of mothers, previous conceptions of children's nurses were questioned and, to a significant number of residents, white women seemed a viable solution.

The market revolution had an impact on who was hired as children's nurses, though the occupation involved work that the gendered ideology of the market had redefined as "love" taking place in the home, apart from "real work." In response to this impact, urban southerners emphasized a racialized difference between black women and working white women, and between young and old workers. In raising their opinions of older white working women in particular, however, employers sometimes were confronted by their employees' own assumptions about class. When white working women sought more autonomy, that is, a legitimate way of capitalizing on assumptions that their race brought with it superior personality and working traits, they met the resistance of employers who held firmly to their faith in a class-based social order.

New ideas certainly did not bring a complete revolution. Susan Grigsby, who had wanted a dependable white nurse, experienced a change of heart, but not a conversion, as her willingness to return to Jenny when Mrs. Anderson quit suggests. The experiences of such employers and volatility within the definitions of good nurses illustrate the fluidity of this society. Racial, gender, and class stereotypes were in the midst of change and could be challenged from both sides. The debate on who should be minding the children raged on.

## NOTES

1. *National Intelligencer*, 1 August 1833.
2. See Ruth H. Block, "American Feminine Ideals in Transition: The Rise of the Moral Mother, 1785–1815," *Feminist Studies* 4 (June 1978): 101–26.

3. Catharine Beecher, *A Treatise on Domestic Economy* (1841; reprint, New York: Schoken Books, 1977), 13–14, 207–35.

4. *Hillsborough [North Carolina] Recorder*, 27 July 1825, quoted in Guion Griffis Johnson, *Ante-bellum North Carolina: A Social History* (Chapel Hill: University of North Carolina Press, 1937), 61–62.

5. *National Intelligencer*, 1 January 1840.

6. *American Farmer* 8 (21 April 1826): 37, quoted in D. Harland Hager, "The Ideal Woman in the Antebellum South: Lady or Farmwife?" *Journal of Southern History* 46 (August 1980): 411. Hager has found similar attitudes in at least three other southern periodicals.

7. For the quotation see "Fashionable Women," *Southern Cultivator* 17 (August 1859): 252, quoted in Hager, "Ideal Woman." Hager offers one of the strongest arguments that southerners entertained competing messages about the "lady ideal."

8. *Raleigh [North Carolina] Star*, 29 September 1847, quoted in Johnson, *Ante-bellum North Carolina*, 61–62.

9. See, for example, "F.C.J.," "Female Influence," *The Ladies Repository* 4, no. 10 (1844): 312–13, and Trace Talmon, "Papers for the Ladies: Part V, The Mother's Discipline," ibid., 19, no. 3 (1859): 170.

10. A good introduction to the economic demands that structured the assignment of slave labor can be found in Robert W. Gallman and Ralph V. Anderson, "Slaves as Fixed Capital," *Journal of American History* 64 (1977): 24–46. For more on slave children as nurses, see Deborah Gray White, *Ar'n't I a Woman: Female Slaves in the Plantation South* (New York: W. W. Norton, 1985), 92–94.

11. Richard C. Wade, *Slavery in the Cities: The South, 1820–1860* (New York: Oxford University Press, 1964), 20–23, outlines the dimensions of urban slaveholding.

12. The best explanations of this interpretation of southern society can be found in Eugene D. Genovese, *Roll, Jordan, Roll: The World the Slaves Made* (1972; reprint, New York: Vintage Books, 1976), and Elizabeth Fox-Genovese, *Within the Plantation Household: Black and White Women of the Old South* (Chapel Hill: University of North Carolina Press, 1988).

13. *National Intelligencer*, 2 December 1817; Mary McGuire to Mary Anne Claiborne, 18 February 1861, Claiborne Family Papers, Section 46, Folder 5, Virginia Historical Society, Richmond, Va. (hereafter VHS); Susan Tabb Daniel to Raleigh Travers Daniel, 5 August 1831, Daniel Family Papers, Section 3, VHS. See also Mary Diana Harper to Mrs. Robert Harper, 22 September 1815 and 22 July 1817, Mary Diana Harper Letterbook, Maryland Historical Society, Baltimore, Md. (hereafter MHS).

14. Olive to Mrs. August H. Claiborne, 26 July 1853(?), Claiborne Family Papers, Section 6, and Maria Steiger to Elizabeth Shriver, February 1837, Shriver Papers, Box 32, both in MHS.

15. Edward McGuire to Mary Anne Claiborne, [undated—mid 1850s], Claiborne Family Papers, Section 46, Folder 5, VHS; Robert Goodloe Harper to Mary Diana Harper, 25 January 1817, Mary Diana Harper Letterbook, MHS.

16. John Q. Anderson, ed., *Brokenburn: The Journal of Kate Stone, 1861–1868* (1955; reprint, Baton Rouge: Louisiana State University Press, 1972), 8–11; *Narrative of the Life of Frederick*

*Douglass, An American Slave, Written by Himself*, ed. David Blight (New York: Bedford Books of St. Martin's Press, 1993), 56.

17. See Bertram Wyatt-Brown, *Southern Honor: Ethics and Behavior in the Old South* (New York: Oxford University Press, 1982); Steven Stowe, *Intimacy and Power in the Old South: Ritual in the Lives of the Planters* (Baltimore: Johns Hopkins University Press, 1987); and Fox-Genovese, *Within the Plantation Household*, 112 (though she notes for female children that this power to command was necessarily backed up by the presence of the child's father). Anna Rubbo and Michael Taussig develop a similar point in "Up Off Their Knees: Servant-hood in Southwest Columbia," in *Female Servants and Economic Development*, Michigan Occasional Paper, no. 1 (Ann Arbor, 1978), 22. Grace Elizabeth Hale, *Making Whiteness: The Culture of Segregation in the South, 1890–1940* (New York: Pantheon Books, 1998), 100–101, 116, discusses the continued importance of black nurses to white children in the years after the Civil War.

18. Sarah Ruggles to Ellen Green, 1 August 1839, Green Family Papers, Filson Club, Louisville, Kentucky. A sense of slaves' corrupting influence on children also upset Fanny Kemble. See Frances Ann Kemble, *Journal of a Resident on a Georgia Plantation in 1838–1839*, ed. John A. Scott (Athens: University of Georgia Press, 1984).

19. Willie Lee Rose, "On the Domestication of Domestic Slavery," in *Slavery and Freedom*, ed. William W. Freehling (New York: Oxford University Press, 1982).

20. William Wirt to Peachy Gilmer, 4 August 1804, Volume 1, William Wirt Papers, Manuscript Division, Library of Congress, Washington, D.C. (hereafter WWP); George W. Anderson to his wife, 4 April 1830, Anderson Family Papers, Folder 3, Margaret I. King Library, University of Kentucky, Lexington, Ky.; Henderson quoted in Fox-Genovese, *Within the Plantation Household*, 136–37. Fox-Genovese (*Within the Plantation Household*, 112) ascribes to up-country planters such as Gov. Joseph Brown of Georgia the idea that children should be separated from slave nurses in order to learn better work ethics. See also Catherine Clinton, *The Plantation Mistress: Woman's World in the Old South* (New York: Oxford University Press, 1982), 48.

21. Agnes Gamble Cabell to Henry Coalter Cabell, 17 October 185[?], Cabell Family Papers, Section 7, VHS.

22. This assumption that between the eighteenth and nineteenth centuries a stronger sense of motherhood developed among southerners is based in part on Julia Cherry Spruill's description of colonial motherhood in *Women's Life and Work in the Southern Colonies* (1938; reprint, New York: Russell & Russell, 1969), 55–59.

23. Fox-Genovese, *Within the Plantation Household*, 279–80, argues that plantation women generally did not believe that using wet nurses and slave nurses to tend infants and toddlers was a contradiction to their primary obligation as mothers.

24. White, *Ar'n't I a Woman?*, 44–61. In this section I am arguing for a middle ground between the implication that "mammy" was a Lost Cause creation and Fox-Genovese's assessment that "mammies indisputably existed." For the former position, see Cheryl Thurber, "The Development of the Mammy Image and Mythology," in *Southern Women: Histories and Identities*, ed. Virginia Bernhard, Betty Brandon, Elizabeth Fox-Genovese, and

Theda Perdue (Columbia: University of Missouri Press, 1992), 87–108. Thurber and Hale, in *Making Whiteness*, 85–119, make a good case for viewing southerners' dramatic romanticization of mammies during the first decades of the twentieth century, as they solidified their respect for the benefits of slavery, as support for a return to the racial hierarchy of the past. Fox-Genovese (*Within the Plantation Household*, 137, 147–62, 291–92) maintains that the mammy image was one effort by white planters to allay their fears of slaves' perceived overt sexuality and hostility. In mammy, nurturing and love displaced such characteristics. Although I agree such an image helped anxious whites, I think it was constructed as attacks on slavery were increasing in the 1850s. Most of Fox-Genovese's evidence comes from the 1850s and from slave narratives dictated in the 1930s by ex-slaves who could not recall much about southern society before the last decade of the antebellum period, the time period from which comes the evidence I found on the same subject.

25. Fox-Genovese, *Within the Plantation Household*, 136.

26. Susan Tabb Daniel to Raleigh Travers Daniel, 5 August 1831, Section 3, Daniel Family Papers, VHS.

27. Sarah Bonetta Valentine to Edward V. Valentine, 19 November 1859, Sarah Bonetta Valentine Papers, Valentine Museum, Richmond, Virginia.

28. For example, the contradiction between the romanticized view of mammies and their status as household property becomes clear in an exchange during the U.S. Senate debate over the Kansas-Nebraska bill. Senator George Badger of North Carolina asked: "If some southern gentlemen wishes to take the . . . old woman who nursed him in childhood, and whom he called 'Mammy' . . . into one of these territories for the betterment of the fortunes of his whole family—why, in the name of God, should anybody prevent it?" To which Senator Benjamin Wade of Ohio replied: "We have not the least objection . . . to the senator's migrating to Kansas and taking his old 'Mammy' along with him. We only insist that he shall not be empowered to sell her after taking her there" (cited in James M. McPherson, *Ordeal By Fire: The Civil War and Reconstruction*, 2d ed. [New York: McGraw-Hill, Inc., 1992]). I am indebted to Carol Lasser for bringing this remarkable exchange to my attention.

29. For more on the complexities of urban border society, see Stephanie Cole, "Servants and Slaves: Domestic Service in the Border Cities, 1800–1850" (Ph.D. diss., University of Florida, 1994). See also Ira Berlin, *Slaves without Masters: The Free Negro in the Antebellum South* (New York: Oxford University Press, 1974); Leonard Curry, *The Free Black in Urban America, 1800–1850: The Shadow of a Dream* (Chicago: University of Chicago Press, 1981); Claudia Dale Goldin, *Urban Slavery in the American South, 1820–1860* (Chicago: University of Chicago Press, 1976); Christopher Phillips, *Freedom's Port: The African-American Community of Baltimore, 1790–1860* (Urbana: University of Illinois Press, 1997); Wade, *Slavery in the Cities*; and T. Stephen Whitman, *The Price of Freedom: Slavery and Manumission in Baltimore and Early National Maryland* (Lexington: University Press of Kentucky, 1997). Whitman offers a very important analysis of "term slaves," and his study is particularly revealing of the difficulties slaveowners encountered as they attempted to secure the peculiar institution in a new economy.

30. Cole, "Servants and Slaves," 54–98; for more on free black restrictions see Wade, *Slavery in the Cities*, 106–10; Berlin, *Slaves without Masters*, 209–12; and Curry, *Free Black in Urban America*, 83–90; for more on labor-law restrictions of "free" workers, see Robert J. Steinfeld, *The Invention of Free Labor: The Employment Relation in English and American Law and Culture, 1350–1870* (Chapel Hill: University of North Carolina Press, 1991), 147–72, and Christopher L. Tomlins, *Law, Labor, and Ideology in the Early American Republic* (New York: Cambridge University Press, 1993), 232–93.

31. A good theoretical explanation of this process is Evelyn Nakano Glenn, "From Servitude to Service Work: Historical Continuities in the Racial Division of Paid Reproductive Labor," *Signs* 18 (Autumn 1992): 1–43. Karen Tranberg Hansen, *Distant Companions: Servants and Employers in Zambia, 1900–1985* (Ithaca, N.Y.: Cornell University Press, 1989), 3, 9–11, 85–137, discusses the way in which cultural factors, along with economic structures, determined who would work in whites' homes in Zambia. Relying in large part upon the theoretical work of Anthony Giddens, she argues that "human-made distinctions, construed as essential differences in culture, race, class, and sex, turned the servant's personhood into otherness." See also Sandra Lauderdale Graham, *House and Street: The Domestic World of Servants and Masters in Nineteenth-Century Rio de Janeiro* (Cambridge: Cambridge University Press, 1988), and Tera W. Hunter, *To 'Joy My Freedom: Southern Black Women's Lives and Labors after the Civil War* (Cambridge, Mass.: Harvard University Press, 1997).

32. I created this sample by reading four months of issues, chosen at random, out of every fifth year of one newspaper from each of the five border cities. For each city I began sampling newspapers for the year closest to 1800 and continued with 1805, 1810, and so forth through 1850, making necessary accommodations for gaps where they existed. For a fuller analysis of changes in advertisements regarding domestic help illustrated in this source, see Cole, "Servants and Slaves," 59–98.

33. In order to gain as much information as I could from newspaper advertisements, I essentially coded them for content analysis, using a software program called SPSS/PC+. I asked several questions for each ad, including whether it was a "help-wanted" or a "situation-wanted" advertisement; whether the advertiser sought a slave, slave-for-hire, or a free person; what race, gender, and age the servant might be; and what skills were important. I attempted to compensate for missing information by making guesses based upon textual clues (a request for a "likely" servant probably concerned a slave), but I kept track of those guesses and have taken those ads out of the following comparisons when it seemed appropriate. For an extended description of the database and coding process see Cole, "Servants and Slaves," 280–86.

34. Of the 419 advertisements for cooks, 263 clearly concerned African Americans, 244 concerned slaves, and 405 concerned females.

35. Elizabeth Wirt to Catherine Gamble, 5 June 1831, WWP, Volume 4. On a more significant scale illustrating the tolerance employers could summon for a good cook, almost half of all ads noting that the domestic had a child concerned a cook, while none of these ads concerned nurses. As Goldin argues in *Urban Slavery* (63), city-dwelling slave-

holders considered a small child a "net loss" and insisted on compensation for the burden in the price of the sale. Advertisers frequently termed servants with children "inconvenient" or "troublesome." See *National Intelligencer*, 29 November 1802, 10 December 1806, 11 November 1807, 15 March 1814, and 12 September 1814, and the *Louisville Daily Journal*, 3 December 1836.

36. *National Intelligencer*, 4 August 1819. Barbara G. Carson, *Ambitious Appetites: Dining, Behavior, and Patterns of Consumption in Federal Washington* (Washington, D.C.: American Institute of Architects Press, 1990), 97–98, argues that elite southerners highly valued their cooks, and actually preferred men. My evidence does not support that that preference was as prevalent as Carson implies. See *National Intelligencer*, 6 and 10 January 1831, 5 June 1834, and 1 December 1847.

37. Between 1815 and 1850 the proportion of ads that were unclear in regard to the race and status of the person whom the advertiser sought rose from 5.2 to 23.8 percent. In part this increase was a function of my own conservatism in certifying ads without direct references to slavery as free worker ads. Thus, as more free workers entered the pool of workers, what I saw as unclear wording in advertisements increased proportionately. The problem was not entirely in the coding, however. Imprecision also reflected employers who cared less about who they hired. The number of "white or colored" references in advertisements increased as well, hence my argument that a growth in ads unclear regarding the race or status of a prospective employee might also have reflected increasing ambivalence in border residents about whom they wanted to hire.

38. Account book of Ann Mackenzie Cushing, 1835–42, MHS.

39. About 80 percent of the ads still concerned African American women. See Tables 4.1–4.5. All tables were prepared without guesses about missing information, so statistics are slightly different from those that appear in the text, which include guesses.

40. Of the 396 advertisements for house servants, 296 concerned African Americans, 274 were for slaves, and 301 were for females.

41. For the period 1800 to 1850, 10 percent of the advertisements analyzed were unclear. This percentage reflects the high number of slaves in this occupation, because advertisements concerning slaves were usually the most clearly written. As described above, my ability to ascertain confidently the status of an individual who clearly was not a slave was often limited.

42. See Table 4.2 for comparison of ages across skill categories.

43. Of the 195 house servants who were eighteen or younger, 136, or 70 percent, were slaves. In addition, 84 percent of the house servants who were slaves were under age eighteen.

44. Of the 212 advertisements for or by nurses, 211 clearly concerned females, and 105 concerned free workers. Almost an equal number of advertisers were white (55) as were black (62). But these aggregate statistics are particularly deceiving of how the occupation changed in nature over time, as I argue below.

45. The average given for nurses was 22.3 years, with a standard deviation of 11.8 years.

46. Of 212 ads, 114 listed an age or approximate age.

47. The average age for slave nurses was just under sixteen years; the average age for free nurses was just over twenty-four. I should note, however, that while the average age of advertised white nurses was 24.6 years, the standard deviation was 12.9 years. Calls for older white nurses were more frequent than for younger white nurses, but white girls remained appealing to many border city residents.

48. Two, almost simultaneous, ads from the Baltimore *Sun*, 9 and 27 September 1845, provide an example of the contrasting interests expressed in advertisements for nurses.

49. Every ad for a nurse in the period between 1800 and 1815 mentioned an African American; only 44 percent did so in the years 1830–50. Table 4.5 shows the movement toward hiring free and white nurses. Comparing the lambda ($\lambda$) statistics reported for the movement toward free labor in each occupation illustrates that the shift toward free and white servants in the occupation of children's nurse was stronger than for any other occupation. That is, knowing the status of a nurse, you could reduce the error of guessing the period her ad ran by 18 percent, but knowing the status for either of the other occupations did not reduce errors at all. In addition, knowing the race could reduce guessing errors by 22 percent for nurses but not at all for cooks or house servants. (See Tables 4.3–4.5.)

50. *Sun*, 27 February 1845.

51. Susan Shelby Grigsby to Virginia Shelby Breckinridge, [n.d., 1850s], Grigsby Collection, Filson Club, Louisville, Kentucky (hereafter GC). John Tayloe, a substantial slave-holder who lived in Washington and on an estate in Virginia, employed a white woman from Philadelphia as nurse (Carson, *Ambitious Appetites*, 94, 191 n. 56).

52. *Sun*, 2 June 1845. See also *National Intelligencer*, 2 June 1848.

53. Quotation appears in *National Intelligencer*, 30 March 1833. Similar wording appears in many other advertisements. See, for example, ibid., 1 August 1833, 15 March 1843, and 15 October 1846; *Sun*, 17 April 1850; and the *Louisville Daily Journal*, 29 June 1836.

54. None of the studies of domestic service in the North indicates that employers placed a premium on hiring older nurses. See Faye E. Dudden, *Serving Women: Household Servants in Nineteenth-Century America* (Hanover, N.H.: Wesleyan University Press, 1983), 147–54, and Carol Lasser, "Mistress, Maid, and Market: The Transformation of Domestic Service in New England, 1790–1870" (Ph.D. diss., Harvard University, 1982). David Katzman, *Seven Days a Week: Women and Domestic Service in Industrializing America* (New York: Oxford University Press, 1978), does not identify such a pattern for the years between 1870 and 1920.

55. Fox-Genovese, *Within the Plantation Household*, 279–80, notes that southerners did not customarily associate good motherhood with participating in its daily, menial tasks.

56. See Table 4.5. The quotations appeared in the *Sun*, 23 January 1850.

57. I am particularly indebted to Carol Lasser for helping me develop this point.

58. For background on this issue, see Victoria E. Bynum, *Unruly Women: The Politics of Social and Sexual Control in the Old South* (Chapel Hill: University of North Carolina Press, 1992), 7–8, 88–110, and Martha Elizabeth Hodes, *White Women, Black Men: Illicit Sex in the Nineteenth-Century South* (New Haven: Yale University Press, 1997).

59. Charles Howard to Elizabeth Howard, 20 February 1833, Howard Papers, Box 11, MHS.

60. To cite one now famous example, Sally Hemmings was originally a nurse to Thomas Jefferson's daughter. See also Catherine Clinton, "Caught in the Web of the Big House: Women and Slavery," in *The Web of Southern Social Relations: Women, Family and Education*, ed. Walter J. Fraser Jr., Frank Saunders Jr., and Jon L. Wakelyn (Athens: University of Georgia Press, 1985), and Catherine Clinton, " 'Southern Dishonor': Flesh, Blood, Race, and Bondage," in *In Joy and in Sorrow: Women, Family, and Marriage in the Victorian South*, ed. Carol Bleser (New York: Oxford University Press, 1991).

61. Cushing Account Book, 10 September 1839, MHS.

62. Catherine Wirt to Elizabeth Wirt Goldsborough, 14 September 1833, WWP.

63. Ibid., 26 September and 16 October 1833. For a more extensive discussion of the Wirts' concern about "troublesome airs" among white women servants, see Anya Jabour, *Marriage in the Early Republic: William and Elizabeth Wirt and the Companionate Ideal* (Baltimore: Johns Hopkins University Press, 1998).

64. Susan Grigsby to Virginia Breckinridge, [n.d., 1850s], Folder 95, GC.

65. Because Susan and her mother did not date the series of letters between them in which this story unfolds, it is difficult to determine in what order she expressed her range of feelings on the subject of nurses. But even so, no one course is ever mentioned twice, suggesting that this befuddled mother could not decide what to do. See Susan Grigsby to Virginia Breckinridge, [n.d., 1850s], Folders 94, 95, and 96, GC.

66. Evidence that residents of other southern cities experimented with imposing their views of racial and gender hierarchies on diverse labor pools can be found both in personal narratives and scholarly studies that discuss the impact of immigration and increasing numbers of free African Americans in southern cities. See, for example, Daniel E. Sutherland, ed., *A Very Violent Rebel: The Civil War Diary of Ellen Renshaw House* (Knoxville: University of Tennessee Press, 1996), xviii; Harriet E. Amos, *Cotton City: Urban Development in Antebellum Mobile* (Tuscaloosa: University of Alabama Press, 1985), 93–113; Barbara L. Bellows, *Benevolence among Slaveholders: Assisting the Poor in Charleston, 1670–1860* (Baton Rouge: Louisiana State University Press, 1993), 135–38, 186; Walter J. Fraser Jr., *Charleston! Charleston! The History of a Southern City* (Columbia: University of South Carolina Press, 1989), 227–29; Lawrence H. Larsen, *The Urban South: A History* (Lexington: University Press of Kentucky, 1990), 45–48; Robert C. Reinders, *End of an Era: New Orleans, 1850–1860* (Gretna, La.: Pelican Publishing Company, 1963), 17–31; and Thomas C. Parramore, *Norfolk: The First Four Centuries* (Charlottesville: University Press of Virginia, 1994), 125.

## Spheres of Influence:
## Working White and Black Women in
## Antebellum Savannah

TIMOTHY J. LOCKLEY

The vast majority of southern women worked. About three-quarters of all white southern families did not own slaves on the eve of the Civil War, and consequently women in these families generally shared with black women the necessity of working.[1] Whatever else may have divided them, and there was much, black and white women regularly toiled in the fields to produce goods for the market and for the dinner table. They worked in the home caring for children and occasionally producing handicrafts. And in urban areas, as this essay will demonstrate, they pursued a variety of wage-earning occupations. As Stephanie McCurry has demonstrated, this was true in some slaveholding families as well. In coastal South Carolina, it was the work of the wives and daughters that helped to secure the economic independence of yeoman households, even those owning as many as ten slaves. Only a small number of elite white women in the South enjoyed the leisured lifestyle popularized in twentieth-century mythology.[2]

Any study of the lives of antebellum women faces problems because most sources are written by men, about men, and for men. Official statistical compilations, for example, frequently overlooked the part that women played in southern life. But our ignorance of women's lives and experiences in the antebellum South is gradually being reversed. Since the 1970s the historiographic anonymity of southern women has been overcome to some extent by scholars such as Suzanne Lebsock, Elizabeth Varon, and Catherine Clinton, among others, but the focus has tended to be on elite women rather than ordinary women.[3]

Moreover, scholars have examined the domestic lives of women in far more detail than their public lives, and, with a few exceptions, rural women in preference to urban women. The domesticity that was the norm for rural elite women has been termed the woman's "sphere." But, as this essay will demonstrate, women's "spheres" were not only domestic. In fact, a woman's work, paid or unpaid, has perhaps an equal claim to be termed a "sphere" because it dominated the normal day-to-day existence for so many women.[4] By broadening our interpretation of the "woman's sphere" we can explore in greater depth the interaction of race, class, and gender in the antebellum South.

This essay is a case study of the lives of working women in Savannah, a city that dominated the Georgia low country, acting as a focal point for the coastal rice and cotton trades. In addition, as an entrepôt, it was the only place where low-country residents could hope to have a modicum of purchasing choice. The population of the city was large, rising from five thousand in 1800 to more than twenty-two thousand in 1860, and cosmopolitan, with slaves and free blacks making up between a third and a half of the urban population. Among whites, more than half did not own slaves and a large number were immigrants.[5] Determining the size of the female workforce in Savannah is not straightforward. The best source is the 1860 federal census, which listed 1,578 white women and 228 free black women with occupations in Chatham County, the vast majority of whom would have been resident in Savannah. No comparable occupational data was collected for bondwomen in 1860, but the city tax records show that there were 7,712 slaves in Savannah in 1860, allowing us to estimate the female slave population at 3,856. Since previous city censuses show that bondwomen constituted about 60 percent of the urban slave population, the female slave population of Savannah in 1860 was probably more like 4,600. Of these women, we also know that just over half of them were aged over fifteen, thus the adult female slave population in Savannah in 1860 was perhaps about 2,300.[6] Nearly all of these slave women would have worked.[7]

Perversely, the best documented of all Savannah's female groups is also the smallest, namely free black women. In 1817 the city registered as many free black men and women as it could find (and judging from the much larger number counted by the census, city officials did not try particularly hard), repeating the task periodically during the remainder of the antebellum period.[8] This register usually included occupational data, and therefore free black women constitute the only female population in the city whose occupations can be traced and analyzed over a period of time.

In 1817 only nineteen free black women were given an occupation in the register: nine sold "small wares," another seven were cooks, two were laborers, and one was a washer. Seven years later, in 1824, free black women were starting to congregate in certain occupations, with women occupied as "seamstresses," "washerwomen," and "vendors of small wares" collectively accounting for 60 percent of the workforce. Yet small numbers of free black women continued to find work in more unusual situations, as shopkeepers and gardeners.[9] However, by 1829, two-thirds of Savannah's free black women were working as seamstresses or washerwomen, and the proportion of women involved in retailing had halved from 20 percent to 10 percent of the workforce.[10] The trend among free black women therefore seems to be one of greater occupational specialization, with fewer and fewer women employed outside their own homes. It seems likely that free black women were making informed choices about exactly which occupations suited their individual and collective circumstances. Certainly free black women could be responsive to the needs of the labor market. Over a number of years, several women moved from washing to cooking, or from selling to sewing, no doubt making careful decisions about which pursuits brought the most regular income. Nancy Goudling, for example, retailed goods in 1829 but was a pastry cook in 1860. Other free black women settled on jobs early and stuck with them. Mary Sheftall, born in Savannah in 1799, was first registered as a washerwoman in 1824 and was still doing laundry work in 1860. Most of these women earned sufficient incomes to maintain their families, but women such as Priscilla Moody, who earned enough as a vendor of small wares to eventually purchase her own shop, were few and far between.[11]

Significant differences existed between white and free black working women in Savannah. For example, of more than 3,500 white women in Savannah in 1860 between the ages of twenty and fifty-nine, roughly 1,300 of them, or just over a third, were assigned occupations in the federal census. In stark contrast, more than four-fifths of free black women of a similar age worked.[12] The racial differences are even more marked among women over sixty and those under twenty. Only about one in six white women in these age groups was working, compared with more than one-half of free black teenage women and three-quarters of free black women over sixty.[13] From this evidence it is clear that the length of the working lives of free black women significantly exceeded those of white women. Nancy Johnson was apparently still working as a nurse in Savannah at the age of 103. Women lacking occupations were not necessarily idle. Married women with young children, for instance, may well have spent all their time in child care and housework.[14] Given that fewer than half of Savannah's households owned slaves, and that a number owned just one slave, it is perhaps fair to estimate that only about a quarter of white women in the city were ladies of leisure.[15]

The reasons that so many of Savannah's women worked no doubt varied greatly, but the available evidence suggests that most women, of all social groups, worked simply to survive.[16] Two-thirds of working white women and nearly 90 percent of free black women in 1860 were either the principal or sole breadwinners in their households.[17] More than half had dependents, so not working, in a society where social welfare was nonexistent and charity provided only the most basic level of support, was simply not a viable option.[18] Women were particularly vital to the sustenance of free black families in Savannah. Chatham County's free black community had a female majority, and consequently there was a particular onus on free black women to earn sufficient income to support their families.[19] Moreover, whereas a third of working white women had husbands living with them, only about 10 percent of free black women were in the same situation. It is entirely conceivable that many husbands and fathers of free black women and children were slaves; indeed, the relatively high proportion of free black women who had children but no husbands suggests this was the case. Such husbands would have been unable to contribute with any degree of regularity toward their families' incomes.[20] Therefore, many free black women in Savannah would have worked principally to avoid starvation and destitution for themselves and those who depended on them. Some of these women built themselves a reputation for skill and competency by word of mouth—Asphasia Mirault's bakery and ice-cream store, for instance, gained a legendary status among Savannah's youth—but for many there was little security beyond the casual business they themselves could drum up, perhaps by going door to door.[21]

Black and white women in Savannah had work in common because they experienced similar economic pressures regardless of race. But the purpose of this essay is not only to establish that a large number of women worked in antebellum Savannah; it also seeks to show what actually determined a woman's occupation. The southern racial hierarchy seemingly dictated that black people should undertake only the most menial occupations, yet the evidence from this southern city suggests that race was only one occupational determinant. Women grouped themselves in certain occupations because they shared common family backgrounds, ages, and ethnicities as well. The spheres of occupational influence in antebellum Savannah were actually determined by a number of complex variables that interacted and intersected with each other.

Race was obviously one factor that could influence the employment of women in Savannah. Some occupations were generally not open to black women whether they were enslaved or free. For example, in 1860 there were thirty-one white women employed as teachers, a job that black women were legally excluded from. Among white women, there were also 122 boardinghouse keepers, twenty-five shopkeepers, three hoteliers, a brass and iron foundress, a doctoress, and an actress. These jobs were generally white occupational spheres because the vast majority of black women in the city would not have had access to the capital necessary to set themselves up as independent businesswomen, necessarily entailing the purchase of stock and the purchase or rent of premises. Furthermore, most free black women would have known this and few would have wasted time, effort, and perhaps money in trying to get a foothold in such occupations. Of course, for every such generalization there is an exception. Rachel, the slave of Patrick Ryan, applied to the Southern Claims Commission after the Civil War for $1,659 in recompense for loss of property during the Union occupation of Savannah. She claimed that "I always hired my own time from the time I was a woman grown" and when her daughters were old enough she hired their time as well. With the profits of their labor, Rachel first rented and subsequently purchased a large sixteen-room house and took in boarders. Evidently, this woman believed that one needed to be neither white nor free to pursue such an occupation, and local white residents who knew about this arrangement apparently agreed, even writing in support of her claim.[22]

Despite Rachel's case, there were clearly significant hurdles to overcome if a black woman was to be so visibly financially independent. Far more common was for black women to engage in economic activity that was not so high profile, but significant nevertheless. Black women came to dominate market trading despite the distrust of the city authorities. As several scholars have shown, the informal slave economy was probably at its most vibrant in the Georgia and South Carolina low country, with slaves taking advantage of the task-labor regime of rice plantations to engage in their own pursuits on their own time.[23] Probably the most common occupation for those slaves motivated to work in their free time was in the gardens provided for them on most plantations. Bondwomen in particular were expected to tend to the garden, growing a wide variety of vegetables and rearing livestock, especially chickens.[24] As production increased, and surpluses were produced, a visit to the weekly market in Savannah became necessary.

The Savannah city market was held daily in Ellis Square, and as early as 1775 slaves had adopted Sunday as the day they brought produce to market to trade.[25] The best description of the market in Savannah comes from a New Englander resident in Georgia for eight years. Emily Burke came to teach at the Savannah Female Asylum in 1840 and on her very first morning in Savannah was awakened before dawn by the noise from the market, which her hotel overlooked. Her vivid description of the market is worth quoting at length.

> In the morning . . . I saw a great many colored persons . . . assembled together under a sort of shelter. That, from the appearance of things, I soon judged to be the city market. . . . This building is furnished with stalls, owned by individuals in the city who send produce there to sell.
>
> In each of these stalls stands a servant woman to sell her master's property, who is careful to deck out his saleswoman in the most gaudy colors to make her as conspicuous as possible that she may be successful in trade. I once heard a gentleman, whose saleswoman had not been successful say, "he must get her a new handkerchief for her head and see if she would not sell more! . . ."
>
> The market is free for trade from five o'clock in the morning till ten. Then the bell rings and all are obliged to disperse and take with them their unsold articles, for everything that remains on the ground after ten o'clock belongs to the keeper. Trade is not allowed in the market excepting on Saturday evening, when it is more crowded than at any other time. For the people come then to purchase for the Sabbath, and many go just because they want to see a great crowd. It has been estimated that on some pleasant evenings there are no less than four thousand people in the market at one time. Here almost every eatable thing can be found. Vegetables fresh from the garden are sold the year round. All kinds of fish, both shell and finny, may be had here; birds of all kinds, both tame and wild; and the most delicious tropical fruits, as well as those which are brought from cold countries. People travel a great distance for the purpose of buying and selling in the market. I have known women to come one hundred miles to sell the produce of their own industry.[26]

As a newcomer to Savannah, Emily Burke could not have realized that most of the goods retailed in the market were in fact produced by slaves in their own gardens. As to the agency of owners in decking out their bondwomen, Burke later contradicted herself by noting that slave women themselves took every opportunity to dress up in bright colors.[27] This description of the city market shows it to be the vibrant hub of the city's commercial and retail life.

Most, if not all, of the public market trading in the Savannah City Market was undertaken by women—just as it was in Charleston and throughout the Caribbean Islands and in West Africa.[28] In the nineteenth century the market was a female sphere, but this had not always been the case. In 1792 a male slave was fined by the city council for selling vegetables without a badge, and four years later bondman Cato was ordered to be whipped for forestalling in the market.[29] However, after 1800 there is no evidence that bondmen were retailing regularly, though some free black men continued to work as butchers in the market.[30] Several observers commented on the black women who traded in low-country markets, one traveler being particularly impressed by their "great quickness in reckoning and making change [with] rarely an error in the result."[31] The dominance of bondwomen in the city market is also shown by the number of licensed slave vendors. In 1801, the Savannah City Council granted thirty vending badges to slaves, twenty-five of which went to bondwomen.[32]

The sheer number of slave women bringing their garden produce to Savannah meant that they began to dominate the market. White and free black traders were effectively excluded from the market most likely because they did not have the same regular supply line direct from the plantation.[33] Even if white and free black women were able to procure supplies, slave women were able to undercut their competitors because their prices reflected the fact that their owners continued to be the main providers of the necessaries of life. It was not long before the market had become a sphere for black women, a development that the Chatham County grand jury believed would be "highly injurious to the citizens."[34]

The jury's prediction was correct, because once slave women had secured their monopoly position in the market, they began to increase their prices to white shoppers. This was effectively racial discrimination: prices offered to fellow slaves or to free blacks apparently did not increase at the same rate as those offered to whites, and to ensure that civic authorities were powerless to prevent it, slaves apparently sold much of the best farm produce before the Sunday market officially opened. In 1814 the Chatham County grand jury cited "numerous Negro sellers" for "forestalling in purchasing large quantities of eggs, poultry, etc. and vending them at a higher rate to the inhabitants."[35] Four years later the grand jury cited "as an evil of great magnitude, the ordinance granting badges to colored and black women, for the purpose of hawking about articles for sale. These women monopolize in divers ways, many of the necessaries of life, which are brought to our market, by which the price is greatly enhanced, and the poor inhabitants of our city, proportionately distressed."[36] Evidently a new ordinance passed in 1817 that limited the hours that trading could occur in the market was neither observed by slave vendors nor rigorously enforced by city officials.[37] Much of the trading between bondwomen relied on personal contacts, often to the exclusion of white people, rich and poor alike. Apparently a ploy used by slave women working as domestics in Savannah was to pretend that purchases were for their white families, when in reality they were buying for their own consumption.[38] This is not to say that white people did not purchase at the market. When trying to regulate Sunday trading in 1829, the city council itself acknowledged that it was customary for "the poorer class of white persons who generally receive their wages in the evening of Saturday . . . [to] . . . require a short time on Sunday morning to preserve the usual food for their families."[39] Indeed, we can probably go further and say that most of the white people who made purchases in the market would have been women. These women were most likely to have been nonslaveholders who did not have slave domestics to purchase for them. Unfortunately, no direct testimony survives from these women describing how they felt negotiating with black women for groceries and most likely being forced to pay over the odds. Moreover, it is also likely that black and white women who regularly visited the city market became familiar in a way that was not common in the South.

The disquiet felt in some quarters of Savannah society about the activities of market women resulted in crowds of white people gathering to use "the most offensive and undecorous language [to] insult and abuse females and others who have articles to sell." Such was the threat to the peace of the city that the grand jury requested that the city watch be posted at the market during the early hours of the morning to arrest "all persons so offending."[40] On another occasion the mayor specifically ordered the arrest of "all colored females, who may be selling in and outside the market, with or without badges when not authorized by the ordinance regulating badges."[41] Female vendors selling their goods on the streets of the city were also criticized. The grand jury complained that while white people were engaged in Sunday worship, "the multitude are crying small wares about our streets," and it likened the number of slave vendors in Savannah to an infestation.[42] The Sabbath Union, formed by evangelicals to end Sunday trading in the city, also complained that those "sequestered in the temple of the most high" were compelled "to listen to the rude cry of the blacks offering their articles for sale, under the very windows of the churches."[43] Clearly the slave vendors caused much disquiet in the city; one grand jury went so far as to claim that "they encourage theft; deprave our domestics, and by their evil influence and dissolute lives endanger the safety of the city."[44]

During the 1840s and 1850s the monopoly position of slave vendors was challenged by some white women. Several observers reported that white women from the countryside surrounding Savannah brought their own farm produce to the city.[45] Rural white women, while they could sell their produce in a local country store, perhaps preferred the Savannah city market because it gave them the chance to purchase a wider variety of items, at good prices, than they normally had access to. Emily Burke noted that groups of up to six women would travel together upward of a hundred miles in order to retail in Savannah: "When they arrive, they go directly to the market place, tie their mules round about upon the outside of the market square, kindle up little fires in the street near the market and cook their suppers . . . instead of sleeping in their carts, they camp down upon the cold, damp bricks in the market with no other bed than what one coarse blanket makes for them."[46]

Frederick Law Olmsted similarly observed in 1854 that the women's preferred modes of transport were "small one horse carts."[47] In addition to these periodic visitations from rural white women, some urban white women were prepared to retail goods on the streets and in the market. Five white women in 1860 were listed as retailing such goods as milk, candy, and poultry. But although their activity may have broken the black monopoly on trading, the effect of just five white women would have been minimal. One white woman, conscious of the dominance of black women in the market, decided that the only way she could retail successfully was to "black her face." Eighteen-year-old Euphemia Hover earned herself a $3 fine for her trouble.[48] Undoubtedly, black women continued to dominate the city market until the Civil War—they had made it their sphere and preserved it as such.

If black women wished to obtain goods that were not for sale in the market they had to visit one of the city's shops, twenty-five of which in 1860 were owned by white women. We know that white female shopkeepers in Savannah were perfectly prepared to retail to slaves, even in violation of municipal laws. Women such as Sophia Austin, Mary Garnet, Sarah Falligrant, and Catherine Prendergast regularly appeared before council in the 1820s, 1830s, and 1840s on charges of retailing liquor without a license, violating the Sabbath ordinances, or "entertaining Negroes."[49] Indeed, white female shopkeepers located their establishments in the western areas of the city most densely populated with African Americans.[50] Sarah Falligrant even petitioned the city council for a permit to retail goods in the market square, where bondwomen were generally congregated.[51] Bondwomen wishing to purchase at these shops may well have been forced to pay higher prices for cloth, groceries, tobacco, or liquor than white customers, reversing the pattern of trading seen in the market. Shop-keeping was, by 1860, an exclusively white pursuit.

Either through legal discrimination or through ingenuity and enterprise some areas of employment therefore became almost racially exclusive. White women would have found it as hard to become market traders in Savannah as black women would have trying to become teachers. Considering that race was one of the key social determinants in antebellum Savannah, this is not entirely surprising. Still, many other jobs women held in the city were not determined by race but by other factors such as age, nativity, and family status.

The youngest working women in Savannah generally occupied the most menial positions. Among white women, the vast majority of them were not native southerners; indeed, more than half of all working white women in Savannah in 1860 had been born in Ireland, easily outnumbering the combined totals of those born within the state of Georgia and those from the rest of the United States.[52] The Irish women working in Savannah in 1860 were generally under thirty, and they dominated the least skilled areas of employment. They constituted, for example, nearly 70 percent of white washers and ironers, nearly 80 percent of white domestics and servants, and more than 80 percent of white chambermaids. In part these figures reflected the age, and presumably the skill level, of these women. Irish servant women were, on average, just twenty-four, and the youngest of them, Mary Manning, was just eleven. Many of these women would have lacked the skills to earn a living in any other way. Young white girls had long been employed in such capacities. Between 1811 and 1830 the Savannah Female Asylum bound out sixty girls to domestic work in the city, all of whom were under eighteen.[53] By 1860 most of the city's hotels and boardinghouses employed Irish girls in preference to free black women or bondwomen, most likely because they were cheaper. Slaves who might have worked on hire in such establishments had to pay their owners a weekly fee earned from their income and could not afford to take jobs that offered board and lodging instead of wages.[54] Moreover, hired slaves were not totally dependent on their employers; they always had recourse to their owners if they were dissatisfied with their positions. Young Irish women most likely had nowhere else to go, and employers may well have reasoned that they had more of an economic hold over their white employees than their black ones. White women may have constituted 95 percent of the city's free-labor servants, according to the *1860 Census*, but they shared certain characteristics with their free black counterparts.[55] Nearly all young servant girls, regardless of race, were young and single and lacked family ties (according to the *1860 Census* only one Irish servant girl was married and only five had children) and this made them particularly attractive to employers. These women had no other demands on their time (for example a husband or children), and they would accept employment in return for board and lodging rather than the cash wages that women who were bread-winners required. On occasion white servant women even worked alongside black women. Three Irish girls worked with Ann LaRoach, a thirty-year-old free black woman, as servants in Maria Dickson's boardinghouse, for example.[56]

Women who worked as domestics in private homes were significantly older than those who worked as servants in boardinghouses (on average, twenty-nine years old as opposed to twenty-four for white women, thirty-five as opposed to twenty for free black women), and their family situations were completely different. Eight out of ten white domestics were married, and more than two-thirds had children. The trend was not so marked for free black women, but they were still three times more likely than servant women to be married with children. These women most often worked as resident domestics, living together with their own children in their employers' households. The type of work white female domestics were employed to do evidently included child care in addition to cooking and cleaning, all pursuits that could be completed while they cared for their own families. The flexibility offered by domestic work was probably what made it particularly attractive to working mothers.

The demand for white domestics, in a traditionally black occupation, varied over time. Many antebellum low-country planters who owned homes in Savannah had no need for white domestics since they would have brought a number of their female slaves to town to act as cooks, maids, nurses, and washerwomen. The large number of carriage houses still standing behind the big houses in Savannah is testimony to that. House-servants often worked long hours, and owners no doubt found it more economical to use either older female slaves who were no longer productive in the fields or young girls rather than to pay white women. Other city residents hired black domestics, particularly in the early part of the nineteenth century, when the number of young immigrant women was small. William Curry, for example, negotiated with "black Betty" to cook for him in return for a weekly wage.[57]

By 1820 the bondwomen's stranglehold on domestic work had begun to weaken under pressure from the rapid immigration of Irish women.[58] Employers started to advertise for domestics, claiming that they were "not particular to age or color," requiring only that applicants be "of good disposition, and accustomed to children."[59] Other employers did not specify race in their advertisements for servants.[60] Indeed, the early 1820s saw an increase in the number of advertisements from families in Savannah seeking white women as domestics, and from young white women themselves seeking employment.[61] The fact that employers were increasingly interested in white domestic servants is perhaps a confirmation of Stephanie Cole's argument, presented elsewhere in this volume, that parents were becoming worried about the formative influence that domestic servants, especially nurses, were having on their children. Unlike Upper South residents, however, residents in Savannah remained open to employing black women to care for their children. In 1860 one advertisement sought "a competent nurse for a child, to remain in the city, white or colored."[62] The principal concern for this employer was competency, not skin color.

City residents who did not have a large number of idle slaves, or merchants permanently resident in the city who did not own a plantation, were prepared to employ white girls ahead of their slave counterparts. To these people, or to the aspiring middle classes, the wages paid to a white Irish girl were far less than the expense of purchasing a slave, and her labor was fundamentally more flexible. She could be hired at short notice and dismissed easily if her work was not up to scratch or her services were no longer required.

The only occupation that employed white and free black women in roughly equal numbers was laundry work.[63] These women shared more than their occupations, being collectively the oldest working women in the city.[64] Moreover, white and free black washerwomen had to compete with some bondwomen who hired themselves out to do laundry. One visitor to Savannah in 1848 commented that slave women "hire themselves of their masters, and pay them so much a month. They do washing, at fifty cents a dozen, and go for the clothes and return them."[65] All women undertaking this work would have had to compete on price, speed, and competency in order to gain a regular clientele.

By far the most popular occupations among free women in 1860 were in the clothing trade: dressmaker, seamstress, milliner, and mantua maker.[66] More than 40 percent of working white women in Savannah, and over half of the 228 free black women with jobs in 1860, worked in the clothing trade.[67] Although there was a wide range of occupational specialties within the clothing industry, such as vestmaker, shirtmaker, and mantua maker, the vast majority of women in this line of work described themselves either as dressmakers or as seamstresses, with the latter outnumbering the former by a ratio of two to one among white women and ten to one among free black women.[68] It is therefore evident that white and free black, and most likely a small number of slave, women must have competed for this work.[69] However, any such competition would have been rather unequal. While clothing work was equally important to free black and white women in terms of the proportion employed, the sheer number of white women in the labor pool ensured that they would dominate this sphere. Indeed the *1860 Census* shows that there were six times as many white women working in the clothing business as free black women.

What made the clothing trade attractive was that the volume and regularity of the work, and therefore the income, was fairly constant—people always needed their clothes repaired. Moreover, it didn't require a significant investment in raw materials, and since many women worked from home, they did not have to rent a separate workspace. This last point was particularly important. Seamstressing could be readily combined with child care, and this almost certainly influenced the type of women who worked in the clothing trade. Most seamstresses in 1860 were in their early thirties, and two-fifths had children, a higher proportion than in any other profession. Black and white seamstresses also shared similar backgrounds. More than half of all Savannah's seamstresses were born in Georgia or South Carolina, whereas foreign-born women constituted less than a third of dressmakers and seamstresses. Locally born women had certain advantages over immigrant women. They had long experienced the economic conditions of the city, they knew the best suppliers and the best retail locations, and most important they had had the time to build up a wide clientele. It is perhaps for these reasons that native-born women were more likely to be in better paid, more skilled occupations than immigrant women.

It is also possible that seamstressing work in Savannah was divided along racial lines. White people may well have preferred to visit white seamstresses, while black people patronized black seamstresses. Moreover, it is possible that female slaves were allowed to choose a seamstress to repair the clothing of a white family. Apparently the "most opulent inhabitants of Charleston, when they have any work to be done, do not send it themselves, but leave it to their domestics to employ what workmen they please; it universally happens that those domestics prefer men of their own color and condition; and as to a greatness of business thus continually passing through their hands, the black mechanics enjoy as complete a monopoly, as if it were secured to them by law."[70] It is possible that similar networks operated among black women in Savannah.

It is unlikely that white seamstresses could rely on their race alone to secure them sufficient employment in this competitive market. Their skill and competency had to be sufficiently eminent to attract and retain customers. That some white women never achieved this degree of proficiency is shown by the formation of the Needle Woman's Friend Society in 1849. The stated aim of the society was "to give employment to poor women" by soliciting needlework from city residents and by retailing the finished products in a city store. One Savannah newspaper praised the "unquestionably legitimate" aims of the society "to prevent the masses of our race from a perpetual endurance of the miseries of want."[71] The first annual report of the society in 1850 was fairly positive about what the members had achieved. About 70 women were being helped by the society, which had attracted more than 300 paying subscribers to fund its workfare program. Of particular note was that the Central Railroad had placed an order with the society for "Negro clothing," which kept several white women in employment. However, the directresses had been forced to relocate from the society's central store on Bay Street to one "far from convenient," due to the high rents. In subsequent years the reports would not be so positive. In 1851 the directresses acknowledged that they struggled to win the support of residents, generally because the work completed by the women was so shoddy. The work was of poor quality in part because "the class who are most in need of our aid are women generally unable to do other than coarse and plain work, [and] often careless in executing even that." Consequently, during the 1850s the number of subscribers more than halved and the society struggled to stay afloat despite emotive pleas in the city press regarding the "industrious needlewomen who daily call [for work]."[72] It seems that competency rather than race was the overriding determinant of success for seamstresses. Although there was most likely a difference in quality and price of goods between white seamstresses who owned a shop and those, both black and white, who worked from home, any seamstress who earned herself a reputation for good quality work would have made a reasonable living.

Several other occupations employed women in small numbers. About 200 women, mainly young Irish girls and native-born free black women, earned their living from prostitution.[73] Older women, which in antebellum Savannah meant women in their early forties, tended to work as nurses, or as midwives. Like seamstressing, laundry work, and domestic servitude, these were employments that suited the skill or family circumstances of Savannah's white and black working women. In all cases, it appears that race was not particularly relevant.

The principal spheres in which working women found themselves in Savannah were in part defined by race. If we consider skilled businesswomen as constituting the upper end of the occupational scale and unskilled workers the lower end, then white women were, overall, more likely to be found in the top end and black women at the bottom end. Moreover, exclusivity worked both ways: some occupations remained solely white, but that was balanced by white

women's exclusion from the city market by slave women. However, the picture
is far more complex than this simple racial typology makes out. Other factors
cut across racial lines; older women had better jobs than younger women;
native-born women worked in better-paid professions than immigrant women;
married women were more skilled than single women. Age, status, experience,
and nativity just as much as race therefore determined to which occupational
sphere working women in Savannah would belong.

## NOTES

1. John B. Boles, *Black Southerners, 1619–1869* (Lexington: University Press of Kentucky,
1983), 75.

2. Stephanie McCurry, *Masters of Small Worlds: Yeoman Households, Gender Relations, and the
Political Culture of the Antebellum South Carolina Low Country* (New York: Oxford University
Press, 1995), 59, 72–83.

3. Suzanne Lebsock, *The Free Women of Petersburg: Status and Culture in a Southern Town,
1784–1860* (New York: W. W. Norton, 1984); Elizabeth R. Varon, *We Mean to Be Counted:
White Women and Politics in Antebellum Virginia* (Chapel Hill: University of North Carolina
Press, 1998); Catherine Clinton, *The Plantation Mistress: Woman's World in the Old South* (New
York: Pantheon Books, 1982).

4. On spheres see Barbara Welter, "The Cult of True Womanhood, 1820–1860," *American Quarterly* 18 (Summer 1966): 151–74, and Nancy F. Cott, *The Bonds of Womanhood:
"Women's Sphere" in New England, 1780–1835* (New Haven: Yale University Press, 1977).

5. Claudia Goldin, *Urban Slavery in the American South* (Chicago: University of Chicago
Press, 1976), 52–53. For more on the demography of the low country see Lockley, *Lines in
the Sand: Race and Class in Lowcountry Georgia, 1750–1860* (Athens: University of Georgia Press,
2001), 1–28.

6. Betty Wood, *Women's Work, Men's Work: The Informal Slave Economies of Lowcountry
Georgia, 1750–1830* (Athens: University of Georgia Press, 1995); City of Savannah, Tax
Digest, 1860, Georgia Historical Society, Savannah (hereafter GHS). Residents paid $3 for
each slave aged between twelve and sixty. Younger or older slaves were taxed at the rate of
$1.50. The comparative statistics are taken from two city censuses of 1825 and 1835. In
both years 62 percent of slaves were female, and in the later year, when age was noted, 57
percent of slaves were aged over fifteen (Savannah Board of Health Minutes, 21 September
1825 and August 1835, GHS). Tax records have been used in preference to census records
because they differentiated between city slaves and county slaves.

7. A slave census from Charleston in 1848 reveals that the vast majority of bondwomen
worked as domestic servants (87.6 percent) or as ordinary laborers (9.7 percent). Very small
numbers worked as washerwomen (0.8 percent), seamstresses (0.5 percent), cooks (0.3
percent), or hucksters (0.4 percent) (Goldin, *Urban Slavery*, 43). These figures may be

skewed by women who worked in a skilled capacity but were reluctant to admit it to census enumerators because they lacked the required badge from the city council.

8. In 1830 the census counted 393 free blacks, 239 women, and 154 men resident in Chatham County, significantly more than the 246 registered by the city in 1828 (*Daily Georgian*, 10 March 1828). Census statistics are available at //fisher.lib.virginia.edu/census.

9. City of Savannah, Register of Free People of Color, 1817 and 1824, GHS.

10. This register was published by the *Daily Georgian*, 24 September 1829. Of 96 women with jobs, 60 were either washerwomen (27) or seamstresses (33); only 9 were retailers.

11. All of this information is taken from the Register of Free People of Color, 1817 and 1824; *Daily Georgian*, 24 September 1829; and *The 1860 Census of Chatham County, Georgia* (Easley, S.C.: Georgia Historical Society, 1980) (hereafter *1860 Census*). According to the 1860 Savannah Tax Digest, only nine free black women owned property.

12. The actual figures are 3,585 white women aged twenty to fifty-nine, 1,305 (36.4 percent) of whom were working. Of 187 free black women aged between twenty and fifty-nine, 154 (82.4 percent) were working. These and subsequent statistics are all taken from *1860 Census*.

13. Among white women under twenty, 16.1 percent worked; among women over sixty, 16.2 percent worked. Comparable figures for free black women are 49.3 percent and 74.4 percent, respectively.

14. Jane H. Pease and William H. Pease, *Ladies, Women, and Wenches: Choice and Constraint in Antebellum Charleston and Boston*. (Chapel Hill: University of North Carolina Press, 1990), 41–45.

15. The proportion of nonslaveholders varied from 51 percent to 61 percent among Savannah taxpayers (Savannah Tax Digests, 1809–60, GHS).

16. See Timothy J. Lockley, "A Struggle for Survival: Non-Elite White Women in Low-country Georgia, 1790–1830," in *Women of the American South: A Multicultural Reader*, ed. Christie Ann Farnham (New York: New York University Press, 1997), 26–42.

17. Among working white women, 65.3 percent were unmarried; among free black women, 87.3 percent were.

18. 50.3 percent of white women and 53.5 percent of free black women were supporting other members of their families.

19. In 1860, 54 percent of Chatham County's free black population was female.

20. See Whittington B. Johnson, "Free African-American Women in Savannah, 1800–1860: Affluence and Autonomy amid Adversity," *Georgia Historical Quarterly* 76 (1992): 262. Among free blacks, unmarried mothers outnumbered married mothers by a ratio of four to one.

21. William Harden, *Recollections of a Long and Satisfactory Life* (New York: Negro University Press, 1968), 48–49. Asphasia Mirault was recorded as a pastry cook in the 1829 Register of Free People of Color.

22. Case of Mrs. Rachel Brownfield, #13361, Southern Claims Commission, Settled Claim, RG 217, Chatham County, Georgia, GHS.

23. For a discussion of the task system see Philip D. Morgan, "Work and Culture: The

Task System and the World of Lowcountry Blacks, 1700–1880," *William and Mary Quarterly* 39 (1982): 563–99. See also Philip D. Morgan, "The Ownership of Property by Slaves in the Mid-Nineteenth Century Lowcountry," *Journal of Southern History* 49 (1983): 399–420.

24. Wood, *Women's Work*, 31–52.

25. Grand Jury Presentment, *Georgia Gazette*, 21 June 1775.

26. Emily Burke, *Pleasure and Pain: Reminiscences of Georgia in the 1840s* (Savannah: Beehive Press, 1991), 8–10.

27. Ibid., 24.

28. Wood, *Women's Work*, 91–92 and 105–18. Robert Olwell argues that the Charleston marketplace was almost the exclusive preserve of slave women and that they defended it as "their space." See Robert Olwell, "Loose, Idle and Disorderly: Slave Women in the Eighteenth-Century Charleston Marketplace," in *More than Chattel: Black Women and Slavery in the Americas*, ed. David Barry Gaspar and Darlene Clark Hine (Indianapolis: Indiana University Press, 1996), 97–110.

29. City Council Minutes, 21 March 1792 and 20 June 20 1796, GHS.

30. See the protest about black butchers in the *Savannah Republican*, 20 April 1820.

31. Eugene L. Schwaab, ed., *Travels in the Old South*, vol. 2 (Lexington: University Press of Kentucky, 1973), 326.

32. City Council Minutes, 26 January and 9 February 1801. About 100 badges were given to slave women between 1790 and 1810 (Wood, *Women's Work*, 87).

33. In 1829 nine free black women were registered as retailers, but by 1860 there were none (*Daily Georgian*, 24 September 1829, and *1860 Census*).

34. *Columbian Museum and Savannah Advertiser*, 21 October 1796.

35. Ibid., 13 January 1814.

36. *Daily Savannah Republican*, 17 January 1818. See also *Daily Georgian*, 26 April and 31 October 1826.

37. The new ordinance was passed on 20 October 1817 (City Council Minutes, 25 August 1817 and 2 July 1829).

38. *Daily Georgian*, 26 April 1826.

39. Ibid., 2 July 1829.

40. Ibid., 31 October 1826.

41. City Council Minutes, 24 July 1820.

42. Chatham County Superior Court Minutes, Book 7, 1804–8, April Term, 1808, Georgia Department of Archives and History, Atlanta; *Columbian Museum and Savannah Advertiser*, 13 January 1814.

43. Report of the Petition of the Sabbath Union, *Daily Georgian*, 2 August 1828.

44. *Savannah Republican*, 17 January 1818.

45. Frederick Law Olmsted, who observed women driving cartloads of produce to Savannah, commented that "the household markets of most of the Southern towns seem to be mainly supplied by the poor country people." For his entertaining description of the rough manners of these women see his letter under the pseudonym "Yeoman" to the *New York Daily Times*, 14 June 1853.

46. Burke, *Pleasure and Pain*, 76–77.

47. Mills Lane, ed., *The Rambler in Georgia* (Savannah: Beehive Press, 1973), 211.

48. Savannah Recorders Court, Mayor's Fine Docket, 1856–57, 3 September 1857, GHS. By 1860 Euphemia Hover had decided it was safer to earn her living as a seamstress. See *1860 Census*.

49. City Council Minutes, 1823–45. Sophia Austin was fined $175 for eight trading offenses between 24 September 1829 and 2 July 1840. Mary Garnet was fined $315 for fifteen citations between 13 November 1823 and 8 November 1827. Sarah Falligrant was fined $1 for "entertaining Negroes" on 7 December 1826. Catherine Prendergast was fined $10 for two citations on 19 December 1839 and 20 February 1845.

50. Of five grocery shops owned by women in 1849, all were within three blocks of West Broad Street in heavily black areas (*City Directory for Savannah, 1849* [Savannah: Edward C. Councell, 1849]).

51. City Council Minutes, 4 May 1818.

52. Of the 1,578 working white women in Savannah in 1860, 798 (50.6 percent) were Irish. Of the remainder, 328 (20.8 percent) were born in Georgia and 273 (17.3 percent) were born elsewhere in the United States. The others were from a number of Western European countries. In contrast, of 228 free black women, 197 (86.4 percent) were from Georgia, 26 (11.4 percent) were from elsewhere in the United States, 3 (1.3 percent) were from the West Indies, and 2 (0.9 percent) were from Africa.

53. Savannah Female Asylum Records, Minutes, 1811–30, GHS.

54. For more on slave hire see Wood, *Women's Work*, 101–21.

55. Exact figures are 269 white servants and 11 free black servants. These figures differ greatly from the findings for Charleston, where in 1848 domestic occupations were deemed exclusively African American. See Pease and Pease, *Ladies, Women and Wenches*, 51–53.

56. *1860 Census*.

57. Savannah Cash Book, 1806–10, entry for 29 November 1806, Hargrett Rare Book and Manuscript Library, University of Georgia Libraries, Athens, Georgia. Betty's wages were set at 37 pence per week.

58. In 1820 the immigrant population of Savannah rose rapidly in response to an appeal for laborers to rebuild after the fire of 11 January 1820. See Lockley, *Lines in the Sand*, 36–37, and Edward M. Shoemaker, "Stranger and Citizens: The Irish Immigrant Community of Savannah, 1837–1861" (Ph.D. diss., Emory University, 1990), 31–43, 73–86.

59. *Savannah Republican*, 8 January 1819, 19 April, 21 May 1820; *Daily Georgian*, 28 January 1820.

60. See advertisements for a cook, washer, and ironer; a pastry cook, washerwoman, and chambermaid; a cook; and a child's nurse in *Daily Georgian*, 27 November 1828 and 12 March 1829; and *Daily Morning News*, 18 December 1854 and 17 May 1860, respectively.

61. See advertisements in *Savannah Republican*, 19 April 1820 (seeking a "cook, washer and ironer, a white person would be preferred"); 26 April 1820 (a "smart white girl" seeking employment); and 17 January 1821 (seeking a cook/chambermaid); in *Daily Georgian*, 21

April 1821 (from a "young woman"); and in *Columbian Museum and Savannah Advertiser*, 23 June 1821 (wanting a "healthy young white woman of good character" to act as a wet nurse).

62. *Daily Morning News*, 7 June 1860.

63. Forty-five white women and forty-one free black women did laundry work according to the *1860 Census*.

64. White washerwomen averaged thirty-seven years and free black washerwomen averaged forty-six years, respectively seven and nine years above the average for all working women.

65. Entry for Wednesday, 12 January 1848, in D. Nason, *A Journal of a Tour from Boston to Savannah* (Cambridge, Mass.: D. Nason, 1849), 33

66. These jobs had differing specializations. Dressmakers catered to exclusively female customers, seamstresses to either gender. Milliners made hats and mantua makers made coats.

67. Exact figures are 642 white women (40.7 percent) and 120 black women (52.6 percent).

68. There were 178 white and 9 free black dressmakers and 364 white and 110 free black seamstresses in Savannah in 1860.

69. At least three fugitive bondwomen who had been seamstresses were advertised in Savannah during the 1820s. See the advertisements for Celia, Mary Ann, and Jane in the *Daily Georgian*, 8 January 1825, 13 March 1827, and 12 July 1828, respectively.

70. Petition of Sundry Mechanics of the City of Charleston, General Assembly Papers, 0010 003 1811 00048, South Carolina Department of Archives and History, Columbia, South Carolina.

71. *Friend to the Family*, 22 March 1849.

72. *Daily Georgian*, 7 March 1849 and 8 March 1850; *Savannah Morning News*, 24 February 1851, 24 February 1855, and 5 March 1857; *Savannah Republican*, 2 March 1858.

73. Lockley, "Crossing the Race Divide: Inter-racial Sex in Antebellum Savannah," *Slavery and Abolition* 18 (1997): 166–70. In 1856 the mayor of Savannah reported that there were 93 white and 105 free black prostitutes, one for every 44 men in the city (William W. Sanger, *The History of Prostitution: Its Extent, Causes, and Effects throughout the World* [New York: Medical Publishing Company, 1910], 612–13).

*Chapter Six*

## Patient Laborers:
## Women at Work in the Formal Economy
## of West(ern) Virginia

BARBARA J. HOWE

Together with the stories of the hundreds of women who are the subjects of other essays in this volume, those of Deborah, the fictional cotton mill picker described by Rebecca Harding Davis, and of Mary C. Key Leech and Elizabeth Key, two successful businesswomen in the clothing trade in western Virginia, enrich our understanding of the roles of white women in the antebellum textile and clothing industries in the Upper South.[1] (For the purposes of this essay, the word "industries" also refers to the work of milliners and dressmakers, who made and sold clothing.)

Deborah, a character in Rebecca Harding Davis's "Life in the Iron Mills," published in 1861, was a picker at a cotton mill who lived a harsh life in Wheeling, the largest city of western Virginia.[2] After standing "twelve hours at the spools," she was weak and aching by the time she joined the "crowd of half-clothed women . . . going home from the cotton-mill" about 11:00 P.M. one night.[3] There may not have been a real Deborah, but Davis was one of the nation's earliest fiction writers to base her stories in the reality of nineteenth-century urban life (and her descriptions conjure up Dickensian images of a wage worker's life in the textile mills).

Mary C. Key Leech, on the other hand, left a long record of her life as a businesswoman. Her family was from Baltimore, and she started in the clothing business about 1835. Her husband, John, was a merchant tailor in 1839, and Thomas Hughes apprenticed for him. She inherited half of John's estate in 1844 and took over his business. In 1845, although Thomas Hughes conducted the business, Leech was considered the "responsible party." She bought her goods from a master tailor in Baltimore and supposedly turned over all active involvement with her clothing business to Hughes by 1849, although the two were in business together for many years. Hughes, who became one of Wheeling's prominent merchant tailors, employed women as seamstresses and tailoresses. Leech also had a millinery business that she turned over to her sister-in-law, Elizabeth Key, in the 1850s.[4]

All of the women considered in this essay lived in Wheeling, Martinsburg, Parkersburg, and Charleston, the four cities of western Virginia (and later West Virginia) in the mid-nineteenth century, cities that varied rather dramatically in racial and ethnic composition. The Ohio River city of Wheeling grew rapidly after the National Road reached it in 1818 and achieved city status by 1830.[5] Located in Virginia's northern panhandle, Wheeling was north of the Mason-Dixon line. It counted very few slaves and many immigrants; across the Ohio River was freedom from slavery.[6] Wheeling claimed only 31 slaves in 1860. Critics there argued that slavery "was incompatible with a commercial and industrial based economy" because immigrants would avoid the state if they had to compete with slaves.[7] Wheeling's economy was based on paper, glass, textile, and iron manufactories, as well as related trade. Martinsburg and Parkersburg were cities by 1860. The county seat of Berkeley County, Martinsburg was a regional marketing center that gravitated toward the Baltimore & Ohio Railroad. Culturally, it was the most southern of the four cities. It also boasted the largest slave population and was the least industrialized of the four.[8] The county seat of Wood County, Parkersburg was located on the Ohio River at the mouth of the Little Kanawha. The city became an early important shipping center at the terminus of the Staunton-to-Parkersburg Turnpike and the Northwestern Virginia Railroad, and a regional center for the oil and gas industry when oil was discovered nearby in 1860. Its population was overwhelmingly native born and white.[9] Charleston, at the junction of the Kanawha and Elk Rivers gained city status by 1870. The county seat of Kanawha County, it was a local center of the salt industry, which brought many slaves to the area before the Civil War. This city had the highest percentage of African American residents after the war and the lowest percentage of foreign-born residents.[10] Population boomed after the war as Charleston became the state capital in 1870 and as city leaders anticipated the arrival of the Chesapeake and Ohio Railroad the next year. (This story ends in 1870, when the state was poised for rapid economic expansion based on improved transportation and the exploitation of natural resources.)

These four cities do not feature prominently in studies of southern urban

history, nor is the history of the South's antebellum clothing and textile industries well known (even though women had long been responsible for supplying
their family's clothing needs). However, the overwhelming majority of western
Virginia's female urban industrial workers were employed in the textile trades,
making cotton, woolen, and silk cloth and yarn. Indeed, more of western Virginia's urban women were employed in jobs related to textiles, sewing, and
clothing than in any other occupations, except domestic service.[11] This essay,
then, first examines the women who made their living as factory workers in
cotton, wool, and silk factories, as did Deborah; second, it highlights seamstresses and tailoresses, particularly in merchant tailor operations; then, it identifies the mantua makers (making long cloaks for women), dressmakers, and
milliners, who sometimes owned their own shops and were considered independent businesswomen in the R. G. Dun & Co. credit records, such as Elizabeth Key; and, finally, it illuminates those who, like Mary Leech, owned businesses related to clothing or textile production.

Neither ladies nor slaves, these women worked in a part of Virginia usually
ignored by historians of the Old South (because existing published scholarship
on women's history in transmontane Virginia is still too sparse to be included in
general women's history texts and because the state of West Virginia split from
Virginia to join the Union in 1863). Historians of Appalachia study West Virginia but too often ignore urban and industrial history. For example, Mary K.
Anglin has looked at women's work in western North Carolina at this time but
focused on rural women.[12] Wilma Dunaway noted Wheeling's economic importance but did not include businesswomen or merchant tailors who hired women
as tailoresses and seamstresses.[13] Historians long have defined urban economies
only in terms of men's jobs, but few have looked at the history of small businesses, and even fewer have looked at women in business.[14] Therefore, moving
the usual geographic focus away from New England and large cities to examine
how women earned their livings in small nineteenth-century southern cities
better integrates these urban women into the broader national story of women's
employment.[15]

Many of the other essays in this volume focus on the intersecting stories of
white and black women. However, but for a few exceptions, the women we can
document in the sewing, clothing, and textile industries in these western Virginia cities were whites, either native or foreign born. Martinsburg had the
largest black population before the Civil War, but there seem not to have been
textile mills that employed women, be they enslaved or free, white or black.
While enslaved women probably did some sewing for their owners' families, we

have no record of women of color working in the textile mills or merchant tailor firms in any of these cities. Nor is there any evidence of women of color owning any millinery shops or working as dressmakers, serving white or black women.[16] Immigrant women were more prevalent in Wheeling's work force than in other western Virginia communities. In 1860, approximately 24 percent of the city's females were foreign born, which approximates the percentage of foreign-born women in the textile and clothing industries and businesses nationwide, with most foreign-born women coming from Ireland and Germany.[17]

These women workers involved in the clothing trade participated in a regional economy because residents of surrounding rural areas or smaller towns came to cities to buy clothing and because the textile mills and merchant tailor firms served customers beyond the city limits. Due to the paucity of sources, the extent of the market for the area including the four western Virginia cities considered here can only be inferred. Milliners regularly advertised that they had "gone East" or gone to Cincinnati to learn the latest fashions and buy goods for their local customers. Newspapers also document the competition that these women faced; they regularly published ads for businesses in Baltimore, Pittsburgh, and Cincinnati that would ship goods to any town along the Baltimore and Ohio Railroad, Ohio River, or Chesapeake & Ohio Railroad.

Since this essay focuses on the formal economy, it does not address the informal networks that almost certainly existed among these women engaged in the textile and clothing-related business and their broader communities. Although Wheeling, in particular, was an ethnically diverse city, extant sources make it difficult to say whether racial or ethnic identity played a role in either customers' decisions about what businesses to patronize or in manufacturers' hiring considerations. But for a few references to relatives working together as milliners or dressmakers, records are too sparse to document other informal relationships among workers, for example, whether textile workers helped their relatives find work in the mills. Because Wheeling was not a textile mill town, like the mill towns in Georgia Michele Gillespie has studied, for instance, family concentrations in the mills are not easily found. Nor were men in Wheeling farming while women worked in the mills, as was the case in the typical mill village.[18] Likewise, scanty sources make it difficult to determine the connections between formal and informal economies, or to document the modalities of rural women's participation in the former, as Susanna Delfino has done for the iron and mining industries.[19]

By concentrating on a surely formal type of economy, which allows for women's official visibility, this essay also provides one methodology for looking at the complexity of women's work in a community. Jobs in the formal economy can be documented through sources such as census records, city directories, newspaper ads, R. G. Dun & Co. records, wills, and deeds, although it is important to acknowledge the problems with documentation inherent in working with small towns and marginal workers.[20] For example, there are no extant factory records or mill girls' correspondence to use for the four western Virginia towns considered here, as Thomas Dublin had for Lowell, or as Bess Beatty found for the Salem Manufacturing Company and Cedar Falls Manufacturing Companies.[21] And, of course, as happened everywhere else in the country, census takers and city directory compilers were not very consistent or thorough in their documentation, leading to some problems in identifying all possible wage earners. Moreover, patent discrepancies between the information provided by the census and that obtainable from other sources about women's employment in the textile and related trades, as illustrated in this essay, dramatically raise the problem of interpreting the reasons for the invisibility of women's work even in traditional and socially acceptable occupations as these were.

Because of the range of occupations they held, these western Virginia women almost certainly represented every urban social class, especially in Wheeling. Although there is no evidence to show what milliners or dressmakers earned, compared to the monthly pay rates documented in the census for textile workers, the fact that some advertised regularly in the newspapers and received praise from the R. G. Dun & Co. credit reporters are indicators that they had reasonably stable businesses. Although it is hard to determine the amount of their income, it is likely that Elizabeth Bradley and Mary Leech were the wealthiest of the women in this story, since both owned property and companies. The records do not provide information on class mobility, either; for example, on textile mill workers who may have become owners of millineries or on milliners who became textile mill workers.

As the largest city, Wheeling offered women the widest range of ways to earn a living, including the widest range of jobs within the textile, sewing, and clothing industries, and it is in Wheeling, then, that this story must start. In the early nineteenth century, the American cotton industry employed far more women than men. Virginia's was no exception, employing 275 females and 143 males in 1831. Nationally, women furnished a smaller proportion of the labor force in the woolen industry than in cotton manufacturing.[22]

At least three cotton mills employed women before the Civil War.[23] These mills were such short-lived operations that a usually thorough local historian gave no names and just noted that "like a flower, [they] bloomed only for a season."[24] The Wheeling Cotton Mills opened in 1846.[25] In 1850, the factory employed 78 females and 34 males to produce muslin and batting, making it the largest industrial employer of females in western Virginia. The women earned an average of $8.82 per month, while the men earned an average of $16.47. Tingle and Zane's Franklin Cotton Mill employed 30 females and 10 males to make cotton yarns that year. The women earned an average of $6.67 per month, while the men averaged $20.[26] Together, in 1856, the two mills made such items as sheetings, cotton yarns, cotton warps, cotton twines, cotton chain, coverlid yarns, and cotton battings.[27] Both mills were out of business under those names by 1860, leaving only J. W. Gillis & Co. as a cotton factory, where 70 women and 25 men produced sheeting and batting. Wages had improved to $7.71 as a monthly average for women and $22.40 as a monthly average for men.[28] While women workers averaged 62 percent of the national monthly income in 1860, Wheeling averaged 74 percent.[29]

A few Wheeling women found employment in John W. Gill's short-lived silk-making venture, which opened about 1845.[30] Since the first silk factories had begun to appear in 1829, raising silk worms and reeling and preparing the silk had been encouraged as particularly good jobs for women and children employed in factories. Gill's female employees may very well have been responsible for unwinding the silk cocoons after they had been placed in water heated by steam, but the whole silk-making process was highly labor intensive.[31] Gill's factory produced 2,000 shirts and drawers and 800 pairs of hose, as well as other products. In 1850, Gill employed 10 females and 10 males; nationally, the industry average was 62.5 percent female. He paid his women workers an average of $6 a month, while the men averaged $20.[32] Gill invited the "curious in such matters" to "call and see the process of manufacturing." He did not describe the process, unfortunately, except to say his employees made "velvets, satins, vestings, dress silks, fringes, cravats, handkerchiefs of white, black, plaid, figured and printed, all the newest styles, made of best twined silk, twilled and plaid," as well as "shirts, drawers, and half hose for gentlemen," which he sold at his adjoining store or through local merchant tailors.[33]

Women who wanted job security would have been wise to work at the Bradley Woolen Factory, for although small, this company lasted longer under one family's ownership and in continuous operation than any other textile factory in Wheeling. Small woolen mills were located throughout the state, using local wool to serve local needs, and Bradley's Mill fit this pattern. William Bradley, an Englishman, was known as a hardworking and honest businessman. His factory employed four females and four males to process wool into yarn in 1850. He paid the women an average of $6 a month. During the 1850s, the company made woolen stocking yarn, and that specialty continued until about 1864.[34] William died in early 1858, leaving an estate of at least $15,000 clear of debt. By his will, he directed that his wife, Elizabeth, act as executrix of the estate and conduct the business during her lifetime and until their children reached the age of majority.[35]

Pennsylvania born Elizabeth Bradley was about forty years old when her husband died, leaving her with eight children, who ranged in age from newborn to nineteen. The head of her household in 1860, when her occupation was listed as a "manufactory" in the census, she was one of only a few women known to have owned manufacturing establishments in western Virginia before the Civil War.[36] The R. G. Dun & Co. judged Elizabeth fully capable of conducting a careful business and in good credit; she sold her goods away from Wheeling to unspecified destinations. In 1860, she employed thirteen men and nine women to make yarn and flannel. The women earned an average of $12 a month, while the men averaged $36.[37] The census enumerators identified no women specifically as operatives.

Since most Wheeling factory women were only identified in the census as "operatives," it is not often clear what specific work they did or where they worked. Spinning, which had traditionally been part of women's household activities, also became their work in the factories. A city directory identified Fanny Gorrell as a spinner in 1851.[38] One operator on an improved mule spindle could operate 1,200 spindles by midcentury, but this person usually had to be a male because women were "so much impeded by their skirts" in trying to follow the mule.[39] Women had dominated power loom weaving since those looms had been introduced in Waltham in 1814, and they continued to dominate weaving until automatic looms replaced them late in the nineteenth century. "Dressing," or sizing the yarn, was one of the best-paid occupations for women in the mills until 1866, when the slasher, a new machine for this purpose, was introduced.[40]

While there are many caveats involved in using manuscript census returns, it is possible to draw broad conclusions about these factory operatives. Just six women, all of whom were white, were labeled operatives in cotton factories in Wheeling in 1860, far fewer than the J. W. Gillis & Co. supposedly employed. None were heads of households. Four of the six were born in Virginia, one in Pennsylvania, and one in Ireland. Four lived in households headed by females, while two lived in male-headed households. Five lived in households where the head had the same last name as theirs. Two lived in the city's Fourth Ward, and four lived in the Fifth Ward, the two wards that had the highest number of industrial workers among the city's six wards and adjoined South Wheeling.[41]

Wheeling's female textile mill workers left no evidence of the motivations behind their job choices. Perhaps they chose cloth making because it was traditionally "women's work." More likely, it was because that was the most readily available occupation for women. There were so many other job opportunities for men in Wheeling—in the glass and iron industries, for instance—that men may have avoided the low-paying cotton mill jobs, leaving more opportunities for women who sought these jobs to avoid the even lower-paying domestic service or sewing jobs. Wheeling newspapers carried very few ads for businesses seeking employees, so one can only assume that women found these positions by word of mouth or by going directly to the factories.

Women's working conditions in Wheeling's most dangerous factories are also poorly documented. In all probability, factory owners there, as elsewhere, sealed windows to keep humidity levels high so that threads did not break. Dust and noise from the machines filled the buildings. Friction from the machines as well as the dust from the raw materials likely sparked fires. Yet whereas Lowell mill hands organized to protest their working conditions, there is no evidence of any organized labor activity in the Wheeling factories.

Textile production, though, was not the largest source of industrial employment for urban women in antebellum western Virginia. Nationally, and in Wheeling, the vast majority of industrial needleworkers were the seamstresses who did plain sewing, generally as piecework for labor contractors or clothing manufacturers such as merchant tailors. This work included basting, lining, seaming, trimming, making buttonholes, sewing on buttons, and, often, laundering the clothing when finished. Sewing women, according to Ava Baron and Susan E. Klepp, were "more exploited than any other wage laborers in America."[42]

As the production of men's clothing moved out of the home and into the shop in cities, seamstresses and tailoresses worked for master tailors or, in western Virginia, merchant tailor firms. Tailors advertised in Wheeling newspapers as early as 1830. Eight merchant tailor firms employed 229 women and 111 men in 1850, and one, Thomas Hughes & Co. (Leech's company), employed 100 women and 35 men. By comparison, just 161 women worked in other sewing, clothing, and textile jobs, and a total of 21 worked in other industries that year.[43]

Merchant tailors stocked ready-made clothing, mostly for men and boys, to serve their fashion-conscious new urban customers who also wanted less expensive apparel. They also made clothing to order from a wide variety of domestic and imported fabrics. Wheeling merchant tailors boasted that their clothing, the work of seamstresses and tailoresses, reflected the height of fashion. Women working for Stephen Rice in 1853, for example, helped him "make up to order at the *shortest notice*, in the *best manner*, and *latest style* the "Plain and fancy CASSIMERES; Silk, Satin, and all kinds of VESTINGS, etc." that he had selected on his trip to "Eastern cities."[44] There are no records to document whether these women sewed at home or in the tailors' shops, but most tailors advertised that they had workshops and stores, indicating some work was done on the premises.

To reduce labor costs, merchant tailors eventually changed the way clothing was made and marketed. During the 1830s and 1840s, as Wheeling's merchant tailoring business grew, a "proportional measurements" system developed in the ready-made clothing industry. This system assumed that bodies had a set of proportional measurements so that knowing one, such as chest size, automatically yielded a series of other measurements. Clothing made for anonymous customers could then be marketed in specialty stores or new department stores, although Wheeling merchant tailors continued to advertise that they could supply custom-made, as well as ready-made, clothing. These industrywide changes, Baron and Klepp have noted, "contributed to the development of the garment industry as a capital enterprise . . . increased the labor supply, reduced labor costs, and transformed the craft work by increasing its profitability." Thus, "both the formal and real subjection of seamstresses to the capital mode of production" began before the sewing machine was in common use.[45] This also seemed to be the case in Wheeling, as some women earned as much as $10 to $16 a month in 1850, whereas Thomas Hughes paid only an average of $6 a month in 1860.[46]

Sewing machines dramatically changed clothing production, since fewer women could make more clothing faster. In 1846, Elias Howe patented the lockstitch and a machine that could sew straight seams for a short distance. His machine could sew five seams faster than a hand sewer could do one.[47] Isaac M. Singer then produced the first practical sewing machine for domestic use in 1851.[48] Ads for sewing machines could be found in Wheeling, Martinsburg, and Parkersburg newspapers by 1860. The 24 March 1860 issue of the *Parkersburg Gazette* alone advertised New York's Globe Manufacturing Company's patent lever sewing machines for $50; Lester's Improved Shuttle Lock-Stitch Sewing Machines, available through a Baltimore agent; and the Eureka Shuttle Sewing

Machine, also sold through a Baltimore agent for $50.[49] These ads also touted the sewing machines for tailor shops, whose cost, at $50, equaled about eight months' wages for one of Thomas Hughes's workers in 1860.

Nationally, manufacturers had no problem finding workers, for seamstresses, according to Baron and Klepp, unlike the young single women who formed most of the workforce in the nineteenth century, were more likely to be widows, women abandoned by their husbands, or women with disabled husbands. This was a job that could be done at home with a flexible schedule to accommodate child care. One did not need to invest the capital needed to start a boarding-house or shop. Also, sewing was acceptable women's work, a skill girls were expected to learn from their mothers.[50]

In the case of western Virginia, it is easier to document employers than individual workers, as names of workers in city directories and manuscript census returns rarely specify places of employment. However, some of the earliest known needleworkers were listed in the 1839 Wheeling city directory and fit Baron and Klepp's model. Elizabeth Swyler manufactured saddle pads and was a cloth stitcher; a widow, Swyler shared her residence with her daughter Olevia, a tailoress. Maria Wallace, also a widow, worked with her daughters as mantua makers, manufacturers of saddle pads, and cloth stitchers. Ann Mary Fogle and Martha A. Taylor, both widows, were mantua makers and milliners.[51] The fact that some of these women were both seamstresses and tailoresses or tailoresses and mantua makers may mean that they did not work exclusively for one employer and may have worked at home, where they could also earn additional income as independent businesswomen. (While Wheeling would be home to two orders of Roman Catholic nuns before the Civil War, the Sisters of Saint Joseph and the Sisters of the Academy of the Visitation were members of nursing and teaching orders; there is no evidence that they engaged in the specialized needlework that produced income for the Oblate Sisters of Providence in Baltimore.[52]) Only one of the 24 seamstresses in the 1851 city directory, Margaret Wade, could be identified with the same occupation as in 1839.[53] In addition, three documents compiled in Wheeling in 1860 do not appear to be for the same city. The 1860 city directory compilers identified 12 dressmakers, 3 mantua makers, only 1 seamstress, and 2 tailoresses, while census enumerators found 17 dressmakers, 14 mantua makers, 128 seamstresses, and 8 tailoresses. The Products of Industry schedule recorded 100 women working in Thomas Hughes & Co., the only merchant tailor firm listed that year, but the enumerators did not specify job titles for these women. The same census schedule found just 79 in other sewing, clothing, and textile jobs, and just 20 in other industries.[54]

In 1860, according to the census of population, Wheeling women who worked as seamstresses or tailoresses or in other sewing trades, as dressmakers, milliners, and mantua makers, and as factory workers and weavers made up 24.6 percent of the total number of women with occupations. The seamstresses and tailoresses were overwhelmingly *not* the heads of their households, as one might expect widows or abandoned women to be.[55] All were white, although directory compilers found one African American seamstress in Wheeling in 1851. They spanned a range of ages, with household heads older than non-heads.[56] The percentage of foreign-born seamstresses was just slightly lower than the percentage of foreign born in the city as a whole, although household heads were more likely to be foreign born than those who were not household heads.[57] Almost all the seamstresses lived in Wheeling's Fourth Ward or Fifth Ward, as did the majority of the tailoresses.[58]

Clothing production in Martinsburg and Parkersburg was not concentrated in merchant tailor firms, so women who sewed for a living probably worked more often for private families. As a group, seamstresses in these two cities in 1860 were much like those in Wheeling. In Martinsburg, 68 of the 86 seamstresses were not heads of households. Almost all the nonheads were under 30, while the largest number of household heads were 50 and older. Most were born in Virginia, but the next highest groups of nonheads were born in the neighboring states of Pennsylvania and Maryland; there was a higher percentage of foreign-born women in this job than in the population as a whole, presumably because slaves dominated domestic service, the usual entry job for immigrant women.[59] Parkersburg had only 11 seamstresses, 7 of whom were not household heads; "sewing" was the occupation for 4 more women who were not household heads. All were native born.[60]

Women who had more resources could start clothing-related businesses. Such shops provided urban women with the largest number of jobs in the business world as milliners, mantua makers, dressmakers, and clothing shop owners. (The term "mantua-maker" disappeared from common usage by about 1860, although it showed up occasionally in the census listings, and was replaced by "dressmaker.") Dressmakers were the female equivalents of tailors, as they measured and cut material; seamstresses then often did the sewing. By combining millinery and dressmaking, "married women or women who chose to remain single could make a comfortable living as respected and valued members of small towns."[61] (Census takers, though, knew that women might use legitimate occupations like dressmaking to hide illicit activity, although there is no documented evidence of this happening in these cities.)

The earliest evidence of nineteenth-century Wheeling businesswomen comes from an 1815 newspaper account in the *Wheeling Intelligencer*. In describing Wheeling at that date, it noted that "Black Rachael had a millinery shop [and]. . . [Mr. Mandale] died and his wife and daughters became milliners."[62] Unfortunately, neither "Black Rachael" nor Mr. Mandale's wife and daughters were recorded by full name. If "Black Rachael" was one of the city's free African American women, she was unique in owning a shop.

Although they had to have some resources to be in business, most Wheeling businesswomen owned small, short-lived businesses and usually had "very small means," to use an R. G. Dun & Co. phrase. Indeed, the most common adjective R. G. Dun & Co. used to describe these businesses was "small." Most cannot be traced for long. Some undoubtedly failed during economic depressions, but they may also have failed due to poor management or lack of access to adequate credit at a time when commercial banking was in its infancy. The fact that relatively few of today's small businesses last more than about five years helps give perspective on the constant appearance and disappearance of women-owned small businesses.[63] At the same time, other women were in business for many years, as traced through marriages, different occupations, and, in at least two cases, different cities. Almost all were native born, but a high percentage were not from Virginia, especially in Wheeling, where many came from the bordering states of Ohio and Pennsylvania.[64] The few foreign born were from English-speaking countries. All were either single, married, widowed, or, rarely, divorced.[65] At least seventeen women were milliners or owned millinery stores from 1851 through 1860; six of them were identified as "Miss" and six as "Mrs."; five had no indication of marital status; and only one was identified as a widow.[66] Household heads were older than nonheads.[67]

Most dressmakers worked at home or went to clients' homes, but a few had shops and advertised for business in the local newspapers. Miss M. A. Dugan moved to Wheeling from Philadelphia and opened "a Dress and Cloak making Establishment" above "Mrs. Boles Shoe Store" in April 1856. Dugan promised "to execute orders in her line of business and on the most reasonable terms," and she sought apprentices. Mrs. Randall invited "the ladies of Wheeling" to her shop at the "Ladies' Parlor of the Metcalf House" in 1858. She advertised that "Cutting has been reduced to a mathematical exactness.—Patterns accurate cut. No charge is made where complete satisfaction is not given."[68]

Wheeling was large enough before the Civil War that the city could support a few more specialized clothing stores. Maria Cochrain, for instance, had a children's furnishings store in the city in 1859.[69] Women who ran millinery stores also sometimes sold notions, which included needles, thread, pins, braid, tape measures, and other sewing supplies, or they combined millinery and fancy goods stores, where they sold trimmings for hats, lace, etc. If they chose to concentrate on millinery, women might be able to gain "status and an income much envied by working-class and lower middle-class women."[70] A few women combined millineries and confectioneries, but, in general, food and clothing businesses were kept separate. One notable exception was a business owned by two women in 1839 in Wheeling in which they manufactured corsets and sold fruits and confectionery.[71]

The fact that married women could not legally own their own businesses if they lived with their husbands did not stop a few wives from starting their own businesses, but it did mean that R. G. Dun & Co. had to continually warn potential creditors that husbands were responsible for wives' debts. Mrs. S. B. Shallcross was a Wheeling milliner whose husband was a U.S. mail agent in the 1850s. He reportedly owned real estate worth $3,200 in 1851; her business and credit were fair according to the credit records. In 1856, the creditors reported that he "lives with her & is considered liable for her debts." By 1859, she owned a bonnet store. By 1860, she was an industrious, good businesswoman, and the next year, creditors could loan Mrs. Shallcross money "if endorsed by her husband . . . who is rich & assists her."[72]

Wheeling city directory references are often too confusing to determine whether a woman who was listed as a milliner also operated a millinery shop, worked out of her home, or worked in another's millinery shop. Miss Jane Crymble was in business as either a milliner or owner of a millinery shop from at least 1856 until long after 1870.[73] Mrs. Florence kept a millinery shop that almost rivaled Crymble's in longevity, although the R. G. Dun & Co. never identified her by first name and she was never listed in the city directories as a milliner or millinery shop owner in any way that would identify her as a woman. She had a very small establishment by September 1855. The R. G. Dun & Co. dutifully reported for some twenty-three years that she had little or no means of credit and ran a very small business.[74]

Ohio-born, thirty-year-old Elizabeth Key opened her "Fashionable Millinery" in the spring of 1856.[75] She stocked a "splendid assortment of new Paris styles of Bonnets, of different varieties, together with her own manufacture" and also sold ribbons, caps, headdresses, and laces.[76] The wife of Abner Key was continuing a very small business that her sister-in-law, Mary C. Key Leech, Hughes's partner, had operated.[77] Elizabeth and her husband lived frugally and paid their debts. She even merited the praise of being described as "a hardworking industrious woman" who was doing a fair amount of business by 1860.[78]

Miss Elizabeth and Miss Mary Marsden, both English born, were straw and fancy milliners in 1859 in Wheeling.[79] That fall they had "on hand a large and fashionable assortment of every variety of WINTER BONNETS" and "a large variety of LADIES' DRESS CAPS, which they offer to the public on reasonable terms." The sisters asked the "public, especially the ladies, . . . to call and examine their stock before making their purchases."[80] Elizabeth told the census taker she was twenty-five in 1860, but when she married John Wallis (probably Walters) in 1861, she told the county clerk she was thirty.[81]

Other women also ran businesses for a few years at a time. Mrs. C. Harrison and her family moved to Wheeling so that she could get a new start in life after her husband's business in Cumberland, Maryland, was destroyed about 1849, and he absconded to England. Her brother started her in a millinery business in Wheeling, presumably because she had no means of her own to do so, and she opened her shop by the fall of 1852. Mrs. Harrison's husband returned to the family, but he came back as poor as when he had left. By January 1853, "nothing could be made" of either Mr. or Mrs. Harrison, and she was out of business by February 1854.[82]

Mrs. John E. Wade got her start in the millinery business in 1849, when her husband went to California as part of the gold rush. He had operated a boot store from at least 1846 until his departure. Wade reportedly accumulated "quite a little fortune" by digging gold; he returned to Wheeling by February 1852 worth $7,000. He did not take up his old business or any business when he returned. Instead, his wife continued her millinery shop "on a modest scale." Wade returned to California by July 1852. By July 1854, with her husband still gone, Mrs. Wade had quit her business, perhaps to join her husband.[83]

William Bole, a boot and shoe dealer, had absconded to Australia by November 1853, leaving behind his wife, Margaret, and some children "in penury." The family's life may have improved after William left, for he was reported to have been frequently intoxicated and, while inebriated, once stated that Roman Catholics, through his wife, were robbing him. When he left town to sober up on one occasion in 1853, he left the store "in charge of his wife, who has always been 'the salesman' or rather Saleswoman." She continued to run her husband's business for a short while after he left.[84]

Margaret Bole's friends then helped her open "another little store," but she conducted the business as an agent for Mrs. Keating, who ran a confectionery, "to prevent the stock being attached for her husband's debt." Bole received her requested divorce in the spring of 1854. By July of that year, she was still conducting a small business as Mrs. Keating's agent but was in business in her own name by November, when she was reported to be doing "quite a snug little business," although her only means were those borrowed from friends. Mrs. Bole ran a shoe store in 1856 but was insolvent and out of business by November 1857.[85]

Mrs. A. W. Hassell operated a millinery store at 162 Main Street in Wheeling in the 1850s.[86] In April 1856, she announced that she had "just returned from the East with a choice and well selected assortment of Fashionable Articles of Millinery" and asked "her friends, the ladies of Wheeling and vicinity," to come to her opening on the 15th. She "engaged a first-class Eastern Milliner" and was "prepared to make up any goods to order, on the shortest notice." If women did not want hats, they could also purchase "Ladies and Children's Gaiters, Boots and Shoes" at her shop.[87] Once identified as "a poor widow," she was in business until at least April 1860.[88]

Women's occupational choices were more limited in Martinsburg by 1860. Because of the prevalence of slavery, whereby slave women mostly performed domestic chores, the occupational structure for white women differed from that found in the Ohio River cities. Unlike in cities with fewer slaves, where immigrant women worked as domestic servants, the largest percentage (68.3 percent) of Martinsburg women in 1860 were identified as seamstresses. Foreign-born women comprised a higher percentage (14.5 percent) of the seamstresses, mantua makers, and milliners in Martinsburg than the percentage of total foreign born in the county (4.0 percent).[89]

A few Martinsburg women had millinery and dressmaking businesses.[90] Mrs. Elizabeth D. Hughes sold millinery and fancy goods, including bonnets, ribbons, cloaks, raglans, and shawls at her "Emporium of Fashion."[91] Miss Jane Gemmell, working from her father's house, took orders to make dresses.[92] There were fewer consumers to support the specialized stores then thriving in Wheeling, and the city was close enough to Baltimore that people could order goods from there.

Opportunities for businesswomen in Parkersburg were also limited before the war. Of the 100 women identified with an occupation in the 1860 census, 11 were seamstresses, with 9 working as dressmakers or milliners. Two dressmakers, both born in Scotland, were the only foreign-born women in the group of 20.[93] Mrs. S. F. Duvall advertised that she was "prepared to fit and trim to order, and in the latest and most approved style, every variety of work in the Millinery line." She solicited "a liberal share of horse patronage and orders from a distance."[94] Mrs. Maria Elliott, a thirty-seven-year-old Ohio native, moved her "Fashionable and Fancy Dress-Making" business to Parkersburg in 1860 and was one of the few dressmakers to open a shop.[95] R. G. Dun & Co. did not identify any antebellum businesswomen in Parkersburg.[96]

Women continued to find employment making and selling clothing during the Civil War. Across the country, women entered factories to make the textiles and clothing needed for the armies, but there is no evidence that any firm had contracts to supply clothing, cloth, or related supplies for the Union army, even after West Virginia became a Union state in 1863.[97] Also, the scattered and uneven local records make it difficult to know whether opportunities increased in these cities.

At least two Wheeling women made shoes during the war. Lucinda Heston was a shoe binder, while Mary Briggs, "a young widow woman, . . . bosse[d] a sewing machine" at Mr. Anderson's boot and shoe establishment. Briggs met a Confederate soldier imprisoned in jail and occasionally supplied him with contraband. In one of the few descriptions of a sewing woman, the newspaper reporter commenting on her crime noted that "she is about thirty years of age, rather stoutly built, and although by no means an unattractive woman, she is a most uncompromising rebel."[98]

By May 1862, all but one of Wheeling's merchants had sworn an oath of allegiance to the U.S. government and the Restored Government of Virginia, whose capital was Wheeling. Taking the oath was both a precondition for staying in business and a way to avoid sending taxes to Richmond.[99] If Mary Leech, Elizabeth and Abner Key, and Thomas Hughes took that oath, they did so for expediency, since all were known Confederate sympathizers.[100] Leech and Hughes, under the firm name of M. C. Leech, officially dissolved their "copartnership" on 19 October 1863, although Hughes remained in the merchant tailor business.[101] Mrs. M. C. Leech thanked the public "for the very liberal share of patronage bestowed upon her during the 28 years she has been engaged in the clothing business in this city."[102] Although officially dissolved, the business partnership between Leech and Hughes continued in some fashion after the war, as they continued to own property together. Hughes was one of her heirs and the executor of her estate when she died in 1868.[103]

Unless the directory compilers were simply more efficient in their record keeping, it seems that the number of milliners increased during the war in

Wheeling. Elizabeth Key's millinery business suffered, though, and she was worth very little by April 1865.[104] The Marsdens were in the millinery business as E. Walters and M. Marsden, then operated separate shops after Mary married John B. Colvig in April 1863.[105] Elizabeth Hughes left Martinsburg and relocated to Wheeling after "having suffered much in the loss of property, and otherwise, by contending armies."[106] By April 1864, Hughes was advertising as "Mrs. E. D. Hughes & Co."[107]

During the war, a few Wheeling women inherited clothing businesses when their husbands died or they took over management of the company when their husbands were no longer capable of running the businesses (during the war), but there is no evidence that the war was a factor in their circumstances. When Mrs. Therese Auber's husband died, she inherited his boot and shoe store, which she ran from at least 1864 until 1870.[108] Alex Graham, who had a dying business, was "considered bad" in 1863. In R. G. Dun's January 1864 records, on a page which is torn and thus partly unreadable, there is a tantalizing reference to "is from his wife with another woman." His wife, Ann, had taken over her husband's business by April 1864. She was apparently a better businessperson than her husband.[109]

There is very little information extant about wartime employment for women in Martinsburg or Parkersburg. No R. G. Dun & Co. records exist for Martinsburg during the war years, probably because the city changed hands so many times that it was too dangerous to try to collect credit reports, and only intermittent records exist for Parkersburg. Not many extant newspapers provide information about ads for businesswomen in either city, although one ad promoted Mrs. W. Scales's "Millinery Establishment" in her home on Market Street in Parkersburg. Scales was "determined" to sell her large and varied stock "lower for CASH than can be bought elsewhere in town."[110]

After the war, women continued to find employment options in the textile and clothing industries, but their options were no longer as limited. Opportunities for married women improved in 1868, when West Virginia passed its first Married Women's Property Act. Now, a woman living apart from her husband could " 'in her own name, carry on any trade or business,' and keep her earnings."[111] West Virginia married women who lived with their husbands, however, still could not legally own their own businesses. While this did not stop a few wives from starting their own businesses, it did mean that the R. G. Dun & Co. had to continually warn potential creditors that these women could not be responsible for their debts; creditors needed to know if the husbands had assets to cover their wives' debts. For example, although Ann Graham was carrying on the family's dying business in her own name in March 1868, the R. G. Dun & Co. noted, her husband was a "drunken useless fellow."[112]

By 1870, the four cities offered employment to 53.6 percent of the state's 226 women in the clothing and textile industries, as documented in the Schedule and Products of Industry. The vast majority of these jobs were in Wheeling. Of the 175 Wheeling women listed for all the industries, the census enumerators found 107 Wheeling women working in textile and clothing industries. These 107 women primarily worked for merchant tailor firms; they represented 33.2 percent of all the West Virginia women in industry and 47.3 percent of all the women in textile and clothing industry firms listed in the census. Other Wheeling women found employment making paper or working in the tobacco and cigar industries, in the glass industry, in a brewery, or in a tack factory, but these opportunities were far fewer in comparison to those in textiles, clothing, and sewing firms.[113]

By 1870, the number of textile manufacturers was declining. In 1868, the last year that Elizabeth Bradley was identified with the firm, E. Bradley & Son employed women in at least five positions.[114] But Bradley & Co., which employed twenty females, eleven males, and one child/youth to produce flannels and yarns, was the only Wheeling textile manufacturer listed in the census in 1870, except for Susan Miller's small carpet weaving firm.[115] Six women worked with two men and three children at Parsons, Appleton & Co.'s new Kanawha Woolen Mill in Charleston in 1870.[116] Only one woman worked as a weaver in that woolen mill, twenty-two-year-old Caroline Roy.[117] Some of those women may have worked in the laundry that was part of the mill—a common practice since women could wash both the cloth and the clothes.

Merchant tailors employed fewer tailoresses and more seamstresses than before the war, as clothing production moved out of Wheeling to larger cities and the remaining Wheeling firms began to use sewing machines. Wheeling had twelve merchant tailor firms in 1870, but the total number of females employed, according to the Schedule and Products of Industry enumerators, was only 84, fewer than Thomas Hughes employed a decade earlier.[118] The Wheeling population census enumerators found only 21 tailoresses in 1870, 18 women whose occupations were listed as a variety of sewing jobs, and 232 seamstresses, clearly far more than worked in the merchant tailor shops, so maybe some worked for the 15 dressmakers also identified that year.[119] As in 1860, these women were overwhelmingly not heads of households. The majority of them were Virginia born, and the next largest groups came from Pennsylvania and Ohio. The majority of the seamstresses lived in male-headed households (113), with 83 in female-headed households.[120]

By 1870, Martinsburg and Parkersburg were large enough to support small merchant tailor businesses, but each had only one small firm employing four females.[121] Census enumerators found 12 seamstresses in Martinsburg, all native born; some may have been working for dressmakers or in private homes.[122] Three seamstresses and 4 "sewing" women, all native born, worked in Parkersburg, but there is no way to know if the sewing women were employed by W. H. Bush, the merchant tailor there.[123] Charleston had no seamstresses identified in the 1870 census at all.

Dr. James E. Reeves, Wheeling's public health officer, expressed great concern for the needleworkers: "Among all the trades which are carried on in the city, there are none more unhealthy or which yield, according to the number employed, a higher death return than the several classes of sewing women— dress makers, milliners, and those engaged in and for the several large tailoring establishments. Many of these patient laborers live in small, ill-ventilated houses, and on foggy or smoky days work by gas light. Consumption, shattered nervous system, disease of the liver, dyspepsia and uterine trouble are some of the accompanying bitter fruits of their toils." No wonder, then, that Reeves praised the sewing machine as "that God-send to women," for "it has increased the probability of life of needle-women by giving them comparative freedom and comforts in place of *white slavery* and destitution."[124]

Women continued to own small clothing stores and to work as dressmakers and milliners. Wheeling continued to support the most specialized stores, with 7 women, all white, dealing in "retail notions" in 1870.[125] Mrs. Jno. E. Walters (Elizabeth Marsden Walters) still had a millinery in May 1866 but may have been in business with her husband.[126] Mrs. E. Newcomb, one of several milliners in Martinsburg after the war, moved to the city from New York City and opened her "Millinery and Mantua-making establishment" in 1866.[127] Mrs. J. C. Collins opened her Parkersburg millinery in 1866.[128] Mrs. C. Heinsfurter, a "sole trader" whose husband was living in July 1869, did a moderately fair business with her millinery, liquors, and billiards business in Parkersburg but, by September 1870, was "of no account" due to suits pending against her.[129]

Seven women had millineries or worked as mantua makers in Charleston in 1870.[130] Mrs. Mary A. Booton, a "stranger," arrived in Charleston in the spring of 1870 and opened a millinery. She was thirty-five and headed a household that included Louisa Booton, aged twenty-six, and Fanny Atkinson, then nineteen; all three were Ohio natives and milliners. Mary Booton advertised that she was "experienced in the business" and "prepared to furnish the latest styles of hats, bonnets, &c." on "short notice, and on reasonable terms."[131] She bought at least part of her stock in Cincinnati.[132] Mrs. Rebecca Force ran a "first class millinery store" and proudly proclaimed that her hats were "not done up in slop-shop style." She may also have been the same woman identified in the R. G. Dun & Co. records as "Mrs. R. Force," a milliner engaged in "a very small business worth about nothing" in May 1866 in Wheeling and out of business in December 1867.[133]

These postwar businesswomen, like their antebellum sisters, were also native-born white women.[134] Unfortunately, existing records do not indicate whether they were widowed as a result of the war and started a business to support themselves and their families. Nor is it possible to know whether women may have stayed in a business like dressmaking or millinery longer as a single woman because the war had decimated the ranks of eligible men to marry.

By 1870, although Deborah's cotton mill had closed and Mary C. Leech and Elizabeth Bradley had died, the clothing and textile industries in West Virginia cities continued to provide more employment opportunities for white women than any other sector of the economy except domestic service. This was especially true in the smaller cities of Martinsburg, Parkersburg, and Charleston, where there were few other options for white women and where, in Martinsburg and Charleston, black women dominated the ranks of domestic servants.[135] Wheeling needleworkers may even have kept some of these other urban women out of the needle trades since the city's merchant tailor firms advertised in Charleston and Parkersburg newspapers that they could supply clothing to those cities, which undercut the need for local firms to develop.

New opportunities would come through national companies that recruited women (and men) to sell the $18 sewing machines that displaced seamstresses and moved machine sewing into the home, promising $75 to $200 a month plus expenses or a commission, but no women were identified with that job by 1870 in these cities.[136] Good opportunities for urban women in western Virginia to serve an increasing number of customers remained available if they had the skill and financial resources to be milliners and dressmakers, could afford the sewing machines, and had the talent to make hats and read patterns. However, the ready availability of sewing machines also encouraged women to make their own clothing, and dressmakers would be the next to face competition—this time from the soon-to-emerge women's ready-made clothing trade.

No sector of the formal economy, except domestic service, offered white women in western Virginia more employment. The official record of white women at work in textile and clothing-related trades in nineteenth-century western Virginia shows us that opportunities were most prevalent in the largest and most economically and ethnically diverse cities where free labor predominated. Yet white women's work within these industries was amazingly diverse. First and foremost, significant stratification across class was represented in the enormous contrast between women who owned their own businesses and women who were employed in the merchant tailor shops and textile mills. Moreover, great diversity existed among the members of the women wage-earning class itself as represented in the very nature of their work, in respect to the skills required, number of fellow women workers, amount of wages earned, degree of job security, working conditions, and women wage laborers' age, nativity, and household composition. The fragmented information about these women, business owners and wage workers alike, tantalizes us with hints about their fascinating life stories, which not only remain to be explored more fully in all their complexity but whose counterparts in other parts of the South (or the rest of the nation) have yet to be examined to allow for more comparative analysis.

## NOTES

1. See, for instance, the essays by Timothy J. Lockley, Bess Beatty, and Michele Gillespie in this volume.

2. West Virginia officially became a state on 20 June 1863. When discussing pre-1863 events, I use "western Virginia" to refer to those counties that became part of the new state. I am indebted to Lori Hostuttler, whose research in newspapers enriched this article. Deborah's story is told in Rebecca Harding Davis, *Life in the Iron Mills, or The Korl Woman* (Old Westbury, N.Y.: Feminist Press, 1972).

3. Ibid., 19, 15.

4. Ohio County Will Book, vol. 3, p. 276, Ohio County Court Clerk's Office, Wheeling, W.Va.; Virginia, vol. 34, p. 182, R. G. Dun & Co. Collection, Baker Library, Harvard Business School, Boston, Mass. (hereafter R. G. Dun & Co. Collection); "To the Public," *Wheeling Daily Intelligencer*, 15 November 1863. The 1835 date comes from the fact that she said she had been in business for twenty-eight years by 1863.

5. For most of the nineteenth century, the census used 8,000 as the definition of "city." By 1900, that number had dropped to 4,000. By 1920, when the census takers declared the nation to be over 50 percent urban for the first time, the number was down to 2,500, and that is the number historians have continued to use.

6. Wheeling's population was 5,221 in 1830; 7,885 in 1840; 11,435 in 1850; 14,100 in 1860; and 19,280 in 1870. The city had only 11 male slaves and 33 female slaves in 1850 and a total

of 31 slaves in 1860. There are no figures on foreign-born residents before 1860 because the census did not document birthplaces for all residents before 1860, but, in that year, there were 2,764 foreign-born men and 1,746 foreign-born women in Wheeling (24.2 percent of the total of 7,226 women). In 1870, the total number of foreign-born residents was 4,153 (21.5 percent).

7. Robert Harold Simmons, "Wheeling and the Hinterland: An Egalitarian Society?" (Ph.D. diss., West Virginia University, 1990), 67.

8. Martinsburg's population was 3,364 in 1860, including 240 slaves and 110 free blacks. The county had only 630 foreign-born residents in the county (4.0 percent) that year, so there were no separate figures for the city. The city's population was 4,863 in 1870, including 476 blacks and 488 foreign-born residents.

9. Parkersburg's population was 2,493 in 1860; technically, Parkersburg's population was just short of the 2,500 mark, but it is too close to ignore here. The number of foreign-born residents in 1860 was not calculated separately since there were only 708 in the county (4.4 percent of the county's population). There were also no separate records kept of slaves in the city, but there were 176 slaves in the county. The city had 60 free blacks and 2,433 whites in 1860. In 1870, Parkersburg's population was 5,546, including 4,298 whites, 447 blacks, and 801 foreign-born residents.

10. Charleston's population was 3,162 in 1870, including 761 blacks (24 percent of the population) and 214 foreign-born residents (6.8 percent of the population).

11. In 1850, there were 658 women in the counties that would be West Virginia who were working in industries; 556 (84.4 percent) were in sewing, clothing, or textile industries. Of these, 390 (70.1 percent) worked in industries in Wheeling. There were no women identified in these industries in Parkersburg or Martinsburg in 1850 and only 166 in the 10 other counties in which women were working in industries. The 1860 Products of Industry schedule identified 298 women in industries; 273 (91.6 percent) were in sewing, clothing, or textile industries. Of these, 179 (65.6 percent) were in Wheeling, with none in Parkersburg or Martinsburg and 94 in the 10 other counties that identified women in industries. All figures are from U.S. Census, Schedule 5, Products of Industry, Fiscal Year 1849–50, vol. 2, Ohio County.

12. Mary K. Anglin, "Lives on the Margin: Rediscovering the Women of Antebellum Western North Carolina," in Mary Beth Pudup, Dwight Billings, and Altina Waller, eds., *Appalachia in the Making: The Mountain South in the Nineteenth Century* (Chapel Hill: University of North Carolina Press, 1995), 185–209.

13. Wilma Dunaway, *The First American Frontier: Transition to Capitalism in Southern Appalachia, 1700–1860* (Chapel Hill: University of North Carolina Press, 1996).

14. See, for example, Mansel G. Blackford, *A History of Small Business in America* (New York: Twayne Publishers, 1991).

15. The region that became West Virginia in 1863 was 3.1 percent urban in 1830 (5,221 residents of 166,537 total), 3.5 percent urban in 1840 (7,885 residents of 224,477 total), 3.8 percent urban in 1850 (11,435 residents of 301,505 total), and 5.3 percent urban in 1860

(19,957 residents of 376,688 total). In 1870, the four cities had a total of 32,851 residents, 7.4 percent of the state's 442,014 residents.

16. In contrast to this "all-white" story, see Lockley's essay in this volume.

17. Among the 167 women who can definitely be identified in the clothing and textile industries, using only the 6 cotton factory operatives instead of all possible operatives, 48 were foreign born, with 18 born in Ireland and 16 in Germany. Among the native-born women, the largest groups were born in Virginia (45), Pennsylvania (34), and Ohio (25). All figures are from the U.S. Census, Census of Population, Ohio County, Wheeling, 1860.

18. See Gillespie's essay in this volume.

19. See Susanna Delfino's essay in this volume.

20. See, for example, Margo J. Anderson, *The American Census: A Social History* (New Haven: Yale University Press, 1988).

21. Thomas Dublin, *Transforming Women's Work: New England Lives in the Industrial Revolution* (Ithaca, N.Y.: Cornell University Press, 1994), 77–118; Beatty's essay in this volume.

22. Helen L. Sumner, *History of Women in Industry in the United States*, vol. 9 of *Report on Condition of Woman and Child Wage-Earners in the United States* (Washington, D.C.: Government Printing Office, 1910), 55, 52, 58.

23. One could have been David Hull's Eagle cotton factory in 1839, but there are no further records on this factory (J. B. Bowen, *The Wheeling Directory and Advertiser* [Wheeling: John M. M'Creary, Printer, 1839], 47).

24. J. H. Newton, G. G. Nichols, and A. G. Sprankle, *History of the Pan-Handle: Being Historical Collections of the Counties of Ohio, Brooke, Marshall, and Hancock, West Virginia* (Wheeling: J. A. Caldwell, 1879), 243. Unincorporated businesses did not need to file records of ownership, nor did manufacturers always pay license taxes to the Commonwealth of Virginia, or, if they did, the records do not include company names or type of business. License taxes through the spring of 1861 are filed with the Auditor of Public Accounts records at the Library of Virginia, Richmond, Virginia. License records do not survive for the Restored Government of Virginia (1861–63) or the State of West Virginia.

25. Ohio County Deed Book, vol. 29, p. 29, Ohio County Courthouse, Wheeling, W. Va.

26. U.S. Census, Schedule 5, Products of Industry, Fiscal Year 1849–50, vol. 2, Ohio County.

27. "Wheeling and Franklin Cotton Mills," *Wheeling Intelligencer*, 3 January 1856.

28. U.S. Census, Schedule 5, Products of Industry, 1860, Ohio County (Wheeling).

29. Sumner, *History of Women in Industry*, 56.

30. Newton et al., *History of the Pan-Handle*, 244.

31. Sumner, *History of Women in Industry*, 60; Charles H. Singer et al., eds., *A History of Technology* (Oxford: Clarendon Press, 1954–58), 4:308–13. Singer identifies the workers who unwound the cocoons as female, hence that assertion here.

32. U.S. Census, Schedule 5, Products of Industry, Fiscal Year 1849–50, vol. 2, Ohio County; Sumner, *History of Women in Industry*, 60–61.

33. "City Business," *Wheeling Intelligencer*, 28 August 1852.

34. Virginia, vol. 34, p. 59, R. G. Dun & Co. Collection; U.S. Census, Schedule 5, Products of Industry, Fiscal Year 1849–50, vol. 2, Ohio County.

35. Bradley obituary cited in Carol A. Scott, *Marriage and Death Notices of Wheeling, Western Virginia, and the Tri-State Area*, vol. 2, 1858–65 (Apollo, Pa.: Closson Press, 1987), 44, with reference to *Wheeling Intelligencer*, 12 January 1858.

36. U.S. Census, Census of Population, Ohio County, Wheeling, 1860.

37. U.S. Census, Schedule 5, Products of Industry, 1860, Ohio County (Wheeling); Virginia, vol. 34, p. 59, R. G. Dun & Co. Collection.

38. Oliver I. Taylor, *Directory of the City of Wheeling & Ohio County, Comprising the Names, Occupations and Residences of the Inhabitants, with a History of the Settlement, Progress, Resources and Public Institutions of the City and the Statistics of the County, as Exhibited by the Census of 1850* (Wheeling: Printed at the Office of the Daily Gazette, 1851), 50.

39. T. K. Derry and Trevor I. Williams, *A Short History of Technology* (Oxford: Oxford University Press, 1960), 564; Edith Abbott, *Women in Industry* (New York: D. Appleton & Co., 1910), 91.

40. Abbott, *Women in Industry*, 93, 95, 96, 99.

41. South Wheeling was part of the city of Wheeling by 1870. All figures are taken from the U.S. Census, Census of Population, Ohio County, Wheeling (including South Wheeling), 1860.

42. Ava Baron and Susan E. Klepp, " 'If I Didn't Have My Sewing Machine . . .': Women and Sewing Machine Technology," in *A Needle, a Bobbin, a Strike: Women Needleworkers in America*, ed. Joan M. Jensen and Sue Davidson (Philadelphia: Temple University Press, 1984), 22, 23.

43. The 1850 firms were A. M. Adams (60 women, 12 men), Aub & Corder (10 men, 5 women), Thomas Hughes Jr. (30 women, 12 men), Henry Kurtz (3 women, 5 men), Stephen Rice (50 women, 50 men), Alexander Rogers (50 women, 6 men), Warden & Edwards (6 women, 11 men), and Christian Kammerer (20 women, 10 men). The 21 other women worked for Armstrong & Crowl, a paper manufacturer (8), Hobbs Barnes & Co., a glass manufacturer (2), C. D. Lambdin & Co., a paper manufacturer (10), and J. N. Zimmer, a baker (1) (U.S. Census, Schedule 5, Products of Industry, Fiscal Year 1849–50, vol. 2, Ohio County).

44. "Spring and Summer Clothing," *Wheeling Intelligencer*, 26 May 1853.

45. Baron and Klepp, " 'If I Didn't Have My Sewing Machine,' " 29, 28.

46. According to the Products of Industry schedule, Henry Kurtz, Stephen Rice, and Alexander Rogers paid an average of $10 per month to women, while Christian Kammerer paid $12 and Warden & Edwards paid $16. A. M. Adams, though, paid only an average of $2 per month to women, while Aub & Corder paid $4.50 and Thomas Hughes Jr. paid only $1. Wages for men were higher, at $22, $25, $32, $10, $25, $26, $16, and $16.67, respectively.

47. Baron and Klepp, " 'If I Didn't Have My Sewing Machine,' " 31.

48. Derry and Williams, *Short History of Technology*, 575; Abbott, *Women in Industry*, 219, 221.

49. "The Ne Plus Ultra of Sewing Machines," *Parkersburg Gazette*, 13 March 1860; "Les-

ter's Improved Shuttle Lock-Stitch Sewing Machines," ibid., 24 March 1860; "The Eureka Shuttle Sewing Machine," ibid., 14 March 1860.

50. Baron and Klepp, "'If I Didn't Have My Sewing Machine,'" 23.

51. Bowen, *Wheeling Directory and Advertiser*, 50, 37, 77.

52. See Diane Morrow's essay in this volume.

53. Taylor, *Directory of the City of Wheeling & Ohio County*, 82; Bowen, *Wheeling Directory and Advertiser*, 80.

54. Mears and Snavely, comps., *The Wheeling Directory, Containing the Names of the Inhabitants, A Subscribers' Business Directory, and an Appendix of Much Useful Information* (Wheeling: "Intelligencer Office," 1860); U.S. Census, Census of Population, Ohio County, Wheeling, 1860. The 20 women in other industries worked for Armstrong & Co., a paper manufacturer (5), Bassett & Co., a paper mill (10), Daniel Cushing, a paper manufacturer (4), and Wm. Ewing, a printer (1) (U.S. Census, Schedule 5, Products of Industry, 1860, Ohio County [Wheeling]).

55. The 785 women identified in the Wheeling census of population in 1860 included 32 teachers/nuns; 448 domestics, nurses, and cooks; 59 washerwomen and laundresses; 130 seamstresses, tailoresses, or those in sewing trades; 38 dressmakers, milliners, and mantua makers; 15 business owners; 25 factory workers and weavers; 11 boardinghouse keepers and hotel keepers; and 27 in other occupations. In addition to the 6 workers in the cotton factory, 1 worked in the paper mill, but the others were just identified as "operative" or "operative-factory." Ninety-five of the seamstresses were not heads of households, and only 33 were household heads. Seven tailoresses were not heads of households, and 1 was a household head. All figures are from the U.S. Census, Census of Population, Ohio County, Wheeling, 1860.

56. In 1860, in Wheeling, among seamstresses who were not heads of households, 27 were 19 and under, 38 were 20–29, 10 were 30–39, 12 were 49, and 6 were 50 and older. Among household heads who were seamstresses that year, 3 were 25–29, 12 were 30–39, 12 were 40–49, and 6 were 50 and older. The Wheeling tailoresses who were not heads of households that year were 19 and under (2) and 35–39 (1); the household heads were 19 and under (4) and 40–44 (1). The seamstress was Letty McKee (Taylor, *Directory of the City of Wheeling & Ohio County*, 67).

57. The total population of Wheeling in 1860 was 32 percent foreign born (4,510). Only 25 (26.3 percent) of the city's 95 seamstresses who were not heads of households were foreign born (3 in England, 8 in Ireland, 11 in Germany, and 3 in France). Of the 33 household heads who were seamstresses, 14 (42.4 percent) were foreign born (1 in England, 4 in Ireland, 4 in Germany, 3 in Scotland, and 1 in France). Only 3 tailoresses in Wheeling were foreign born (2 in Ireland and 1 in Germany); none were heads of households. All figures are from U.S. Census, Census of Population, Ohio County, Wheeling, 1860.

58. U.S. Census, Census of Population, Ohio County, Wheeling, 1860.

59. 10 of the 68 seamstresses (14.7 percent) who were not heads of households were foreign born (7 in Ireland and 3 in Germany); among the 18 household heads who were

seamstresses 27.8 percent were foreign born (3 in Ireland and 2 in Germany). All 12 Martinsburg seamstresses in 1870 were native born. The 1860 census of population for Martinsburg found that, among seamstresses who were not heads of households, 28 were 19 and under, 34 were 20–29, 4 were 30–39, 3 were 40–49, and 1 was 50 or older. Among household heads, none was 19 or under, 5 were 20–29, 4 were 30–39, 2 were 40–49, and 10 were 50 and up. The 1860 seamstresses who were not household heads were born in Virginia (40), Pennsylvania and Maryland (14 each), Ireland (7), Germany (3), and New Jersey (1). Those who were household heads were born in Virginia (10), Maryland and Ireland (3 each), and Germany (2).

60. The 1860 census of population for Parkersburg found that among seamstresses who were not heads of households, 1 was 19 or under, 4 were 20–29, and 4 were 30–39. The 2 household heads were 50 or older. Parkersburg's seamstresses were born in Virginia (3 nonheads, 2 heads), Pennsylvania (2 nonheads, 1 head), New York (2 nonheads), and Maryland (1 head). Five lived in households where the head's name was not the same as theirs, while just 2 lived in households where the head's name was the same. All figures are from U.S. Census, Census of Population, Wood County, Parkersburg, 1860.

61. Joan M. Jensen, "Needlework as Art, Craft, and Livelihood before 1900," in Jensen and Davidson, eds., *A Needle, a Bobbin, a Strike*, 9–10, 11.

62. Newton et al., *History of the Pan-Handle*, 183–84, 187.

63. Blackford, *History of Small Business in America*, 122.

64. The 1860 census of population documented that the Wheeling dressmakers were born in Canada (1 nonhead, 1 head), Ohio (2 nonheads, 1 head), Virginia (2 nonheads), Pennsylvania (1 nonhead), Maryland (1 nonhead), and Ireland (1 head). Only 3 milliners in Wheeling were foreign born: 2 in England (1 nonhead, 1 head), and 1 household head in Ireland. Only 2 mantua makers that year were foreign born (1 in England and 1 in Ireland); both were household heads. In Parkersburg in 1860, the only foreign-born businesswomen were 2 dressmakers born in Scotland (1 household head and 1 nonhead). In 1870, the 2 women in the "millinery &c." business were born in Germany. All the other businesswomen were native born. In Martinsburg in 1860, the only foreign-born businesswoman was one household head who was a mantua maker born in Ireland. All the businesswomen were native born in 1870.

65. The 1860 Wheeling census of population identified 10 dressmakers (7 who were not heads of households and 3 who were), 14 mantua makers (11 not heads of households and 3 heads), and 14 milliners (9 not heads of households and 5 heads).

66. The single women were Miss Sarah Crowley, Miss Mary Crowley, Miss Mary Jane Jepson, Miss Nassell, Miss H. Plimpton, Miss S. B. Stanton. The married women were Mrs. Anne E. Frost, Mrs. Jane Loe (widow of William), Mrs. Martha H. Pugh, Mrs. C. Wells, Mrs. Hassell, Mrs. Elizabeth Lindsay. The ones with no marital status indicated were Emma Hawkins, Jane Lowe, Elizabeth Marsden, Kate Rickett, and Emily Sweeney. These names (with the exception of the last four, which were listed in the 1860 census) come from the R. G. Dun & Co. records for Ohio County; Taylor, *Directory of the City of Wheeling & Ohio County*; C. S. Williams, *Williams' Wheeling Directory, City Guide, and Business Mirror*, vol. 1,

1856–57 (Wheeling: John H. Thompson, 1856); and George H. Thurston, comp., *Directory of the City of Wheeling and Vicinity; Embracing the Adjoining Towns of Benwood, Lagrange, Bellaire, Kirkwood, Bridgeport, Martinsville and Fulton. For 1859–60* (Wheeling: Daily Intelligencer Office, 1859); and U.S. Census, Census of Population, Ohio County, Wheeling, 1860.

67. The nonheads among the 1860 Wheeling dressmakers were 19 and under (1) and 20–29 (6). The household heads in that group were 20–24 (1) and 30–34 (1). The nonheads among the 1860 Wheeling mantua makers were 19 and under (4), 20–29 (6), and 35–39 (1). The one household head who was a mantua maker was 45–49. The nonheads who were milliners in Wheeling in 1860 were 19 and under (4), 20–29 (4), and 35–39 (2); the household heads were 20–24 (1) and 35–39 (3).

68. "Miss M. A. Dugan," *Wheeling Intelligencer*, 21 April 1856; "Dress Cutting," ibid., 16 August 1858.

69. Thurston, *Directory of the City of Wheeling and Vicinity*, 21. Sometimes her last name was spelled "Cochran."

70. Jensen, "Needlework as Art," 12.

71. Bowen, *Wheeling Directory and Advertiser*, 16.

72. Thurston, *Directory of the City of Wheeling and Vicinity*, 100; Virginia, vol. 34, p. 53, R. G. Dun & Co. Collection.

73. She was listed as having a millinery shop in the 1856–57, 1859, 1864, 1868–69, 1872–73, and 1875–76 Wheeling city directories but as a milliner in 1862 and 1880–81. By 1875–76, her shop was a millinery and fancy goods shop.

74. Virginia, vol. 34, p. 105, R. G. Dun & Co. Collection.

75. U.S. Census, Census of Population, Ohio County, Wheeling, 1860.

76. "Opening of Fashionable Millinery," *Wheeling Intelligencer*, 8 April 1856; Williams, *Williams' Wheeling Directory*, 121, 125; Thurston, *Directory of the City of Wheeling and Vicinity*, 56, 59.

77. Williams, *Williams' Wheeling Directory*, 121, 125; Thurston, *Directory of the City of Wheeling and Vicinity*, 56, 59.

78. Virginia, vol. 34, p. 165, R. G. Dun & Co. Collection.

79. Thurston, *Directory of the City of Wheeling and Vicinity*, 21.

80. "Millinery," *Wheeling Intelligencer*, 17 November 1859.

81. Ohio County Marriage License, vol. 4, p. 34, Ohio County Court Clerk's Office.

82. Virginia, vol. 34, p. 66, R. G. Dun & Co. Collection.

83. Ibid., 154.

84. Ibid., 80. The credit reports are conflicting as to when Bole absconded, for the reports for Margaret indicate he left in, perhaps, 1851, while those for William indicate that he was in the store in mid-October 1853 but had left by November 4.

85. Williams, *Williams' Wheeling Directory*, 29; Virginia, vol. 34, p. 80, R. G. Dun & Co. Collection.

86. Williams, *Williams' Wheeling Directory*, 103.

87. "Millinery," *Wheeling Intelligencer*, 21 April 1856.

88. Virginia, vol. 34, p. 102, R. G. Dun & Co. Collection.

89. The 101 women identified in the Martinsburg census of population in 1860 included 2 teachers; 5 domestics; 20 washerwomen; 69 seamstresses; 3 milliners and mantua makers; and 2 boardinghouse keepers. The foreign-born mantua makers and seamstresses were from Ireland (11) and Germany (5). There were 51 seamstresses who were not heads of households and 18 who were household heads. All figures are from the U.S. Census, Census of Population, Berkeley County, Martinsburg, 1860.

90. There were two milliners who were not heads of households and two who were heads. The milliners were Almyra and Virginia Apsy, Louise Bast, and Annie C. Smith. Bast and Smith were household heads, while the Apsys lived in Bast's household. All four were born in Virginia. The Apsys were twenty and twenty-three years old, while Bast was forty-four and Smith, twenty-five. All figures are from U.S. Census, Census of Population, Berkeley County, Martinsburg, 1860.

91. "Emporium of Fashion," *Martinsburg Advertiser and Gazette*, 27 March 1860. Hughes was not identified with an occupation in the census.

92. "Dress-Making," ibid., 24 March 1860.

93. The 100 women identified in the Parkersburg population census in 1860 included 3 teachers; 62 domestics, nurses, hotel employees, and cooks; 12 washerwomen and laundresses; 11 seamstresses, tailoresses, or those in sewing trades; 9 dressmakers and milliners; 1 business owner; and 2 boardinghouse keepers. Four dressmakers (Maria Elliott, Jane Morehead, Sarah Robinson, and Isabel Young) and 2 milliners were not household heads; 2 dressmakers (Scottish-born Rosena Smoot and Elizabeth Young) and 1 milliner were household heads. 4.4 percent of the county's population was foreign born. Smoot, Morehead, and Robinson were born in Virginia. All were white. Smoot was 36, Elizabeth Young, 30, Isabel Young, 25, Morehead, 19, and Robinson, 21. Morehead and Robinson lived in a household where the head's name was not the same as theirs. All information is from the U.S. Census, Census of Population, Wood County, Parkersburg, 1860.

94. "Millinery! Millinery!" *Southern Methodist Itinerant* (Parkersburg), 16 May 1860.

95. "Fashionable and Fancy Dress-Making," ibid., 2 May 1860.

96. U.S. Census, Census of Population, Wood County, Parkersburg, 1860.

97. The Quartermaster's Records in the National Archives, Washington, D.C., contain no such contracts.

98. "A Romantic Adventure with a Dismal Ending," *Wheeling Daily Intelligencer*, 15 April 1864.

99. Hewetson Ault, "Wheeling in the Civil War" (master's thesis, The Ohio State University, 1930), 8. The one who did not take the oath was probably Dr. Alfred Hughes, a brother of Thomas Hughes (Leech's partner), since he was an active Confederate.

100. Hughes stayed in business, but he was no longer Leech's agent by the summer of 1863 (Virginia, vol. 34, p. 182, R. G. Dun & Co. Collection).

101. "Dissolution," *Wheeling Daily Intelligencer*, 15 November 1863, 3:6.

102. "To the Public," ibid., 2:6.

103. Ohio County Will Book, vol. 4, pp. 430–32, Ohio County Court Clerk's Office.

104. Virginia, vol. 34, p. 165, R. G. Dun & Co. Collection.

105. Ohio County Marriage License, vol. 6, p. 40, Ohio County Court Clerk's Office.

106. "Something for the Ladies," *Wheeling Intelligencer*, 1 May 1863.

107. "Attention Ladies," ibid., 13 April 1864.

108. Virginia, vol. 34, pp. 35, 209; vol. 35, p. 306, R. G. Dun & Co. Collection; city directories for 1864 to 1868–69.

109. Virginia, vol. 34, pp. 170, 171, R. G. Dun & Co. Collection.

110. "Millinery Establishment," *Parkersburg Gazette*, 11 February 1864.

111. Donna J. Spindel, "Women's Legal Rights in West Virginia, 1863–1984," *West Virginia History* 51 (1992): 30–31.

112. Virginia, vol. 34, pp. 170, 171, R. G. Dun & Co. Collection.

113. The other employers, with the number of females employed in each, were Buchfield & Co., ink, 2; B. F. Caldwell, tinner, 2; D. Cushing, paper, 5; Eberling, Beck & Pebler, tobacco, 5; Central Glass Co., glass, 25; M. Marsh & Son, tobacco, 2; G. Mendel & Co., unknown product, 1; E. F. Moore, cigars, 2; Norway Tack Co., tacks, 9; A. Reymann, brewer, 10; Henry Vaas, cigars, 5 (U.S. Census, Schedule 4, Products of Industry, 1870, Ohio County [Wheeling]).

114. These women can be identified in Williams & Co., comp., *Williams' Wheeling Directory for 1868–9; fourth issue* (Wheeling: A. W. Paull & Co., 1868). For Bradley's career, see Virginia, vol. 34, p. 59, R. G. Dun & Co. Collection. Mrs. Bradley was in partnership with John Eckhart Jr. in 1865–66, advertising the factory as Bradley & Eckhart in 1867–68 and as E. Bradley & Son in 1868 (Andrew Boyd, comp., *The Wheeling Directory: Containing the Names of the Inhabitants of Wheeling; Centre Wheeling; North, South and East Wheeling; and Wheeling Island, A Business Directory and an Appendix of Much Useful Information. 1865–'6* [Wheeling: J. C. Orr & Co., Booksellers, n.d.], 79; and *Williams' Wheeling Directory, for 1867–'8. 3rd Issue* [Wheeling: J. C. Orr & Co., 1867], 65; and Williams & Co., comp., *Williams' Wheeling Directory, fourth issue*, 53).

115. Miller was a carpet weaver in 1868–70 and employed three women to work on her three looms. The 1870 census enumerators found four women working as carpet weavers but none named Susan Miller (U.S. Census, Census of Population, Ohio County, Wheeling, 1870).

116. U.S. Census, Schedule 4, Products of Industry, 1870, Kanawha County (Charleston), 1.

117. Roy was born in West Virginia; neither parent was foreign born. She lived in a household where the head did not have the same last name (U.S. Census, Census of Population, Kanawha County, Charleston, 1870).

118. U.S. Census, Schedule 4, Products of Industry, 1870, Ohio County (Wheeling), identified the following merchant tailor firms in Wheeling: A. M. Adams (6 females, 10 males, 6 sewing machines), Henry Dailer (3 females, 1 male, 1 sewing machine), John Foos (7 females, 5 males, 2 sewing machines), Christian Hess (3 females, 9 males, 2 sewing machines), Thomas Hughes (35 females, 40 males, 10 sewing machines), Henry Kurtz (2 females, 4 males, 2 sewing machines), Herman Lingen (4 females, 3 males, 2 sewing machines), Charles Pfaffenbach (3 females, 4 males, 2 sewing machines), John S. Rice

(8 females, 12 males, 3 sewing machines), Conrad Schambra (3 females, 3 males, 2 sewing machines), J. H. Stallman (7 females, 8 males, 2 sewing machines), and Philip Winter (3 females, 3 males, 1 sewing machine). There were no children or youth reported as working in these firms that year.

119. These titles were "sewing for tailor," "sews for tailor," "sews in tailor shop," or "works for tailor" (4) and "works in tailor shop" (2). There were a total of 1,320 women identified with occupations in the census of population for Wheeling in 1870, including 54 teachers and nuns; 788 domestics, nurses, hotel employees, and cooks; 95 washerwomen and laundresses; 282 seamstresses, tailoresses, and sewing trades; 40 dressmakers, milliners, and mantua makers; 25 business owners; 23 factory workers and weavers; 7 boardinghouse owners and hotel keepers; and 6 in miscellaneous occupations. All figures are from U.S. Census, Census of Population, Ohio County, Wheeling, 1870.

120. In 1870, 194 of the city's seamstresses were not heads of households; only 38 were household heads. The figures for tailoresses were 17 and 4, respectively. The population was 21.5 percent (4,153) foreign born. Only 19 of the 194 seamstresses who were not heads of households were foreign born (5 in Ireland, 9 in Germany, 3 in Scotland, and 2 in Holland), but about one-half had fathers who were foreign born and/or mothers who were foreign born. The 38 household heads who were seamstresses included 16 foreign-born women (1 in England, 7 in Ireland, 5 in Germany, 1 in Scotland, 2 in Holland, and 1 in Wales). The 4 tailoresses who were household heads included 3 foreign-born women (1 in England, 1 in Ireland, and 1 in Scotland).

Among the seamstresses who were not heads of households, 83 were 19 and under, 87 were 20–29, 20 were 30–39, and 3 were 40 and older; among household heads, 8 were 20–29, 18 were 30–39, 4 were 40–49, and 8 were 50 and up. All figures are from the U.S. Census, Census of Population, Ohio County, Wheeling, 1870.

121. The Martinsburg firm was Henry Kratz's, with 4 females, 8 males, and 0 sewing machines (U.S. Census, Schedule 4, Products of Industry, 1870, Berkeley County [Martinsburg], 2). The Parkersburg firm was W. H. Bush's, with 4 females, 3 males, and 1 sewing machine (U.S. Census, Schedule 4, Products of Industry, 1870, Wood County [Parkersburg]). Neither firm reported employing children or youth.

122. The 215 women in Martinsburg with occupations included 9 teachers; 162 domestics, nurses, hotel employees, and cooks; 15 washerwomen and laundresses; 12 seamstresses; 13 dressmakers, milliners, and mantua makers; 1 business owner; and 3 boardinghouse keepers/hotel keepers. None of the 12 seamstresses were heads of households. All figures are from the U.S. Census, Census of Population, Berkeley County, Martinsburg, 1870.

123. The 3 seamstresses were all white women born in Virginia of native-born parents; none were heads of households. The census enumerators found 272 women with occupations, including 24 teachers and nuns; 208 domestics, nurses, hotel employees, and cooks; 3 washerwomen and laundresses; 7 seamstresses, tailoresses, and in other sewing trades; 23 dressmakers, milliners, and mantua makers; 1 factory worker; 5 boardinghouse keepers/

hotel keepers; and 1 clerk in a store. All figures are from the U.S. Census, Census of Population, Wood County, Parkersburg, 1870.

124. James E. Reeves, *The Physical and Medical Topography, Including Vital, Manufacturing and Other Statistics of the City of Wheeling* (Wheeling: Printed by order of the City Council by Daily Register Book and Job Office, 1870), 26–27.

125. U.S. Census, Census of Population, Ohio County, Wheeling, 1870.

126. Credit listings referred to both husband and wife at times (Virginia, vol. 34, p. 40, R. G. Dun & Co. Collection).

127. "Millinery and Mantua-Making," *The Martinsburg New Era*, 20 September 1866.

128. "Millenery [*sic*]," *Parkersburg Daily Times*, 5 June 1866.

129. Virginia, vol. 54, p. 594.Y24, R. G. Dun & Co. Collection.

130. The census enumerators identified 186 women with occupations in Charleston in 1870, including 4 teachers; 170 domestics, nurses, hotel employees, and cooks; 1 washer-woman; 10 dressmakers, milliners, and mantua makers; and 1 factory worker. The 2 mantua makers who were not household heads were born in Ireland; all other businesswomen were native born. All figures are from the U.S. Census, Census of Population, Kanawha County, Charleston, 1870.

131. "Millinery," *West Virginia Journal*, 27 April 1870; Untitled, ibid., 6 April 1870; "New Advertisements," ibid., 6 April 1870; U.S. Census, Census of Population, Kanawha County, Charleston, 1870.

132. "Millinery," *West Virginia Journal*, 1 June 1870.

133. Untitled, ibid., 15 June 1870; Virginia, vol. 34, p. 195, R. G. Dun & Co. Collection.

134. This conclusion is based on listings for dressmakers, milliners, mantua makers, and "millinery &c." workers in the U.S. Census, Census of Population, Ohio County (Wheel-ing), Berkeley County (Martinsburg), Wood County (Parkersburg), and Kanawha County (Charleston), 1870.

135. In Martinsburg, 71 of 179 women in positions as chambermaids, domestic servants, cooks, house cleaners, housekeepers, nurses, and washerwomen (39.7 percent) were black or mulatto in 1870 (U.S. Census, Census of Population, Berkeley County, Martinsburg, 1870). Blacks made up 9.8 percent of the city's population that year. In Charleston, 98 black or mulatto women (57.6 percent of the 170 total women in these jobs) had jobs as chamber-maids, dining room servants, domestic servants, nurses, or washerwomen, according to the U.S. Census, Census of Population, Kanawha County, Charleston, 1870. Blacks made up 24 percent of the population that year.

136. "Wanted—Agents," *West Virginia Journal*, 23 March 1870; Baron and Klepp, "'If I Didn't Have My Sewing Machine,'" 35–37.

*Part Three*

·  ·  ·  ·  ·  ·  ·  ·  ·  ·  ·  ·  ·  ·  ·  ·  ·  ·  ·  ·  ·  ·  ·  ·  ·  ·  ·  ·  ·  ·  ·  ·  ·  ·  ·  ·

Women as Unacknowledged Professionals

*Chapter Seven*

. . . . . . . . . . . . . . . . . . . . . . . . . . . . . . . . . .

# Depraved and Abandoned Women:
# Prostitution in Richmond, Virginia,
# across the Civil War

. . . . . . . . . . . . . . . . . . . . . . . . . . . . . . . . . .

E. SUSAN BARBER

Historically, prostitution has often been a viable employment option for poor and working-class women and at least a few men in a variety of regional settings, often in times of economic despair but, occasionally, as a matter of personal preference, and, in this, nineteenth-century Richmond, Virginia, was no exception. Historical studies of sexual commerce, however, have seldom paid much attention to the profession in the colonial, antebellum, or wartime South. Histories of the Civil War, if they mention prostitution at all, usually point to a paucity of sources and dispense with the topic in a few brief sentences. Both of these omissions indicate not only the difficulty in researching this topic but also, perhaps, a reluctance on the part of earlier scholars of southern history to grapple with issues of interracial sex.[1]

Instead, most examinations of prostitution in the nineteenth-century United States have typically focused on two specific areas: antebellum sex workers in urban locations, frequently New York City, or the madams, dance hall girls, and "soiled doves" who trekked to the West to satisfy the sexual needs of an isolated male population composed of silver and gold miners and other frontier adventurers.[2] And, with the exception of Anne Butler's examination of western prostitution in the United States and Judith Walkowitz's study of prostitutes in English port towns in the nineteenth century, few of these studies make the important links between the prevalence of prostitution and the availability of nearby garrisons of soldiers or sailors who provided a virtually inexhaustible supply of willing clients.[3] This essay contributes to the growing body of research on prostitution by examining the shifting visibility of sex work and its connections to race and class in Richmond, Virginia, from the late 1850s to 1870—the end of Reconstruction in Virginia. It also draws comparisons between Richmond prostitutes and sex workers in New York City and the West during the same period of time.

In 1855, Richmond, Virginia, was a city whose social structure and economic base reflected its southern slaveholding roots but also hinted at its possible northern aspirations. Much of the city's economy was driven by the processing of agricultural products that were grown by slaves in the surrounding countryside and shipped to the city where they were processed by a labor force composed of urban slaves and free blacks. Along the banks of the James River, slaves and free blacks processed tobacco in one of the city's fifty tobacco factories or milled wheat at the Gallego Mill, the largest supplier of flour to South America.

In addition to agricultural processing, by 1860 Richmond possessed a thriving commercial and manufacturing economy that rivaled the economies of some northern cities. The manufacturing schedule of the 1860 census reveals a total of eight lumberyards, six brick-making establishments, three flour mills, a nail factory, fifty-two tobacco processors, eight box factories, four textile mills, and the largest iron foundry in the South. Of the 332 businesses listed in the census, 90 employed between twenty and a hundred workers, each. Fourteen more, including the Old Dominion Iron and Nail Works, the Eagle Machine Foundry, the Haxall and Crenshaw flour mills, Tredegar Iron Works, and seven large tobacco processors, hired crews that were sometimes well in excess of a hundred laborers.[4] At Tredegar Iron Works, hundreds of slave men worked alongside recent German and Irish immigrants to produce the iron rails and locomotives that provided much of the region's developing transportation network. Richmond itself was an important rail center, linking five or six independent lines in a series of tracks that crisscrossed the downtown metropolis.

As Timothy Lockley's essay in this volume demonstrates, poor white and black women in southern urban settings worked outside the home throughout the antebellum period in a variety of occupations. As early as 1814, white and black Richmond women and girls found employment at the Richmond Cotton Manufactory while others labored at occupations that made use of their domestic talents. Enterprising Richmond women of both races baked pies and cakes and sold them to hungry passersby in the city's Capitol Square. Others stitched and sold hats, cloaks, and dresses from their homes or in tiny shops. Still more women took in laundry, rented out rooms, worked in family shops, or labored at one of the cotton textile factories in the working-class town of Manchester on the other side of the James River.[5]

By midcentury, a number of educated white women—Elva M. Jones, Margaret Brander, Grace Bennett, Mary C. Gordon, and Antonietta and Marietta Erba, to name just a few—had taught English, vocal music, and piano at one of the city's six schools for elite white girls. Others, including Ellen Mordecai, Harriet Hall, Jessie Gordon, and Mary Anderson, offered lessons in their homes for younger elite white children of both sexes. By 1856, thirty-four-year-old Mary Jackson had obtained a license to sell veal in the city market. And behind the curtained windows of those elite Richmond homes in communities like Church Hill, slave women provided countless hours of domestic labor that enabled the city's more affluent white women to engage in an array of social activities centered on church and family.

Prostitution was also an occupational alternative for poorer women in antebellum Richmond. By the 1850s, the term "Cary Street woman" was commonly used as a term of opprobrium for women whose behavior was deemed to be sexually promiscuous. But the prostitution that existed in Richmond in the decades before the war was hidden from view and often far more clandestine in nature than it would be during the 1860s. During the antebellum period, the city's sexual commerce seldom intruded on the consciousness of Richmond's respectable elites or its more upstanding working-class citizens. Concrete evidence for the antebellum period is, thus, difficult to obtain. Most histories of the city dispense with the subject in one or two sentences, if they mention it at all.

Information about prostitutes, thus, can be obtained only for these women when they ran afoul of the law and, therefore, usually is derived from sources such as court records, docket books, and newspaper accounts that frequently reflect middle-class criticisms of the poor and working class as being dirty, intemperate, and improvident. In addition, the charge of "keeping a disorderly house" appears to have been used as a catch-all term for establishments that engaged in a wide variety of activities that included illegal gambling, selling liquor without a license or selling liquor to negroes, prostitution, or simply holding raucous parties and engaging in brawls that disturbed the peace on a Saturday night. At times, then, it is difficult to distinguish between individuals who were engaged in prostitution from those who were involved in other forms of disorderly conduct. The fact that prostitution was a largely invisible occupation that relied on the anonymity of dark alleys or the back rooms of tippling houses and the women's frequent use of aliases to disguise their identities further complicates the research.

Despite these biases and ambiguities, it is clear that more than 180 Richmond women were involved in sexual commerce of some kind between 1853 and 1868. In the decade before the Civil War began, white, slave, and free women of color appeared before the mayor's court to answer charges that ranged from "street strolling," to public nudity and drunkenness, to keeping a "house of ill name, fame, and reputation." For example, Willie Ann Smith, a free woman of color, was found guilty in September 1854 of operating a brothel on 3rd Street that was inhabited by Maria Willis, Rebecca Williams, and Sarah Ann Pleasants.[6] In January 1855, Mrs. Margaret Connerton, a white woman, made her second appearance before the court for keeping a disorderly house.[7] In 1856, Frances Waddle and Anne Clarke were hauled into court for soliciting sex in the First Market.[8] In May 1857, Lydia Brooks, identified as "a slave going at large," was arraigned before the mayor and charged with "keeping a disorderly and bad house where whites and blacks congregate."[9] Two months earlier, Alice Hardgrove, described as "a frail damsel from 12th Street," was brought before the mayor's court for streetwalking. When arrested, Hardgrove was attired in a sailor's uniform, perhaps a disguise that allowed her to practice her profession while concealing her identity from the police. Wearing men's clothing also permitted Hardgrove to roam through the seamier sections of the city that would have been off-limits to respectable ladies.[10]

Houses of ill repute seem to have been scattered throughout the antebellum city, but by the late 1850s some Richmond locales, such as "Solitude," "Sugar Bottom," and "Pink Alley," had acquired colorful names and dubious distinctions for their heavy concentrations of sex workers. In 1855, a reporter for the *Richmond Whig* described Pink Alley as being "as notorious in the police annals of Richmond as are the Five Points in those of New York," a reference to an area of New York City where many prostitutes plied their trade.[11] By April 1860, a report in the *Richmond Dispatch* identified the rooms over the Wall Street Stables as the resort of "thirty females of bad character."

Evidence of a more concrete nature can be found in the 1860 Richmond census. By 1860, at least four brothels operated in this city of approximately 39,000 white and black free citizens.[12] Historians of prostitution are evolving a vocabulary to delineate the various types of sex workers and establishments contained within this broad occupational category, and it seems appropriate at this juncture to define some of these terms before continuing with a more detailed discussion of prostitution in Richmond. A "brothel" is defined as any sort of house where various forms of heterosexual and homosexual sex are bought and sold. Cross-dressing male prostitutes sometimes worked as streetwalkers but also could be found working in brothels with heterosexual female prostitutes.[13] Brothels—especially those that catered to an elite clientele—were not specifically built as houses of prostitution. These houses were often tastefully decorated with chandeliers and carpets. Many had parlors with pianos where prostitutes greeted their guests before retiring to an upstairs bedroom. Some of these were referred to as "parlor houses."[14]

A "house of assignation" refers to a hotel or boardinghouse where prostitutes arranged to meet their customers for sex, after first negotiating the "assignation" at some other location. This negotiation could include an exchange of notes carried by a slave or servant or a verbal agreement on a city thoroughfare. A "crib" is often defined as the most degraded kind of prostitution house, which consisted of numerous small six-foot-by-eight-foot rooms designed solely for sex. Each of these rooms opened on the street by either a door or a window. Prostitutes in these cribs are often the ones described as standing at the door, often semiclad to attract customers.[15] A "panel house" was a house with a movable panel or wall, which enabled prostitutes working with accomplices to rob unsuspecting customers through the use of a sliding door or panel. While the couple was engaged in sex, the accomplice would sneak in through the sliding panel and steal the customer's wallet.[16]

Most historians also define a "hierarchy" of prostitution that ranges from sex workers in elite brothels who catered to the city's more affluent men, to dance hall pickups—frequently identified in the literature as "hurdy gurdy women"—to streetwalking prostitutes who provided sexual services to working-class clients.[17] "Madams" were women who operated the brothels, providing shelter, food, and protection in exchange for a portion of the fee. Madams typically did not engage in prostitution themselves, since that would put them in competition with women under their employ and weaken their ability to wield power over recalcitrants. Included in this broader definition of "prostitutes" are women we would define today—and who were defined then—as "mistresses," individuals who traded sex, and occasionally love and affection, with men in sometimes long-term relationships, in exchange for housing, food, and clothing.[18] Various colorful euphemisms for prostitutes also permeate the literature, including "soiled doves," "nymphs du pave," "frail sisters," and "cyprians," to name but a few.[19]

With a little bit of practice, larger brothels are relatively easy to locate in the manuscript census. Their household arrangement was distinctive from other households of the time. Most contained between eight and fifteen women, who usually ranged in age from their late teens to their early thirties. Most of the women had surnames that were different from each other and, in cases where the place of birth was provided, at least a few of the women occasionally came from different parts of the country or from abroad. In addition, there were usually very few children living in the home, since many prostitutes with children arranged for them to be cared for by others. Another telltale sign is that most of the women listed an occupation such as domestic, or washerwoman, or seamstress as a means of concealing their true profession. In her study of prostitution in Nevada, Marion Goldman has noted that such occupations as chambermaid, servant, domestic, seamstress, laundress, hotel keeper, and boardinghouse keeper were often "tinged with disrespectability," in part because "a number of fast women were recruited from those ranks."[20] By contrast, typical family households included individuals with a range or ages, most of whom shared one or two surnames.

I began my search for Richmond brothels by working backward, with the name of a woman arrested for prostitution in 1863. In the 1860 manuscript census, that woman—Josephine DeMerritt—appears in a brothel in Richmond's Second Ward whose composition defined what I soon discovered would be a fairly typical residence pattern. Once I identified the brothels, I was then able to verify that these were indeed houses of prostitution by cross-matching the names of other women in these households with their subsequent arrests on the charge of engaging in sex for hire.

Although this process is fairly effective for locating larger brothels, it is not foolproof and care must be exercised to avoid the presumption that any two or three women sharing a domicile and listing their occupations as washerwomen were engaged in sexual commerce. To do this would be to snare innocent working-class women in the web of prostitution, a fate that all too many of them suffered at the hands of nineteenth-century police. Thus the smaller brothels and independent prostitutes have escaped this historian's detection in the same way that some residents of small houses of prostitution were able to evade apprehension by police in the nineteenth century. In addition, nineteenth-century prostitutes tended to be a transient population in two important ways: they moved in and out of the occupation as circumstances—health, age, marital status, the economy—allowed and they changed houses frequently, perhaps to avoid detection. In addition, many prostitutes used one or more aliases. So it is often difficult, if not impossible, to trace a particular woman through subsequent censuses.[21]

In spite of these limitations, census data concerning four brothels in Richmond's Second Ward helps to shed light on the ages and household arrangements of brothel prostitutes in 1860. In these four brothels, a total of thirty-three white women ranging in age from sixteen to thirty-six shared their living and working quarters with their children and, occasionally, with servants.[22] Twenty-seven-year-old Josephine DeMerritt—the woman with whom I began my investigation—shared a brothel house with eight other white women and four white men between the ages of seventeen and thirty. At least three of the men in DeMerritt's house may have been prostitutes, too. Their names—Frank Leslie, Frank Fargo, and James Moore—all indicate that they were males, but, in the column denoting sex, they were identified by the census taker as "females," an indication that they may have been some of the cross-dressing prostitutes noted in other historical studies. Four-year-old Eddie Lytle also lived in the house. All of the women listed their occupations as domestics, an occupation that was largely performed by slave and free black Richmond women until the end of the nineteenth century.

The house next door to DeMerritt's was a second brothel that was probably operated by thirty-four-year-old Louisa Duncan, the oldest woman in the house, who most likely was also the madam.[23] The remaining seven women ranged in age from seventeen-year-old Kate Jewell to twenty-five-year-old Ellen Franklin. Like the women in DeMerritt's household, all of these women were white and claimed to be domestics. Thirty-six-year-old Elizabeth Hubbard shared a third household with her two teenaged sons and twelve other Virginia and North Carolina women between the ages of sixteen and twenty-five. Two younger children whose surnames do not match the names of any of the female residents also lived in the Hubbard's house: two-year-old Mildred Epps and one-year-old George Davis. Thirty-year-old Anne Stevens, who shared her domicile with ten other white prostitutes between the ages of seventeen and thirty-four, probably owned the fourth house. Two small children lived in this house as well: five-year-old Eugean Bosseaux and four-year-old Christopher Cooper, the son of the thirty-four-year-old Mary Cooper, a free black woman who listed her occupation as "servant."

While the censuses are helpful in providing statistical information, they do little to help us understand the dynamics of the familial relationships those dwellings frequently contained. One wonders, for example, what arrangements were made for the care of Eddie Lytle, Mildred Epps, and George Davis while their mothers entertained clients? And what did Louisa Duncan's teenaged children think about their mother's occupation? Data gleaned from descriptions of court cases—which appeared in the Richmond press—sheds light on other family relations and suggest that, in some houses at least, Richmond prostitutes worked alongside other women with whom they shared bonds of blood. Sisters Mary and Emmeline Martin, for example, prostituted themselves in a house on the south side of the Basin between 1854 and 1859.[24] Mary Sullivan was probably apprenticed into the profession by her mother, Margaret. Between 1857 and 1862, these two women appeared before the mayor's court on at least seven separate occasions for charges related to prostitution.[25]

Information on the realty and personal property of the brothel operated by Ann Stevens is unavailable, and the house managed by Elizabeth Hubbard appears to have been quite modest. But Louisa Duncan's brothel and the one where Josephine DeMerritt worked were, by comparison, quite affluent. The madam of DeMerritt's house reported real estate valued at $4,000 and personal property worth $9,000. In the house next door Louisa Duncan listed her realty and personal assets at $10,000, each, amounts that were the same or similar to those claimed by Virginia governor John Letcher, Richmond lawyer John Crenshaw, merchant William Paine, and Dr. James B. McCaw, all men of affluence in the antebellum city.[26]

Although several historians have recently called attention to the existence and sometimes the tacit recognition of interracial sexuality in the colonial and early-nineteenth-century South, by the late 1850s, laws in many southern states prohibited the sexual mingling of the races.[27] In late antebellum Richmond, the color lines created by the city's black codes appear to have divided sex workers and their customers along racial lines. A few madams, such as the notorious Jane Wright, flaunted the color barrier and provided opportunities for women and men of both races to meet for illicit interracial sex. In September 1854, angry neighbors tore down Wright's house on Brooke Avenue, no doubt as punishment for violating the city's racial norms.[28] Racial divisions such as the ones found in the Richmond census were also the norm for bawdy houses in New York City during the same period of time. Marilynn Wood Hill notes that most New York prostitutes in the 1850s were white. White clients had access to sexual services in either white or black brothels, while black men were denied opportunities for sexual intercourse with any white sex workers.[29]

Marion Goldman and Anne Butler have both pointed to the wide regional and ethnic diversity of western prostitutes—many brothels contained women who were recent Chinese and Mexican immigrants, as well as whites, African Americans, and a few Native Americans. Goldman's study concludes that most workers were divided by race as well, while Butler finds evidence of some racial mixing among the prostitutes, although not necessarily among the clients. In Butler's study, white male clients were free to frequent all of these establishments, regardless of the race of the prostitutes. But Mexican, and especially Chinese, men were prohibited from having sexual intercourse with white sex workers. Their varied ethnicity indicates that many western sex workers were also born outside the region.[30] By comparison, Richmond prostitutes appear to have been largely native born. Only one brothel prostitute in the 1860 census was born outside the United States, and two-thirds of the Richmond women listed their place of birth as Virginia or another southern state, such as Georgia or North Carolina. Of the remaining eleven women, six were born and raised in New York, perhaps an indication of the prevalence of sexual commerce in that state and hence its importance to historians as a source of information about nineteenth-century sex work.

Nearly 70 percent of the Richmond women in 1860 were between the ages of sixteen and twenty-four, a finding comparable to Marilynn Hill's statistics for New York City prostitutes between 1850 and 1855. By comparison, prostitutes working Nevada's Comstock region in 1875 indicates that later, Richmond and New York City prostitutes were frequently five years younger than their western counterparts, which leads to the conclusion that some prostitutes in East Coast cities may have followed their male clients westward when the Civil War was over.[31]

On the eve of the Civil War, then, Richmond prostitution could be characterized as a relatively invisible occupation that divided prostitutes and their clients along racially specific lines. Women like Jane Wright who transgressed these lines were subject to public censure. During the Civil War, however, prostitution became a highly visible occupation in which prostitutes competed for public space with more respectable elements of the white and black population. In addition, postwar brothels challenged notions of racial mixing by providing sexual services to black and white Union soldiers by both black and white prostitutes. In the climate of racial hostility surrounding the end of slavery, these racially mixed bawdy houses may have contributed to emerging anxieties about interracial sex between white women and black men that fueled racial violence in the postwar South.

As other past and future wars had done and would continue to do, the American Civil War temporarily broadened southern and northern women's opportunities for work, both in traditional areas such as sewing, food preparation, and caring for the sick and in nontraditional work such as clerking and making ammunition. Once Richmond was chosen to be the capital of the Confederate States of America, thousands of southern men converged on the city to work in war-related industry or for the Confederate government, or to train in one of the military camps that dotted the city in preparation for deployment to the field. The presence of so many virile men in uniform also helped to transform the city into what one historian has called a "true mecca for prostitutes."[32] Although not regular "government work," prostitution nevertheless provided services to Confederate soldiers far from the conjugal comforts of home.

Accurate numbers for prostitutes in wartime Richmond are impossible to obtain; no city censuses were taken during the war years, when the population tripled from 40,000 to 120,000. And none of these Richmond sex workers have left written records of their own. But evidence from newspapers, eyewitnesses, and the Richmond courts supports the assertion that wartime Richmond attracted large numbers of prostitutes who brazenly went about the business of providing sexual services to Confederate soldiers quartered in the city. In so doing, they rendered prostitution more visible. They also transgressed the moral and social boundaries of the city that divided respectable citizens from its more disreputable denizens.[33] In May 1862, for example, a letter to the editor of the *Richmond Dispatch* complained that "shame-faced prostitutes of both sexes" were "disporting themselves extensively on the sidewalks and in hacks, open carriages, etc. . . . to the amazement of sober-sided citizens."[34] Less than six months later, the editor of the *Richmond Enquirer* charged that prostitutes were using public conveyances to engage in sexual commerce to such an extent that "[r]espectable ladies are actually afraid to be seen in a public hack, from the dread of being mistaken for these painted wretches."[35] Observations such as these were virtually absent from the antebellum Richmond papers and suggest the ways in which the presence of a large, aggressively virile male population transformed the profession from an invisible occupation based on anonymity to a more public exchange that penetrated the boundaries separating respectable Richmonders from the city's coarser elements.

Marilynn Hill has noted that New York prostitutes frequently had tacit agreements with many theater owners that permitted the women to claim the upper balcony or "third tier" of most theaters as a place where they could meet prospective customers or entertain themselves on their "off hours."[36] But by 1863, prostitutes had begun to share the private boxes of the dress circle of the Richmond Theatre with Confederate officers, an area of the theater normally reserved for respectable Richmond ladies.[37] Richmond prostitutes cavorting in the dress circle were usually arrested and made to appear before the mayor's court, where they were fined as much as $200 to $300 for violating this zone of respectability that had the potential to call into question the reputation of any woman attending an afternoon matinee. At other times, the theater manager simply ejected them.

Richmond prostitutes also invaded the gardens and walkways of Capitol Square, an area of greenery around the governor's mansion and the Virginia State House traditionally off limits to any but the most respectable white Richmond families.[38] In August 1864, the *Examiner* reported that "gaudy unblushing strumpets" strolled "among the decent women and children" in Capitol Square, listening to martial music while leaning on the arms of Confederate soldiers.[39] Richmond mayor Joseph Mayo was appalled at the growing number of "lewd women" thronging to the city and, in 1862, attempted to curtail their spread through a strict application of the city's vagrancy laws. In 1863, Mayo stepped up his campaign by ordering the city police to arrest all prostitutes streetwalking in Capitol Square. These measures led to the arrest of a number of the city's "public women," but they also flooded the city's overloaded court system. Many cases were dismissed for lack of evidence, and others resulted in fines that were hastily paid by women eager to return to their profitable trade.[40] By January 1864, prostitution in Richmond had become so great a problem that a separate department was set aside in Castle Thunder—a prison housing Confederate deserters, Union sympathizers, free negroes, and those convicted of espionage—for the city's "depraved and abandoned women."[41]

Although the mayor's efforts succeeded in removing a number of streetwalkers from circulation, brothels continued to flourish. Hospitals filled with convalescent soldiers, miles from home and desperate for a little feminine comfort, often provided an important source of business. In May 1862, for example, the managers of the YMCA hospital for sick and wounded soldiers complained to the city's provost marshal about a group of "lewd females" operating a brothel directly across the street. From the brothel's windows and doors, the women gestured and displayed themselves "in a half-nude state, divert[ing] the convalescent soldiers' attention from their legitimate business of sickness." A few of the patients ventured across the street, returning a few hours later in a drunken stupor brought on by too much sex.[42]

Prostitution was a dangerous and frequently violent occupation in the wartime capital. In the brothels that lined Main and Cary Streets in the eastern end of the city, Confederate soldiers broke up furniture and occasionally engaged in murderous brawls. Emma Brown and Maggie J. Jones operated a "low brothel" on East Main between 23rd and 24th Streets where James A. Kelly of the First Louisiana Regiment, New Orleans, was stabbed to death with a stiletto on the morning of 16 February 1864.[43] William Downes and Patrick Kelley, both soldiers in Read's Artillery, were killed in a brothel fight on 9 May 1862.[44] Benjamin Delarme was killed on 16 August 1864 in a brothel on 21st Street between Main and Cary that was managed by Catherine Blankenship.[45]

Some prostitutes combined sex work with petty theft by robbing the men who were their clients. Eliza Liggon and Albertine Coephas, who were described in the *Richmond Examiner* as "prostitutes of a low order," shared a house in Lombardy Alley near 14th Street with Jennie Richardson and Anne Jackson. Liggon and Coephas appeared in court in April 1864, after being involved in a violent and bloody brawl that erupted after Liggon stole money and a pocket-knife "of sentimental value" from one of her male customers.[46] Mary Sullivan, who operated a brothel in the working-class community of Rocketts, was found guilty in May 1862 of robbing one of her customers of a thousand dollars.[47] Mary Smith and Mary Taylor were arrested in April 1863 for stealing $125 in Confederate Treasury notes from Joseph Kepler, an "emaciated-looking German," who had visited the two women at their house on Wall Street with his friend Horatio Sutherland.[48]

Descriptions of prostitutes appearing in the courts shed light on the hierarchy contained within the profession as well as class assumptions by middle-class observers, based on the women's appearance. Prostitutes from "low brothels" were often described in extremely unflattering terms that stripped them of any shred of feminine beauty. Catherine Blankenship was described as being "smoke dried and embrowned out of all semblance of female comeliness" and "as garrulous as a crow on a dead limb in corn-planting time."[49] When Eliza Liggon appeared in court to protest her innocence in the theft of her customer's pocketknife, she was described as "a short fat girl of eighteen, with very vulgar features" and wearing "very common clothes." Her partner, Albertine Coephas, was described as being "considerably older, but no prettier," her face "a perfect patchwork of sticking plasters" from the injuries she received in the fight. According to the court reporter, she was "arrayed like Solomon in all his glory," wearing a black silk dress, a black velvet cape, and "a bonnet that was a triumph of military taste," an insinuation that Coephas was thought to be dressing above her class in that her attire was considered too fine for a woman of ill fame.[50] Well-dressed prostitutes not only were guilty of blurring the lines between themselves and the city's respectable women, they also offended middle-class sensibilities by providing evidence that sex for sale was a profitable business. Mary Smith was apparently more appropriately dressed when she came before the Hustings Court in May 1863. Described in the press as "a fat, flabby-looking girl of eighteen . . . with a small vulgar nose situated on her face like a full moon," she was wearing a pink calico dress and "a blue silk bonnet, ten fashions old." The jurors found Smith innocent, saying that Kepler got what he deserved for "going into such an abominable hole as the woman Smith lived in."[51]

Some madams who catered to Confederate officers and highly placed government officials found prostitution to indeed be an extremely profitable occupation in a military enclave like Richmond. By 1862, Josephine DeMerritt had left the house where she had worked in 1860 and had established a brothel of her own. By 1863, she was a woman of considerable means and influence who was able to avoid prosecution through the use of high-priced lawyers and an entourage of well-placed character witnesses.[52] Although she appeared in court several times during 1862 and 1863, her connections to influential men in the city, including the former treasurer of the Virginia Medical Society and the city's fire chief, meant that the prosecution usually dropped the charges, or else DeMerritt was ordered to pay a fine. In 1863 she owned three slaves valued at $3,600 and other personal property amounting to an additional $3,000.[53]

Several of the city's other white brothel operators encountered treatment similar to DeMerritt's. Frances Matthews, Margaret Hamilton, Belle Jones, Margaret Taffy, Anna Thompson, and Alice Ashley—all white women—either were found not guilty or received nolle prosequi judgments, suggesting that the court either was too preoccupied with more pressing matters or had decided in favor of leniency in cases of sexual commerce by white women.[54] Black madams were not treated equally, however. Lucy Smith, "a fashionable free negress," was stripped and given twenty-five lashes in August 1862 for keeping "a house of evil fame, shame, and reputation."[55]

While women like DeMerritt appear to have chosen prostitution as a potentially lucrative profession, others—especially streetwalking prostitutes—were probably forced into sexual commerce by utter destitution, a situation not uncommon in a city whose population tripled within three years' time. Fourteen-year-old refugee Eliza Dickinson, for example, after her widowed mother died shortly after the family arrived in the city, roamed the streets of Richmond in April 1862 to earn a living for herself and her two younger brothers.[56] She and her brothers were eventually sent to North Carolina to live with relatives.

On 3 April 1865, Richmond fell to Union forces who marched into the Confederate capital and immediately went to work restoring order and putting out the fires set by Confederate soldiers complying with government orders. Military rule under federal Reconstruction, which lasted from 1865 to May

1870, did little to stem the tide of Richmond's sexual commerce, in part because the city continued to be a military capital overrun with men. Eight weeks after the city's surrender, white and black prostitutes were perched in the rear windows of the Virginia Towing Company, joking and laughing with prisoners across the street in Libby Prison. To the outrage of at least one eyewitness, the Libby inmates responded by "frequently . . . exposing their persons in the most indecent manner."[57]

Libby at this time contained southern soldiers incarcerated by the federal government, so it might be possible that the Richmond courtesans outside the prison were providing a little entertainment for the inmates as a demonstration of southern solidarity. But other prostitutes appear to have abandoned their patriotism and yielded to market forces by "sleeping with the enemy," either out of economic necessity or a keen eye for business. Mary Massey has observed that prostitutes traveling with Confederate troops on battle maneuvers seldom evacuated the field with retreating Confederates. Instead, they simply waited for Union soldiers to arrive. According to one eyewitness, they were "as willing to extend their gentle favors to the National officers as to their late Rebel protectors."[58]

Eyewitness accounts from irate Richmonders support Massey's claim. "The Yankee officers are in the constant habit of riding out on horseback, and in open barouches with women of the pavé," fumed Lucy Walton Fletcher in July 1865. "As I walk the streets, I never see a familiar face, but am continually jostled by Yankees, negroes, Dutch, and Jews, while negroes and courtesans ride gaily by . . . with the most shameless effrontery."[59] Five days after Fletcher's blistering critique, the officer commanding the district of Henrico in Richmond, Virginia, issued a general order condemning "the disreputable conduct of officers . . . in driving up to houses of ill fame in government ambulances [or] . . . permitting their horses to be held by orderlies in front of said disreputable places." He ordered the chief of police and the provost marshal to "detail a guard whose duty shall be to arrest all officers stopping at such places" and report them to headquarters.[60]

Despite this order, which applied only to Union officers, the city's "fallen women" continued to cavort on public streets with citizens and soldiers of both races. In 1867, for example, a petition signed by twenty-two residents living near the intersection of 4th Street and Clay pleaded with the city's Common Council not to permit the circus to perform in their neighborhood. "From the arrival of the first wagon, truck, or elephant, the petitioners wrote, "the femmes de pave . . . take possession of every available space in and around the premises and it requires no lively imagination to conjecture the scenes and acts of this unfortunate class of people—in fact they render our neighborhood for the time a perfect Hell on Earth."[61] In fact, it might have served Union officials' purposes to look the other way when Union troops frolicked with the city's "femmes de pave." Richmond's depraved and abandoned women were no doubt a more acceptable outlet for the soldiers' sexual appetites than the winsome white daughters of the Confederacy.

On 16 January 1868, nine white and mulatto prostitutes, including Emma Wilson, Adelaide Johnson, and Carrie Jones, were arrested in a bawdy house operated by Betsy King, a mulatto madam. With them were eleven white men, including eight soldiers in army blue.[62] And in January 1870, a police raid on a dance hall owned by John C. Clarke resulted in the arrest of five U.S. soldiers, four civilian males, and ten black prostitutes.[63] The arrests at Betsy King's and John Clarke's brothels suggest another way in which the Civil War may have transformed prostitution in Richmond. Although most prostitutes in antebellum Richmond appear to have worked in racially segregated brothels, by the late 1860s women of both races shared the same houses and, often, the same clients. The end of the Civil War, then, and Richmond's occupation by black and white Union troops may have led to a redrawing of the color lines in the city bawdy houses.

In May 1870, the federal government withdrew its occupation forces, leaving Richmond once more in the hands of its white citizens. To Richmonders' great delight, a number of the city's prostitutes went with them, perhaps to take up places in the brothels lining the mining and military camps in the American West. But the city they left behind had been changed, perhaps forever. During the antebellum period, prostitution in Richmond had been a relatively invisible occupation, hidden from the public gaze in the shadowy haunts of dark alleys and theater balconies where the women plied their trade. Respectable Richmond men and women could remain more or less ignorant of its existence by avoiding the places where prostitutes lived and worked. But by the late 1860s, prostitutes competed for public space with the city's white elite. The presence of thousands of Confederate and, later, Union soldiers had brought the profession into the light. No longer hidden from view, prostitution was now a highly visible occupation that challenged Richmonders' notions of female sexuality and racial purity as it exposed them to public spectacles of bold-faced harlots of varying hues who cavorted in public spaces with the city's black and white men.

NOTES

1. Bell Irvin Wiley, *The Life of Johnny Reb: The Common Soldier of the Confederacy* (1943; reprint, Baton Rouge: Louisiana State University Press, 1978); Emory M. Thomas, *The Confederate State of Richmond: A Biography of the Capital* (Austin: University of Texas Press, 1971); Virginius Dabney, *Richmond: The Story of a City*, rev. ed. (1976; reprint, Charlottesville: University Press of Virginia, 1990); George Rable, *Civil Wars: Women and the Crisis of Southern Nationalism* (Urbana: University of Illinois Press, 1989); Victoria E. Bynum, *Unruly Women: The Politics of Social and Sexual Control in the Old South* (Chapel Hill: University of North Carolina Press, 1992); Drew Gilpin Faust, *Mother of Invention: Women of the Slaveholding South in the American Civil War* (Chapel Hill: University of North Carolina Press, 1996). James M. McPherson does not discuss the subject in either *Ordeal by Fire: The Civil War and Reconstruction* (New York: Knopf, 1982) or *Battle Cry of Freedom: The Civil War Era* (New York: Oxford University Press, 1988), and George Rable's discussion of Richmond prostitutes in *Civil Wars* (194–95) adds nothing new. Drew Faust makes only two references to prostitution in *Mothers of Invention*: Benjamin Butler's General Order No. 28 (p. 212) and a discussion between a husband and wife about him visiting "fancy women" while in the army (pp. 124–25).

2. New York women have been the subject of numerous studies; see Marilynn Wood Hill, *Their Sisters' Keepers: Prostitution in New York City, 1830–1870* (Berkeley: University of California Press, 1993); Christine Stansell, *City of Women: Sex and Class in New York, 1789–1860* (New York: Knopf, 1986); and Timothy Guilfoyle, *City of Eros: New York City Prostitution and the Commercialization of Sex, 1790–1920* (New York: W. W. Norton, 1992). They also occupy a major portion of William W. Sanger's massive study of prostitution, *The History of Prostitution* (1859; reprint, New York: Arno Press, 1972). Barbara Meil Hobson's study, *Uneasy Virtue: The Politics of Prostitution and the American Reform Tradition* (1987; reprint, Chicago: University of Chicago Press, 1990), focuses on women in Boston, Massachusetts. Scholarly works on prostitution in the American West include Anne M. Butler, *Daughters of Joy, Sisters of Misery: Prostitutes in the American West, 1865–1890* (Urbana: University of Illinois Press, 1985); Marion S. Goldman, *Gold Diggers and Silver Miners: Prostitution and Social Life on the Comstock Lode* (Ann Arbor: University of Michigan Press, 1981); and Jacqueline Baker Barnhart, *The Fair but Frail: Prostitution in San Francisco, 1849–1900* (Reno: University of Nevada Press, 1986). Popularized accounts of western prostitutes include George Williams III, *The Redlight Ladies of Virginia City, Nevada* (Riverside, Calif.: Tree by the River Publishing, 1984), and Mary W. Remmers, *Going Down the Line: Galveston's Red-Light District Remembered* (N.p.: n.p., 1997). Some of the best European studies are Judith R. Walkowitz, *Prostitution in Victorian Society: Women, Class, and the State* (1980; reprint, Cambridge, Eng.: Cambridge University Press, 1983), and Alain Corbin, *Women for Hire: Prostitution and Sexuality in France after 1850*, trans. Alan Sheridan (Cambridge, Mass.: Harvard University Press, 1992).

3. Marilynn Hill's study of prostitution in New York City does address prostitutes' relations with the military, and neither Barnhart's study nor Anne Butler's examination of

prostitutes in the American West deals with any potential changes to prostitution as a result of the Civil War.

4. The Tredegar Iron Works employed more than 800 men; the Old Dominion Iron and Nail Works, 225 (Manufacturing Schedule for the 1860 Census, Richmond, Virginia, National Archives and Records Administration, Washington, D.C.; hereafter NARA).

5. *Richmond Whig*, 24 January 1860.

6. *Richmond Dispatch*, 7 September 1854.

7. Ibid., 17 January 1855.

8. Ibid., 29 July 1856.

9. Ibid., 6 May 1857.

10. Ibid., 25 February 1857.

11. *Richmond Whig*, 29 August 1865.

12. Manuscript Census for Richmond, Virginia, 1860, NARA.

13. Guilfoyle, *City of Eros*, 135–38.

14. Barnhart, *Fair but Frail*, ix–x.

15. Ibid., ix.

16. Guilfoyle, *City of Eros*, 173; Vern Bullough and Bonnie Bullough, *Women and Prostitution: A Social History* (Buffalo, N.Y.: Prometheus Books, 1987), 217.

17. Hobson, *Uneasy Virtue*, 15.

18. Barnhart, *Fair but Frail*, ix–x; Bullough and Bullough, *Women and Prostitution*, 175.

19. Goldman, *Gold Diggers and Silver Miners*, 57–58; Bullough and Bullough, *Women and Prostitution*, 175 and 220.

20. Goldman, *Gold Diggers and Silver Miners*, 29. See also Bullough and Bullough, *Women and Prostitution*, 170.

21. Goldman, *Gold Diggers and Silver Miners*, 59.

22. Richmond, at this time, was divided into three wards. I was not able to identify any brothels in the other two wards. I also do not know the precise location of these brothels.

23. I am drawing this conclusion from the fact that Duncan's name is listed first, in the place usually occupied by the head of the household.

24. *Richmond Dispatch*, 18 July 1854, 26 June 1858; *Richmond Whig*, 18, 19, 20 July 1854.

25. *Richmond Dispatch*, 29 June, 25 July 1857; 13, 15 February, 15 October 1858; 2, 3 November 1859.

26. In the 1860 census, Letcher reported $13,750 in realty and $10,000 in personal property. Although their real estate holdings were more extensive, Crenshaw, Paine, and McCaw all listed the value of their personal property as $10,000 (Manuscript Census for Richmond, Virginia, 1860, NARA).

27. See the essays by Diane Miller Sommerville, Kirsten Fischer, and Virginia Meacham Gould in Catherine Clinton and Michele Gillespie, eds. *The Devil's Lane: Sex and Race in the Early South* (New York: Oxford University Press, 1997).

28. *Richmond Dispatch*, 5 September 1854.

29. Hill (*Their Sister's Keepers*, 55–56) reports that between 1850 and 1855, only two of the

eighty brothels in two New York City wards were black. In 1853, one of these brothels, operated by Sarah Sweet—a mulatto madam originally from Rhode Island—played on fantasies of interracial sex by advertising itself as a resort where "Southern gentlemen . . . will feel quite at home."

30. Goldman estimates that two-thirds of all prostitutes in Comstock in 1875 were foreign born. By 1880, this number had declined to 54 percent (*Gold Diggers and Silver Miners*, 67–68; Butler, *Daughters of Joy*, 3–12).

31. Manuscript Census for Richmond, Virginia, 1860, NARA; Goldman, *Gold Diggers and Silver Miners*, 65.

32. Wiley, *Life of Johnny Reb*, 51–55.

33. *Richmond Examiner*, 22 August 1864. Bell Wiley has blamed Richmond prostitutes for the increased incidence of syphilis and gonorrhea in the Army of Northern Virginia and other troops garrisoned in and around the Confederate capitol (*Life of Johnny Reb*, 53–57). Emory Thomas (*Confederate State of Richmond*, 68–69) relies heavily on the information Wiley provides. Judith Walkowitz's study of prostitution in nineteenth-century England indicates that prostitutes tended to concentrate around the port towns of Southampton and Plymouth, in order to serve the British sailors (*Prostitution and Victorian Society*). Regarding the incidence of venereal disease among northern soldiers, Rudolph H. Kampmeier estimates that there were 73,382 cases of syphilis and 109,397 cases of gonorrhea among white soldiers in the Union armies between June 1862 and June 1866 ("Venereal Disease in the United States Army, 1775–1900," *Sexually Transmitted Diseases* 9, no. 2 [April–June 1982]: 100–108). Barring recurrences or cases in which soldiers contracted both syphilis and gonorrhea, this means that one in every eleven Union soldiers might have been suffering from venereal disease, although not all of the cases, of course, were the result of visiting prostitutes.

34. *Richmond Dispatch*, 13 May 1862.

35. *Richmond Enquirer*, 21 October 1862.

36. Hill, *Their Sisters' Keepers*, 199–206; Stansell, *City of Women*, 173–75; Goldman, *Gold Diggers and Silver Miners*, 143; Guilfoyle, *City of Eros*, 67.

37. *Richmond Examiner*, 27 April, 2 June 1863. According to Marilynn Hill (*Their Sister's Keepers*), permissive attitudes about the "third tier" as the prostitute's domain were on the decline by the end of the 1850s, and theater managers by this time more frequently ejected the women or barred their entry. If this was also the case in Richmond, the presence of prostitutes in the dress circle must have been a real affront to Richmond society.

38. Black codes that were enacted in Richmond in the 1850s, for example, prohibited blacks from appearing in Capitol Square, unless they were slaves on errands for their owners.

39. *Richmond Examiner*, 22 August 1864.

40. Ibid., 27 April 1863.

41. Ibid., 19 January 1864; Alan Lawrence Golden, "Castle Thunder: The Confederate Provost Marshal's Prison, 1862–65" (master's thesis, University of Richmond, 1980).

42. *Richmond Dispatch*, 6 May 1862.

43. *Richmond Examiner*, 7 February 1864.

44. Ibid., 13 June 1861; 17 February, 22 August 1864; *Richmond Dispatch*, 12 May 1862.

45. *Richmond Examiner*, 22 August 1864.

46. Ibid., 18 April 1864.

47. *Richmond Dispatch*, 9 May 1862.

48. *Commonwealth v. Mary Smith*, Richmond City, Hustings Court Suit Papers, April 1863 term, Library of Virginia, Richmond, Virginia (hereafter LV).

49. *Richmond Examiner*, 22 August 1864.

50. Ibid., 18 April 1864.

51. Ibid., 27 May 1863; *Commonwealth v. Mary Smith*, Richmond City, Hustings Court Suit Papers, April 1863 term, LV.

52. *Commonwealth v. DeMerritt et al.*, Richmond City, Hustings Court Suit Papers, July 1863 term, LV.

53. Virginia, Personal Property Tax Records, Richmond City, 1863, LV.

54. *Commonwealth v. Belle Jones*, January 1863 term; *Commonwealth v. Margaret P. Taffey*, March 1863 term; *Commonwealth v. Alice Ashley*, March 1863 term; *Commonwealth v. Margaret Hamilton*, July 1863 term; *Commonwealth v. Frances Matthews*, July 1863 term; *Commonwealth v. Anna Thompson*, n.d. 1863 term, all in Hustings Court Suit Papers, Richmond City, LV.

55. *Richmond Enquirer*, 15 August 1862.

56. Dickinson's father had died some time earlier. See ibid., 29 April 1862.

57. E. G. Westcott, Adams Express Company, Richmond, to the Provost Marshal, 10 June 1875, Isaac Howell Carrington Papers, William R. Perkins Library, Duke University, Durham, North Carolina (hereafter DU).

58. Quoted in Massey, *Bonnet Brigades* (New York: Knopf, 1966), 73 n. 7.

59. Entry dated 3 July 1865, diary for 27 April 1865–94, Lucy Muse (Walton) Fletcher Papers, Mss. 1-01-1, DU.

60. General Order No. 53, July 8, 1865, in *General Orders, Division of the James, Department of Virginia, 24th Army Corps*, in Record Group 153, Records of the Judge Advocate General's Office, NARA.

61. Letter from Thomas W. Brockenbrough and attached petition to Richmond Common Council, 12 September 1867, Bundle dated 6 September 1867, Richmond City Papers, Minutes of the Common Council, LV.

62. *Richmond Enquirer and Examiner*, 16 January 1868.

63. *Richmond Whig*, 8 January 1870.

*Chapter Eight*

. . . . . . . . . . . . . . . . . . . . . . . . . . . . . . . . .

# The Female Academy and Beyond:
# Three Mordecai Sisters at Work in the Old South

. . . . . . . . . . . . . . . . . . . . . . . . . . . . . . . . .

EMILY BINGHAM AND PENNY RICHARDS

One day in 1818, Jacob Mordecai, proprietor of a noted female academy in the small town of Warrenton, North Carolina, picked up his quill and signed a document selling his school for ten thousand dollars. With nearly a hundred girls enrolled, the institution was thriving. The business had hauled Mordecai out of debt and made him a success after years of financial struggle as a store-keeper. Now he could retire in comfort.[1]

The names of three of Jacob Mordecai's daughters, Rachel (1788–1838), Ellen (1790–1884), and Caroline (1794–1862), did not appear in the contract transferring the academy's ownership. Nor did the women receive any proceeds. Yet, as hundreds of family letters attest, the school was central to their lives, and as teachers and managers, they had been vital to its success. Though scholars have argued that few southern women saw emotional, intellectual, or financial benefits in the instruction of youth, these three women did. And the school's sale did not close such avenues; the sisters' labor as teachers can be traced over the course of five decades. Their motivations and the meanings they took from their teaching offer fresh angles from which to assess the historical categories of southern women's labor, categories that have obscured the work of Jacob Mordecai's daughters almost as effectively as the deed of sale he signed that day in 1818 did.

Southern education history has had less to say about teachers than about schools and their role in knitting together communities and elite female identity.[2] Yet the Mordecais (and thousands of other women in the antebellum South) worked teaching children.[3] Among paid teachers in the South, in 1850 some 35 percent were women.[4] Yet how do we reconcile this with a regional ideology that supposedly shackled respectable white women to pedestals? By working for money, a woman shamed male relations, exposing their powerlessness to support or subdue their social and sexual dependents.[5]

The careers of Jacob Mordecai's daughters call for a more nuanced interpretation of southern women's work. The Mordecai sisters taught for different reasons at different times: out of family duty, financial need, personal ambition, and the desire to escape dependence. Their labor was not always remunerative. Indeed, at times it was not paid at all, which both increased its invisibility and raises questions about the sharp distinction labor historians have typically drawn between women's paid and unpaid work.[6]

Despite the image of women's work shackled by gender and class ideology, the teaching work of the Mordecai sisters was to some degree elastic. They and their family taught differently at different times to suit different conditions. The first part of the essay examines the roles Rachel, Ellen, and Caroline played in their family's business from 1809 until 1818 and their centrality to its success as a for-profit enterprise. Their unpaid work during those years highlights tensions surrounding women's labor in a period when separate-sphere ideology (the proposition that woman's "natural" place was private and nurturing while men's was public and economic) began to crystallize within the elite and middle classes. The second part of the narrative follows each sister's experience after 1820. One never married, and of the two who did, one was widowed early. When they pursued paid teaching posts not mandated by financial need (as their work for the family in Warrenton had been) their father and brothers protested, sometimes angrily. The women found varying ways of explaining their labor to themselves and others. They called up enlightenment concepts of female intellectual ability, the social importance of education to a strong nation, the value of being "useful" to society, and a notion that the Mordecais, as a family, were simply "put here to keep school and born smart on purpose."[7]

. . .

Had Jacob Mordecai succeeded as a country merchant, he would never have embarked upon the family educational venture, and probably his daughters would not have become teachers.[8] Born to Jewish parents in Philadelphia, Jacob migrated south after the Revolution and opened a store. His first wife, whose father was a New York silversmith, died after childbirth in 1796, leaving him with six children under eleven. Jacob sent his three girls to nearby Richmond, Virginia, where maternal aunts and uncles took them in for several years, during which time Jacob married his sister-in-law. She bore seven children over the next two decades. The town's only Jews, the Mordecais did not follow orthodox practice. (Eventually, many of Jacob's offspring intermarried and several converted to Christianity.) Jacob won appointment as justice of the peace for Warren County, a post of some stature, but, in 1805, in a scenario all too common to the nineteenth century, a financial panic threw him deeply into debt. Jacob lost the store and his home to creditors.[9]

Their social and financial status thrown into uncertainty, family members took comfort in intellectual and literary pursuits. The Mordecais considered themselves above the bulk of their neighbors—even the wealthy ones—when it came to things like learning, cultivation, and sensibility. Jacob and his wife had exchanged Goethe's *The Sorrows of Young Werther* during their courtship, and they instilled a love of books and ideas in nearly all their children. Jacob demanded their "perseverance and attention" at school. Studying hard would gratify him, he told them. More important, he said, the knowledge they gained would bring them countless "pleasures" and "advantages." And education did not end with school. Jacob quizzed anyone who finished a book what new things she learned from it. By the time Jacob's affairs went awry, his teenage daughters studied, read, conversed, and corresponded for their own gratification. Such genteel pursuits also offered a soothing distraction from religious difference and rickety financial status.[10]

Meanwhile, Jacob Mordecai's sons, Moses and Samuel, had completed their formal education at Warrenton's male academy and left town for promising apprenticeships in law and business. Rachel, the eldest girl in the family, often wished that she, too, could do "something for my own support."[11] Rachel sewed clothes for the still-growing family and pledged to keep her spirits up for her father's sake. This was the appropriate thing for a daughter to do. But it did not suffice when hard cash was needed.

Only such pressing financial concerns can explain Jacob's request for his daughter Rachel's assistance in a new business venture, a "boarding school for young ladies." Profits could repay his debts and after that be invested and put aside, and Jacob projected that ten years' work would fund a comfortable retirement. Jacob appointed his wife, Rebecca, supervisor of the school's domestic arrangements. Twenty-year-old Rachel would teach. She rejoiced to think she would be not a burden but rather "a blessing" to the father she loved. Rather than "occupying uselessly a space on this planet," she would employ herself by improving the minds of others.[12]

The position had drawbacks—drawbacks arising from resistance (which was hardly exclusive to the South) to public work for elite women. For instance, Rachel shrank from engaging in competition with the other school for girls in Warrenton. Whatever the deficiencies of that institution, threatening its success seemed hard, impolite, and unladylike. (But a husband-and-wife team staffed the school, making Rachel neither the town's first nor its only female teacher.)[13] Rachel understood further that, while female education was gaining support throughout the United States, so-called learned women risked being seen as asexual and unfeminine.[14] In committing to her father's new endeavor, Rachel might postpone, or even forfeit, her chance to marry. The nineteenth-century's high anxiety about spinsterhood manifested itself in Rachel's psyche through a haunting nightmare. She would take her seat in the schoolroom for the first time only to find "her forehead all wrinkled, her hair all grey," her hand paralyzed with rheumatism.[15] Truly, society—including her prosperous Richmond cousins and childhood schoolmates—would consider Rachel's fate unfortunate, since it drew her from the standard life course of privileged women. Rachel had no beau, however, and doubted she ever would. Meanwhile, her family was in need and her earnings would go directly to its support. Teaching did not require her to abandon her home (though it did take her outside the strictly domestic sphere). Most important, in becoming a schoolteacher, she did a daughter's duty by obliging her father's request.

But was she qualified? Rachel's formal schooling consisted of a few years of indifferent instruction at Mr. Hodgson's School for Young Ladies in Richmond.[16] Rachel dreaded to think of the "thousand faults" her pupils would soon detect in her. She labored over lesson plans and turned to her sixteen-year-old brother Solomon, whose schooling far outstripped hers, for "a competent knowledge of Geography and the use of the Globes."[17] But at the end of her first day in the schoolroom, Rachel laughed at her fears, having "found the reality much less terrible than the anticipation."[18]

In fact, Rachel found that she enjoyed being a teacher. School life held a pleasant regularity, and her time, rather than hanging heavily, flew. When her pupils succeeded in impressing the audience at the school's first public examination, she "actually wept for joy."[19] Not only did the future of the school seem secure, Rachel's own labors won general applause. She had pleased her parent and proven herself—two immensely satisfying accomplishments.

When the Mordecai school first opened, Ellen Mordecai's feelings about the family's business were far more mixed than her elder sister's. Applying econometric language similar to Rachel's, Ellen grieved that she had been given no "task," no means of alleviating the "tax" her existence levied on the family.[20] And, though she had nearly the same education as Rachel, Ellen never taught at the academy. Perhaps their father hoped to spare Ellen, or thought she was more likely than Rachel to marry. Rachel once suggested Ellen was too spirited for "scholastic labours." Whatever the reasoning, Ellen felt hurt. She never overcame the sense of being a burden to her family, and it followed her in later years, when she did teach. Nevertheless, Ellen did fill an important role at the school. Her stepmother had charge of the students' nonacademic life: their comportment outside class, cleanliness, meals, and laundry. When Rebecca became pregnant with her fifth child (and Jacob's eleventh) during the school's first year, Ellen assumed these responsibilities. The arrangement became permanent.[21]

With an average of eighty-one boarders per session, no one would claim Ellen did not materially contribute to the academy's success.[22] Indeed, parents of the boarding scholars required assurance that their daughters led comfortable, closely regulated lives at school. Yet supervising the cleaning, laundry, and cooking work of slaves, proctoring mealtimes, and individually inspecting students for proper grooming gave Ellen little joy and did not in an intellectual family confer the respect teaching could—and had for Rachel.

The status attached to teaching depended, however, on the sex of the teacher. At sixteen, Solomon, Jacob's fifth child, graduated from the local boys' academy. Rather than enter college as his father had hoped or apprenticing himself as his older brothers had, Solomon joined the Mordecai school faculty.[23] Steadily increasing enrollment and the family's effort to keep expenses down by not hiring outsiders justified Solomon's move. The Mordecai children's unpaid labor kept overhead low when a suitable teacher would demand three hundred dollars a year, or more.[24]

As it happened, Solomon was needed to stabilize the institution. In addition to taking over most of Jacob's classes, he assumed the accounting work. Laboring together with their father, the Mordecai children had observed his outright "aversion to trade," a quality that did not inspire their confidence. Affection muffled their frustrations, but the children were, in a sense, Jacob's business partners in the academy.[25] Perhaps because he was accustomed as a merchant to extending credit to his customers, Jacob had not required full tuition payment at the time of enrollment and substantial sums went uncollected. Solomon put an end to that.[26] Welcome as his intervention was, the family spoke of Solomon's work as a detour in his path to a suitably genteel career in law, medicine, or business. Schoolteaching paid too poorly for a man to support a family accord-ing to the standards the Mordecais strove to meet, and instructing girls further decreased the work's status.[27]

The inadequacy of schoolteaching as a male pursuit had a profound effect on Jacob's third daughter, Caroline, who began her career at the school as a fourteen-year-old student and later made her "debut in the classroom" teaching history, reading, and parsing in 1817, when Solomon contracted tuberculosis.[28] By that time, Caroline was in love with another male teacher, Achille Plunkett. In 1812, the Mordecais had hired Plunkett, a widowed refugee from the slave uprising in Santo Domingo, to teach French, drawing, painting, music, and dancing, "feminine accomplishments" much in demand as extra-academic of-ferings.[29] More than his Catholic background, his age (more than twenty years Caroline's elder), or his three children, Plunkett's chosen career, with its limited income, rendered him an unacceptable suitor in her family's eyes. The Mor-decais continually tried to get Caroline to drop Plunkett, yet he remained as a teacher and became one of three purchasers of the school in 1818.

For years, the Mordecais had projected the close of what Ellen impatiently called their "sessions of trouble without cessation."[30] By 1818, annual prof-its reached $7,500.[31] Earnings had been tapped from time to time. Jacob's daughters received fabric for new dresses and paid visits to family and friends in nearby cities. Larger withdrawals financed Solomon's recuperative tour of northern spas and another brother's attendance at the United States Military Academy at West Point. Thousands more dollars of the school's earnings went to their merchant brother, Samuel, to be invested. In 1819, Jacob was not only free of his old debts but rich enough to retire from the "anxieties" of business, to purchase slaves, and to move with his wife, daughters, and youngest son to a farm north of Richmond, Virginia.[32] The following year, Solomon departed for medical school in Philadelphia with the understanding that his father would cover his expenses. Samuel, who had been embarrassed by his unmarried sisters' "perpetual labour" and his own inability to see to their "comfort," heaved a sigh of relief.[33] They would sew, ride, enjoy society, correspond, improve them-selves by leisurely reading and study, and make a happy home for their father—avocations befitting their sex and class.

But teaching also formed part of the plan. Well before the school closed, another mode of educational work appeared in the Mordecai household: family teaching. Three years earlier, Rachel had begun privately instructing her five-year-old half-sister, Eliza. When the Mordecais moved to Virginia, Caroline and

Ellen had charge of yet another younger half-sister: six-year-old Emma.[34] Because the history of education has generally been told from an institutional vantage point, with schools at the center, women teachers have appeared almost exclusively in private academies or public school systems. From this angle, Rachel and Caroline Mordecai can be seen pioneering schoolteaching two generations before Catharine Beecher promoted it as the consummate profession for respectable single women. Yet such an angle obscures other educational work. Because family teaching took place in the home and involved no cash transactions, historians interested in feminism and its links to workforce participation have also ignored it. The Mordecai case exposes a practice that may have been both more common and more important to women as teachers and students than historians have thought. As long as middle- and upper-class women's work outside the household was discouraged, home teaching could supply an alternate pedagogical domain.[35]

Home education had its own history in the Mordecai family. While most parents considered teaching young children "too burdensome for the parent and too fatiguing for the child," Jacob's first wife committed herself to her children's mental development. Jacob was proud of Judith and recalled how her early successes with Ellen and Rachel had elicited "the admiration of strangers."[36] His second wife showed no such aptitude or interest, for which her stepchildren often criticized her. Indeed, Rachel and her sisters derived considerable gratification when they taught their younger half-sisters, Eliza and Emma. In a single stroke they followed in their mother's footsteps, pleased their father, and thrust their stepmother (and the little girls' own mother) to the family's margins.

It made sense for other reasons, too. For years, Rachel, Ellen, and Caroline had earned Jacob's praise by contributing to the school's success; home education promised to extend paternal gratitude. Jacob never had to pay tuition for Eliza or Emma—a savings of at least one hundred dollars a year per child.[37] Rachel, Ellen, and Caroline's time and skills not only saved Jacob money in the academy and in the education of his youngest daughters. The teaching materials they developed during the era of the school and later—handwritten textbooks on mythology and geography, hand-copied music lessons, and penmanship samples for emulation—were for years afterward used with siblings, nieces, nephews, and paying students.[38]

Because of its private nature, family teaching did not cast Jacob as a poor provider who pressed his daughters into the labor force. It did not make their brother Samuel feel guilty. Finally, family or home education did not bind the teacher to the routine of school; lessons could halt for short periods or easily shift location. In at least one respect, little had changed from the school days. The elder Mordecai sisters received no payment for their labor.

Family teaching had its pitfalls. Perfectionism was one. Ellen complained that Emma did not reward her efforts, and Eliza distressed Rachel, sometimes to the point of despair. Conflicts between student and teacher that might have dissipated in a school setting often rankled when they involved siblings in a household. The Mordecais had never idealized schoolteaching. It was a job. Home education was a mission of sorts. Perhaps because the labor of family teaching at home was even less connected to the cash economy, it required greater proof of success to be satisfying. Solomon predicted darkly that "retirement" from the school might not bring his sisters the happiness they anticipated. "A governess of four," he warned, might easily have "as much care and anxiety" as "a governess of four score."[39]

The rhythms of farm living and family teaching were still new when Rachel, Ellen, and Caroline learned that their "retirement" stood in jeopardy. A brilliant year of tobacco trading in 1818 led Samuel to think he could make his father not just comfortable but rich. He invested extensively in western lands and tobacco, the value of which evaporated in the panic of 1819. Forced to cut costs, Jacob fired the overseer and began managing the farm work himself. Dumbfounded, Ellen, Caroline, and Rachel watched their "hard earned little store . . . wasting gradually in supporting the negroes and improving the land."[40] Just as they had after their father's bankruptcy fifteen years before, these Mordecai daughters found themselves at the mercy of forces they could not control, dependent on men whose investments they had never been asked to approve. But they were not helpless. In the summer of 1820, Rachel, Ellen, and Caroline decided to apply their skills strategically and do "something for our own profit and comfort."[41]

They would go back to teaching school. The farm should be sold or rented out and the family would move to Richmond, where Rachel, Ellen, and Caroline would open a small female academy. They sounded resigned, but disappointment bred a new determination. In effect, they re-enacted the birth of the school in Warrenton, with the roles reversed. The daughters asked the father to serve as the school's principal, but only in order to avoid indelicately exposing themselves to the public. No duties and no authority came with Jacob's post.[42] Even more striking, under the 1820 plan, the profits, rather than going into a family pool to support the farm, to repay Samuel's debts, or to cover Solomon's tuition, would be "independently ours, Rachel's, Caroline's, and mine." The women would save or spend the money as they saw fit. For the first time they disentangled their educational labor from female duty and male prerogative—and the protections it supposedly offered. Though they were women and lived under their father's roof, they would not work for free.[43] The plan won Jacob's regretful approval. It never went into effect, however, for within a year, Rachel and Caroline left home to marry.

. . .

Rachel had already once rejected a proposal of marriage from Aaron Lazarus, a widower with seven children, but she reconsidered it in the summer of 1820 as she and her sisters contemplated opening another school. Aaron Lazarus was not "the man [her] youthful fancy would have portrayed as the arbiter of [her] destiny": he was not learned, but plain, solid, acceptable.[44] Interestingly, a significant factor in Rachel's decision to marry was her vision of the ideal teaching life. As an avid follower (and correspondent) of the Irish novelist and educational theorist Maria Edgeworth, Rachel believed true education to be very different from the schoolroom instruction she had imparted in Warrenton. Edgeworth cautioned that institutional education introduced children to bad habits, enforced discipline inconsistently, and rewarded rote learning over understanding. Thus, when speaking of "Education," with a capital "E," Rachel did not mean school. Rather she confined her "thoughts to our own family, perhaps I ought to say to one member of it, my little Eliza."[45] Because of her intellectual aspirations regarding domestic teaching, starting another school held little real interest for Rachel, no matter the compensation. A stable home supported by Aaron Lazarus's mercantile business came nearer to her ideal setting. There, Rachel felt she could focus on the home-based instruction she valued so highly. The couple wed in March 1821, and Rachel moved to Aaron's Wilmington, North Carolina, home, taking Eliza along in order to complete her education. She never again taught in a classroom.

As a sister, stepmother, and later mother, Rachel attempted what she understood to be her most important teaching. A log of her work with Eliza ran to over two hundred pages in two volumes.[46] Rachel also took responsibility for teaching several of her Lazarus stepdaughters. The realities of teaching her own children did not, however, match her expectations, which seemed to rise in proportion to the nearness of the relationship. While her siblings predicted that Rachel's first child, Marx, would "be one of the best managed children of the age," Rachel found "the task" of teaching him "as difficult . . . as if I were a complete novice."[47]

Isolation and lack of control over reproduction also severely undermined the teaching Rachel undertook in Wilmington. Aaron supported but did not enter into his wife's pedagogical ideals and would have been satisfied to send his children to schools. At times, family teaching at Spring Farm had been challenging, but at least Rachel had Ellen or Caroline at hand to supply solace or advice. In Wilmington, Rachel found almost no one to share her sense of mission as a teacher, even though advice manuals increasingly harped on mothers' instructional duties. Meanwhile, Rachel's sense of inadequacy to the task of teaching her own children mounted with each successive pregnancy. She complained that her intellect was shriveling from exhaustion and neglect. Ten years into marriage, Rachel was forty-three, the mother of four. Her youngest was under a year old. She "pray[ed] to have no more children. I may possibly be able to do those I have some degree of justice, but . . . the care and solicitude and fatigue inseparable from [their] nurture and education" was too much for her to contemplate ever embarking anew on such a labor.[48]

Motherhood forced Rachel to reconsider the pronouncements Maria Edgeworth (who never married) leveled against schools; Rachel came to feel "that the good and evil may be said to be nearly balanced."[49] Eventually, all her children would attend lessons in a classroom setting, and son Marx would be placed at a boarding school. In 1835, Rachel opposed the commands of her husband and father and privately embraced Christianity. At that point, her strong desire to educate her children rightly became a torture. If she taught them the thing she most deeply believed they should know—that Jesus was the messiah—Aaron threatened to remove them from her care.[50] This stress, among others, wore on Rachel, and in 1838 she died at the age of fifty, leaving young daughters still to be educated.

In Warrenton, Rachel had found success as a schoolteacher. But she sought to be a teaching sister and mother in the Edgeworth mold. She was knowledgeable and reflective about education and always ready to advise Mordecai siblings in both school- and home-based teaching methods. Marriage looked more attractive than school life and spinsterhood for this gifted and committed educator who saw in family life itself a challenging teaching space. But her ideals remained out of reach. The demands of managing a household (including stepchildren and slaves), separation from like minds, unwanted pregnancies, and a tearing religious crisis all sapped Rachel's energies and her time. Rachel's story highlights the ambitions and realities that could attach to motherhood and teaching in the early nineteenth century and points to another interpretation for the lives of teachers who "left" to marry: many may never really have left their educating work at all.

. . .

Perhaps in part because of her sense of being overlooked as a teacher at the Mordecai school and her relegation to less creative work counting linens and supervising meals, Ellen never relished teaching. Indeed, Ellen would repeat her mode of life at the Mordecai school through her long career, working very hard but never really finding the status or fascination it provided her sisters. Within the family she taught as a spinster sister and aunt out of obligation; beyond the family, Ellen taught almost exclusively for money, which, again as a single woman, she saw as almost her only security against a dependent old age.[51]

Whereas Rachel entered into the work of educating her half-sister Eliza with energy and dedication, Ellen was less than enthusiastic about playing the same role in young Emma Mordecai's upbringing. In 1822, Ellen reluctantly turned down a teaching post paying $800 a year because her father wanted her to remain at home.[52] She conceded that sometimes it was "very gratifying to be so useful to" Emma and "so much beloved" for it. But more often the work felt thankless, burdensome, and unfairly imposed.[53] Ellen occasionally vented against Emma, as when she observed that teaching "might be the amusement of some of my hours, the interesting duty of my life," though not with "so thoughtless and inattentive a child."[54] Stepmother Rebecca became the real focus of Ellen's anger. In her journal, Ellen sharply criticized Rebecca for being a mere reproducer: "[N]either the mistress of her house, the mother of her children, nor the companion of her husband—helpless in the extreme she does nothing for herself nor for her children but bring them into the world."[55]

Not surprisingly, Rebecca sometimes resented her stepdaughters' child-rearing assistance. She did not like Rachel keeping Eliza in Wilmington for three full years. She also complained when eleven-year-old Emma accompanied Ellen to Warrenton to tend Caroline (then pregnant, widowed, and keeping school). Ellen retorted sarcastically that Emma received "regular instruction" in Warrenton, and were it not for Caroline's immediate needs, Ellen would dedicate her entire time "to the improvement of my younger sisters." "Far be it from me my dear girl to wish or expect that your life should be" thus "devoted," Rebecca replied tartly, reminding her stepdaughter that hers was a "voluntary task."[56] Within weeks of this exchange, Jacob took his wife's side and ordered thirty-three-year-old Ellen home from Warrenton, perhaps effectively deciding the question of whether her teaching was, in his family, a "duty" or a "voluntary task."[57]

Ellen believed only time would release her from this obligation. If she lived long enough to "make Emma an amiable, useful, and well-informed woman," Ellen planned to "sit down with an easy conscience and with the retrospection of a useful life to cheer my future days."[58] She found, though, that her family and her own goals would require her to teach long past Emma's needs. In 1827, just as Emma had grown independent of Ellen's supervision, the family's fortunes again grew precarious. Ellen and her eldest half-sister, Julia, proposed opening a school at Spring Farm. Two thousand dollars would be allotted to "the support of the family," while the sisters would divide any further proceeds. It was hardly the angry declaration of independence of the summer of 1820, when Ellen thought all income should go to the teachers, but she felt confident that the school could "be a good little income for us."[59]

In this and the rest of Ellen's teaching ventures, there is little mention of her enjoying teaching; indeed she felt unsuited "to the task of a country schoolmistress." Ellen considered herself "by nature fitted for a different station"—marriage. Such happiness was not to be, however, and teaching, "after a youth of toil is destined to be my walk in life."[60] In fact, Ellen did teach for many more years, in a variety of settings. Several nieces and nephews would fall under her care in the 1830s. In 1843, she tried working as a governess in New York, but the boys in her charge were disagreeable and she soon returned to Virginia. In 1845, she was instructing female convicts in Richmond with a charity organization. The next year, against her brothers' advice, she considered an offer to teach in a girl's school in New Orleans, but the plan collapsed. Soon, she was back in the New York area as a governess, this time in a better situation, where she stayed for nearly two years. In 1851, Ellen, then a woman of sixty, taught at Mrs. Hackley's school in Richmond.

In all her paid teaching positions, Ellen made calculations about the duration necessary to obtain the sum she sought, with a restful future always in view: "I am working for $1000," she informed a brother in 1848. The hire of her slave, Jenny, along with teaching, would allow her to reach that mark, she thought, "in two or three years." Then she went on in her best spinster humor that "after I have seen Niagara Falls I will go home and sit down and visit you all and eat mush to my satisfaction."[61] Wary of underselling her labor, Ellen more than once decided against helping sister Caroline in her school because the money was insufficient; later, when one of her New York students moved, she consulted her brother about whether her compensation should be adjusted. Even a position at a religious school (Ellen, too, converted to Christianity) was considered primarily for its financial opportunity. "Mine is not a missionary inclination," she wrote of her motivations.[62]

Throughout her life, Ellen taught not by desire (as Rachel largely had) but by resignation to "destiny"; because her family needed money and could command her labor; and because she wanted somehow to earn her hoped-for respite— "that I may sit down with an easy conscience." Ellen might have rested from her labors earlier, but she shrank from living anywhere without paying her portion of expenses and only reluctantly accepted gifts of money from her prosperous brother, George.[63] Both Ellen and her younger sister, Caroline, were profoundly fearful of economic dependency, scarred, perhaps, by their early experiences of their father's bankruptcy. Rachel, more mature when Jacob fell into debt, bounced back more easily, and had even assumed with her teaching duties a direct role in helping the family escape the threat of poverty. Ellen and Caroline never forgot the feeling of insecurity and powerlessness that seized them. In the 1840s and 1850s, Ellen also tried her hand at an alternate career—writing—but without success and returned to the schoolroom.[64] "If I could afford to live without it," she confessed to Caroline of teaching, "I never should do it for pleasure nor goodness."[65]

. . .

Like Rachel, Caroline wed and started a family in the early 1820s. Like Ellen, she would spend most of her life alone and teaching. And, like many late-twentieth-century professional women of her class, Caroline elected to combine paid work with motherhood. Caroline's career in teaching was more public, more independent, and somehow both sadder and more joyful than those of her sisters. Widowed young, Caroline had burdens and choices her sisters never faced. That she lost all her children in their infancy made Caroline's lifelong involvement with other peoples' children all the more poignant.

Caroline moved to Spring Farm with the rest of the family in 1818, while Achille Plunkett remained in Warrenton as part owner of the former Mordecai school. She was included in the sisters' plan to open their own institution in Richmond, but the unexpected happened: Caroline's lovelorn misery and Plunkett's repeated proposals eventually wore on Jacob, who at last consented to their quiet marriage in 1820. (Caroline's only regret was leaving Emma, whose tutelage she shared with Ellen.)[66] Within the year, the Plunketts became sole proprietors of the school in Warrenton. Again, Caroline was engaged as a teacher in a family enterprise. "[N]ow you must not say or even think *poor C* once," she commanded her sisters, "but rather happy C who truly feels herself so in . . . being able to assist her beloved husband and family."[67]

Caroline did seem happy, though at times exhausted and struggling. Two sons were born, through which, to the dismay of many, she kept up her school duties. If marriage did not always disqualify a genteel woman from work outside the home, motherhood assuredly did, and in later years school systems enforced policies prohibiting married women from teaching in public schools.[68] But Caroline pressed on cheerfully. While "sitting in the school room I often think what a delight awaits me in the house, the sweet child," she told Ellen. Rachel considered the arrangement very bad, indeed. "I sometimes wonder how you can attend to your daily duties without neglecting dear little Frank," Rachel chided. Her own firstborn "engrosses every moment I can spare," and Rachel had no classes to teach. As Caroline's second pregnancy advanced, she appealed to Ellen to relieve her by teaching in Warrenton. "I . . . fear everything should not go on as it ought and when I will have another child to attend to either" the baby or the school "must be neglected."[69]

Then, in 1823, a shattering year began for Caroline: both her sons fell ill and died suddenly. In January 1824, Achille also died, leaving Caroline pregnant, grieving, and in debt. A year later, her last-born perished, as well. Writing to Ellen, Rachel blamed Caroline's "pains" in part on her work—and on the marriage that made teaching necessary. "[M]ight not maternal care and prudence (had circumstances permitted their exertion) have preserved our sister's little Frank from the illness that deprived [his parents] of their darling?"[70]

Though it upset her family, Caroline taught through these repeated bereavements—and for years afterward. When Achille died, the family begged her to give up the school and preserve her own health. She had best, they said, return to her father's home. Or she could go to Raleigh to teach her brother Moses's three orphans at the home of their aunts. Brother George Mordecai could not understand Caroline's apparent determination "to continue a slave during the rest of her days," yet still she taught and kept school: to pay off debts, to distract herself from grief, to remain independent, and, initially, to stay in Warrenton where her loved ones lay buried. "I cannot leave this spot," she would repeat when any move was suggested.[71]

At times, she wished for her sisters to join her and share the responsibilities, citing her "awful situation" as "a lone female . . . before the public." But at other times, she seemed almost giddy with satisfaction. To avoid hiring a paid assistant, she studied arithmetic and sciences and taught the subjects herself. Four years after her husband's death, Caroline was "out of debt . . . and out of danger" and approached the coming term "with a heart as light as my purse." Caroline eventually found her Warrenton school unprofitable and left there in 1831.[72]

She did not, however, leave teaching. She spent a year in Raleigh, tutoring her niece and nephews at their home. Caroline had been educating the children of Moses Mordecai in Warrenton for six years by that time, and she was strongly attached to her charges. Yet Caroline, like Ellen, found family teaching frustrating. She especially resented having to share control of the children she was expected to educate so intensively. Living with the children's aunts in Raleigh was unbearable, in part because they made her feel her economic "dependence," which was "more shocking to me than the hardest day's work," and in part because the aunts pointedly asserted their authority over the children's lives. Caroline was crushed that they refused to let her take her pupils along when she decided to open a school in Wilmington. She never again taught relatives in a home setting, perhaps because she could not bear another emotionally difficult attachment to someone else's children.[73]

Caroline's commitment to teaching in schools, however, remained unflagging long after her financial state had ceased to require it. Caroline's insistence on putting her own name in the newspaper advertisement for her school made Rachel shudder. She considered it "unpleasant publicity."[74] "Mrs. Plunkett's School for Young Ladies" in Wilmington thrived. Restless, Caroline left for the Tennessee frontier in 1833.[75] There she helped several Mordecai alumnae run schools in LaGrange and Brownsville. Despite "the roughness of the country," Caroline enjoyed her work, and the academies flourished.[76] In 1837, she relocated to Mobile, Alabama, where she remained for many years. Caroline lived alone, even though brother Solomon (who practiced medicine in Mobile) offered to house her. She maintained a small school to amuse herself and feel useful—always against the pleas of family urging a more proper and retiring life. But, as she said, "few things interest me more than the remarks of children."[77] At age sixty she reported taking "great delight" in the "improvement" of "four pretty nice little girls." That her pupils might improve and, as they said, "love me dearly," seem in Caroline's writings to have been all the reward necessary for her teaching in later years.[78] Indeed, in 1854 she said she felt "something like degradation" when collecting tuition money, a statement that brought her full circle to the impropriety of paid work with which the Mordecai women had contended since 1809.

But lest this endpoint imply too saintly an image, Caroline's whole career in teaching reveals that, while she did love children and enjoyed instructing them, she also sought them as a refuge from a life of pain and tragedy, and from the "shocking" possibility of dependence on her family. More specifically, school-keeping kept children in her life without exacting the emotional toll of family teaching. In meeting her own needs, Caroline exasperated her siblings; eccentric was one of the kinder terms they found to describe her choices.

· · ·

Not exactly ladies and clearly not slaves, Rachel Mordecai Lazarus, Ellen Mordecai, and Caroline Mordecai Plunkett aspired to and in most ways achieved social respectability as teaching women in the Old South. Their introduction to educational labor occurred because of a patriarch's pressing needs in a disintegrating household economy. Jacob Mordecai discovered that Rachel, Ellen, and Caroline, along with his son, Solomon, were extraordinary economic assets, and, however regretfully, he employed them to great benefit. As young women, the sisters worked at the Mordecai school in Warrenton out of duty toward and affection for their father. They succeeded in helping Jacob reclaim his pride, repay his creditors, and (so they all thought) assure his financial security—as well as their own while they remained in his household. During the decade the Mordecais operated their school, Rachel, Ellen, and Caroline performed labor that was not, in a pure sense, "public." Indeed, in that they worked under the direction of their father, side by side with other family members, without salaries, and in a setting that integrated home and business, the academy offered a hybrid space between the developing market and the fading household economy. In gratifying Jacob's wishes, each of his daughters, through educational work, developed strategies to gain security, focus individual identity, and pursue ambition.

The school operated during a period when teaching was just being advanced as an acceptable vocation for middle-class women. Jacob and his elder sons regretted that Rachel, Ellen, and Caroline performed labor that boosted the family's cash income. To what degree their regret reflected their generic patriarchal disapproval, a particular regional proscription, or their sensitivity as religious outsiders to inviting public notice is not yet clear. The unspoken assumption, however, was always that the women's "school work" was a temporary necessity to be performed seriously and with dignity. Still, the lesson that female educational labor had significant monetary value could not be unlearned.

But that was rarely its only value. For Rachel, whose role as head teacher in Warrenton brought her public recognition, teaching allowed her both to prove her devotion to her father and to exercise her intellect. She did not mind trespassing into "male" territory, such as provisioning, hiring, expanding, and recruiting for the school.[79] But her vision of domestic life enlightened and intellectualized by study and family teaching called for a retreat from the public realm. Home and marriage, Rachel felt, offered more potential for true self. Because she married a man with the means to support her—and because he survived, Rachel could follow this dream. It is not coincidental that the men in her life applauded her education of Eliza and of the children she had with Aaron Lazarus. Family teaching avoided contact with the market and did not directly challenge Rachel's economic dependence on the men she loved. The most idealistic of the sisters when it came to the purpose of education and pedagogical practice, Rachel nevertheless followed the most traditional path.

Ellen and Caroline, on the other hand, grated against this dependency. The school in Warrenton proved that teaching could pay (even though it did not pay them), and in later years when family members protested that they did not need to earn an income and should not live or work away from home, Caroline and Ellen violated social norms by making their own decisions in such matters. Doing so in North Carolina, Virginia, Tennessee, and Alabama may have provoked more criticism than it would have in the North. But patriarchal rhetoric cannot be fairly assessed without assessing its effects upon those at whom it was directed. And Ellen and Caroline soldiered on. They found friends, remained in close contact with their family, yet lived independently. Like teachers from other parts of the country, Ellen and Caroline found vastly different rewards from their work. And, like leading female women educators such as Emma Willard and Catharine Beecher, they explicitly rejected women's political equality as articulated by Margaret Fuller or Elizabeth Cady Stanton. If Rachel justified her teaching in idealistic and philosophical terms, Ellen and Caroline found other explanations for their work. They excused their continual recurrence to the classroom as a force beyond their control. Ellen, who felt unable to rest unless her ease were paid for out of her own pocket, considered teaching her own unfortunate "walk in life." The success of the family's educational enterprise in Warrenton and the number of Mordecais who engaged in teaching over the years made it possible for Caroline to think of educating as a family trait. This trait might not have been pleasant—she called it a "disease" and "the Mordecai bite"—yet, she seemed to say, "so it is, don't blame me."[80]

Whatever the justifications, these three southern women spent much of their lifetimes teaching in schools and in homes, with and without pay. Indeed, this essay strongly suggests the need for a broader conception of education that includes other, often unpaid, pedagogical work like family teaching and home education. The sisters labored in all stages of life, as daughters, sisters, mothers, spinsters, wives, and widows. Their values (which included deference to their father, hard work and high standards, willingness to sacrifice for their family and dedication to its success, self-improvement, and independence) also hint at the ways in which middle-class ideology bled across the Mason-Dixon line. True, some planters and their wives scorned teachers as too "learned" (and therefore too base) to be ladies—and linked such women's work to bondage. A Mordecai brother who married into the planting elite considered Caroline's schoolteaching a sort of self-enslavement, and Ellen pretended to adopt a slave dialect when writing to him from her governess post in the North.[81] The siblings remained close, in spite of such tensions. Moreover, planters throughout the antebellum period wanted respectable teachers for their daughters and sent them to schools like the Mordecais's academy.

Not all women who taught suffered from "guilt and self-consciousness," as historians who describe a hegemonic planter aristocracy have suggested.[82] It seems worth considering whether some southern women who taught found a certain status in a culture where literacy formed an important line demarcating black from white, "savage" from "civilized." An early historian of education in Richmond detected a degree of "condescension" toward teachers, but she also concluded that "the teacher of mental ability, of high character, of attractive personality, was not only esteemed in Richmond, he—or it might be she—was even revered."[83] As the history of gender, work, and region gains depth and nuance, it will be easier to determine how common or rare the Mordecai women's educating labor really was. It will be possible to judge the "status" of largely invisible female teachers in the South—those who taught in schools and those who taught in domestic settings—and determine the flexibility of their work, the way it changed over time, and how it differed from that of women who taught in other regions.

## NOTES

1. Sale, Rachel Mordecai (later Lazarus) (RML) and Solomon Mordecai (Sol) to Samuel Mordecai (SM), 5 August 1818, Pattie Mordecai Papers (PMP), North Carolina Division of Archives and History (NCDAH), Raleigh; Enrollment, fig. 3.4 in Penny Leigh Richards, "'A Thousand Images, Painfully Pleasing': Complicating Histories of the Mordecai School, Warrenton, North Carolina, 1809–1818" (Ph.D. diss., University of North Carolina at Chapel Hill, 1996). This essay draws from Richards and from Emily Simms Bingham, "Mordecai: Three Generations of a Southern Jewish Family, 1780–1865" (Ph.D. diss., University of North Carolina at Chapel Hill, 1998).

2. Christie Anne Farnham, *The Education of the Southern Belle: Higher Education and Student Socialization in the Antebellum South* (New York: New York University Press, 1994); Steven Stowe, "The Not-So-Cloistered Academy: Elite Women's Education and Family Feeling in the Old South," in *The Web of Southern Social Relations: Women, Family, and Education*, ed. Walter J. Fraser Jr., R. Frank Saunders Jr., and Jon Wakelyn (Athens: University of Georgia Press, 1985).

3. Quantitative data is lacking, but historians suggest that most of the Old South's female teachers were not really "southern" in that they were not native to the region (Farnham, *Education of the Southern Belle*, 97). Indeed, many women from Emma Willard's academy came southward—and many remained there. Dolly Lunt Burge grew up in the North but taught, got married, and taught some more in the South. A Kentucky native, Julia Ann Tevis established the state's best-known antebellum girl's school, Science Hill. See Christine Jacobson Carter, ed., *The Diary of Dolly Lunt Burge, 1848–1879* (Athens: University of Georgia Press, 1997), and Julia A. Tevis, *Sixty Years in a School-Room: An Autobiography of Mrs. Julia A. Tevis, Principal of Science Hill Female Academy* (Cincinnati: Western Methodist Book Concern, 1878). Possibly, there were more southern women teaching than historians have thought. If not, the experience of the Mordecais may shed light on why more southern women did not fill the teaching posts in the growing number of academies throughout the region.

4. John L. Rury, "Who Became Teachers: The Social Characteristics of Teachers in American History," in *American Teachers: Histories of a Profession at Work*, ed. Donald Warren (New York: Macmillan, 1989), 17.

5. This patriarchal ideology is expressed in Victoria Bynum, *Unruly Women: The Politics of Social and Sexual Control in the Old South* (Chapel Hill: University of North Carolina Press, 1992), 6–7, 161 n. 19. The incongruity between teaching and the ideal of the southern lady is repeated throughout the literature. See, for example, Barbara M. Solomon, *In the Company of Educated Women: A History of Women in Higher Education in America* (Boston: Houghton-Mifflin, 1979), 21; Anne Firor Scott, *The Southern Lady: From Pedestal to Politics, 1830–1930* (Chicago: University of Chicago Press, 1970); Bertram Wyatt-Brown, *Southern Honor: Ethics and Behavior in the Old South* (New York: Oxford University Press, 1982), 228–29, 238–39; Farnham, *Education of the Southern Belle*, 32; and Elizabeth Fox-Genovese, *Within the Plantation Household: Black and White Women of the Old South* (Chapel Hill: University of North Carolina Press, 1988), 46, 404 n. 16.

6. Jeanne Boydston's *Home and Work: Housework, Wages, and the Ideology of Labor in the Early Republic* (New York: Oxford University Press, 1990) examines how women's social status has been damaged by the gendered division between paid and unpaid work.

7. Eliza K. Mordecai Myers to Caroline Mordecai Plunkett (CMP), 11 January 1828, Jacob Mordecai Papers (JMP), Duke University Rare Books, Manuscripts, and Special Collections Library, Durham, N.C.

8. It was not, however, uncommon for women to turn to teaching when a family hit hard times. Emma Willard opened her first school following her husband's "political and financial reverses" (Solomon, *In the Company of Educated Women*, 18).

9. "Unpleasant," RML, Memories, Myers Family Papers (MYFP), Virginia Historical

Society, Richmond, Va. The Mordecais had hired slaves to work as domestic servants since coming to the South, but there is no record of their owning slaves in Warrenton until after the school was established.

10. Goethe, Judith Myers to Jacob Mordecai (JM), 11 March 1784, Little-Mordecai Collection (LMC), NCDAH; love of books, JM to Moses et al., 20 July 1796, MYFP; "perseverance" and "pleasures," JM to RML and Ellen Mordecai (EM), 10 December 1796, JMP, quoted in Sussman, "Our Little World: The Early Years at Warrenton," paper submitted to Dr. Jacob Rader Marcus, n.d., American Jewish Archives, Hebrew Union College, Cincinnati, Ohio; Jacob's quizzes, [EM], "Past Days, A Simply Story for Children" (1840–41), 82–83, MYFP. During this period, family correspondence became a marker of an expanding American middle-class culture. See Konstantin Dierks, "Letter Writing and the Diffusion of Family Responsibility in America, 1750–1800" (Ph.D. dissertation in process, Brown University, 2002).

11. "Support," RML, Memories, MYFP.

12. "School," RML to SM, 13 July 1808, JMP; "blessing," [EM], "Past Days," 52, MYFP; "occupying," SM to RML, 4 May 1809, Mordecai Family Papers (MFP), Southern Historical Collection, University of North Carolina, Chapel Hill (SHC). See also advertisement for "Female Education in Warrenton," dated 18 August 1808, MFP, SHC.

13. "I am constantly told we owe something to ourselves," Rachel told a brother, "and cannot be expected to sacrifice our own good from delicacy" (RML to SM, 13 July 1808, JMP). On the Falkener school, see Lizzie Wilson Montgomery, *Sketches of Old Warrenton* (Raleigh: Edwards and Broughton, 1924), 129–31, and Farnham, *Education of the Southern Belle*, 41–42.

14. The sense of tension between learning and femininity is apparent in RML to SM, 27 February 1814, PMP; RML to Moses Mordecai, 4 October 1817, MFP, SHC; and EM to Sol, 12 February 1818, JMP. In the 1850s, women teachers were advised not to teach longer than three or four years, as their independence threatened to render them "repugnant" to men. See Geraldine Joncich Clifford, "Man/Woman/Teacher: Gender, Family, and Career in American Education History," in Warren, ed., *American Teachers*, 325–26.

15. [EM], "Past Days," 77, MYFP.

16. Rachel noted how far education had come since her days as a pupil in RML to EM, 5 January 1823, MFP, SHC.

17. "Thousand" and "geography," RML, Memories, MYFP.

18. RML to SM, 1 January 1809, MFP, SHC.

19. RML, Memories, MYFP. The examinations the Mordecais held and teachers' ecstatic relief upon their completion were typical of nineteenth-century education. See Sari Knopp Biklen, *School Work: Gender and the Cultural Construction of Teaching* (New York: Teacher's College Press, 1995), 66–67.

20. EM to SM, 12 September 1808, MFP, SHC.

21. RML, Memories, MYFP. Ellen, Rachel claimed, could not confine "her attention where nothing agreeable called for it" ("scholastic labours," EM journal entry, 1 October 1815, PMP).

22. Mordecai school register, LMC, NCDAH. For the ratio of boarders to day students, see Richards, "Thousand Images," 46, fig. 3.5.

23. Jacob dreamed of sending Solomon to Princeton, but the family could not afford tuition. See RML to SM, 28 May and 5 July 1809, MFP, SHC.

24. Hiring, SM to RML, 30 December 1810, MFP, SHC. On salary see RML to SM, 11 February 1810, PMP.

25. RML, Memories, MYFP; "aversion," JM to Sol, 28 November 1817, JMP.

26. Lax business practices, SM to RML, 30 December 1810, MFP, SHC. For Solomon's efforts to collect overdue tuition, see RML to SM, 8 December 1811, ibid. Jacob retained the role of head of school. He presided at ceremonies, oversaw provisioning, upkeep, and construction projects, and communicated with parents. See Richards, "Thousand Images," 95–105.

27. On men's experience of teaching in the nineteenth century, see Clifford, "Man/Woman/Teacher," 319, 324; Barry H. Bergen, "Only a Schoolmaster: Gender, Class, and the Effort to Professionalize Elementary Teaching in England, 1870–1910," *History of Education Quarterly* 22 (Spring 1982): 1–21; Jackie Blount, "Spinsters, Bachelors, and Other Gender Transgressors in School Employment, 1850–1990," *Review of Educational Research* 70 (Spring 2000): 83–101; and Farnham, *Education of a Southern Belle*, 110.

28. "Debut," CMP to [?], 7 July 1817, JMP. Caroline's pre-1817 contributions to the school are referred to in family correspondence, though their nature is not explicit. See RML to CMP, 11 February 1811, JMP; RML and Sol to EM, 20 March 1814, and SM to RML, 7 March 1815, MFP, SHC.

29. On ornamental subjects, see Farnham, *Education of the Southern Belle*, 33–40.

30. EM to SM, 25 June 1815, MFP, SHC.

31. SM to RML, 29 March 1818, JMP.

32. SM to JM, 17 February 1815, JMP. Slaves, RML to SM, 20 January 1817, JMP.

33. "Perpetual," SM to [?], 7 March 1815, MFP, SHC; "comfort," SM to JM, 9 March 1815, ibid. For Samuel's resistance to his sisters' work, see EM journal entry, 31 July 1820, ibid.

34. Rachel's journal of her education of Eliza has been published in annotated form by Jean E. Friedman, *Ways of Wisdom: Moral Education in the Early National Period, Including the Diary of Rachel Mordecai Lazarus* (Athens: University of Georgia Press, 2001), 155–240. An earlier version of Friedman's interpretation of Rachel's teaching can be found in "The Politics of Pedagogy and Judaism," in Christie Ann Farnham, ed. *Women of the American South: A Multicultural Reader* (New York: New York University Press, 1997). Also see Emily Bingham, " 'Not Just as I Endeavored to *Make Her*': Experiencing Home Education in a Southern Family, 1815–1825," paper delivered at the Fourth Southern Conference on Women's History, Charleston, S.C., 1997.

35. Alison Prentice and Marjorie R. Theobald point to the invisibility of women who taught "in domestic settings" in "The Historiography of Women Teachers: A Retrospect," in *Women Who Taught: Perspectives on the History of Women and Teaching* (Toronto: University of

Toronto Press, 1991), 8–9. On Beecher's campaign see Kathryn Kish Sklar, *Catharine Beecher: A Study in American Domesticity* (New Haven: Yale University Press, 1973), 168–83.

36. For "burdensome" and "admiration" and more on Judith Myers Mordecai's home teaching, see JM to Moses et al., 20 July 1796, MYFP.

37. In 1809, the Mordecais charged $105 for annual tuition and board, not including music or other ornamental instruction. Female academies in Richmond cost that much or more; see Margaret Meagher, *History of Education in Richmond* (Richmond: n.p., 1939), 16–17.

38. Mythology text (in Ellen Mordecai's hand), manuscript music text, and principal place book, LMC, NCDAH. The "principal place book" composed by Rachel was mentioned as still being used by paying pupils some twenty years after Rachel used it to instruct her son Marx (EM to Ellen Mordecai II, 2 May 1848, MFP, SHC). Penmanship samples, strips of paper on which geography phrases were written in large, careful handwriting, can be found also in LMC, NCDAH.

39. Solomon and RML to SM, 28 June 1818, JMP. Solomon was thinking of the strain on the teachers, but evidence suggests that learning at home presented difficulties for the students, as well. No classmates winced sympathetically when Rachel reproved Eliza. Eliza dared not complain to her parents about her teacher (her own sister) as paying students might. On the final day of her lessons, Eliza betrayed no particular emotion. "I said nothing," Rachel reported, although she was deeply hurt. To withhold affection was perhaps the only weapon Eliza wielded in a relationship that was far more freighted than that between most students and their instructors (RML to EM, 29 February 1824, MFP, SHC).

40. EM journal entry, 6 May 1820, MFP, SHC. On Samuel's gains, debts, and losses, see George Mordecai (GM) to SM, 15 November 1818; SM to Sol, 8 June 1820; SM account with JM, 1 October 1819; and RML to Sol, 11 January 1821, all JMP.

41. EM journal entry, 6 May 1820, MFP, SHC.

42. On the role of male principals in female schools, see Farnham, *Education of the Southern Belle*, 107, 98–99.

43. EM journal entries, 6 May and 31 July 1820, MFP, SHC; for the plan to sell the farm, see SM to Sol, 16 August 1820, JMP. In 1861, another Jewish father was deeply embarrassed to invade his middle-class daughter's wages—a sign, perhaps, of women's advancement in relation to public work. See Elliot Ashkenazi, ed., *The Civil War Diary of Clara Solomon: Growing Up in New Orleans, 1861–1862* (Baton Rouge: Louisiana State University Press, 1995), 58–59, 164.

44. RML to Sol, 23 August 1820, JMP.

45. RML to SM, 25 February 1816, MFP, SHC. See Edgar E. MacDonald, ed., *The Education of the Heart: The Correspondence of Rachel Mordecai Lazarus and Maria Edgeworth* (Chapel Hill: University of North Carolina Press, 1977). The central Edgeworthian educational text is Maria Edgeworth and Richard Lovell Edgeworth, *Practical Education* (1798), the themes of which Maria expanded in popular writings for children. See essays by Mitzi Myers: for instance, " 'Anecdotes from the Nursery' in Maria Edgeworth's *Practical Educa-*

*tion* (1798): Learning from Children 'Abroad and at Home,'" *Princeton University Library Chronicle* 60 (Winter 1999): 220–50, and "Romancing the Moral Tale: Maria Edgeworth and the Problematics of Pedagogy," in *Romanticism and Children's Literature in Nineteenth-Century England*, ed. James Holt McGavran Jr. (Athens: University of Georgia Press, 1991).

46. Rachel's journal of Eliza's education, Virginia Historical Society, Richmond.

47. "Best," Julia Mordecai to GM, 4 August 1823, LMC, NCDAH; "task," RML to EM, 2 April 1826, MFP, SHC.

48. RML to EM, 2 August 1831, ibid.

49. RML to CMP, 12 May 1828, JMP.

50. EM to Sol and CMP, 3 July 1838, MFP, SHC.

51. Monetary motivations were hardly unusual, despite nineteenth-century paeans to women's innate capacity for nurture (Lee Chambers-Schiller, *Liberty, a Better Husband: Single Women in America: The Generations of 1780–1840* [New Haven: Yale University Press, 1984], 140–41).

52. Caroline and her husband owned the Mordecai school and pled with Ellen to join the teaching staff (CMP to EM, 18 November 1822, and EM to CMP, 30 November 1822, JMP).

53. EM to RML, 5 November 1819, JMP.

54. EM to Sol, 16 April 1824, JMP.

55. EM journal entry, 1 April 1819, MFP, SHC.

56. EM to Rebecca Mordecai, 22 February 1824, and Rebecca Mordecai to EM, 7 March 1824, ibid.

57. JM to EM, 13 March 1824, ibid.

58. EM to SM, 20 December 1823, JMP.

59. EM to Sol, 8 November 1827, JMP.

60. EM to CMP, 31 March 1828, JMP. Ellen turned down one suitor and harbored a lifelong passion for her brother, Solomon. She also had severe doubts about marriage. Writing to Rachel, who was exhausted with her duties and teaching, Ellen expressed her hope that her sister's infant girl would be her "last pupil and that you may live to see her grown—shall I add and married too? I believe not for matrimony can be a monstrous hobble" (EM to RML, 19 August 1831, JMP). Also see EM to CMP, 18 July 1832, JMP.

61. EM to GM, 20 November 1848, MFP, SHC.

62. Helping Caroline, EM to CMP, 14 November 1822, JMP; student moves, EM to GM, 29 January 1849, George Washington Mordecai Papers (GMP), SHC; "missionary," EM to GM, 9 December 1845, ibid.

63. See GM to EM, 18 December 1841, PMP; EM to GM, 5 February 1843, GMP; EM to Ellen Mordecai II, 6 February 1843, MFP, SHC.

64. Ellen published *Past Days: A Story for Children* (New York: D. Appleton, 1841) under the pseudonym Esther Whitlock. Her papers include manuscripts and correspondence with publishers.

65. EM to CMP, 19 September 1832, JMP.

66. CMP to Sol, 10 December 1820, JMP.

67. CMP to EM, 5 September 1821, JMP.

68. See Robert J. O'Brien, "Persecution and Acceptance: The Strange History of Discrimination against Married Women Teachers in West Virginia," *West Virginia History* 56 (1997): 56–75; Madelyn Holmes and Beverly J. Weiss, *Lives of Women Public Schoolteachers: Scenes from American Educational History* (New York: Garland Publishing, 1995), 170; and Kathleen Weiler, *Country Schoolwomen: Teaching in Rural California, 1850–1950* (Stanford: Stanford University Press, 1998), 182–85.

69. "Sweet," CMP to EM, 20 January 1822, JMP; "wonder," RML to CMP, 29 May 1822, JMP; "fear," CMP to EM, 1 January 1823, PMP.

70. RML to EM, 3 August 1823, MFP, SHC.

71. "Slave," GM to EM, 19 October 1826, MFP, SHC; "spot," CMP to SM, 9 January 1825, JMP.

72. "Lone," CMP to EM, 12 October 1828; arithmetic, CMP to EM, 23 March 1828; "debt," CMP to EM, 16 November 1828; and unprofitable, CMP to EM, 20 August 1830, all JMP.

73. Unbearable, CMP to EM, 27 September 1831, and JMP and GM to JM, 2 September 1831, GMP, SHC; "shocking," CMP to EM, 20 August 1830, JMP.

74. For Rachel's disapproval of women advertising their business, see RM to EM, 10 September 1828, MFP, SHC. The public announcement of a woman's paid work was a very sensitive issue. See, for instance, the violent reaction of Petersburg teacher Anna Campbell's husband, John, when she proposed placing a notice for her school in the paper (Suzanne Lebsock, *The Free Women of Petersburg: Status and Culture in a Southern Town, 1784–1860* [New York: W. W. Norton, 1984], 32).

75. Caroline's school had more than fifty scholars in December 1832 (RML to EM, 2 December 1832, MFP, SHC). Caroline left North Carolina heartbroken in the wake of a failed romance and stinging from her father's anger at her conversion to Christianity. She had fallen in love with her botany tutor, a young New Englander named Moses Ashley Curtis, who later became an Episcopal bishop. See RML to EM, 19 September and 14 February 1832, ibid. He proposed, and she refused but regretted it and grew depressed. She left for the West, thinking her father wished her away from the rest of the family. (They eventually reconciled.) See RML to EM, 14 April 1834, JMP.

76. CMP to EM, 1 April 1834, JMP.

77. CMP to EM, 13 January 1838, MFP, SHC.

78. CMP to EM, 25 February 1854, LMC, NCDAH.

79. She wrote unladylike "business" letters but cheerfully defended her violation of form (RML to SM, 28 May 1809, MFP, SHC).

80. CMP to EM, 2 November 1828, and JMP and CMP to Mary Catherine Lazarus, 11 January 1848, GMP, SHC.

81. EM to GM, 10 February 1848, ibid.

82. Wyatt-Brown, *Southern Honor*, 229. Also see note 5, above.

83. Meagher, *History of Education in Richmond*, 14.

*Chapter Nine*

# Peculiar Professionals:
## The Financial Strategies of the New Orleans Ursulines

EMILY CLARK

Twenty-one women gathered together on a March night in 1798 to decide the future of two women who were excluded from their meeting. Therese Farjon, mother superior of the Ursuline convent of New Orleans proposed to her fellow nuns that they sell a bondwoman named Celeste "because of her bad conduct and licentiousness." All agreed that Celeste should go. On the same night, the women voted to buy a young woman named Denise, "as she was needed for the plantation. Another reason was that she might marry one of our slaves who had begged us to allow him to do so." The nuns agreed to purchase Denise, who married Charles, the son of two Ursuline bondpeople, later that year.[1]

This is a provocative vignette. It tells us that a body of religious women in late colonial North America owned and managed slaves and a plantation, and thus participated in a realm of activity in which women, particularly spinsters, rarely appeared. The source for the story is a volume of chapter minutes that record the communal decisions of the nuns, most of them related to the economic management of their multiple enterprises. The women did not delegate the management of their financial assets to an outside male adviser, nor did they look to an internal leader. Instead, they administered their wealth themselves, as a team. On one level, the nuns' communal approach seems an appealing exception to the individualistic, market-driven behavior that guided business decisions elsewhere in antebellum America. On the other hand, decisions like the exchange of the wayward Celeste for the virtuous Denise expose how deeply the nuns were enmeshed in the ideologies of race and class that pervaded antebellum southern society. The boundaries of the community of decision makers were quite conventionally drawn: only the well-born, white, choir nuns of the convent participated in chapter meetings.[2] Neither converse nuns, whose fathers were farmers, artisans, and wage workers, nor enslaved women had a voice in the management of convent affairs. Gender had no power to trump social status within the monastic enclosure.

And yet their gender and their religious vocations placed the Ursuline choir nuns beyond the norms of southern plantation society in a variety of ways. The nuns owned a plantation but grew no staple crops. Instead, their farm supplied some of the provisions for the large boarding school from which their cash income derived. That school, in turn, depended on the labor of the nuns for its financial success. The teaching nuns were not wage earners, but unlike the married counterparts of their class, they did receive cash for the work they did. The women were slaveowners, but the contribution of slaves to the convent economy was limited and in the end depended predominately on the marginal cash earnings of female slaves. Furthermore, the sexual morality that influenced the nuns' acquisition and sale of bondpeople was at odds with the motives of profit and pleasure that usually underlay transactions in the slave market. Among convent bondpeople, mothers and fathers married one another in the church, saw their children do the same, and knew that their mistresses would honor matrimonial connections.

Like other slaveowners throughout the plantation belt, the Ursuline nuns exercised control over their bondpeople at even the most intimate level. But unlike many southern masters who used that power to feed their own sexual appetites, the sisters used it to punish sexual relations outside of wedlock and to promote sacramental marriage and slave families. This behavior put the nuns in direct opposition to some of the emerging norms and presumptions that shaped southern slaveholding society. They encouraged the bonds of nuclear family among slaves and seem to have placed them before financial considerations that led other slaveowners to disregard and even discourage such ties. Perhaps more important, when they imposed the ideal of a moral Catholic family on their bondpeople, they conferred on enslaved women something resembling the domestic ideal that defined the lives of free, upper- and middle-class women. Ursuline slave women were expected to be good wives and mothers, not sexual objects with neither the will nor the capacity to attain feminine virtue.

The professionalism of the nuns was perhaps at even greater odds with the social and economic currents of their time than was their unusual approach to slave morality. The "separate spheres" paradigm has become a virtual tautology in the historiography of early America that relates to gender. The familiar argument suggests that as the colonies met and overcame the challenges of encounter and the frontier to advance to social and economic maturity on the eve of the Revolution, women were ineluctably enclosed within a separate sphere of domestic activity. Experiments in erasing the boundaries between male and female domains—the evangelicalism of the Great Awakening and the quickening of female political activity during the Revolutionary age—died in the young republic. In the years between the Revolution and the Civil War, America reconciled the aggressive capitalism of its economic maturity with its social conscience by assigning each attribute to a different gender. Men and women shared the same household but acted in separate spheres, allowing Americans to nurture two dissonant constituents of their identity without integrating them. In the South, where slavery widened the compass of white male authority, the Ursulines diverged markedly from the ideological script of separate spheres and female submission. They lived in a household without men and earned their own way by teaching and investing, relying on their own labor and wits to elude the confining paradigm of dependent domesticity that was at the heart of the slaveowners' republic. Theirs is a story that unfolds in counterpoint to the dominant narrative of the Old South in which women are visible only when wearing the mantle of plantation mistress or slave.[3]

• • •

Twelve Ursuline nuns came to New Orleans in 1727 under contract to Louisiana's proprietors, the Company of the Indies, which had arranged for the nuns to operate the colonial military hospital. Although the women remained in charge of the hospital for nearly forty years, their chief object in traveling to Louisiana was to establish a school for girls. The size of their community ebbed and flowed over the next 125 years, with as few as six nuns in the early years, but averaging about twenty sisters as the American era dawned and throughout the antebellum period. Their student body grew along with the colonial city, from twenty-seven boarding students in 1729 to about sixty boarders and more than a hundred day students, free and enslaved, at the end of the colonial period and into the nineteenth century. The students were a diverse group, with daughters of wealthy French Creole planters taking lessons beside the children of English-speaking merchants, and heiresses sitting down to dinner in the boarding school with girls whose fathers were blacksmiths and glaziers. Free girls of color attended the boarding school, and enslaved women and girls filled the convent's free school. When Louisiana came under the aegis of the new American republic in 1803, it is likely that most girls living in New Orleans, whatever their race or social standing, spent some time at school among the Ursulines.[4]

This impressive female educational enterprise was the product of a distinctive French religious legacy. The Ursulines had been founded in the mid-sixteenth century as a small congregation of female catechizers in northern Italy. In early-seventeenth-century France, they grew rapidly and became an important arm of the Catholic reform movement. Their premise was that the propagation of Catholicism and its defense against the Protestant heresy rested with mothers, the first and best teachers of the young. The association of literacy with Protestantism's advance helped the Ursulines justify an educational program that reached beyond religious instruction to reading and writing. Asserting that universal salvation depended on making good Catholic mothers of all girls, the French Ursulines established schools that educated the daughters of laborers as well as those of lawyers, ignoring earlier traditions of educational privilege. In New Orleans they not only taught girls drawn from every social stratum but opened their doors to Indian and African girls as well.[5]

In Louisiana the Ursulines' educational mission represented more than a pious endeavor for the nuns. It was their livelihood, and this set them apart from their French predecessors and from other colonial American women. The Ursulines' ledger for 1802 reveals an enterprising community of women who may have exercised more economic independence than any of their contemporaries. That year, they earned 62 percent of their income through teaching and other services they provided.[6] French Ursulines, by contrast, ultimately derived most of their revenue from the dowries their families gave upon their entry into religious life. At the Ursuline convent of Dieppe, for example, income from investments of dowry capital made up 79 percent of revenues in 1716. Fees paid for services rendered brought the Dieppe nuns only 21 percent of their earnings that year.[7] French nuns commanded significant financial resources, but their wealth was ultimately dependent upon the largess of fathers, who provided for their daughters through the traditional mechanism of the dowry.

Anglo-American women of the colonial era who enjoyed control over substantial assets depended on inherited, rather than earned, wealth. In the English colonies, financially powerful women were invariably widows who preserved and exploited the material legacies of fathers and husbands, not spinster entrepreneurs or planters. The colonial New Orleans nuns, all well-born daughters of prominent French and colonial families who labored in the classroom to support themselves, were closer in their financial autonomy to the working girls of the antebellum industrial North than they were to the ladies of the French salon, the merchant's townhouse, and the southern plantation. And while they resemble in many ways such antebellum female educators as Mount Holyoke's founder, Mary Lyons, their enterprise anticipated hers by more than a century and supported itself through financial strategies that were distinctly southern.[8]

The nuns are remarkable not only for their financial independence but for the tortuous path they took to achieve it and the unusual way they maintained it. The Ursulines followed the planter's route to economic security through land and slaves for a time in the mid-eighteenth century, only to retreat at precisely the time plantation agriculture became truly lucrative in the colony. Although there is no evidence that they ever participated in staple-crop agriculture, for about fifty years they regularly exploited opportunities to make money by the sale of land and slaves. As part of the terms of their service in Louisiana, the women received a plantation and eight adult male slaves from the colonial proprietors in 1727. They negotiated the purchase of a second plantation in 1734. In the 1740s, they borrowed money to purchase twenty slaves to help maximize the return on plantation produce. They sold six slaves in 1756, and probably used some of the proceeds to rent eight slaves and a plantation with an orchard of wax-producing myrtle. In 1758, they tried to borrow the large sum of 24,000 livres "to be invested in blacks to increase the value of our plantation." The next year they sold three slaves and with the proceeds purchased a family of seven, including a teenage daughter on the threshold of her childbearing years.[9]

This restless pattern of trading land and slaves was typical for planters who tried to squeeze prosperity and profit from Louisiana's unyielding environment during the French regime, which lasted from 1699 until the mid-1760s. Inhabitants staked their hopes on one staple crop after another—tobacco, indigo, rice—only to have the climate and soil betray their trust in the colonial dream of easy riches. These commodities could be produced in Louisiana but could match in neither quality nor quantity those supplied by competitors in the Chesapeake, low-country South Carolina, and the Caribbean. Slim profit margins and the heat and humidity of the Lower Mississippi Valley thus made slaves key to even modest planter success for most of the eighteenth century. While the Ursulines did not join in the scramble to identify and exploit a staple crop, their active participation in the New Orleans slave market attests that they understood the value of this peculiar form of capital and relentlessly sought to expand it. In 1770, with nearly seventy slaves, the nuns were among the top 6 percent of slaveholders in the Lower Mississippi River valley.[10]

Then, rather suddenly, the nuns diverged from the planter's path. While others in the colony invested in increasing their slaveholdings in the late eighteenth century, the Ursulines scaled back their participation in plantation slavery. In 1776, they rented their main plantation and the thirty-five slaves who worked it to another planter. A year later, they sold the slaves and the land to different owners. Instead of buying a new plantation, they bought a small dairy farm to supply the convent's needs. They made no move to replace the thirty-five slaves they had sold, though they represented about half of their total holding.[11] Indeed, for the rest of the colonial period their involvement in the slave market decreased markedly from what it had been earlier. They acquired thirty-two (74 percent) of the forty-three slaves they purchased during the colonial era before 1780, and 89 percent of their colonial slave sales transactions took place before this date. After 1780, they were much more likely to emancipate or sell slaves than they were to purchase them, and more likely to manumit bondpeople than to sell them. When they did participate in the market, financial motives did not predominate. In the last two decades of the eighteenth century, the nuns sold only nine slaves, in nearly every instance citing some moral defect in the bondperson. They acquired eleven slaves during the same period, and in three of these cases they made the purchases in order to unite couples and children.[12]

The Ursulines' involvement in the slave market declined at a time when it was on a dramatic upswing for other planters, who redoubled their efforts to make Louisiana tobacco pay under new protectionist policies enacted by the Spanish, who took over the government of the colony in 1767. Newly enslaved Africans poured into the Lower Mississippi Valley in the closing decades of the eighteenth century to meet increased demand from planters trying to make the most of a more favorable trade environment. After the perfection of a new process for refining sugar in the 1790s, Louisiana's fate as a slave society was sealed as the profitability of sugar spurred investment in the large labor force that cane cultivation required.[13]

It would be heartening to find some evidence indicating that the nuns turned from slavery because they found the institution morally uncomfortable. In fact, however, their apparent retreat probably simply represented a return to more familiar financial strategies with less onerous management requirements. French nuns favored investing their dowry money in financial instruments and urban real estate over farming and rural tenants. The New Orleans Ursulines came to the colony with no capital. Their order's rules required that they leave their dowries with their original convents. The plantation and slaves provided them by the colonial proprietors, in addition to their fees, were the only means they had to create and expand the convent wealth necessary to sustain their American mission.[14]

This changed in the late 1770s, when the Ursulines again gained access to dowry capital, and it was the freedom this gave them to pursue other investment strategies that led them away from the plantation. More than a dozen wealthy French Creole[15] women and postulants from Havana entered the convent between 1775 and 1800, and all brought dowries that the Ursulines promptly invested in urban real estate.[16] The religious women of Louisiana, in the end, did not find the seigneurial life and the financial rewards of staple-crop agriculture seductive enough to overcome their bourgeois roots. They were, by tradition and upbringing, suited to being teachers and urban landladies, and they relinquished the unaccustomed planter's mantle as soon as circumstances allowed.

The Ursulines never turned into female versions of the archetypal antebellum plantation master, yet a subtle transformation had nonetheless taken place that distanced the New Orleans nuns forever from their French predecessors. Dowries enabled the colonial nuns to pursue their favored form of investment but did not alter the essential calculus of the New Orleans convent's economy. The colonial nuns derived most of their income from their own labors, not from endowments provided by men or other indirect sources. The French nuns of Dieppe, for example, earned only one-fifth of their revenue in 1716 from their teaching, compared to more than three-fifths earned by the New Orleans sisters in 1802.

Although the Ursulines increased their wealth chiefly through their teaching, they nevertheless retained slaves until emancipation and continued to draw cash income from their labor. At the close of the colonial period, male slaves were more likely than bondwomen to contribute to the convent coffers, but on the eve of the Civil War, positions were reversed and female slaves were the only source of such cash income. This shift contributed to an inversion of gender roles that would have been striking in the Old South: women earned and managed all of the cash that came to the convent in the final antebellum decade.

The nuns were never among the largest slaveholders of nineteenth-century Louisiana, and while they remained among the minority who owned significant numbers of bondpeople, their account books reveal that from 1800 to the Civil War they drew only a small part of their income from the labor of their slaves. In 1802, the sale of produce grown by slaves, together with the earnings of a slave blacksmith and shoemaker the nuns rented out, made up only 12 percent of their income that year.[17] The proportion of the contribution of slave labor and the occasional sale of a bondperson to the convent economy remained

TABLE 9.1. Convent Revenue Sources as Percentage of Total, 1820–1855

|  | Investments | Fees for Services | Derived from Slaves | |
|---|---|---|---|---|
|  |  |  | All | Women Only |
| 1820 | 41% | 53% | 6% | n/a |
| 1825 | 42 | 49 | 9 | <1% |
| 1830 | 21 | 62 | 17 | 1 |
| 1835 | 51 | 37 | 12 | 2 |
| 1840 | 45 | 45 | 10 | 1 |
| 1845 | 43 | 45 | 12 | 2 |
| 1850 | 57 | 41 | 2 | 2 |
| 1855 | 49 | 49 | 2 | 2 |
| Average | 43.6 | 47.6 | 8.75 | 1.5 |

*Source*: Accounts, June 1806–October 1869, Ursuline Convent of New Orleans Archives, New Orleans, La.

relatively small throughout the antebellum years, averaging about 9 percent, as Table 9.1 illustrates.

Prior to 1845, the major contribution of bondpeople to the revenue stream originated in the sale of farm and dairy products derived from their labor on the nuns' rural property, and profits from these sources grew considerably between the turn of the century and the Civil War. From just over $800 in 1802, receipts from milk and produce ranged from $2,000 to $3,300 between 1830 and 1850.[18] Although a substantial proportion of the proceeds came from dairying, in which women may have assumed the primary role, men certainly participated in raising the vegetables and chopping the firewood that accounted for the remainder. The notation "reçu de l'habitation en denrées" (received from the farm for produce) that regularly appeared in the annual recapitulation of convent revenues was the joint contribution of bondmen and bondwomen to the nuns' cash flow.[19]

Beginning in 1850, "reçu de l'habitation en denrées" disappeared from the ledger, and the revenue categories shrank to three: rent from urban property, student fees, and "blanchissage de nos domestiques" (laundering by our house servants).[20] In the final decade of antebellum New Orleans, none of the cash flowing into the monastery was produced by the labor of men. With respect to bondpeople, this represents the reversal of an earlier pattern. Male slaves, particularly a skilled blacksmith and shoemaker, had brought in a steady stream of monthly fees for the rental of their services outside the convent in the late 1790s and early 1800s. During these same years, the nuns regularly paid rent to others for additional bondwomen to accommodate the polishing of church furniture and ornaments and the laundering of sacramental linen. The shift away from deriving cash from the labor of male slaves seems to have begun around 1811, when the nuns sold their blacksmith, François. In subsequent years, rental fees for skilled slaves disappeared from convent accounts. Cash dependence on male slaves disappeared altogether when farm produce ceased to be a revenue stream for the convent in the 1850s.[21]

There are several possible explanations for this evolution in the participation of slaves in the cash economy of the convent. The large population of free people of color practicing trades in New Orleans may have decreased demand for the services of skilled slaves.[22] In addition, the convent moved in 1824 to a new site beyond the city limits, where they were distant from the urban center of population and activity that generated work for their bondmen. Competition and geography thus probably combined to reduce the contribution of skilled bondmen to convent revenue. The cessation of cash from slave agriculture obviously had different roots. Perhaps the nuns found it increasingly difficult to differentiate among the produce their slaves raised to provision the convent and school, the surplus that was to be sold, and that raised for the slaves' own consumption. On a sugar or cotton plantation, slave provision plots for produce were geographically distinct, and slaves' cultivation of them could be easily monitored and separated from their labor in the cane and cotton fields. Such was not the case on the convent farms. It may have been more trouble than it was worth to the nuns to negotiate with their bondpeople on what portion of the farm produce should go to market and be sold to benefit the convent. Or perhaps the change was simply the result of a favorable shift in the monastery balance sheet. There was a cash surplus of more than $5,000 in 1850. Perhaps the nuns felt they no longer needed the cash income from farm produce.[23]

The Ursulines continued, however, to collect cash income from the laundry maintained by convent bondwomen, and this enterprise actually grew from very small beginnings in the 1820s to a significant business from the mid-1830s until the Civil War. In 1825, the laundry brought in only eighty dollars, less than 1 percent of the convent's revenue. By 1830, it was bringing in nearly triple that amount, and after 1835 it averaged earnings of about $500 annually. Although the laundry never contributed more than 2 percent of convent revenues, it was a consistent source of cash. (See Tables 9.1 and 9.2.)

Of the various factors that shifted the earning burden from male to female

TABLE 9.2. Convent Income Derived Directly from Slaves, 1820–1855

| Year | All Slave Sources | Laundry Only |
|------|-------------------|--------------|
| 1820 | $1,262 | n/a |
| 1825 | 1,115 | $80 |
| 1830 | 3,355 | 230 |
| 1835 | 3,331 | 536 |
| 1840 | 4,232 | 409 |
| 1845 | 3,094 | 543 |
| 1850 | 459 | 459 |
| 1855 | 535 | 535 |

*Source*: See Table 9.1.

slaves at the convent, geography was probably chiefly responsible. When the Ursulines moved in 1824 some three miles downriver from their original site in the heart of New Orleans, the relationship between the convent and the city became attenuated. It no longer made sense for the nuns to own bondpeople who might easily find paying work in the town just outside the monastery walls. At the same time, their ability to derive income from the labor of their slaves depended on a ready market. In their new location, the most likely customers for their slaves' labor were not townspeople in need of shoemakers and black-smiths but the students living within the convent compound who needed personal services. The girls boarding at the convent during the antebellum years paid extra for their baths.[24] Staying at the rather isolated convent, far from the townhouses and servants of their families, it is likely that they also paid to have their laundry done by convent bondwomen. It was more difficult for the convent, now located some distance from town, to pick up the extra domestic help it needed to manage the laundry and cleaning demands of a large girls' boarding school. The convent had to maintain its own labor source for these tasks. Laundresses thus became the bondpeople most indispensable to convent operations, but even they were peripheral to the economic engine that the nuns themselves represented.

The Ursulines were never typical major slaveowners. They did not preside over a plantation realm built on profits from sugar or cotton produced by their bondpeople and measure their capital wealth in units of human life. Slaves did not represent the source of labor essential to their enterprise; their chief capital investment was their sprawling complex of dormitories and classrooms. At the same time, these well-born women were clearly dependent upon slaves for the success of their business. Bondwomen cleaned, cooked, and laundered, freeing the nuns to teach and creating the comfortable environment parents expected for their daughters.

The Ursulines departed in yet another way from the template of the typical southern planter. Throughout the colonial and antebellum periods, they insisted on sacramental marriage among their bondpeople and showed no tolerance for bondwomen who produced offspring without benefit of matrimony. The degree to which the Ursulines supported the institution of sacramental slave marriage is particularly interesting because of the potential that it had to undermine the financial and social underpinnings of slavery. Although slave marriage was recognized and the slave family somewhat protected under the French colonial regime, they lost the support and protection of civil authority in the Spanish and American periods.[25] The Ursulines, however, continued to promote marriage among their slaves, and as the eighteenth century closed and the nineteenth dawned and advanced, their example became increasingly exceptional.

It is impossible to know whether slave families began to form during the Ursulines' first years in the colony. Their contract with the Company of the Indies stipulated that they be given eight adult male African slaves in 1727 to work their plantation, but there is no record of female slaves before 1733, and no evidence that their slaves were marrying and bearing children until 1756. That year, a group of six slaves in three families stood accused of theft, and the nuns voted in chapter to sell them. Among them were two married couples and a Creole boy in his teens. One of the couples was also Creole, but the husband of the other was known by an African name, Equé, in addition to the Christian name he had been given. This evidence suggests that the nuns were promoting sacramental marriage among first-generation African, as well as Creole, slaves.[26]

One might hypothesize that the nuns imposed marriage on their bondpeople without taking individual choice and affection into account, forcing unions among those living in their convent and on their plantation to marry one another. While this may have been the case in some instances, there is no direct evidence for it. On the other hand, the nuns' chapter minutes reveal that they did act to bring together bondpeople in love who were kept apart by separate ownership. In 1758, a woman who wanted to enter the convent as a permanent boarder offered her bondwoman, Victoire, as part of her entrance dowry. Originally, the nuns were to receive only Victoire and a cash sum, but instead they negotiated to have the money diverted to a third party to obtain ownership of Victoire's husband, Leveillé. The two lived together at the convent until Victoire's death.[27] Much later in the century, the nuns continued such interventions. In April 1795, they purchased a thirty-three-year-old woman named Victoria and her two-year-old son so that she could marry the father of her child, an Ursuline bondman named Ramon. The two were wed in a July ceremony, and the sacramental register carefully notes that the child, also named Ramon, was legitimated by the marriage.[28] And in March 1798, the convent council approved the purchase of Denise so that she could marry their bondman Charles.[29]

Sometimes the Ursulines could carry their promotion of slave marriage to unlikely extremes. Between 1798 and 1804 they were embroiled in an investigation to determine the validity of the marriage between two of their bondpeople. Theresa had originally been married to another of their slaves, Mathurin. While on a trip up the Mississippi in 1776, Mathurin disappeared, and although his body was never found, he was presumed dead. The "widowed" Theresa married again, and when her second husband died she took a third, Estevan, from among the nuns' slaves. In 1798 word reached the Ursulines and ecclesiastical officials in New Orleans that Mathurin had been sighted in Havana. Theresa and Estevan were separated, pending the outcome of official inquiries that involved notarized depositions of slaves in Havana and the intervention of the archbishop himself.

In 1804, six long years into the inconclusive investigation, the mother superior wrote to the bishop asking that he close the case and pronounce Mathurin dead, "for the long separation is very harmful to the family of Theresa, her children and her husband who has always considered her as his legitimate wife." She went on to say that the husband was "desperate and is continually asking me to let him marry another woman if he cannot have Theresa back. I do not know what to do to tranquilize him." This episode reveals the Ursulines' continuing insistence on legitimating slave sexual relationships through sacramental marriage and suggests that the slaves themselves had either assimilated their values on the matter or knew that acting against them would bring an unwanted reaction.[30]

The New Orleans slaveholding population as a whole did not match the Ursulines' unwavering commitment to sacramental marriage among their bondpeople during the eighteenth century. Slave marriage was fairly common during the French period.[31] During the Spanish period, however, sacramental slave marriage almost disappeared. The proportion of slave children born in wedlock dropped precipitously, to 7 percent in 1775, 3 percent in 1785, and 2 percent in 1795. The change probably occurred for several reasons. Spanish law did not prescribe slave marriage as French law had, and clerics in the later eighteenth century charged such high fees for performing weddings that many people, white and black, settled into common-law relationships to avoid the cost.[32] It may also be that what one historian calls the "re-Africanization" of Louisiana's slave population contributed to the decrease in slave marriage, since it is likely that Creole slaves practicing Catholicism would be more likely to ask for the sacrament than new Africans.[33] Almost unique among the slaves of late-eighteenth-century New Orleans, the bondpeople of the Ursulines regularly knelt before the altar to receive the nuptial blessing and ceremonial veiling at the hands of Catholic clergy. The four slave children born to married parents and baptized in 1785 were all Ursuline bondpeople, as were three of the four whose baptisms were recorded in 1795.[34]

The nuns no doubt insisted on sacramental marriage for their bondpeople for reasons of social control as well as religious morality. Settled families were likely to produce stable, reliable workers. There is at least one example of the deterioration of a bondman's behavior upon the loss of his family.[35] Pragmatism, however, does not explain several instances when they tried to help families stay together until children were grown, even when it did not serve their financial interests. In 1777, they sold thirty-five slaves. All of them, except two bondmen in their late twenties, belonged to one of seven family groups.[36] The act is notable because, unlike French law, Spanish slave statutes in force at the time did not require that children below the age of fourteen be sold only with their parents.[37] Later in the century, the nuns acted to preserve the cohesion of an enslaved family on the threshold of freedom. In 1789, when Louis and Cecelia approached the convent chapter asking to purchase their freedom and that of their four children, the nuns negotiated with them on the cost and payment terms so that the entire family was freed in a single act of manumission.[38]

The nuns continued to enable the marriage of enslaved lovers in the nineteenth century. In 1845, they bought Louis Carcie, who had married their slave Helen in 1842. In another instance, after a two-year campaign of opposition by his own mother, the Ursulines' slave Michel married Helene, a slave belonging to a man named D'Aquin. The nuns approved of the marriage because D'Aquin was a neighbor of the convent and a good Catholic with whom it would be possible to "arrange matters if circumstances should require it. As for example if Mr. D'Aquin should want to sell his Negress or that we should want to sell our Negro so as not to separate them." The nuns indeed later purchased Helene, in 1850. On at least one occasion they sold one of their slaves to a free mate; in

1840 they agreed to sell to free man of color, Louis Chesneau, their slave Marie Jeanne and their child for the relatively low sum of $350.[39]

The result of the Ursulines' promarriage stance was a slave community marked by family groupings and networks. During the last four decades of colonial rule, ten families of Ursuline bondpeople were linked to one another through marriage. These families often sustained a multigenerational presence at the convent, so that children born at the end of the eighteenth century might be surrounded by uncles, aunts, and grandparents. For example, the children of Alexis and Marguerite—Augustin, Santiago, and Adelaide—would have known their maternal grandmother, Therese, and their paternal grandparents, Jacob and Louise Eulalie, who remained on the Ursuline plantation that Jacob managed for fifteen years after he was freed in 1796. Augustin, Santiago, and Adelaide would also have grown up surrounded by their cousins Maria Theresa, Louis Gonzague, and Maria, the children of Louis Gonzague Sr. and Marie Henriette. And all of these children lived among a number of aunts and uncles.[40]

The Ursulines continued to promote marriage among their slaves in the antebellum years. The record book they started in 1824 when they moved to a new convent records the marriages, births, and baptisms of slaves owned by the nuns between 1824 and 1865 and notes twenty marriages between convent bondpeople. Baptismal records from the Ursuline Convent Chapel for 1834–53 suggest that families headed by legitimately married couples continued to be the norm for the nuns' slaves. During this period, only two of the twenty children born to slaves owned by the Ursulines and baptized at their chapel were of illegitimate birth.[41] Nuclear families related to multigenerational networks of kin continued to dominate the Ursuline slave community until emancipation.[42]

Sacramental records attest that in the three decades before the Civil War, the Ursulines' promotion of sacramental marriage and two-parent families among slaves was unusual. Of the 457 infant slave baptisms at the Ursuline Convent Chapel between 1834 and 1853, 91 percent were of children born to unmarried mothers. Only 9 percent were of children born to married slave parents. Of those, twenty, or nearly half, were baptisms of children born to married slaves of the Ursulines. (See Table 9.3.)

For more than a century, through the French, Spanish, and American periods, the Ursulines supported sacramental slave marriage with equal vigor as those around them moved away from it. In the French period, the nuns were part of a respectable minority of slaveowners whose slaves married. Under Spanish rule, they became exceptional. Their behavior was even more notable in the antebellum period, when supporting slave marriage not only ran against the

TABLE 9.3. Slave Baptisms at Ursuline Chapel, 1835–1853

|  | Number | Percent |
|---|---|---|
| All slave baptisms | 457 | 100 |
| Children of unmarried mothers | 415 | 91 |
| Children of married parents | 42 | 9 |

*Sources*: "Ursuline Convent Chapel Baptismal Register, 1835–1837"; "Ursuline Convent Chapel Baptismal Register, 1837–1845"; "Ursuline Convent Chapel Baptismal Register, 1845–1853," Ursuline Convent of New Orleans Archives, New Orleans, La.

norm but undermined racist stereotypes that proclaimed the moral inferiority of slaves and condemned the sexual exploitation of bondwomen. With the advent of proslavery ideology and racism in the decades leading up to the Civil War, the Ursulines served as public exemplars of values that had disappeared or gone underground in most of the antebellum South. Slaveholding New Orleanians continued to be confronted by the nuns' steadfast promulgation of a moral stance that contested the behavior of masters who put profit before the bonds of family.

The nuns' condemnation of bondwomen who bore children out of wedlock challenged antebellum racism on a different front. The Ursulines refused to accept the characterization of all slave women as natural seductresses who tempted white masters and fellow bondmen alike into fathering illicit off-spring.[43] Their insistence on prenuptial chastity reached back to the colonial period. In 1797, the convent chapter minutes record that a young woman named Touton was sold because of her "vices" and another named Celeste in 1798 because of her "licentiousness." Eloise and Catherine, blood sisters, were sold in 1803 for "bad conduct." The vices, licentiousness, and bad conduct noted in the minutes left tangible proof in two cases. Celeste went to her new mistress with a month-old infant whose father was unknown, as did Catherine.[44] Sometime around 1828, the seventeen-year-old Gogotte Brigitte, herself the illegitimate daughter of an Ursuline slave who later married, was sold along with her bastard son Victoir. In 1843, shortly after her illegitimate child was baptized, the community separated Marie Marthe from their other female slaves and rented her out until she could be sold.[45]

The Ursulines' promotion of marriage could obviously have its unpleasant side for women like Celeste, Gogotte Brigitte, and Marie Marthe who were banished from the community in which they had grown up when they bore children out of wedlock. Yet, on balance, the nuns' bondwomen derived some clear benefits that most of their contemporaries did not share. Because the nuns did not participate in cotton or sugar cultivation, their bondwomen were spared the most punishing forms of physical labor. The Ursulines' promotion of marriage guaranteed slave mothers the companionship and partnership of a husband and father. Perhaps not least, mistresses vowed to chastity posed no obvious threat of sexual abuse.

. . .

This essay shows how some white women from privileged backgrounds eluded the imposition of the rigid framework for the genders that was so much a feature of antebellum America. The economic history of the Ursuline convent in New Orleans illustrates that a distinct cultural endowment survived its Atlantic crossing and produced an alternative to domesticity, in both its ideological and its practical manifestations. The variety and proportions of revenue streams flowing into the New Orleans convent at the end of the eighteenth century were dramatically different from what they had been in France, and beyond the imagination of Anglo-American women who had only begun to pioneer careers in professional service in the antebellum era.[46] Thrown very much on their own resources, the New Orleans nuns embraced plantation agriculture quickly and relentlessly exploited its potential for a time. They were marked forever by the encounter—slaves and the product of slave labor would contribute to the convent economy until the Civil War brought emancipation—but it did not produce a profound and lasting shift in the structure of convent finances. The most significant transformation was actually far more radical.

Teaching, nursing, and providing social services brought the New Orleans nuns a degree of prosperous financial autonomy long before other American women of middling status exploited the opportunities created by reform and benevolence. At the end of the colonial period, the New Orleans nuns' economic base rested on their teaching. Supported by their own skill and labor, they transgressed gender norms for women of their class and their era, resembling the startlingly independent mill girls of Lowell more than the learned matrons of post-Revolutionary America. While these well-bred daughters of the legal and merchant elite never abandoned the social and racial hierarchy that exempted them from hard physical labor and endowed them with authority over the women of lower social status in their community, they nevertheless stepped into a role that was truly new, indeed, revolutionary in colonial and early national America.[47]

These financial migrations, together with the nuns' religious values, ultimately molded the Ursulines into unusual southern slaveholders and influenced the experience of their bondwomen in distinct ways during the antebellum era. As professional women who relied on their own skills and labor for their economic security, the nuns never became typical antebellum masters who counted their wealth and calculated their prospects in terms of human capital. Their enterprise also ultimately led them away from relying on the labor of male slaves for any of their cash income. And their religious morality extended protection from sexual exploitation and the security of marriage and family stability to their bondpeople even in the final years of the antebellum South.

The Ursulines inhabited a role that mirrored neither the republican patriarch of the slave South nor the Protestant ideal of married womanhood. Peculiar female professionals who eluded the bonds of domesticity to confound the separate spheres of the Protestant republic and to challenge the racist tropes of slave immorality with their model slave families, the nuns testify to the diversity of feminine possibilities in the Old South and help lift the cloak of invisibility woven by a series of shopworn dichotomies: dependent, independent; rich, poor; leisured, working; lady, slave.

## NOTES

1. "Délibérations du Conseil," Ursuline Convent of New Orleans Archives, New Orleans, La. (hereafter UCNOA), 81; Ursulines to Augustin Griffony, sale of a slave, 11 April 1798, Acts of Francisco Broutin, vol. 47, Notarial Archives of New Orleans (hereafter NANO), 321; "Libro primero de matrimonios de negros y mulatos de la parroquia de sn. Luis de la Nueva Orleans; en 137 folios. Da principio en 20 de enero de 1777 y acaba en 1830" (hereafter SLC-M3), Archives of the Archdiocese of New Orleans (hereafter AANO), 42 bis.

2. The Ursuline order comprised two ranks of nuns. Choir nuns, so-called because of the requirement that they sing daily office in chapel, were born of aristocratic or bourgeois families, brought dowries with them upon entering the convent, took solemn, perpetual vows, and performed the educational work for which the Ursulines were known. Converse nuns were drawn from farming, artisanal, and laboring backgrounds. They provided no dowries, took simple vows, and served the convent as housekeepers, nurses, gardeners, and messengers.

3. The historiography on which these summary sentences is based is vast, and the following citations are merely representative. On the sexual exploitation of bondwomen see Frances S. Foster, "Ultimate Victims: Black Women in Slave Narratives," *Journal of American Culture* 1, no. 4 (1978): 845–53; and Deborah Gray White, *Ar'n't I a Woman: Female Slaves in the Plantation South* (New York: W. W. Norton, 1985).

On the "separate spheres" paradigm and the cult of domesticity see Barbara Welter,

"The Cult of True Womanhood, 1820–1860," *American Quarterly* 18 (Summer 1966): 151–74, for one of the earliest contributions to this historiography. Scholars of early America have focused on the colonial era as a period of possible transition from more integrated gender roles and greater autonomy for women toward more constraining forms of patriarchy and domesticity in post-Revolutionary America. The progress of this historiography can be traced in these exemplary studies: Nancy F. Cott, *The Bonds of Womanhood: "Women's Sphere" in New England, 1780–1835* (New Haven: Yale University Press, 1977); Cornelia Hughes Dayton, *Women before the Bar: Gender, Law, and Society in Connecticut, 1639–1789* (Chapel Hill: University of North Carolina Press, 1995); Susan Juster, *Disorderly Women: Sexual Politics and Evangelicalism in Revolutionary New England* (Ithaca, N.Y.: Cornell University Press, 1994); and Stephanie McCurry, *Masters of Small Worlds: Yeoman Households, Gender Relations, and the Political Culture of the Antebellum South Carolina Low Country* (New York: Oxford University Press, 1995).

4. *The Letters of Marie Madeleine Hachard, 1727–1728*, trans. Myldred Masson Costa (New Orleans: Laborde Printing Company, 1974), 59; Bishop of Louisiana to José Caballero, 13 October 1800, Archivo General de Indias, Audiencia de Santo Domingo, Seville, Spain, microfilm copy, Historic New Orleans Collection, legajo 2645, f. 419,. In 1795, there were 284 girls of European descent in New Orleans; 245 young women boarded at the convent between 1798 and 1803. There were just under 400 girls of color, enslaved and free, in the city in 1795, and five years later, about 100 of them were in attendance on a given day at the free classes at the convent. "1795 Census of New Orleans," Archivo General de Indias, Papeles Procedentes de la Isla de Cuba, Seville, Spain, legajo 211, July 1795, microfilm copy, Historic New Orleans Collection, is the basis for the population figures. On the diversity of the convent school's student body see Emily Clark, "A New World Community: The New Orleans Ursulines and Colonial Society, 1727–1803" (Ph.D. diss., Tulane University, 1998), 95–106.

5. Elizabeth Rapley, *The Dévotes: Women and Church in Seventeenth-Century France* (Montreal: McGill-Queen's University Press, 1990), and Linda Lierheimer, "Female Eloquence and Maternal Ministry: The Apostolate of Ursuline Nuns in Seventeenth-Century France" (Ph.D. diss., Princeton University, 1994), provide the best discussions of the origins and proliferation of the Ursulines in France and the student population in their schools. Archives des Colonies, Correspondance Général, Louisiane, Archives National de France (hereafter AC), Series C13A, 11:273v–274; and *Letters of Marie Madeleine Hachard*, 44, 49, 50, 56, 59, discuss the student population in New Orleans.

6. "General Accounts, 1797–1812," UCNOA.

7. "Recettes et dépenses, 1707–1716 [Dieppe]," Folio D345, Archives Départementales de la Seine-Maritime, Rouen, France (hereafter ADSM).

8. See, for example, Elizabeth Fox-Genovese, *Within the Plantation Household: Black and White Women of the Old South* (Chapel Hill: University of North Carolina Press, 1988), 203–6, and Lois Green Carr and Lorena S. Walsh, "The Planter's Wife: The Experience of White Women in Seventeenth-Century Maryland," *William and Mary Quarterly*, 3d ser., 34 (October 1977): 542–71.

9. See AC, Series C13A, 10:75–77v, for terms of the contract with the Company of the Indies. A census in 1770 reported that the Ursulines maintained a herd of forty-two cattle and a flock of twenty-five sheep on their main plantation (Albert J. Robichaux, Jr., comp. and trans., *Louisiana Census and Militia Lists, 1770–1789, Vol. I: German Coast, New Orleans, Below New Orleans and Lafourche* [Harvey, Louisiana: Dumag Printing, 1973], 95). Convent accounts for the late eighteenth century record profits from the sale of produce only ("General Accounts: October 1797–October 1812," UCNOA). Land and slave sales transactions are recorded at "Délibérations du Conseil," 18, 32, 37, 42, 44, 45, 47, 49, UCNOA, and AC, Series C11A, 86:274v.

10. John G. Clark, *New Orleans, 1718–1812: An Economic History* (Baton Rouge: Louisiana State University Press, 1970), 161–80, 183–249; Gwendolyn Midlo Hall, *Africans in Colonial Louisiana: The Development of Afro-Creole Culture in the Eighteenth Century* (Baton Rouge: Louisiana State University Press, 1992), 276–77; Daniel H. Usner Jr., *Indians, Settlers, and Slaves in a Frontier Exchange Economy: The Lower Mississippi Valley before 1783* (Chapel Hill: University of North Carolina Press, 1992), 159, 188–90, 216–18, 278–85.

The census of 1770 records the Ursuline slaveholding as sixty-one ("1770 [January] State of the Habitations of the coast of the River below [the city] beginning at the habitation of Madame Widow Lachaise up to the environs of the Prairie aux Moucle both of the [Right] shore as well as of the left shore," in Robichaux, *Louisiana Census and Militia Lists*, 95). There were probably at least ten bondpeople serving at the convent in the city, as well.

11. "Délibérations du Conseil," 57, UCNOA, records the nuns' decision to sell their plantation and thirty-five slaves to Francisco Bouligny. Acts of Garic, vol. 8 (January–December 1777), 8 November 1777, NANO, records the act of sale for the slaves. Acts of Garic, vol. 10 (June–December 1778), 30 July 1778, NANO, records the sale of the plantation by the Ursulines. "Délibérations du Conseil," 77, UCNOA, records the convent chapter's decision in 1779 to purchase a piece of property on the same side of the river as the convent. Carlos Trudeau, Certification of ownership and survey, 25 July 1780, UCNOA, describes and situates the new plantation.

12. Victoria and her two-year-old son were purchased in 1795. Her child was acknowledged by Ursuline bondman Ramon when they married that year (SLC-M3, 13, no. 77, 14 July 1795, AANO). Pedro was sold in 1796 for bad behavior ("Délibérations du Conseil," 75, UCNOA); Touton was sold in 1797 because of her "vice" (ibid., 79); Celeste was sold for "bad conduct and licentiousness" in 1798, and Denise was purchased in 1798 and married Charles soon afterward (ibid., 81; "Achat de Denise/Venus," act of sale notarized by Carlos Ximenes, 16 May 1798, UCNOA; SLC-M3, 16, no. 42 bis, AANO); Eloise and Catherine were sold in 1803 "because of their bad conduct." Catherine had an infant whose father was unknown ("Délibérations du Conseil," 88, UCNOA).

13. Hall, *Africans in Colonial Louisiana*, 275–309. See also note 9, above.

14. For French Ursuline investment patterns see "État du Revenu des Ursulines de Diepe [*sic*] donné en la visite faite du monre par ordre de monsgr L'archeveque le 15 Juin 1692" and "Recettes et dépenses, 1707–1716 [Dieppe]," Folio D345, ADSM. Cissie C. Fairchilds, *Poverty and Charity in Aix-en-Provence* (Baltimore: Johns Hopkins University Press,

1976), 58–60, 63–64, discusses investment strategies of French charities more generally. Jane Frances Heaney, *A Century of Pioneering: A History of the Ursuline Nuns in New Orleans, 1727–1827*, ed. Mary Ethel Booker Siefken (New Orleans: Ursuline Sisters of New Orleans, Louisiana, 1993), 35, 128, discusses the absence of dowries at the New Orleans convent. Dowry contract of Marie Marguerite Catherine de Pontcarré, Rouen, 1 January 1725, Folio D418, ADSM, is an example of a French Ursuline dowry contract that stipulates that the funds remain with the convent of profession.

15. The word "Creole" is used in this essay to denote persons born in American colonies but descended directly from persons born in Europe or Africa. The adjectives "French," "Spanish," and "African" used with "Creole" specify the Old World ancestry of Creoles.

16. "Livre de l'entrée des filles de choeur," UCNOA, 13–14v, 20–21b, 29b; "Délibérations du Conseil," 83–85, 95–96, 104, UCNOA; Acts of Mezange, vol. 4 (July–December 1781), 962; Acts of Ximenes, vol. 3 (July–December 1792), 363–64v; and ibid., vol. 11 (July–December 1796), 388, NANO.

17. When they moved to their new convent in 1824, the nuns began a register of their slaves with the names of the twenty-three bondpeople who moved to the new site with them. By 1858, the number had grown to sixty, largely through natural increase. Figures derived from "Livre ou sont les noms et les annés de la naissance des Nègres et Négresses qui sont venus au Couvent sur notre habitation le 2nd Octobre 1824"; "Ursuline Convent Chapel Marriages, 1834–1837"; "Ursuline Convent Chapel Baptismal Register, 1837–1845"; "Ursuline Convent Chapel Baptismal Register, 1845–1853"; and "General Accounts, 1797–1812," UCNOA.

18. In 1802, the monetary unit was the Spanish silver piastra, also known as the dollar. Although the standard silver weight of the U.S. dollar differed very slightly from that of the Spanish milled dollar (371.25 grams of silver in the former, compared to 377 grams of silver in the later), the two units were so close in value that it is reasonable to make a comparison between late Spanish colonial and nineteenth-century American dollar amounts. The new American republic adopted the dollar as its monetary unit during the Revolutionary War. From 1779 to 1782, the units were equivalent: one United Colonies dollar equaled one Spanish milled dollar. In 1785, Congress resolved that the dollar, divided on a decimal basis, would be the monetary unit of the United States. The Spanish silver dollar remained legal tender in the United States until 1857 (Arthur Nussbaum, *A History of the Dollar* [New York: Columbia University Press, 1957], 35–37, 47, 53, 84).

19. "General Accounts, 1797–1812," and Accounts, June 1806–October 1869, UCNOA.

20. Accounts, June 1806–October 1869, UCNOA.

21. "Livre du coffre à trois clefs," 22, UCNOA, records the sale of François. For examples of payments received for the blacksmith, shoemaker, and other male slaves, and of payments made for the rental of bondwomen for cleaning and laundering, see "General Accounts, 1797–1812," 287, 290, 295, 301, 307–11, 338, 350, 353, 357, and Accounts, June 1806–October 1869, UCNOA.

22. Kimberly S. Hanger, *Bounded Lives, Bounded Places: Free Black Society in Colonial New Orleans, 1769–1803* (Durham, N.C.: Duke University Press, 1997), 17–87.

23. "General Accounts, 1797–1812," UCNOA.

24. Ibid.

25. Hall, *Africans in Colonial Louisiana*, 168, 183.

26. Costa, trans., *Letters of Marie Madeleine Hachard*, 20; "Délibérations du Conseil," 44, UCNOA.

27. "Délibérations du Conseil," 45, 64, UCNOA.

28. Ibid., 73; SLC-M3, 13, no. 77, 14 July 1795, AANO.

29. "Délibérations du Conseil," 81, UCNOA; "Achat de Denise/Venus," act of sale notarized by Carlos Ximenes, 16 May 1798, UCNOA; SLC-M3, 16, no. 42 bis, AANO. See the opening paragraph of this essay for more on the circumstances of the marriage of Charles and Denise.

30. The story of Theresa and her three husbands is told in the following: Theresa St. Xavier Farjon to Bishop Luis Ignacio de Peñalver, 6 April 1799; Josef de Basquez to Theresa St. Xavier Farjon, 19 April 1799; Bishop Luis Ignacio de Peñalver to Theresa St. Xavier Farjon, 3 August 1799; Francisco Jese de Bassave to Antonia Monica Ramos, 9 June 1801; Antonia De Santa Monica Ramos to Bishop Luis Ignacio de Peñalver, 21 July 1801; Pedro de Tamora to Bishop Luis Ignacio de Peñalver, 27 July 1801; Bishop Luis Ignacio de Peñalver to Pedro de Tamora, 21 July 1801; Notarized statement of Theresa, 13 September 1802; Notarized statement of Angelica Regis, 15 September 1802; Theresa St. Xavier Farjon to Patrick Walsh, 11 June 1804; Patrick Walsh to Theresa St. Xavier Farjon, 12 June 1804; and Notarized statement of Angelica Regis, 16 June 1804, Catholic Archives of America, University of Notre Dame, South Bend, Indiana, xerox copy of manuscript originals at AANO; translations by Jane Francis Heaney, UCNOA.

31. Baptismal records for three sample years during French domination, 1744, 1760, and 1765, show that between 12 and 19 percent of slave children were born to married parents. Of these years, only 1765 includes the baptisms of Ursuline slaves, so this data illustrates that slave marriage did not take place only or even primarily between the slaves of nuns and clergy. This relatively high rate of slave marriage may be partly attributable to compliance with the directive that slaves be married by the church: Le Code Noir ou Édit du Roi. Servant de Réglement pour le governement & l'Administration de la Justice, Police, Discipline & le Commerce des Esclaves Nègres, dans la Province ou Colonie de la Louisiane. Donné à Versailles au mois de Mars 1724," in *Le Code Noir ou Recueil des reglemens rendus jusqu'à present, concernant le gouvernment, l'Administration de la Justice, la Police, la discipline & le Commerce des Nègres dans les Colonies Françaises* (Paris: Chez Prault, 1742) (hereafter *Code Noir*); St. Louis Cathedral Baptisms II, 1744–53; St. Louis Cathedral Baptisms, IV, 1759–62; St. Louis Cathedral Baptisms V, 1763–66 (hereafter SLC-B5); St. Louis Cathedral Baptisms, VII, 1772–76; "Libre donde se asientan las partidas de bautismos de negros y mulatos libres o esclavos el que dió principio en 17 de junio de 1783 para el Isso de esta parroquial de San Luis de Nueva Orleans en la provincia de la Luisiana" (hereafter SLC-B10); and "Libro quinto de bautizados negros y mulatos de la parroquia de sn. Luis de esta ciudad de la Nueva Orleans: Contiene doscientos trienta y siete folios útiles, y da principio

de primero de octubre de mil setecientos noventa y dos, y acaba [en 1798]" (hereafter SLC-B13), all AANO; *Code Noir*, 325, Article VII of the 1724 version.

32. In 1800, the attorney general of New Orleans complained about the effect on the general public of the Capuchins' refusal to bury or marry anyone until their fees were fully paid (Hanger, *Bounded Lives, Bounded Places*, 90–92; Jack D. L. Holmes, "Do It! Don't Do It!: Spanish Laws on Sex and Marriage," in *The Spanish Presence in Louisiana, 1763–1803*, ed. Gilbert C. Din [Lafayette, La.: Center for Louisiana Studies, 1996], 168–69).

33. Hall, *Africans in Colonial Louisiana*, 277–86.

34. SLC-B10, 120, no. 526, 24 April 1785; 136, no. 584, 6 August 1785; 146, no. 623, 25 September 1785; 152, no. 645, 30 October 1785; SLC-B13, 184, no. 749, 8 March 1795; 201, no. 803, 10 May 1795; 230, no. 911, 20 September 1796, AANO.

35. The nuns sold their carpenter, Laurant, to a new master because he had taken to drink, some years after his wife and child disappeared from the record ("Délibérations du Conseil," 57, UCNOA). Laurant had previously been esteemed enough in the community at large to serve as a godfather, but his wife, Jeanne, bore him only one child, in 1766, and the disappearance of both wife and child from the record suggests that they did not survive long afterward (SLC-B13, 40, 21 September 1755; SLC-B5, 113, no. 3, 13 February 1766).

36. Acts of Garic, vol. 8 (January–December 1777), 8 November 1777, 402, NANO.

37. *Code Noir*, 348–49, Articles XLIII and XLIV of the 1724 version, required that slave families be sold together and that no children under the age of fourteen be sold separately from their mothers. As Hans W. Baade, "The Law of Slavery in Spanish Louisiana," in *Louisiana's Legal Heritage*, ed. Edward F. Hass (Pensacola: Louisiana State Museum, 1983), 54–58, explains, Spanish slave law in Louisiana was not articulated in a single code but took shape through judicial decisions of the governor and municipal officials of the *cabildo*, or town council. The preservation of slave families was neither an aim nor a result of Spanish colonial legal administration. Hall, *Africans in Colonial Louisiana*, 169–71, 304–5, provides several examples of slaves who were inventoried and presumably sold in family groups during the French period but notes that during the Spanish period children younger than eight years of age were frequently sold apart from their mothers.

38. "Délibérations du Conseil," 67, UCNOA; Acts of Perdomo, vol. 16 (June 13–December 1790), 24 March 1790, 143 bis-144 bis, NANO.

39. "Livres ou sont les noms," 2, 81, and "Délibérations du Conseil," 111, 118, 121, 129, UCNOA.

40. See Clark, "A New World Community," app. 3, for a reconstruction of slave family groups and kin networks at the Ursuline Convent based on Sacramental Registers of St. Louis Cathedral, 1744–1830, AANO; Sacramental Registers of the Ursuline Convent Chapel, 1835–53, UCNOA; "Délibérations du Conseil," UCNOA; "Book of Slaves," UCNOA; and Notarial Acts, NANO.

41. "Livre ou sont les noms"; "Ursuline Convent Chapel Baptismal Register, 1835–1837"; "Ursuline Convent Chapel Baptismal Register, 1837–1845"; "Ursuline Convent Chapel Baptismal Register, 1845–1853," all UCNOA.

42. "Ursuline Convent Chapel Baptismal Register, 1845–1853," entries for 28 April 1849 and 25 May 1850, UCNOA.

43. On the sexualization of slave women see Foster, "Ultimate Victims," esp. 846, 848–49, and White, *Ar'n't I a Woman*, 22, 32.

44. "Délibérations du Conseil," 79, 88, UCNOA; "Libro de bautizados negros y mulatos," AANO, 198, no. 1113, 3 January 1791; SLC-M3, 16, no. 43 bis, AANO.

45. "Délibérations du Conseil," 57, 75, 79, 81, 109, 115; "Livre ou sont les noms," leaves 25, 27; "Ursuline Convent Chapel Baptismal Register, 1837–1845," entry for 8 January 1843, all UCNOA.

46. Lori D. Ginzberg, *Women and the Work of Benevolence: Morality, Politics, and Class in the Nineteenth-Century United States* (New Haven: Yale University Press, 1990), traces the rise and ultimate professionalization of Protestant female benevolence.

47. Congregations of working-class women in France, such as the Filles de la Charité, also supported themselves through the provision of services in the seventeenth and eighteenth centuries, but their funds came to them through contracts with civil and ecclesiastical authorities. Their success turned on a single relationship with a male governing body. The colonial Ursulines never relied solely on such an arrangement, and the fees they received from individuals as direct compensation for their teaching skills made up their largest source of income.

*Chapter Ten*

# Faith and Frugality in Antebellum Baltimore:
# The Economic Credo of the Oblate
# Sisters of Providence

## DIANE BATTS MORROW

As free black women, as Roman Catholics, and as institutionalized religious, the Oblate Sisters of Providence formed the antithesis of the white, Protestant family patriarch who typified the empowered citizen in nineteenth-century American society. Organized in Baltimore in 1828, this first permanent sisterhood of African descent in the United States both challenged and responded to social and ecclesial attitudes about race and gender. Oblate Sisters of Providence lived in community, executed their teaching ministry, and defined themselves positively as black women religious, in spite of their experience of social derogation predicated on their identities as black women in the antebellum South. Economic self-reliance inhered in this empowered, positive Oblate self-image.

As the "free Negro capital of America" after 1820, Baltimore offered the Oblate Sisters a potentially critical base of black community support. Between 1800 and 1850 the free black population of Baltimore increased by more than 22,000 people, which represented a growth rate in excess of 800 percent during the first half of the nineteenth century.[1] But the numerical strength of Baltimore's free black population did not represent an equivalent accumulation of wealth: compared to the smaller free black populations in fourteen antebellum cities, Baltimore's free black inhabitants ranked in the bottom quadrant of taxable property holders in the 1850s.[2] The tenuous position of Maryland's free black population—economically essential and socially anomalous—reflected the inherent volatility of Maryland's dualistic slave and free political economy. Racial prejudice routinely restricted most of Baltimore's free black population to the least remunerative and prestigious occupations as unskilled laborers and domestic servants. Gender as well as racial proscriptions further reduced black women to employment almost exclusively as domestic servants and laundresses.[3] As a black teaching sisterhood serving black patrons, the Oblate Sisters challenged existing racial mores by sustaining themselves financially through their religious profession and their literacy skills.

The Oblate Sisters joined three other sisterhoods previously established in the Archdiocese of Baltimore: the Carmelite Nuns (1790), the Visitation Sisters of Georgetown in Washington, D.C. (1800), and the Sisters of Charity of St. Joseph, Emmitsburg, Maryland (1809). By 1837 all four groups maintained missions in the city of Baltimore.[4] The School Sisters of Notre Dame (1847), the Sisters of Mercy (1855), and the Sisters of the Holy Cross (1859) complete the roster of sisterhoods functioning in antebellum Baltimore.[5] Because the Archdiocese of Baltimore committed no financial resources to the maintenance of any of its sisterhoods, business and financial matters formed an integral part of these communities' concerns.[6] While issues of gender woven into the nineteenth-century social context affected the Oblate Sisters of Providence and their peer sisterhoods comparably, the pervasive strands of racism woven warp and woof into the American social fabric ensnared the Oblate community alone. The Oblate Sisters engaged in paid work in a variety of forms within and beyond their household. This essay examines Oblate participation in the market economy. It also considers how issues of race affected economic interactions between the Oblate Sisters and segments of Maryland's black and white antebellum populations.

Two streams of immigration that converged in Baltimore in the 1790s enabled the formation of the Oblate Sisters almost forty years later. As the see, or official seat, of the first diocese of the Roman Catholic Church formed in the United States in 1789, Baltimore proved a logical haven for Catholics fleeing revolutions in France and the Caribbean. The French Sulpician priests arrived in Baltimore in 1791 to educate young men for the priesthood. Beginning in 1793, black and mulatto as well as white refugees fled the slave revolution in the French Caribbean colony of St. Domingue to several port cities in the United States.[7] In Baltimore, shared traditions attracted Sulpicians and San Domingan exiles to each other, bound together by their French language and cultural heritage and their profession of the Roman Catholic faith.

In 1796 the Sulpician priests organized Sunday religious instruction in French for the black San Domingan refugees who congregated in their seminary chapel. In 1827 James Joubert assumed direction of this Sunday religious training and proposed a school to facilitate religious instruction. To staff the school Joubert approached Caribbean emigrants Elizabeth Clarisse Lange and Marie Magdelaine Balas, two educated women of color and experienced teachers who conducted their own school for children of their race in their home. Oblate sources state that even prior to the establishment of the Oblate sisterhood and school, black Caribbean émigré parents "lost no time in placing their children in Miss Lange's school . . . filled with the children of the most intelligent families of Baltimore . . . [as well as] a very large number of the poorer class who had no means of paying their tuition."[8] Lange's school evidently served a broad spectrum of the black Francophone community, from poor families to those enjoying sufficiently comfortable circumstances to finance their children's education at the school. The fact that Lange and Balas had independently established a school in Baltimore demonstrated their determination to address a perceived need for education in their new country without seeking white, male, or institutional sanction to proceed.

During their initial meeting, Lange and Balas informed Joubert of their decade-long desire to fulfill religious vocations. After consulting with Archbishop James Whitfield of Baltimore, Joubert concluded that a black sisterhood would suit his purposes as well.[9] Lange served as the first Oblate Mother Superior; Joubert, as the community's first spiritual director. To counter white society's efforts to circumscribe their existence, black Baltimoreans created a nexus of religious, social, and educational institutions as bulwarks supporting their community life.[10] Historically, black people had marshaled their spiritual resources to assert their personal worth. Whether slave or free, black people in the Protestant tradition utilized religion both on an individual basis and collectively in congregations to counter the onslaughts of a racist society disallowing black humanity. The formation of the Oblate community provided another incarnation of black religious piety. The Oblate Sisters of Providence distinguished themselves as black women in the Roman Catholic tradition by their collective profession and practice of spirituality formalized in the pursuit of religious communal life. As black women religious, the Oblate Sisters claimed for themselves the traditional entitlements of respectability and societal exemption inherent in the religious state. In community, black women felt empowered to transcend mere social opposition to their divinely mandated mission: their own personal spiritual perfection and the education of black children. To women circumscribed and demeaned by white society because of their racial identity, the appeal of membership in such an organization proved significant.

Elizabeth Clarisse Lange had apparently enjoyed a relatively privileged life, including a formal education. Born of racially mixed parentage, probably in the 1780s in either St. Domingue or Cuba,[11] Lange maintained financial independence in the slave city of Baltimore subsidized by her father's estate. Oblate sources assert that "Sister Mary [Lange] especially was very often the recipient of large sums of money, sent from her home in Santiago."[12] Lange had inherited "$2000 left her by Monsieur Lange her father" and had "received in settlement $1411.59 which was due her" in 1832 and 1833, respectively.[13] The Oblate Sisters of Providence did not own slaves. However, Elizabeth Lange, and later the Oblate community through her inheritance, clearly benefited from the institution of slavery that generated planter wealth.

The teaching sisterhoods conducting schools in antebellum American society derived much of their income from tuition. The young ladies' academies established in the Archdiocese of Baltimore numbered among their pupils and alumna the daughters of both Roman Catholic and Protestant planter elite, affluent businessmen, and influential politicians as well as middle-class families. In 1809 the Sisters of Charity of St. Joseph, Emmitsburg, had intended to educate poor girls exclusively but experienced such financial straits within their first year of operation that they reluctantly consented to establish an elite academy. From its inception in 1810 the academy generated sufficient income not only to sustain itself but also to subsidize the sisters' instructional efforts for poor girls as well.[14]

The Oblate Sisters also realized a significant portion of their income from tuition charges, a noteworthy fact in a social context that otherwise relegated black women to the most menial forms of drudgery for economic survival. In 1829 Joubert twice commented, with evident satisfaction, that student enrollment proved sufficient to meet all Oblate expenses.[15] Nevertheless, in contrast to the affluence associated with the white Baltimore-area academies, the racially based comparative economic disadvantage of the Oblate target population restricted both the amount and the regular receipt of tuition income the Oblate Sisters could expect. From the 1830s through the 1850s skilled black artisans and mechanics in Baltimore encountered hostile competition from white immigrants and the number of skilled occupations customarily reserved as an exclusively black preserve steadily eroded.[16]

From the beginning of the Oblate sisterhood, members of the Baltimore black community participated actively in promoting the Oblate cause—from working-class people to the few privileged elite who acted as benefactors. Typically, members of the black community demonstrated their support of the Oblate mission by patronizing the school. The Oblate school's annual charge of

$80—twelve months of board and tuition at $4 a month, an annual medical fee of $24, and bed and bedding for $8[17]—appeared extremely modest compared to the basic charge of $160 assessed by the Visitation Nuns for the Georgetown Academy and that of $147 set by the Sisters of Charity for St. Joseph's Academy at Emmitsburg.[18] The Oblate Sisters responded sensitively and sensibly to the straitened circumstances of many of their parents. In addition to the boarding pupils, the sisters accommodated day scholars, who paid $2 for quarterly tuition and an annual book fee of $0.375.[19] The school offered multiple student discounts to certain parents enrolling more than one child. Still, some parents fell considerably in arrears in tuition payments. The Oblate Sisters engaged in creative financing, tolerated sizable deficits, offered scholarships, and in general made every effort to work with the black community to make an Oblate education as affordable and accessible as possible. In return, members of the black community both in and beyond Baltimore rallied to the support of the Oblate community and proved themselves parents who were "if not wealthy, very respectable, honest, and hard working, thinking no sacrifice too great for the welfare of the children."[20]

Dowries provided a second significant source of income for Baltimore's antebellum sisterhoods. The three white sisterhoods that preceded the Oblate community in the archdiocese had not stipulated specific required amounts for dowries. However, the dowry of £2,000 that candidate Jane Hamersley brought to the Carmelite Nuns in 1794 and that of $3,000 in cash plus real estate holdings that candidate Elizabeth Neale surrendered to the Visitation Sisters of Georgetown around 1818 both reflected and typified the familial ties to Maryland's planter aristocracy and the wealth a significant portion of the membership of these two white communities of women religious enjoyed.[21]

The Oblate Rule required prospective candidates to provide a dowry of $400. Depending on the circumstances and qualifications of the candidate, the community could waive this requirement. The sum could prove prohibitive for black candidates who lacked family affluence and who worked in a society that prejudicially curtailed their economic options. Archbishop James Whitfield, not Joubert or Lange, had fixed the dowry amount. Because financial constraints engendered by the racial identity of the Oblate membership and their proposed clientele had threatened the Oblate project from its conception, Whitfield undoubtedly stipulated the dowry to bolster the community's financial self-sufficiency.[22]

Historian Barbara Misner characterizes one-third of the Oblate membership before 1850 as middle class in socioeconomic background.[23] Black and white populations employed different criteria in determining middle-class status. Generally, black people considered not only family wealth but also free lineage, reputation, education, material possessions, and color in ascribing middle-class status. Baltimore's black community proved exceptional in not privileging color as a criterion of social status. Black barbers, caterers, and tradespeople serving a white clientele exclusively, black entrepreneurs operating shops, boarding-houses, and saloons for black patrons, and black people in personal service to important white business, political, or social elite households formed important elements of the black middle class. Although Baltimore's free black population also supported a small professional elite of physicians, ministers, lawyers, and teachers who served the black community, no evidence documents that Oblate members derived from this portion of the black middle class. Oblate family backgrounds more often included barbers and tradespeople, many of whom achieved a comfortable standard of living in antebellum Baltimore.

Five Oblate Sisters invoked the dowry waiver clause incorporated in the original Oblate Rule during the sisterhood's first decade. Most candidates, however, presented at least a token dowry, if not the full stipulated sum. Some Oblate candidates presenting the full dowry amount had earned the money themselves from working. The Oblate annals' cumulative account from 17 May 1828 through 1 January 1836 cited $4,429.30 income from dowries, representing some nineteen entering candidates, averaging $233 dowry per capita.[24] A sufficient segment of the Baltimore black community acquired the resources to support a private school for girls and the black religious community founded to staff it.

In 1834 and 1835 three members of the Andrew Noel family of Wilmington, Delaware, entered the Oblate community. This exceptional family had risen veritably from rags to riches in the cherished American tradition. Parents Andrew and Laurette Noel arrived in Wilmington in 1804 as slaves in the Garesche household, all San Domingan refugees. After their owner had manumitted them, he endowed them with a significant amount of money. The Noels purchased extensive plots of prime Wilmington real estate. They operated an inn at one end of their property and lived comfortably among "the French nobility and Wilmington wealthy." The enterprising Andrew Noel also opened a barber shop. He secured his position as a respected member of the Wilmington Francophone community by renting one of only fourteen pews—the socially prominent DuPont family rented another—in St. Mary's of Coffee Run, the first Catholic church in Delaware.[25] Noel's untimely death sometime after 1820 left Laurette Jane Noel a prosperous if bereaved widow. For at least five years, from the death of her husband until she joined the Oblate community in 1835, Laurette Noel successfully managed the considerable business interests she had inherited from her husband.

The Noel family endowed the Oblate community with a significant financial estate. The Oblate annals entry of 1 June 1833 noted of the nineteen-year-old Jane Laurette that "if she is received she will bring with her more than the required dowry, her father having left her a small fortune at his death."[26] Two years later in 1835, mother Laurette and daughter Marie Louise Noel applied for Oblate membership. In addition to considerable personal property, the Noel women surrendered to the Oblate community Wilmington real estate valued between $1,500 and $2,000 and total cash assets of approximately $2,000.[27]

Only rarely did Oblate members like Elizabeth Lange and Laurette, Jane, and Marie Louise Noel enrich the community with significant personal wealth. More typically, Oblate candidates paid dowry and other expenses from wage-earning work. San Domingan émigré Betsy Duchemin received a good education in Baltimore, including training as a nurse. While employed in that capacity in the household of the socially prominent Howard family, Duchemin met the visiting British major Arthur Howard who fathered her child, Marie Therese, born in 1809. From at least 1822 Duchemin placed her daughter in the care and under the tutelage of Elizabeth Lange and Marie Balas, whom Marie Therese joined in profession as one of the four charter members of the Oblate Sisters of Providence on 2 July 1829.[28] Betsy Duchemin apparently financed her daughter's education and Oblate dowry from her earnings as a nurse. She declared her own intention to join the Oblate community in September 1829 but delayed her entrance as her "affairs would still keep her in the world for about two years."[29] Evidently, Duchemin had to continue her work as a nurse to amass her dowry, $200 of which she advanced on 9 September 1829.[30] Even after entering the Oblate community as Sister Anthony in 1831, Betsy Duchemin continued to practice nursing professionally.

The Oblate Sisters accommodated a limited number of paying female boarders, more as a service to such patrons than as a source of significant income. Younger women seriously contemplating a religious vocation and elderly pensioners lacking family providers for their care typified the Oblate boarder. Between 1829 and 1839 the sisters received five boarders who paid $6 per month for room and board. From 1829 Betsy Duchemin and Eugenie LeBarth boarded two and four years, respectively, while working in the outside world before joining the Oblate community as members. The elderly Elizabeth DuMoulin boarded with the Oblate Sisters from 1831 until her death in 1837. The terms of their contract stipulated that "besides the care that the Sisters shall give this respectable old lady, they shall also furnish her with fire, nourishment, and do her laundry."[31]

In 1833 Helen Bourgoin, a relative of three Oblate members, arranged to board with the Oblate Sisters, "when the infirmities of age should make it impossible for her to gain a living by working." Helen Bourgoin had worked as a domestic servant for many years and agreed to surrender to the Oblate community all her present and future savings in return for perpetual care. Bourgoin's agreement with the Oblate community stipulated that if she died before taking up residence in the Oblate convent, her heirs would have no claim to her funds. By 17 June 1833 Bourgoin had paid the Oblate community $350.[32] In July 1833 Sister Mary Elizabeth Lange donated $1,411.59 to the Oblate community. In return she requested that the sisters agree to shelter her mother, Nanette Lange, "on the same conditions as Helen Bourgoin."[33] Elizabeth DuMoulin, Helen Bourgoin, and Nanette Lange undoubtedly remained indebted to the Oblate community for providing a viable alternative to the Baltimore municipal almshouse's attic "chronic hospital for aged colored women."[34]

Sewing provided another significant source of income for the Oblate Sisters from 1834.[35] The first Oblate prospectus published in the *Laity's Directory* concluded with the notice: "N.B. At the suggestion of several Right Reverend Bishops and Clergymen who attended the Provincial Council, the Sisters of Providence have taken measures for furnishing the different Dioceses of the United States with Clerical Vestments of all sorts, at the lowest prices, and on the shortest possible notice."[36] Evidently, the Oblate Sisters' skilled needlework displayed at their convent so impressed visiting clergy that it precipitated a business opportunity for the community. The Sulpician priest Pierre Babad had initiated negotiations with the Didier Petit Company in Lyons, France, to supply ornaments and cloth on credit until the Oblate Sisters had made, sold, and received payment for the vestments. When the cloth did not arrive and the clergy began ordering vestments, "the Director [Joubert], after taking counsel with the Sisters, decided to write again to ask them to send the cloth."[37]

This entrepreneurial venture proved a lucrative enterprise for the Oblate Sisters from 1834 to 1844. Oblate member and historian Sister M. Theresa Catherine Willigman recalled in her nineteenth-century accounts that "for a number of years the Sisters had as many orders as they could fill. Sets of vestments of the best material were always on hand, and the writer saw, when a child, a complete set worth hundreds of dollars. As there was no other establishment at this time, of this kind, this was a good revenue for the Sisters." The itemized list of vestments the Oblate Sisters offered in the national Catholic directory from 1836 through 1839 corroborated Willigman's recollection of "vestments of the best material." Items ranged from a complete set of vestments in red damask silk richly embroidered with fine gold, adorned with lace and fine gold fringe, and completely lined in silk for $750 to pastoral stoles edged with mock gold or silk and silk-lined for $5.[38]

The Oblate financial statement of 1 January 1836 listed annual income from sewing as $440, second only to income from boarding students at $540. Sewing formed such a significant aspect of Oblate community life that sometime later in the nineteenth century the Oblate Rule temporarily incorporated it as part of the community's mission: "*Note (a). Sewing* in all its branches has been an auxiliary activity from the beginning, ecclesiastically approved, and occupies those incapacitated to teach and to prevent idleness and to contribute to the support of the community."[39]

In 1835 Louis Deluol, Sulpician Superior of St. Mary's Seminary, proposed that Oblate Sisters manage the household and infirmary duties at the seminary. The custom of procuring the services of women religious to perform domestic duties in seminaries and colleges originated in France. Sisters of Charity of St. Joseph served in this capacity at Mount St. Mary's College at Emmitsburg, Maryland, from 1815 to 1852.[40] The Sulpicians were to pay the Oblate community $120 annually as compensation for the services of two sisters.[41] The Oblate Sisters performed this service at the seminary until 1850. Whether in sewing vestments for male clergy or in assuming domestic household duties at the Sulpician seminary, the Oblate Sisters clearly relied on traditional male economic power and wealth for their self-support. Nevertheless, male clergy paid the Oblate Sisters for their domestic and sewing services, thereby transforming female labor customarily unpaid when performed within domestic households into a market exchange.

The comprehensive financial statement issued on 1 January 1836 represented all the income and disbursements of the Oblate institute from 17 May 1828 to date. The figures portray a picture of sound financial management and fiscal responsibility. Long term, the sisters maintained a deficit of only $5.775, despite a series of real estate transactions, renovations, and building on their Richmond Street property to accommodate the steadily growing Oblate community and school. Short term, the sisters balanced annual expenditures of $1,000 against an annual income of $1,305. Significantly, gifts or donations from external sources amounted to only $360 for the eight-year period; subscriptions, only $40, the smallest source of income listed.[42] Neither large infusions of wealth from generous patrons nor personal fortunes of heiress members loomed large on the Oblate fiscal horizon during the entire antebellum era. The sisters maintained solvency through hard work, discipline, sound management, and self-reliance. The Oblate community sustained its economic self-sufficiency a lesson, a stitch, and a prayer at a time.

In the European tradition, religious orders incorporated three distinct classes of sisters in a socially stratified order. The choir nuns formed the elite who devoted themselves exclusively to prayer and meditation. The lay sisters derived from the servant class and performed all the domestic labor. The externs lived outside the cloister and conducted the community's business affairs.[43] Many American communities of sisters institutionalized no class stratifications, although members of at least six white antebellum communities of sisters nationwide owned slaves.[44] Unlike the white sisterhoods serving the archdiocese of Baltimore—the Carmelite Nuns, the Georgetown Sisters of the Visitation, and the Sisters of Charity—the Oblate Sisters owned no slaves to perform their labor. In fact, Oblate Sisters Chantal (Laurette Noel), Helen Joseph (Mary West), Clotilde (Marie Germaine), and Angelica (Angelica Gideon) all began life as slaves. Of the forty women who entered the Oblate novitiate in the antebellum period, eight had risen from slave origins.[45] The Oblate Sisters of Providence did not consider a candidate's previous condition of servitude a liability for Oblate membership.

Given their anomalous status within both antebellum church and southern society, it proves hardly surprising that the Oblate Sisters neither expressed abolitionist sentiments nor engaged in antislavery activities, whatever their private feelings about slavery might have been. Oblate silence about slavery occurred within the context of an American Roman Catholic Church, whose clergy and hierarchy not only frequently and vociferously defended the institution of slavery but also participated in and profited from it.[46] Under such circumstances Oblate refusal to recognize former slave status as a deterrent to membership merits consideration as an Oblate commentary on the institution of slavery itself.

As a teaching community, the Oblate Sisters endured with other sisterhoods throughout the world who engaged in ministries of service the subordinate status ascribed them in the ecclesial hierarchy. Many sisterhoods incorporated teaching, nursing, or caring for orphans into their missions as their primary means of financial support. Such professions differentiated these active sisterhoods in both the United States and Europe from regular orders of nuns whose substantial endowments allowed them the choice of cloistered contemplation as their exclusive occupation. Church authorities in Rome promoted cloistered contemplation as the preferred model for female religious communities universally. In contending with opposing goals of spiritual isolation and worldly involvement, the Oblate community and its peer sisterhoods with service ministries throughout the world experienced the dynamic tension between the realities imposed by their active ministries and the rigid standards for legitimacy imposed by the church hierarchy.[47]

The arduous daily routine of household chores, teaching responsibilities, and religious observances maintained by these sisters required considerable physical stamina. The Oblate Sisters performed all the cooking, cleaning, and laundry of the household themselves, in addition to their teaching duties, on a rotating basis as far as the skills of the individual sisters permitted. Willigman remembered, "In the first early years of the community it was no uncommon thing to see the Sisters piling wood in the yard, taking care of the stable, milking the cow, and other labors."[48] Far from an escape from harsh realities, Oblate life entailed physical deprivation, arduous labor, long hours, and straitened circumstances.

Business matters remained an important aspect of Oblate community life in the early 1840s. A financial statement prepared in January 1842 included a detailed account of Oblate transactions with the firm Didier Petit in Lyons, France. Making vestments for American clergy continued to be a profitable enterprise for the sisters. Between March 1836 and January 1842 the community had received almost $11,500 worth of merchandise from which they sold over $8,000 worth of vestments and had made, but not yet sold, vestments worth almost $2,000. Between January 1840 and January 1842 the Oblate Sisters had realized a profit of $227 on their vestment venture.[49]

Yet the sisters did not experience unalloyed profit and prosperity in their business transactions. Like other entrepreneurs, the Oblate Sisters encountered the vagaries of the market and the caprice of supply and demand. Their profit margin declined from $440 in 1836 to $227 over a two-year period from 1840 to 1842.[50] The nature of the commodity they produced in part explained this shrinking profitability. Although clothing, vestments resembled durable goods in that their owners reserved them for occasional or ceremonial use, ignored seasonal and fashion trend turnover, and replaced them only in the event of loss, damage, or wear. Prelate John Baptist Purcell of Cincinnati purchased vestments worth more than $3,000 between 1837 and 1839; Samuel Eccleston of Baltimore, more than $1,500 worth of merchandise in 1840.[51] These men undoubtedly considered such purchases capital investments, not annual expenses. Furthermore, many of the clerics ministering to Catholics in the United States had outfitted themselves with vestments before they had emigrated from Europe.

The Oblate Sisters also encountered problems with their supplier. In correspondence with Didier Petit in April 1843, an irate Joubert inquired about a shipment several months overdue. He complained, "I see that I must tell you: everyday new demands are made of the Sisters. They would have sold a large amount after nearly six months, but this is impossible, not being better stocked. . . . It is no longer possible to satisfy these requests. The Sisters lose and you do too." Joubert concluded the letter by threatening "to apply to Paris, or to New York, or to some merchants who will better assist me in continuing this good work."[52]

The itemized list of vestments the Oblate Sisters offered had filled two pages in the national Catholic directory from 1836 through 1839. In the 1840 through 1844 editions of this publication, however, the drastically curtailed advertisements did not mention the Oblate Sisters at all. The notices merely advised that "vestments of different colours and of various qualities and prices may be procured by applying to Rev. H. Joubert, St. Mary's Seminary, Baltimore."[53] Such abbreviated advertising may have reflected the reduced profitability of the vestment-making venture for the Oblate Sisters as much as their reduced inventory of vestments resulting both from sales and from supply problems.

The Oblate community's financial statement for January 1840 to January 1842, figured to the quarter-penny, documented the sisters' continued practice of hard work, discipline, frugal management, and self-reliance. Budget itemizations like "Selling of small articles by Sister Therese—$65.72" and "Particular sewing made by working Sisters—$121" demonstrated Oblate self-reliance. In the 1840–42 interval the sisters managed to retire $569.30 of the principal of their debt that then totaled $1,968.375. To eliminate this debt, the community intended to sell the Noel Wilmington estate, valued at $1,600, and items they had worth $800 for a total of $2,400, leaving "a surplus in our favor."[54]

Certain figures in the 1840–42 financial statement suggest the precarious nature of Oblate solvency in the early 1840s. The Noel family's Wilmington estate represented a major, nonrenewable resource. Although its intended sale would help liquidate an outstanding debt, its loss would deprive the Oblate community of an income-generating asset. Likewise, the $800 in personal property the sisters had inventoried to sell represented a liquidation of nonrenewable assets. Furthermore, Joubert may have optimistically inflated the projected proceeds of $2,400 from the sale of this real and personal property. In 1843 an item he valued at $127 sold for only $41.[55]

Dowries, the second largest source of income for the Oblate Sisters at almost $4,500 from 1828 through 1835, had plummeted in the early 1840s to a single dowry of $200. In spite of the continuing interest in Oblate membership demonstrated by black Catholic women in Baltimore and Washington, D.C., Sister Louise Gabriel Addison remained the only candidate who entered the Oblate community in the 1840s and persevered in her vocation. The limited financial resources of the Oblate community afforded them fewer occasions to waive the dowry requirement for even the worthiest of candidates as the community grew. Conversely, the generally straitened economic circumstances of the black community produced fewer candidates who could pay the full dowry requirement. Declining Oblate admissions in the 1840s proved less a function of diminishing spiritual resources in the black Catholic community than of diminished financial resources.

For the remainder of the antebellum period, no Oblate candidates matched, much less exceeded, the generous financial endowments with which cofounder Lange and the three Noel women from Wilmington had enriched the community. Oblate dowry income remained negligible during the decade of the 1850s. Although the Oblate community received and professed some thirteen candidates between 1849 and 1860, extant Oblate records note one dowry of $180 for these years.[56]

In November 1842 the Oblate Sisters initiated collections at Masses in their chapel to augment income. Collections produced negligible amounts ranging from a high of $3.08 on the first day to a low of $0.28 on Christmas Day 1842, and averaging $0.70 for the four months the Oblate annalist recorded the amounts.[57] Without an endowment or substantial income generating assets, even the most austere and frugal lifestyle, fiscal discipline, and hard work could only forestall the relentless encroachment of insolvency.

Oblate spiritual director James Joubert's death in November 1843 and the subsequent alienation of the Sulpician priests and diocesan authorities from the Oblate community subjected the sisters to trials that tested both their faith and their viability as a community of women religious. For almost four years the Oblate Sisters strictly adhered to their vows and community rules and steadfastly observed religious community life without benefit of clerical direction. Finally, in October 1847 the Redemptorist priests courageously assumed the spiritual direction of the abandoned Oblate community in the person of the newly ordained Thaddeus Anwander.

While enjoying newfound security in the spiritual aspects of their lives during the late 1840s and 1850s, the Oblate Sisters still struggled to maintain solvency. Anwander later noted that when he became Oblate spiritual director in 1847, the sisters had "orphan and school children about 10, some $700 debt, and no income except taking in washing and mending for the Seminary and the Cathedral."[58] However, an untitled and unremarked ledger housed in the Oblate Archives preserves accounts of Oblate business transactions from January 1844 through December 1854. This document provides a more nuanced perspective on the Oblate financial picture than Anwander's terse summary suggests.

The very existence of the ledger bears silent witness to the remarkable stability and continuity of the Oblate experience during the crisis of 1844–47 as the sisters accomplished the routine requirements of conducting their community and school life without benefit of male guidance. Ledger entries reveal that the sisters continued the practice established under Joubert's directorship of depositing sums on a regular basis in an account with Louis Deluol at St. Mary's Seminary. Between January 1844 and October 1849, the sisters had deposited $1,556.81 with Deluol in amounts as small as $3 and as large as $177 on an almost monthly basis. These deposits frequently represented 30–75 percent of monthly Oblate expenses and, not infrequently, an even larger percentage of their monthly income.[59]

In January 1842 the Oblate community had carried a debt burden of $1,968.37.[60] Anwander's prosaic statement that the sisters carried a $700 debt in 1847 masks the extraordinary Oblate achievement of significantly reducing their debt, under the less than propitious circumstances ensuing from Joubert's death in 1843. Oblate discipline, frugality, and funds deposited at St. Mary's Seminary enabled the sisters to retire more than $1,200 of the principal of their debt between 1842 and 1847.

Oblate income exceeded expenses by $170.45 January 1844 through December 1847, including Anwander's first months as spiritual director. The only unencumbered income cited in the ledger for the entire decade 1844–54 appeared in January 1844: a New Year's gift of $10 from Louis Deluol and an anonymous donation of $50. Oblate income consisted almost exclusively of compensation for goods and services provided by the Oblate Sisters and occasional loans.[61]

Ledger information challenges Anwander's contention that the sisters derived "no income except washing and mending for the Seminary and Cathedral." Although a dependable source of income, laundering the cathedral altar linens earned the Oblate Sisters only $3 to $4 a month through 1847. Sewing clerical vestments remained a more lucrative enterprise for the sisters, accounting for an income of $483.67 during the 1844–47 period alone. Between 1844 and 1861, the Oblate Sisters realized more than $2000 in income from sewing vestments.[62]

This ledger proved as informative for its contents as for entries it did not include. It duly recorded four separate entries of $5.00, $2.60, $2.31, and $4.375 as "Cash of Sister Mary for making preserves for Seminary."[63] However, the ledger cited no receipts of the annual $120 the Sulpician priests had contracted to pay for Oblate household managers, although Oblate Sisters Mary Lange and Rose Boegue filled these positions at the seminary until 1850. Sulpician compensation for the six-year period 1844–49 would have totaled $720. Only two months after Sulpician authorities appointed Francis Lhomme superior of St. Mary's Seminary in Baltimore and recalled Louis Deluol to France permanently in November 1849, an Oblate ledger entry under date 1 February 1850 noted, "Cash given for to save [*sic*] to the Redemptorist fathers from Rev. Mr. Lhomme, on the 31st of January $500, when [*sic*] $200."[64] Transfer of $700 from Sulpician to Redemptorist hands as Oblate "savings" may in fact represent delayed compensation for Oblate services rendered the Sulpicians from 1844.

Between 1849 and 1860, Oblate annual expenses exceeded annual receipts every year. The sisters continued to supplement their income from the board and tuition of their students with sewing for both the public and the local religious institutions.[65] The community assumed a more public profile in fund-raising efforts, soliciting contributions in person either from other parishes in the archdiocese or canvassing the households of the Oblate St. Frances Chapel's parishioners. In 1857 the Oblate community solicited "for the benefit of the institution, also for payments of curtains for the Church." Oblate canvassing netted $64 by 1860. The sale of articles from the display case in the Oblate parlour further augmented Oblate income by some $230.[66] At regular intervals between 1857 and 1861 the Oblate community noted such items as "By cash of Sister Scholastica [Bourgoin] from the produce of her Store" in amounts totaling $440. Several members of the Bourgoin family had earned a living as confectioners since the 1830s.[67] Evidently, Sister Scholastica had retained or inherited an interest in or income from her family's business.

Black community support of the Oblate school remained so vigorous that increased school enrollments required two expansions of its physical plant within the Oblate community's first decade, in 1830 and again in 1836.[68] Oblate records document significant black participation in financing the 1836 building project. The black Catholic community remained supportive of the Oblate

Sisters through the 1840s. Black benefactors had provided $1,682.05 of the total $1,968.35 passive debt the Oblate community carried in 1842.

Between 1850 and 1855 the Oblate Sisters of Providence and the St. Frances black Catholic congregation undertook two additions to the Oblate convent, enlarged the chapel and classroom building, and constructed a boys' school and meeting hall at a cost of over $10,000. By 1855, the congregation had liquidated this debt.[69] The Oblate Sisters conducted four schools in Baltimore by 1858, all dependent on tuition income to function. That black pupils had to pay for the Catholic education many white pupils received free constituted another example of the disadvantaged position accorded black people within Baltimore society. The willingness of the black community—the segment of the population with the least discretionary income—to support the Oblate schools demonstrated their commitment both to the promise of a Catholic education and to its agents in Baltimore, the Oblate Sisters of Providence.[70]

Several extraordinary individuals among the clergy had both affirmed and promoted the spiritual mission of the Oblate Sisters of Providence from their inception. Clerical support of this black sisterhood, however, never included significant financial donations equal to those that the white sisterhoods previously established in the archdiocese had received. When the Sisters of Charity of St. Joseph formally affiliated with the Daughters of Charity in France in 1850, the Oblate Sisters of Providence remained the only indigenous, independent community in the archdiocese of Baltimore. Unlike the other archdiocesan sisterhoods, the Oblate Sisters of Providence lacked the potential of a European motherhouse and a network of European benefactors to subsidize their efforts in their American mission. The Oblate community had to rely exclusively on its own resources and the generosity of the lay community—white as well as black—for financial support.[71]

The reality of free black productive labor serving white economic interests formed the basis of antebellum Maryland's toleration of its free black population. However, the Oblate Sisters of Providence, as a black religious society formed to serve an exclusively black clientele, had little to recommend them to antebellum white Baltimore in this regard. The Oblate community appeared economically as well as socially superfluous to white society. The ancillary Oblate objective stated in the original Oblate Rule—to produce servants "trained up in habits of modesty, honesty, and integrity"[72]—may have sufficed to validate the Oblate Sisters as economically productive to white Baltimoreans.

During their first decade the Oblate Sisters encountered incidents of racism, both subtle and overt. The racial identity of the sisters and their students complicated their securing a suitable, permanent residence. Unexpectedly evicted from their first rented property in St. Mary's Court in April 1829, the Oblate Sisters experienced a discriminatory housing market familiar to minority populations in both the nineteenth and twentieth centuries. Joubert reported, "We had to search for another place at a reasonable distance from the seminary. We found several but the price asked was exorbitant; several refused absolutely to let us have them, when they were informed that is was for a school, and still more a school for colored children. I began to lose courage as these good girls [the Oblate Sisters] were all upset."[73] Fortunately for the community, within a month of their eviction notice, Dr. Peter Chatard, a wealthy white San Domingan émigré, offered them his Richmond Street property on generous terms.

In 1834 the Oblate community decided to buy the lot adjoining their Richmond Street location. Evidently, the Oblate neighborhood was not located in a very respectable part of the city. Oblate sources state that in part "the fear of seeing the small wooden house which is on the lot converted into a grocery store, or what would be still worse, a house of ill-repute" prompted the sisters to forestall such an eventuality by buying the property. Joubert noted ruefully that "the persons to whom this house belonged felt the need we had of this lot and sold it more dearly, perhaps, than they would have to anyone else but the Sisters."[74] Whether the racial identity or the religious state of the Oblate Sisters evoked such illiberality from the owners of the property remains unclear. Having to pay premium prices for inferior goods and services proved another experience familiar to minority populations in both the nineteenth and twentieth centuries.

The pervasive debasement of all black people ensuing from the racial basis of slavery in the United States convinced most white Americans of universal black inferiority. The city of Baltimore differed in degree, but not in kind, in this pattern of white thought about black people. Charles Carroll of Carrollton, an exemplar of the antebellum Baltimore Catholic white laity, provides an informative illustration of the impact of racism on white responses to the Oblate Sisters of Providence. A noted patriot and statesman, Charles Carroll was the last surviving signer of the Declaration of Independence. Although a highly successful planter who owned 316 slaves in 1790, Carroll nevertheless introduced an unsuccessful bill for the gradual abolition of slavery in the Maryland State Senate in 1797.[75]

An intimate friend of several Sulpician priests, Carroll proved himself a generous benefactor to Sulpician projects. In 1830 he underwrote the Sulpician St. Charles College, a preparatory school for young Catholics planning to enter the priesthood. Carroll donated the land, procured the charter for the college from the Maryland state legislature, authorized the purchase of additional property up to $6,000 to subsidize the project, and contributed fifty shares of the United States Bank for the construction of the college's buildings. He also contributed $20 annually to the Oblate Sisters of Providence from their inception in 1828 until his death in 1832.[76]

Carroll's actions indicated that he opposed slavery on some level and approved of the concept and mission of the Oblate Sisters sufficiently to subsidize their community at a modest rate. However, in accepting the presidency of the American Colonization Society in 1830, Carroll also endorsed that group's racist assumptions about inherent black inferiority and the necessity of black removal. The convictions allowing Carroll's prolonged and profitable participation in the institution of slavery evidently precluded his allowing the full humanity of black people, slave or free. Charles Carroll's small annual disbursements of $20 to the Oblate community compared to his munificence to St. Charles College represented his attempt to honor the Roman Catholic Church's official position on racial matters: to promote the spiritual but not the social equality of black people. Undoubtedly considerations of gender also explain the disparity between Carroll's respective disbursements to St. Charles College for men and the Oblate school for girls in the nineteenth-century society of the American South.

The Chatards and Ducatels, two wealthy white émigré families from St. Domingue, figure prominently in accounts of Oblate history. In 1829 Dr. Pierre Chatard offered to the sisters the house on Richmond Street that remained their convent until the city of Baltimore bought the property in 1870. Although he did not donate the property to them outright, as some benefactors had for some white sisterhoods, Chatard sold the house to the Oblates for $2,000, absorbing an $800 loss. Dr. Chatard and his sons also provided medical care for the Oblate Sisters, as well as for the other Baltimore religious communities. Mrs. Ferdinand Chatard contributed $190 toward the education of an Oblate student between September 1833 and April 1836. In addition to aiding the subscription begun at the formation of the Oblate community, Mde. Ducatel modestly subsidized some Oblate scholars.[77]

Most accounts of early Oblate history focus exclusively on the Chatard and Ducatel families as resources for the Oblates.[78] But Oblate annals state that in 1829 Joubert decided "to find some charitable friend, some rich person" to subsidize the purchase of a suitable Oblate convent and school. Significantly, he resolved to approach first the eminent Catholic of English ancestry, Charles Carroll of Carrollton. Only the fortuitous intervention of Dr. Peter Chatard with a counterproposal of his own property dissuaded Joubert from approaching Carroll.[79]

Oblate records referred frequently to benefactors with the British surname Williamson. Between 1828 and 1831 Oblate ledgers listed seven modest monthly tuition payments jointly subscribed by Mdes. Ducatel and Williamson. Mr. Charles Williamson, a prominent businessman active in the Baltimore Roman Catholic community, gave the Oblate Sisters an interest-free loan of $500 toward the construction of their new chapel in 1836.[80] Evidently, neither Joubert nor the Oblate Sisters considered themselves the product, preserve, or protégés of the Francophone ethnic community exclusively. Like the universal Roman Catholic Church itself, the Oblate community solicited support from a multi-ethnic constituency.

White Catholics continued to support the Oblate community and its work financially through the 1850s. Archbishop Francis Patrick Kenrick's authorization of an Oblate subscription in January 1853 in support of the boys' school construction prompted Baltimore's weekly newspaper the *Catholic Mirror* to publicize the cause in a feature article in March 1853. Significantly, the Oblate Sisters, the St. Frances congregation, and Father Anwander had secured most of the estimated construction costs before the newspaper appeal, as the reporter maintained, "The Reverend Anwander . . . has not yet realized by about $250 as much as will be required to cover the expenses he has directed." Noting the archbishop's "liberal donation" to the subscription, the reporter enjoined "our Catholic fellow citizens" to follow suit. With evident complacency he enthused, "Quite a number has [*sic*] contributed even ten and twenty dollars each." Several clerics contributed to the Oblate subscription "even ten and twenty dollars": the archbishop and seven clerics contributed a total of $80. Prominent Catholic merchants, with whom the Oblate Sisters conducted a substantial volume of business, as well as manufacturers and bankers donated to the Oblate subscription. Civic-minded Emily Harper, a granddaughter of Charles Carroll who had occasionally subsidized Oblate students at a modest level since 1844, distinguished herself by making the largest single donation—$130—listed in Anwander's subscription book. Several tradespeople—noted as such in the list— donated $10 each. The subscription secured a total of $498 for the Oblate boys' school building.[81]

Significantly, the names Chatard and Ducatel do not appear among the contributors listed in Anwander's subscription book. Furthermore, Oblate ledgers from 1844 through 1861 document the fact that these two families gave money to the sisters solely in exchange for goods or services during this period. In a pattern atypical of touted benefactors, the Chatards and the Ducatels paid for shirts and chemises sewn by the Oblate Sisters on a regular basis; they did not, however, disburse any monetary gifts, donations, or even loans to the Oblate community during these years, according to the extant records.

The level of support white Catholics provided the Oblate Sisters during the 1850s remained low relative to their support of white religious communities. The Sisters of Mercy established a mission in Baltimore in 1855. Mrs. Emily McTavish, another granddaughter of Charles Carroll and generous patron of Catholic causes, purchased a residence for the community sufficiently spacious to house both their novitiate and an academy for girls. In 1862 wealthy donor Charles M. Dougherty presented the Sisters of Charity with a Baltimore mansion in which they established St. Agnes Hospital.[82]

By contrast, when the Jesuit William F. Clarke secured a house in St. Joseph parish for an Oblate school in 1858, he "kindly allowed us to pay no rent until there be a sufficient number of scholars, and then the Sisters will pay only half of the rent."[83] However, in 1855 the *Catholic Mirror* had reported that the free, white parochial St. Joseph's Female School, conducted by the Sisters of Charity, "is pleasantly situated in a commodious house on Barre street, which we are gratified to learn, has been purchased and paid for by the zealous Pastor, Rev. Wm. F. Clark [*sic*], S.J."[84] Just as Oblate pupils paid for a Catholic education provided free by the archdiocese of Baltimore to most white pupils, so the Oblate Sisters ministered to the black community with the least support from white Baltimoreans. The differential levels of support white Catholic Baltimore provided the Oblate Sisters of Providence and communities of white sisters in the 1850s continued to reflect the subordinate position ascribed the Oblate Sisters and the black laity in the Catholic community, predicated on their racial identity.

The Oblate community supplemented its tuition, dowry, and paid work income with a variety of more informal economic transactions, arrangements, and subsidies from the local black and white communities. In financial contributions, patronage of Oblate schools, or in volunteering time, labor, and resources to benefit the Oblate cause, members of the antebellum black community amply demonstrated their conviction of the seminal importance of the Oblate mission.

The Oblate Sisters utilized their communal profession of piety and virtue as currency to validate and legitimize their claim to public recognition and support to an extent unrealizable to individual, secular black women in white antebellum southern society. Baltimore's white citizens demonstrated varying degrees of support for the Oblate Sisters throughout the antebellum period. White support of the black Oblate Sisters never equaled that bestowed on the white sisterhoods in the archdiocese of Baltimore, however, because issues of race and the grip of the institution of slavery on social mores intruded on white responses to this community of black women religious. Yet the fact that the institutional Roman Catholic Church and individual white benefactors among both clergy and laity recognized, promoted, and subsidized the Oblate enterprise at all attests to the viability of Oblate virtue as currency in antebellum southern society.

As professional teachers, the Oblate Sisters challenged white attitudes about appropriate fields of employment for black women in antebellum Baltimore. As a sisterhood functioning beyond the pale of traditional domestic households and the immediate purview of male patriarchy, they earned income from men by providing services customarily under the rubric of female unpaid labor within domestic households. A community of women of faith, the Oblate Sisters adopted as their motto "Providence will provide." However, in their economic endeavors the Oblate Sisters of Providence acted on the essential subtext of their motto: "God helps those who help themselves."

### NOTES

1. Ira Berlin, *Slaves without Masters: The Free Negro in the Antebellum South* (New York: Pantheon Books, 1974), 54–55; Leroy Graham, *Baltimore, the Nineteenth-Century Black Capital* (Washington, D.C.: University Press of America, 1982); Leonard P. Curry, *The Free Black in Urban America, 1800–1850* (Chicago: University of Chicago Press, 1981), 250.

2. Curry, *Free Black*, 267–71; Christopher Phillips, *Freedom's Port: The African American Community of Baltimore, 1790–1860* (Urbana: University of Illinois Press, 1997), 153–55.

3. Seth Rockman, "Women's Labor, Gender Ideology, and Working-Class Households in Early Republic Baltimore," *Explorations in Early American Culture*, a supplemental issue of *Pennsylvania History: A Journal of Mid-Atlantic Studies* 66 (1999): 176, 191.

4. Barbara Misner, *"Highly Respectable and Accomplished Ladies": Catholic Women Religious in America, 1790–1850* (New York: Garland Publishing, 1988), 257, 259–63, 268.

5. Thomas W. Spalding, *The Premier See: A History of the Archdiocese of Baltimore, 1789–1989* (Baltimore: Johns Hopkins University Press, 1989). 142, 168–69.

6. Misner, *Accomplished Ladies*, 252, 255.

7. John T. Gillard, *Colored Catholics in the United States* (Baltimore: The Josephite Press, 1941), 79–80.

8. Sister M. Theresa Catherine Willigman, O.S.P., "First Foundress of the Oblates," 1, typescript copy, n.d., Archives of the Oblate Sisters of Providence (hereafter AOSP).

9. Translation of "The Original Diary of the Oblate Sisters of Providence," vols. 1 and 2, typescript copy, 1, AOSP (hereafter Annals).

10. For thorough treatments of antebellum black communal institutions in Baltimore see Carter G. Woodson, *The Education of the Negro prior to 1861* (New York: G. P. Putnam's Sons, 1915), 138–44; James M. Wright, *The Free Negro in Maryland*, Studies in History, Economics, and Public Law, no. 222 (New York: Columbia University Press, 1921), 200–238; Bettye J. Gardner, "Free Blacks in Baltimore, 1800–1860" (Ph.D. diss., George Washington University, 1974), 49–127; Bettye C. Thomas, "The Baltimore Black Community, 1865–1910" (Ph.D. diss., George Washington University, 1974), 17–39, 57–61, 74–80; Clarence K. Gregory, "The Education of Blacks in Maryland: An Historical Survey" (Ed.D. diss., Columbia University Teachers College, 1976), 64–103, 131–36; Curry, *Free Black*, 154–59, 181; Graham, *Baltimore*, 63–85, 93–135, 216; and Phillips, *Freedom's Port*.

11. Current historical evidence identifying Lange's country of origin proves inconsistent. Information from the United States Census Population Schedules lists her birthplace variably as the West Indies (1850), San Domingo (1860), and Cuba (1870 and 1880) (Seventh through Tenth United States Censuses [1850–80], Population Schedules, State of Maryland, Baltimore City, Ward 12 [1850], Ward 11 [1860–80]).

12. Willigman, "First Foundress," 8.

13. Annals, 1:20, 23.

14. Misner, *Accomplished Ladies*, 71, 115; Spalding, *Premier See*, 57; Ellin M. Kelly, ed., *Numerous Choirs: A Chronicle of Elizabeth Bayley Seton and Her Spiritual Daughters*, vol. 1 (Evansville, Ind.: Mater Dei Provincialate, 1981), 157.

15. Annals, 1:2, 6.

16. Berlin, *Slaves without Masters*, 217–49.

17. See "School for Coloured Girls" advertisement in the *Metropolitan Catholic Calendar and Laity's Directory* (Baltimore: Fielding Lucas, 1834), 69–71 (hereafter *Laity's Directory*).

18. *Laity's Directory*, 1834, 70–71, 67, 69.

19. Ibid., 70.

20. Willigman, "First Foundress," 4.

21. Misner, *Accomplished Ladies*, 110–11, 113–15, 120.

22. Ibid., 70.

23. Ibid., 120.

24. Annals, 1:41, 6; Dowry List of Nineteenth-Century Oblates, AOSP.

25. "Where He Leads," unpublished commemorative pamphlet, n.d., 11, AOSP; Charles G. Herbermann, *The Sulpicians in the United States* (New York: Encyclopedia Press, 1916), 74; *Morning News* (Wilmington), 22 February 1975; Jessie M. Milbourn to Sister Ignatius Toodle, O.S.P., July 1949 and 19 January 1950, typescript copies, Mother Louisa Noel Papers, AOSP.

26. Annals, 1:22.

27. Ibid., 36.

28. Sister M. Rosalita Kelly, I.H.M., *No Greater Service: The History of the Congregation of the Sisters, Servants of the Immaculate Heart of Mary, Monroe, Michigan 1845–1945* (Detroit: Congregation of the Sisters of the Immaculate Heart, 1948), 39; Sisters Diane Edward Shea and Marita Constance Supan, I.H.M., "Apostolate of the Archives—God's Mystery through History," *Josephite Harvest* 85 (1983): 10; Sister M. Immaculata Gillespie, C.I.M., *Mother M. Theresa Maxis Duchemin* (Scranton, Pa.: Marywood College, 1945), 14; Sister Maria Alma, C.I.M., *Thou, Lord, Art My Hope!: The Life of Mother M. Theresa, A Pioneer of the Sisters, Servants of the Immaculate Heart of Mary* (Lancaster, Pa.: Dolphin Press, 1961), 10; Joseph B. Code, "Mother Theresa Maxis Duchemin," *America* 74 (22 December 1945): 317. For 1809 birth year see Diane Batts Morrow, "The Oblate Sisters of Providence: Issues of Black and Female Agency in Their Antebellum Experience, 1828–1860" (Ph.D. diss., University of Georgia, 1996), 50–51 n. 97; and Annals, 1:6, 12, 19–20.

29. Annals, 1:6.

30. "Recette," 9 September 1829, Original Oblate Ledger Sheets, 1828–30 (unpaged), Eagle File Box 44, AOSP.

31. Annals, 1:10, 53.

32. Ibid., 22–23.

33. Ibid., 23, 50; Willigman, "First Foundress," 8–9.

34. Thomas H. Buckler, *A History of Epidemic Cholera as It Appeared at the Baltimore City and County Alms-House in the Summer of 1949* (Baltimore: J. Lucas, 1851), 7.

35. Grace Sherwood, *The Oblates' Hundred and One Years* (New York: Macmillan, 1931), 73; Misner, *Accomplished Ladies*, 47; Maria M. Lannon, *Response to Love: The Story of Mary Elizabeth Lange, OSP* (Washington, D.C.: Josephite Pastoral Center, 1992), 31; Thaddeus J. Posey, O.F.M., Cap. "An Unwanted Commitment: The Spirituality of the Early Oblate Sisters of Providence, 1829–1890" (Ph.D. diss., Saint Louis University, 1993), 273.

36. *Laity's Directory* (Baltimore: James Myres, 1834), 71.

37. Annals, 1:34–35.

38. Willigman, "First Foundress," 11; *Laity's Directory* (Baltimore: James Myres, 1836), 169–70; ibid. (Fielding Lucas, 1838), 146–48; ibid., (1839), 183–85.

39. Annals, 1:42; "Rule and Constitution" (undated), English manuscript copy, 1, Box 41, AOSP.

40. Sister Mary Ewens, O.P., *The Role of the Nun in the Nineteenth Century* (Salem, N.H.: Ayer Company Publishers, 1984), 104; Misner, *Accomplished Ladies*, 262; author's correspondence with John W. Bowen, S.S., Sulpician Archivist Emeritus, 20 October 1996.

41. Annals, 1:42.

42. Ibid., 41–42.

43. Margaret Susan Thompson, "Sisterhood and Power: Class, Culture, and Ethnicity in the American Convent," *Colby Library Quarterly* 25, no. 3 (September 1989): 151–52; Sister Mary Ewens, O.P., "The Leadership of Nuns in Immigrant Catholicism," in *The American Catholic Religious Life: Selected Historical Essays*, ed. Joseph M. White (New York: Garland Publishing, 1988): 14–62.

44. Misner, *Accomplished Ladies*, 75–88.

45. "Where He Leads," unpublished commemorative pamphlet, n.d., 11, AOSP; Manumission Documents, Box 21, AOSP; Marie Germain: St. Peter's Pro-Cathedral Baptisms, 1812–19, M1511-5, p. 230, Archives of the Archdiocese of Baltimore, Baltimore, Md., microfilm, Maryland Hall of Records, State Archives, Annapolis, Md.

46. Diane Batts Morrow, "Outsiders Within: The Oblate Sisters of Providence in 1830s Church and Society," *U.S. Catholic Historian* 15, no. 2 (Spring 1997): 37–38.

47. Mary Donovan, "Spirit and Structure: Historical Factors Affecting the Expression of Charism in an American Religious Congregation." *U.S. Catholic Historian* 10, nos. 1 and 2 (1989): 6; Ewens, "Leadership of Nuns," 105–6; Sister Frances Jerome Woods, C.D.P., "Congregations of Religious Women in the Old South," in *Catholics in the Old South: Essays on Church and Culture*, ed. Randall M. Miller and Jon Wakelyn (Macon, Ga.: Mercer University Press, 1983), 102–7.

48. *New York Sun*, 28 September 1884; James Redpath, "The Colored Nuns of Baltimore," typescript, 3–4, AOSP; M. Theresa Catherine Willigman, O.S.P., "Souvenir of Love and Grateful Remembrance of the Foundress of the Oblate Sisters of Providence, Sister Mary, Established in Baltimore, June 5th, 1828, Made Their Vows July 2nd, 1829, Celebrated Her Golden Jubilee July 2nd, 1879, Died February 3rd, 1882, First Superior of the Oblate Sisters," manuscript copy, n.d., 57, AOSP.

49. Annals, 1:88–92.

50. Ibid., 42, 91–92.

51. Ibid., 89.

52. Annals, 2: 20 April 1843.

53. *Laity's Directory* (Fielding Lucas, 1840), 163; (1841), 209; (1842), 188; (1843), 164; (1844), 181.

54. Annals, 1:91–92.

55. Annals, 2: 20 April 1843.

56. Ibid., 29 November 1859.

57. Annals, 1:41, 91; Annals, 2: 6 November 1842 to 2 April 1843, passim.

58. Anwander to Sourin, 27 March 1876, Anwander Director File, AOSP .

59. Untitled Large Ledger, 1844–54 inclusive, 1844–49 entries passim, AOSP.

60. Annals, 1:91.

61. 1844–54 Ledger, 1844–49 entries, passim.

62. 1844–54 Ledger; "Box 10 #1" labeled Ledger, 1855–61, passim, AOSP.

63. 1844–54 Ledger, November 1844, December 1845, March and November 1847 receipt pages.

64. Christopher Kauffman, *Tradition and Transformation in Catholic Culture: The Priests of Saint Sulpice in the United States from 1791 to the Present* (New York: Macmillan, 1988), 129–30; 1844–54 Ledger, dates cited in text.

65. "Box 10 #1" labeled Ledger, 1855–61.

66. Ibid., Receipts, January, February 1857, January 1860, March 1857–October 1861, passim.

67. Ibid., Receipts, July 1856, November 1857, May and December 1858, April 1859,

January and June 1860, June and October 1861; Richard J. Matchett, *Matchett's Baltimore Directory* (1831), 60; (1833), 33, 34.

68. Annals, 1:8–9, 43.

69. Anwander to Sourin, 27 March 1876, AOSP.

70. For a thorough discussion of the relationship between the Oblate Sisters and their black supporters, see Diane Batts Morrow, "'Our Convent': The Oblate Sisters of Providence and the Antebellum Black Community," in *Negotiating the Boundaries of Southern Womanhood: Dealing with the Powers That Be*, ed. Janet Coryell et al. (Columbia: University of Missouri Press, 2000), 27–47.

71. For a full treatment of clerical financial support of the Oblate Sisters and the white sisterhoods in 1830s Baltimore see Morrow, "Outsiders Within," 39–42.

72. Posey, "Unwanted Commitment," 324.

73. Annals, 1:2.

74. Ibid., 5.

75. Spalding, *Premier See*, 57, 113; James Hennesey, S.J., *American Catholics: A History of the Roman Catholic Community in the United States* (New York: Oxford University Press, 1981), 146.

76. Herbermann, *Sulpicians*, 199–201; Original Oblate Ledger Sheets, 1829–36, Eagle File Box 44, AOSP.

77. Annals, 1:2, 3, 10; Student Registers (1828–33), 5, 55, Eagle File Box 44, AOSP; Original Oblate Ledger Sheets, 1828–30, 11 September 1828, 8 February, 26 April, 5 July, 20 September 1829, 17 January 1830; Original Oblate Ledger Sheets, 1829–36, 116, 97–98, 102, 110; Sherwood, *Oblates' Hundred and One Years*, 15–16, 18–19, 46, 60, 79, 150–51, 161–62, 175, 177; Original Oblate Ledger Sheets, 1829–36, 100, 119.

78. Herbermann, *Sulpicians*, 234; Sherwood, *Oblates' Hundred and One Years*, 15–16; Michael J. McNally, "A Minority of a Minority: The Witness of Black Women Religious in the Antebellum South," *Review for Religious* 40 (1981): 263; Kauffman, *Tradition and Transformation*, 114; Spalding, *Premier See*, 108; Gregory, "Education of Blacks," 84.

79. Annals, 1:2–3.

80. Ibid., 43; Original Oblate Ledger Sheets, 1829–36, 112.

81. "Colored Schools," *Catholic Mirror* (Baltimore), 26 March 1853; Anwander Subscription Book, January 1853, Box 95, AOSP; Spalding, *Premier See*, 223, 243; 1844–54 Ledger; "Box 10 #1" labeled Ledger, passim.

82. Spalding, *Premier See*, 168–69.

83. Annals, 2: 28 May 1858.

84. *Catholic Mirror*, 21 July 1855, 4–5.

*Part Four*

. . . . . . . . . . . . . . . . . . . . . . . . . . . . . . . . . . . . .

# Working Women in the Industrial South

. . . . . . . . . . . . . . . . . . . . . . . . .

# Chapter Eleven

# I Can't Get My Bored on Them Old Lomes:
## Female Textile Workers in the Antebellum South

. . . . . . . . . . . . . . . . . . . . . . . . .

BESS BEATTY

In the fictional antebellum world of Scarlet O'Hara the only women who worked were slaves; not until the collapse of the southern Confederacy overwhelmed her way of life did Scarlet defiantly resolve that she would herself work to assure her family's survival. *Gone with the Wind* remains the most powerful image of the Old South. In it southern women are belles and mammies, not women who worked for wages. Historians continue to challenge the powerful but distorting historical assumptions created by this popular fiction. Anne Firor Scott, for example, has written of the Old South, "The precise meaning of 'work' varied with station in society, economic condition, and geographic location, but women of leisure were hard to find."[1]

In the late seventeenth century Virginian William Byrd wrote of the women in his colony and neighboring Carolina that "all spin, weave, and knit, whereby they make good shift to cloath the whole Family," and that "to their credit be it recorded, many of them do it very completely."[2] Clothing a family completely demanded long arduous hours from females in most colonial households throughout the English colonies. As the girls and women Byrd observed filled their days spinning, weaving, knitting, and sewing, they could have envisioned the lives of their daughters and granddaughters for decades to come. Not until a century after Byrd's observation did the first stirring of an industrial revolution began to slowly transform women's work and, indeed, their lives. The mechanization of textile production, spreading from England to her former colonies in the late eighteenth century, made it possible first for elite women and then increasingly for those of more modest means to buy yarn and cloth. As cloth production moved out of homes into factories, it was easy, indeed obvious, to assume that girls and women would continue to be the spinners and weavers in the first factories. Thomas Dublin, in his study of the Lowell textile factories, explains, "On the one hand, the new mill undermined the primary economic activities of farmers' daughters—the spinning of yarn and weaving of cloth. On the other hand, the mills offered employment to these young women and tempted them to leave their rural homes to work in the growing factory towns."[3]

Some southern farm daughters were tempted to try the factories as well. White girls and women made up the majority of the workforce in the small textile mills built across the southern piedmont in the decades before the Civil War. They carried on work similar to that done by their female forbearers but they did it in a profoundly different environment. In the first southern factories, females learned to use machinery to produce the textiles their families and communities needed; they also learned the nature of a new industrial order and decided how to respond to it.

For some women, bringing the mechanization of textiles into their homes was work halfway between home production and factory production. As late as 1859, for example, W. A. Hester wrote a North Carolina mill owner, "My wife is very much disposed to make a trial of your looms" and asked how they could be obtained.[4] After 1840, however, home labor increasingly gave way to factory work, where girls and women (along with a smaller number of boys and men) took up a familiar task in an unfamiliar environment. After observing a small southern mill in 1840, a northerner traveling through the South described the white females working there as "employed in a usual occupation."[5] Familiar as females employed at the tasks of spinning and weaving was, however, the spectacle of a female workforce did not always seem usual. A visitor to a mill in Augusta, Georgia, in 1849, wrote a friend, "I was sorry when I got there I did not have you and Lou with me to see the gretest sight I ever saw. There is about 100 gales and grown females all employed and such sistem I never saw."[6]

System was not always easy for southern mill men to achieve. Many of them did not understand the machinery they hoped to profit from and accordingly frequently looked north for guidance. They also looked north for guidance in procuring and managing the workers they needed. The Lowell mills, founded north of Boston in the 1820s, soon established the model of working "girls" who were carefully chaperoned in boardinghouses. This early experiment in industrial paternalism became familiar to southerners who sought to emulate the profits of northern textile manufacturers. They were, however, also aware of the concept of family labor that was more common in the small mills of western Massachusetts and Rhode Island; most mill owners eventually followed this model and organized their workforce by recruiting families that could furnish several workers.

Southern mill men were generally guided more by northern advisers and by example than they were by southern norms about proper roles for women. Workers were typically viewed as laborers critical to the monetary success of owners rather than as southern women in need of protection. In 1828 a South Carolina mill man wrote his partner that as their business grew they would need more "of as the Yankeys say 'help.'" Calculations for his mill were based on what one "Yankey girl" could produce.[7] Three decades later James Gregg, one of the most successful southern mill men, also sought to emulate northern mills where female workers "turned off 50 doffs per day regularly." Gregg requested that one of these women be loaned to his mill to demonstrate her work, adding "we will consider it quite a favor if you will take the trouble to select one who will do her best work."[8]

Southerners sought northern ideas about labor, but they also had their own peculiar form of labor that most mill builders were familiar with firsthand. A number of antebellum mill men were slaveholders; many of them considered using slaves, and a smaller number actually did so. Several of the early mills were run exclusively by slave labor; others used a mixed workforce that included slaves working alongside free white men and women.[9] An Englishman visiting a Georgia mill around 1840 wrote, "There is no difficulty among them on account of colour, the white boys working in the same room and at the same loom with the black girls; and boys of each colour as well as men and women working together without apparent repugnance or objection."

The availability of slave labor notwithstanding, most of the early factory workers were white. When cotton prices were high, slaves were considered more valuable working the soil. Furthermore, slave labor was not entirely suited to factory production since the early factories operated only intermittently. Slaves needed to be occupied constantly, whereas white workers could be dismissed when floods or broken machinery brought work to a halt.

Most early mill owners were pragmatic as they sought to exploit the potential profits of manufactured yarn and cloth; dogmas concerning a proper industrial workforce did, however, slowly emerge alongside the new factories. Some powerful defenders of plantation slavery discouraged the development of a free industrial workforce. Away from the Deep South plantation belt, however, factories were frequently advocated as opportunities for poor and indigent whites to support themselves. A few years after Edwin Holt founded the Alamance Factory, his father, Michael Holt, defended his son's enterprise by proclaiming, "In a few years N Carolina may bost of Their independence, spin all our cotton, give employment to the poore white labourers, a kind of separation of Slave Labour and free."[10] In 1849 an Augusta newspaper editor concluded that "the success of Georgia girls in learning to spin, weave . . . is most creditable to their tact, intelligence and industry." Three years later he offered as evidence the story of factory girls who had saved ninety-five dollars, claiming it as "a good indication of fair wages on the one side and prudence on the other."[11] The overseer for a Mississippi mill likewise believed maintaining a white workforce was beneficial for owners and workers alike; he maintained that white labor was superior, "not because black is not equal to the task but because white is cheapest and really more efficient, and it affords the means of an honest living acquired by their owne to many poor destitute families, widows and orphans who would otherwise be compelled to live upon what they get from their friends and from charity."[12] According to South Carolina mill owner James Gregg, millwork could dramatically transform the poor into prosperous citizens; he claimed that thanks to their mill wages, his young female workers "now have singing masters, music teachers, writing masters and silk dresses."[13]

These southerners were, of course, all boosters of southern industrial development. Northerners visiting the South observed working conditions from a different perspective. After visiting the Alamance Factory in the 1840s, historian Benson Lossing reinforced southern industrial advocates' views by proclaiming it "a real blessing, present and prospective, for it gives employment and comfort to many poor girls who might other otherwise be wretched."[14] Frederick Law Olmsted, however, reported after visiting an Augusta mill that the New England girls recruited to work there had all left, "owing to the general degradation of the labouring class."[15]

Both northern and southern observers sometimes simplified the varied patterns of the first southern textile labor force. In the Alamance Factory, girls and women of means sometimes worked alongside those more accurately described as wretched. Nancy Murray, for example, worked in the Alamance Factory in 1860 even though her husband could claim thirty thousand dollars worth of property, making him one of the richest men in Alamance County. Several other women employed there were married to men of above average wealth.[16] Some women chose factory work despite having adult children at home who could support them. Twenty-five women worked in Irdell County, North Carolina, mills as weavers, although they were heads of households that included other adult workers. Martha Griffin, Sarah Morrow, Martha Boston, and Rachel Templeton were all past seventy years old; although born in another century, they were willing to give nineteenth-century-style textile production a try.[17]

Mill men were flexible in whom they hired or compelled to work in the early years, but they were also beginning to develop a theory of labor. Increasingly, they agreed with William Makepeace, a Rhode Island mill man who relocated to North Carolina, who advised, "Get all of the widow women that has got a family of girls or other families that are mostly girls as we do not want many boys."[18] Makepeace considered females more submissive than young men and recognized that they were more dependent because they had few alternatives to mill jobs. He also advised that workers from families dependent on their mill wages were easier to control than single individuals. William Gregg agreed; noting that all "our female help" lived with their families, he claimed, "This is a great moral restraint, and gives us an advantage over those who have to rely on the boarding-house system for help, where large numbers of young females are collected together from a wide range of country, away from parents' care."[19] Southern mill men increasingly heeded Makepeace's advice and Gregg's example, but at the same time they learned that getting and keeping female workers was more difficult than these two men implied.

· · ·

The board of the Salem Factory, located in the Moravian community of Salem, North Carolina, accepted the wisdom of Makepeace's advice, concluding, "Families that can furnish 3 or 4 good hands will remain the most desirable help." They built ten single-family dwellings but also built a boardinghouse for single young women. Their boarders proved particularly troublesome. Salem owners were soon complaining that these individuals were prone to set their own hours and to return home whenever they wished. There was always the possibility that single female boarders would quit altogether soon after they had been trained, leaving the mill with a chronically unskilled labor force. Women living away from family sometimes joined together, replicating the support of family ties. When several women working in the Salem Factory threatened to strike for higher wages, the board resolved that "nothing of this sort ought to be countenanced, even tho' half the mill should stop, because if such demands should become yielded to, there would be no end to exactions." Despite their resolve, however, the managers recognized that the skills their female workers had acquired gave them some power; they as frequently resorted to the carrot as the stick when responding to worker demands. At one point the board became so frustrated with high absenteeism and turnover that it determined that "the female operatives could be induced to be more regular at their work" by written agreements in which each woman would agree to forfeit two weeks' pay if she left before an agreed upon time. Recognizing that these women might be difficult to coerce, the Salem board also promised extra pay at the end of the year to anyone who took no time off. When boarding women demanded laundry service, board members reluctantly agreed to have their clothes washed for free. It was also decided that "if the workers expected it," they would be given Christmas day off. The owners came to understand that they could not compel their workers to follow their own Moravian religion, so they dropped a Sunday school program.[20] Despite these concessions and inducements, however, their workers continued to reject industrial discipline and frequently returned home. The Salem Factory's inability to maintain an experienced workforce was a major reason it eventually failed.

Despite lessons learned from his experience on the Salem board, Francis Fries also confronted constant problems trying to discipline his workers to follow an industrial schedule. He sometimes required enslaved men to work alongside the white women he hired. There is no evidence that the women protested working alongside black men, but clearly they protested the work itself by complaining, staying home, or quitting altogether. On 28 June 1840, Fries recorded that "Jim Billiter's girls come in to spin on hard frames." They returned for the next five days; the day after the Fourth of July holiday, however, he reported, "Girls not come." In March 1842 Fries again recorded that the girls did not come and that as a result, "Eric is nearly out of work." Later that year he wrote again that the girls did not come and that as a result, "myself and Wallace tend looms." When two of Larkin Kennedy's daughters failed to show up, the two men were not able to compensate and Fries had to report, "We are balked." Some women told Fries why they were quitting. Lisana Hauser left "because she can not make wages at weaving." Soon after Hauser left, Fries reported, "Julia Tise, Eliza Stain and Lucy Hinshaw leave being dissatisfied with the rate of wages we pay." Perhaps a raise was agreed to. In any case, Hinshaw returned a week later and within two years Stain was again working for Fries as well. Mill owners needed the labor of young women too much to ignore their grievances altogether. In 1848 when Alabama mill owner Daniel Pratt learned that "the weaving is getting on so badly," he told his superintendent, "You must try and make the weavers satisfied."[21]

Making female workers satisfied never included promoting them to the mills' highest-paying positions. The young females collected from the country could run the machinery in these early southern mills but they could not oversee or manage them. Mill men successfully replicated the general social order of male domination and female subordination mandated by nineteenth-century society. There is no evidence that women held supervisory positions in any mill. When a manager of the Salem Factory gave Susan Croutch what the board considered "more authority than is proper even going so far as to intrust her part of the duties incumbent upon Mr. Banner," he was reprimanded and ordered to dismiss her.[22]

While labor theory evolving in the South assumed that women in families were easier to control, there is also evidence that familial support made it easier to resist arbitrary male power in the workplace. Girls and young women were more likely to seek millwork if they were joined by family members and were more likely to be living with family than were males. For example, in 1843 twelve of the sixteen males working at Falmouth Mill in Virginia did so alone; three sons of the Abbott family were among the minority working with family members. The Abbott daughters as well as thirteen other female employees worked with at least one family member; only four females worked in Falmouth alone. The family labor force that emerged in small mills like Falmouth allowed families flexibility in producing income. The Southards were represented by different family members every year. In 1842 Jane and Sarah worked together; the following year their brother John joined them. By 1844 Jane and Sarah had left and Hannah had joined John. She remained four years; when she left in 1848, John worked with his sister Mary.[23] The Southard daughters may have given up millwork to marry; it is also possible that they simply became tired of the conditions and low pay. Having a number of family members available to earn wages gave each individual some control over his or her response to industrial work.

The Cedar Falls Manufacturing Company in Randolph County, North Carolina, was able to recruit family labor but also found it difficult to build a stable and disciplined workforce. In the 1840s approximately three-fourths of its workers were unmarried females and four-fifths of them lived with at least one parent and worked alongside at least one sibling. Having family members close by may have helped ease the transition to industrial work, but it did not assure the diligence owners needed. Martha Briggs's study of Cedar Falls concludes that women workers were particularly prone to absenteeism; most were absent at least several days each month. Typically, workers remained at Cedar Falls three years, but around one-third of those hired were gone after less than one year. A bookkeeper's comments reveal something about why workers left; notations were made for fifty-four women who were fired or who quit between 1846 and 1865. Thirteen left to marry; although married women were more likely to work in the antebellum years than later, most did not work after marriage. Others left because their help was needed at home. Several women were reported as leaving to help their mothers, two sisters as "out doing the house work," and one woman as away cooking. None of these women was necessarily protesting millwork or was hostile to it. Ten women quit to work in another mill; whether they moved in protest to the conditions at Cedar Falls or for other reasons, they were willing to continue giving millwork a try. Nearly one-third of the reasons given, however, clearly reveal discontent. Eleven women were fired for infractions, including "leaving the mill without leaf to visit," "because she could not doe as she was told," "roales violated," "want work," and "cannot spin." Others quit before they were fired. The bookkeeper quoted one as leaving because "I can't get my bored on them old lomes." One woman "got mad and left the mill," while another simply ran away. Sophia Trogden, who, along with some of her siblings, went to work at Cedar Falls in 1856, made the most dramatic exit. Trogden became so hostile to the mill environment that months after she was hired she cut the belts running the spindles; she was promptly fired. Perhaps Trogden apologized adequately or perhaps the mill was desperate for skilled workers. In any case, a year later Trogden was rehired; she left the mill for good after marrying a man who also worked at Cedar Falls.[24]

Most resistance was not so dramatic. Elizabeth Royal was undoubtedly more typical than Sophia Trogden in her response to industrial discipline. Her father, a chair maker, brought his family of nine girls and one boy to Cedar Falls sometime in the late fifties. The gender imbalance in this family made it a likely candidate for millwork. When the children were old enough, they became mill-workers; apparently their mother worked with them for a short time as well. Elizabeth, the oldest of the children, began working at Cedar Falls in 1849 and continued to do so, on and off, for six years. Despite the proximity of family, however, Royal was not happy with her position. In 1853 she wrote a friend that "the factory is broke hear it broke yesterday." Despite the loss of wages, she seemed relieved, adding, "I am going to quit the mill in five weeks if you will com down y may have my looms." Royal did not quit that year but in 1855 moved with her family to Columbia, South Carolina. When they returned to North Carolina, she joined her mother and several siblings working in the Beaver Creek Factory in Cumberland County. After several months Elizabeth reported, "We are dissatisfied hear but we are making money hear." Despite the wages, however, she concluded, "Beaver Creek is a sorry place. I wish I had never seen it" and longed "that I had the wings of a dove and I would fly home and be at rest."[25]

The Kennedy girls, Sophia Trogden, and Elizabeth Royal were not destitute; they had some support from fathers and husbands. It was easier for them to walk away, quit, even indulge in a Luddite-style protest than it was for indigent women, the widows, and their daughters that Makepeace counseled hiring. Women without male support were sometimes compelled by necessity to heed nonfamilial male authority. Many of them also found ways to resist excessive industrial discipline. Even women desperate for the wages mills offered were not always willing to relinquish authority in their families. In 1849 a recruiter for the Orange Factory reported that he had found a family with three daughters who "can come well recommended as poor smart people" and added, "The madam has agreed to leave her inebriate husband if I would help her to get employment for her children." Desperate as this woman was, however, she refused the mill owners' demand that her girls come immediately, insisting that they must wait until she could come with them. In 1855, Elizabeth Carrigan, a barely literate widow with two teenage daughters, moved to a mill village in Gaston County, North Carolina, because, "i thought Mary and Cornelia cood make more to worke in the factory." Several weeks after they arrived, she reported, "We a pleasant place to live in it is brick home we live in the factory belong Thomas Tate Mr. Tate provide for his hands we have preaching hear every third Sabath he is a methidois but he is a good minister." Carrigan quickly came to view the mill owner as her provider, recognition essential to the smooth-running hierarchical paternalism that mill owners developed through the nineteenth century. She also recognized the limits to this relationship and continued appealing to her extended family for support. Not long after moving to the mill village, she asked a stepson for a loan because, "I have to pay rite smarte for movening heer . . . and every thing is sow deer thate takes all thate one can make to support them."[26] Carrigan's letters reveal the nature of the paternalism developing in southern mill villages as well as something about its limits. Edwin Holt, whose Alamance Factory Lossing visited, added a store, religious facilities, and perhaps occasionally provided schools in an effort to maintain a permanent workforce. He allowed his workers to purchase goods on credit and provided them with necessities such as firewood. In time, most mill men determined that their endeavors were best served by a largely female workforce in a paternalistic environment and followed Holt's example. Images of owners as benevolent paternalists and workers as docile and grateful were fostered by postbellum mill men and reinforced by historians. Broadus Mitchell's work in the 1920s successfully entrenched the image of benevolent owners and docile workers for over half a century. As late as 1979 a study of the nineteenth-century North Carolina textile industry concluded that "mill village paternalism at first developed out of planter-industrialists' traditional sense of social responsibility; their dealings with white operatives were guided by the old grammar of master-slave relations.[27]

More recently, historians studying the southern textile industry from 1880 have successfully challenged images of paternalism and docility and the appropriateness of comparing millworkers and slaves. My study of women working in the antebellum textile industry suggests that the revision needs to reach back into the earlier years. Although Jonathan Prude was describing antebellum New England workers when he wrote that "industrialization in this country was from the outset marked by significant tension," his observation is accurate for the South as well.[28]

The image of privatized grievances and docile behavior has been an especially common way of describing female workers. In the first half of the nineteenth century females in all parts of the country were socialized to be docile. The ideology of female subordination may have been especially powerful in the South where maintaining slavery demanded rigid hierarchical control. This study of female workers in the antebellum textile industry reveals, however, that not all of these females were docile or content. Some girls and women gave the mills a try, sometimes several tries, and then walked away. Others remained for years and raised children to be cotton mill people as well. They worked in a variety of circumstances, and they responded in a variety of ways. Some women of considerable means worked, although most female workers were poor, some desperately so. Some worked with as many as one hundred other girls and women and revealed great system. Others worked alongside only two or three other white women and as many black male slaves; their erratic performance left their owners balked. Many worked alongside family members; a minority came alone to live in company boardinghouses. Whether attached to family or alone, many protested the conditions they found. Owners fired workers, but they also tried to address their grievances. Owners were powerful, but female workers were not powerless to affect their working and living conditions.

What E. P. Thompson has explained concerning eighteenth-century English working people—that "deference could be very brittle indeed, and made up of one part self-interest, one part of dissimulation, and only one part of the awe of authority"—rings true for women working in the South's first textile mills as well.[29] Certainly they had a one part awe of authority, but their deference was also often brittle indeed.

## NOTES

1. Anne Firor Scott, *The Southern Lady: From Pedestal to Politics, 1830–1930* (Chicago: University of Chicago Press, 1970), 28.

2. Quoted in Julia Cherry Spruill, *Women's Life and Work in the Southern Colonies* (Chapel Hill: University of North Carolina Press, 1938), 82–83.

3. Thomas Dublin, *Women at Work: The Transformation of Work and Community in Lowell, Massachusetts, 1826–1860* (New York: Columbia University Press, 1979), 5.

4. W. A. Hester to Webb and Douglass, 9 September 1859, James Webb Papers, Southern Historical Collection, University of North Carolina, Chapel Hill (hereafter SHC).

5. Benson John Lossing, *The Pictorial Field-Book of the Revolution*, vol. 2 (New York: Harper and Brothers, 1860), 388.

6. Elijah Wood to Rosa, 4 April 1849, Elijah Wood Papers, South Caroliniana Library, University of South Carolina (hereafter SCL-USC).

7. D. R. Williams to James Chesnut, 26 October 1828, David R. Williams Collection, SCL-USC.

8. James Gregg to Machinist Association, 7 February 1860, Graniteville Manufacturing Company Letterbook, SCL-USC.

9. Michael Holt to Willie P. Mangum, 25 January 1842, quoted in Henry T. Shanks, ed., *The Papers of Willie Person Mangum*, 3 vols. (Raleigh: n.p., 1950–56), 3:276–77.

10. Quoted in Richard T. Griffin, "The Augusta Manufacturing Company in War and Reconstruction," *Business History Review* 32 (1958): 67.

11. Author unknown to Col. Claiborne, 11 August 1858, Claiborne Papers, SHC.

12. "Report of the President and Treasurer," Graniteville Manufacturing Company, 1854, 2, Graniteville Manufacturing Company Papers, SCL-USC.

13. Lossing, *Pictorial Field-Book*, 388.

14. Quoted in Griffin, "Augusta Manufacturing Company," 67.

15. Frederick Law Olmsted, *A Journey in the Back Country*, vol. 2 (1860; reprint, New York: G. P. Putnam's Sons, 1907), 126–27.

16. Eighth Census of the United States, 1860, Alamance County, N.C.

17. Ibid., Irdell County, N.C.

18. George Makepeace to Webb and Douglass, 11 September 1851, Webb Papers, SHC.

19. Quoted in D. D. Wallace, "A Hundred Years of William Gregg and Graniteville," ms. copy, Special Collections, University of South Carolina–Aiken.

20. Salem Manufacturing Company Minute Book, 27 November 1837; 7, 8 February, 9 May, 28 April, 19 June, 26 November 1838; 11 September 1839; 25 September, 31 October

1840; 1 July, 10 November 1841, Fries Papers, Moravian Archives, Winston-Salem, N.C. (hereafter FP).

21. Francis Fries Diary, 26 March, 28 November 1842; 4 January, 6 December 1847; 15 October 1850, FP; Pratt quoted in Dwight M. Wilheom, *A History of the Cotton Textile Industry of Alabama, 1809–1950* (N.p., n.p.), 57.

22. Salem Manufacturing Company Minute Book, 14 May 1842, FP.

23. Falmouth Cotton Mill Records, Special Collections, University of Virginia.

24. Cedar Falls Manufacturing Company Day Book, 1854–65, North Carolina Division of Archives and History, Raleigh, N.C.; Martha Briggs, "Mill Owners and Mill Workers in an Antebellum County" (master's thesis, University of North Carolina at Chapel Hill, 1975).

25. Elizabeth Royal to Cynthia Blair, 1 January 1854 and 19 March 1857, Cynthia and Mildred Blair Papers, Special Collections, Duke University (hereafter DU).

26. Elizabeth Carrigan to William Carrigan, 2 May 1855, DU.

27. Dwight Billings, *Planters and the Making of a "New South": Class, Politics, and Development in North Carolina, 1865–1900* (Chapel Hill: University of North Carolina Press, 1979), 103.

28. Jonathan Prude, *Coming of the Industrial Order: Town and Factory Life in Rural Massachusetts, 1810–1860* (New York: Oxford University Press, 1983), xiii.

29. Edward P. Thompson, "Patrician Society, Plebian Culture," *Journal of Social History* 7, no. 4 (Summer 1974): 399–400.

. . . . . . . . . . . . . . . . . . . . . . . . . . . . .

# Chapter Twelve

# To Harden a Lady's Hand:
## Gender Politics, Racial Realities, and Women
## Millworkers in Antebellum Georgia

. . . . . . . . . . . . . . . . . . . . . . . . . . . . .

### MICHELE GILLESPIE

"There is nothing in tending a loom to harden a lady's hand," stated Chief Justice Henry Collier, a strong advocate for textile manufactures in the antebellum South. Like many promoters of southern industrialization in the decades before the Civil War, Collier recognized that the employment of white females in textile mills secured an inexpensive, quiescent labor force that not only did not compete with but indeed complemented the dominant agricultural economy and its key labor source—slaves. To compel southern society to embrace white women's employment in the mills, he manipulated the conventions of gender and race in the antebellum South by invoking the southern lady ideal with his statement. Thus Collier was contending that a white female employee could remain a "southern lady," despite the unprecedented experience of toiling for fourteen-hour days in massive buildings filled with noisy machines and choking fibers, because her hands would not be callused by her labors. Her mythical gentility, in other words, along with her virtue, would remain intact, making millwork an ideal pursuit for white women, an implicit contrast to slave women, who were perceived by whites to lack such critical character attributes and whose work was generally agricultural, often extremely arduous, and rarely gender-specific.[1]

When British traveler J. S. Buckingham passed through the region in 1842, he painted a very different picture of factory life in the Old South, one that did not include any reference to southern ladyhood. "The white families engaged in these factories live in log huts clustered about the establishment on the river's bank," he commented after meeting millworkers dwelling along the Oconee River in Athens, Georgia. "The whites look miserably pale and unhealthy; and they are said to be very short-lived, the first symptoms of fevers and dysentaries in the autumn appearing chiefly among them in the factories, and sweeping numbers of them off to death."[2] Even Henry Merrell, a Georgia industrialist who firmly believed in the importance of manufacturing for the welfare of the state and region, admitted factory work did not advance southern women's lot, nor promote her gentility. In speaking of the vagaries of the planter economy in general and the plight of the small planter and his kin in particular, he observed "The hard economy . . . condemns the females of a family to profitless drudgery at the loom." Merrell clearly understood that white female factory workers were all too frequently caught in a web of southern social relations that bound together family needs and commercial developments and left them with dreary lives over which they had too little control.[3]

The majority of factory workers in Georgia in the antebellum era were white women. The truth about their origins and experiences remains largely unexplored, despite the fact that their entry into wage work represented a significant new development in the antebellum era.[4] This essay explores the development of women as a mill labor force in Georgia, a key industrializing southern state in the antebellum period. It takes its cue from those scholars of nineteenth-century southern women's history, most especially Victoria Bynum and LeeAnn Whites, who have insisted on exploring the critical connections between the presumably private world of the home and family and the public world of politics and commerce.[5] In doing so, the essay highlights the interplay between seemingly straightforward economic concerns, perceptions about racial realities, uses of gender ideals, and new constructions of working-class identity that worked together to make paid female labor socially and politically palatable in the Old South.

Women from all walks of life had always toiled in the South prior to the advent of female factory work. Indeed, the vast majority of southern women, white and black, slave and free, worked the livelong day, just not in a factory in front of mechanized looms for wages. Wives, daughters, widows, and spinsters managed the household, hen house, and vegetable and herb gardens, ran the kitchen and the dairy, did the spinning, knitting, and making of cloth and clothes, the cleaning and laundering, and the bearing and caring for children. These same women were invariably expected to work in the fields, pick cotton, serve as midwives to the livestock and each other, break horses and drive cattle, handle the plow, build fences, protect the homestead, and in some cases, work with slaves. Their experiences were framed by arduous and never-ending duties for which they received virtually no fiscal remuneration for their efforts (and, excepting the reality of the slave economy, were reminiscent of their pre-industrial sisters in Europe and the North). Although growing evidence clearly indicates that antebellum southern women maintained an extensive system of informal trade networks and were employed in more sectors of the economy than previously appreciated, as this volume attests, much of their identity as documented in the historical record reflected their place in a patriarchal world rather than their identity as shaped by their skills, duties, and in some cases, even occupations.[6]

Slave women, whose very humanity let alone gender was ignored in the interests of augmenting property and production, failed to receive much recognition in the historical record either. Nor did most slave women secure any form of payment for their superhuman efforts, although recent research does indicate that some slave women hired out their own time, sometimes to their financial advantage, or engaged in informal economies of trade to improve the quality of their lives. Both these latter pursuits, one public, the other clandestine, were usually carried out beyond the master's purview, showing how their involvement in the developing commercial economy could give slave women a modicum of independence and choice as workers and consumers.[7]

Even the so-called southern lady was not immune to work, although often of a decidedly different nature than that of most white and black women in the South. The rewards she received were not necessarily immediately tangible and did not come in the form of wages. But the plantation mistress could revel in the symbolic power of her permanent pedestal in exchange for financial sustenance over the course of her lifetime (or at least until the Civil War), provided she generate a never-ending stream of emotional and religious succor to family, friends, and slaves, entertain her husband's business and political acquaintances, and manage the plantation household as well. All told, these were difficult and demanding duties, if not always physically exhausting or remunerative ones, and certainly required frequent removal of her proverbial white gloves.[8]

The rural world of women's work described here, that of white and black, slave and free, in the southern household during the antebellum period, has become an increasingly well documented subject. The introduction and maturation of industrialization in the antebellum South, along with the impact of the Civil War, slowly but surely brought an end to women's work as it once existed in this agricultural, slaveholding economy, yet this topic has not been a popular avenue for exploration. Southern women's transition from household to factory and market, and the shifts in social, economic, and political relations it created, has received critical attention from historians of the late nineteenth and twentieth centuries, however. These scholars have examined how once privileged women "got by" without paternal protectors and slave laborers. They have begun to analyze how sharecropping and tenant-farming women were confounded by the exigencies of their late-nineteenth- and early-twentieth-century rural lives, which forced them into new kinds of economic exchanges. Many of these postbellum women migrated to cities to earn less than adequate pay as domestics, store clerks, and even prostitutes, while others traveled to mill towns in search of factory work. Such experiences profoundly altered women's understanding of themselves and their place in the world.[9]

The origins of this transition, however, which stretch back into the antebellum era, have essentially gone unexamined. At first, industrialization in the South began as little more than a modest trickle of change in the early nineteenth century. At that time, new industrialists in the South were faced with a dilemma in a region ripe for industrialization. Who would work in the mills? Slaves were needed in the fields, and most white men considered wage work beneath them. The only remaining workforce was that of white women and children, who were perceived to be a readily available, cheap, and malleable source of labor. As Bess Beatty has argued in her work on antebellum industrialization in the North Carolina piedmont, textile mills were so new to the region that mill owners' ideas about who should labor in them and how that labor should be managed proved surprisingly flexible.[10] In this sense, industrialists were quite willing to forego gendered and racialized notions about who should and should not do manual labor in southern society in order to make their machines run and turn a handy profit from the fruits of their labor.

Although reliance on female labor in the fledgling textile industry involved relatively few numbers of women at the outset, especially when compared to the postbellum period, the movement of these women into the paid workforce and the rationales employed to explain this unique development in the region laid the groundwork for women's well-known participation in the southern textile industry after the Civil War (and through most of the twentieth century before most such jobs moved overseas). Mill advocates, largely using gender as explanation, over time carefully constructed the ideological and political frameworks for justifying textile workers' historically poor pay, indifferent treatment, and often dangerous working conditions.[11]

While industrialization's beginnings in the North grew out of a regional agrarian economy in the throes of a commercial revolution, its beginnings in the

South were firmly rooted in a more traditional agrarian economy dependent on slave labor and a trans-Atlantic market.[12] Originating with experiments in textile production at Pawtucket, Rhode Island, followed by the establishment of the Lowell Mills in Massachusetts, northern entrepreneurs, speculators, and politicians quickly came to embrace the textile industry as the key tool with which to break Britain's stronghold on the American economy. Domestic production of cloth and other manufactures meant the U.S. government could erect tariffs against importation and encourage a new measure of economic self-sufficiency nationwide. The Embargo Act and the War of 1812, which forced Americans to resort to home production rather than import manufactured goods from Europe, only served to hasten the industrial revolution's initial impact on New England, the mid-Atlantic and the Midwest; the South was not so eager by contrast. Although women laborers were important in easing the transition to a market economy, including those famous farmers' daughters who made up the first working class in the textile mills of Lowell, the diversifying economy quickly came to rely on male free labor as much and in some cases far more than female free labor.[13]

As the market revolution's industrial manifestations began to take more permanent shape, men of means in the South grew increasingly disenchanted with the results. The advent of the cotton gin and the successful cultivation of short-staple cotton across the extensive southern piedmont—which stretched south from Virginia to Georgia and soon swung west across the up-country of the newer Gulf states—promised quick and impressive profits as long as planters could be assured competitive prices from both European and American buyers. The threat of tariffs augured badly for southerners, who feared that northern manufacturers would be able to buy their formerly lucrative crops at bargain-basement prices by forcing Europeans out of the picture. The rhetorical and legal battles that ensued because of these regional fears profoundly affected the national political discourse that led to secession and civil war. But long before these debates crescendoed into a terrible struggle between brothers, some southern speculators, entrepreneurs, and politicians considered fighting fire with fire. Why not, they pondered, build their own textile mills, thereby thwarting their northern competitors and securing increased economic independence for the region? This consideration led to the tentative beginnings of industrialization in the South and the first substantial movement of southern women into the paid workforce.

In many respects, Georgia led the way in this transformation. Although the state boasted a low-country population of wealthy planters, merchants, and plentiful slaves, the state's real growth and development were occurring in the up-country by the early nineteenth century. A burgeoning population of free whites and black slaves along with plenty of good land secured at Native Americans' expense proved the right recipe for economic expansion. As they migrated westward, farmers became planters and nonslaveholders became slaveholders, and many established thriving plantations and bustling market towns in their wake. In just ten years, from 1810 to 1820, the state's population (341,000) had increased by more than a third. By 1860, the population had more than tripled to over a million inhabitants, three out of five of whom were white.[14]

In Georgia, migration westward created strong demand for internal improvements in communication and transportation as early as the 1820s. Piedmont planters could not get their valuable cotton crop to market without adequate roads, river transport, and, eventually, railroads. Private banks mushroomed across the up-country to finance these ventures; regulated by the state and buoyed by the booming cotton economy, these banks proved surprisingly stable throughout the antebellum era.[15] Entrepreneurs eager to establish textile mills believed the energetic state of Georgia's economy and the increasing regional divisiveness between North and South in the political arena meant the time seemed ideal for introducing manufacturing. Although early investors had hoped to tie Georgia's future to New England's spectacular start by building two textile mills in the heart of the piedmont in 1810, their efforts proved premature. Unfortunately, the conclusion of the War of 1812 and the subsequent lifting of the embargo flooded the countryside with cheap imported cloth and forced them out of business.[16]

The textile movement that transformed Georgia into the Empire State on the eve of the Civil War took hold two decades later with the opening of two factories in reaction to the Tariff of 1828. Within ten years, fourteen more mills had sprung into operation. These factories claimed total capital investments of more than half a million dollars and employed roughly 800 people. By 1851, the state boasted forty mills and by some reports more than 2,000 operatives.[17]

Although scholars have long argued that industrialization lagged in the South, whether due to overinvestment of planter capital in land and slaves or the tenacity of the agrarian ideal, much evidence indicates that industrial development, despite its slow start, was very much on the ascendancy by the 1850s, only to be profoundly disrupted in the post–Civil War era. The cotton industry was a significant factor in this antebellum growth.[18] The expansion of the cotton mill industry was fueled for a variety of reasons. Many civic-minded up-country Georgians believed that the advent of the railroad would enhance the local economy and therefore hastened to ensure its passage through their community. Unfortunately, because the iron horse sped cotton almost directly to the sea, virtually bypassing much of the youthful urban piedmont altogether, it did not always leave new economic opportunities in its wake, despite initial expectations to the contrary. Because the railroad carried manufactured goods from the Northeast deep into the interior of the state for the first time, it actually damaged many local businesses and commercial ventures already in place since they could not compete with these cheaper imports. Town boosters argued that the establishment of textile mills would offset this damage because local manufacturers could use the railroad to ship their newly manufactured local goods across the piedmont. Some boosters even claimed up-country mills would substantially benefit area farmers who could become local suppliers of meat, vegetables, and dairy produce.[19] Thus the construction of new mills ultimately brought renewed hope for the economic viability of piedmont towns—a hope never fully realized until the late nineteenth century.[20]

The impetus for mills grew out of another set of concerns as well. State and local leaders quickly recognized that migration had not stopped at the Chattahoochee River, the state's westernmost border, but had spilled over into the newest plantation lands of Florida, Alabama, and Mississippi in the 1820s and 1830s. In fact, Carolina and Georgia families traveling west were such a common sight that one disgruntled Augusta resident simply referred to them as "the movers."[21] Georgia boosters recognized it would only be a matter of time before the rich cotton lands of Louisiana, Texas, and Arkansas siphoned off yet another generation of "movers" as well. The rapid drop in cotton prices in the 1820s followed by the constant stream of families westward convinced many politicians that industrialization offered an attractive alternative to the plantation economy and might help retain those Georgians who might otherwise look for better opportunities in the new Gulf states.[22]

If measured by the spread of factories, the efforts of state and town leaders to generate industry proved quite successful. By 1850, the state led the way in manufacturing profits and output below the Mason-Dixon line. The up-country towns of Macon, Columbus, and Milledgeville had become manufacturing centers. The up-country city of Augusta alone, which had recently resorted to canal building to ensure adequate water power and encourage more manufactures, had become home to nearly a dozen textile factories, and now sported the beguiling title "The Lowell of the South." During the decade that followed, increasing numbers of new textile plants spread even deeper into the Georgia hinterland. Powered by steam, these mills allowed owners to boast more spindles and higher production rates, and earned Georgia monikers such as "The New England of the South" and "The Empire State."[23]

Although the textile industry was brand-new in the 1830s and 1840s, and local mill owners unsure who in fact constituted the ideal laborer, white women and children quickly became the majority workforce. Census records indicate that by 1850 textile factories employed 873 male and 1,399 female hands (or a 2:3 male to female ratio). By 1860, they employed 1,131 male and 1,682 female hands (the 2:3 ratio of male to female hands remained unchanged). Moreover, many of those male hands were not adults.[24] A Milledgeville reporter offered a detailed description of labor specialization and some hints about its gendered and youthful nature based on his observations of the Eagle Textile Factory in Columbus in 1860. The mill, which employed approximately 250 hands, stood four stories high. Six hands, sex unspecified, operated machines in a picking room in the basement. On the first floor, twenty hands, "mostly boys," operated the carding machines. On the second floor, "70 girls, two overseers, and a few small boys" operated 136 looms, each of which could produce thirty to forty yards of cloth a day. On the third floor, seventy children, sex unspecified, operated thirty spinning frames and 5,000 cotton spindles, as well as rope, cotton yard, and sewing thread machines. On the fourth floor, twenty hands, sex unspecified, worked 140 woolen spindles, warping mills, frames, and beaming engines. The occupations of the remaining employees were not detailed.[25] Adult female laborers received an average of $10 a month in wages, and adult male laborers received an average of $20 a month at the profitable Eagle Mill, a clear indication why owners preferred female over male labor.[26] These unequal wages were not unusual. The Columbus Factory, for example, employed eighty operatives, "chiefly girls," paying them $10 to $12 per month, while men earned substantially more.[27] In 1850, women millworkers' average wage across the state was $7.39, while men earned an average of $14.57.[28] Children earned ten cents a day in the Richmond Factory in the 1840s. By 1859, children were earning $1.00 to $2.00 a week, and women from $3.00 to $5.00 in the nearby Augusta Factory.[29]

Mill owners also preferred women and children as laborers in Athens, a college town and market center in the upper piedmont serving Georgia and Carolina farmers alike.[30] Four textile mills operated within seven miles of the town and were able to take advantage of new transportation opportunities with the arrival of the railroad in 1844. By the late 1840s, the Athens Manufacturing Company, the Princeton Manufacturing Company, the Mars Hill Factory, and the Georgia Factory produced a total of 4,400 yards of cloth a day. Their wares were sold in New York, Philadelphia, North and South Carolina, Tennessee, Georgia, Alabama, and New Orleans.[31] Together these mills employed over 200 operatives; every indication suggests that the majority of them were women. The Athens Manufacturing Company alone, the largest and most profitable of the four mills, employed eighty-five operatives, who were explicitly described by the owners as "mostly female."[32]

Information about these women and their families is sparse, but close analysis of the manuscript returns of the U.S. Census for Clarke County in 1860 suggests theirs was a complicated existence. Ninety-two women were identified as factory workers (an indication of the difficulties enumerators faced in including all residents, since it is all but certain that the number of female operatives was higher). Of these ninety-two, the oldest was forty-five and the youngest eleven. The average age of Clarke County female factory workers in the 1860 census was twenty-one. Over three-quarters (77 percent) of the women were native-born Georgians. The remaining 23 percent came from surrounding states, mostly South Carolina (19 percent), and a handful (4 percent) from Alabama, Tennessee, and North Carolina.[33]

The population schedules show that factory work was a family affair. Eighty-six percent of all female factory workers were joined in the mills by at least one other family member. In some of these households, male heads listed their occupations as farmers, while one or more family members worked in the factory. Yet farming was no longer a productive pursuit in a mature plantation economy like that surrounding Athens, where the high cost of land and slaves, along with taxes, and the ups and downs of the cotton market had hurt all but the wealthiest of planters. Yeomen families, in rough straits, needed additional income to make ends meet. As industrialist Henry Merrell observed, rural families in the Georgia piedmont sent their daughters to the new mills to help their families eke out a rather meager subsistence.[34]

The occupational identity of "farmer" undoubtedly allowed male household heads to save face, for many such "farm" families living in the factory district at the edge of town along the river listed no property in the census returns and hence could not have been truly farmers any longer. For example, N. Aumy, twenty-four, lived with her father, mother, and three brothers in the factory district alongside the Oconee. Her father and oldest brother listed their occupations as farmers but owned no land. They may have hired themselves out as agricultural day laborers to make ends meet but clung to the "farmer" nomenclature despite their reduced circumstances. Another factory worker, Mary Bentley, sixteen, lived alone with her father in the factory district; he, too, claimed to be a farmer, however unlikely. The four Smith daughters, Louisa, Malinda, Mary, and Cornelia, ages sixteen to twenty-nine, lived with their father, also a so-called farmer, and a female boarder who worked in the factory with them. Male household heads who claimed to be farmers despite their lack of land probably had moved their families to the mill district only recently, having been unable to turn a profit on their crops and steer clear of debt in the turbulent agricultural economy of the late 1850s. This family migration pattern from farm to mill town is significant, for it precedes the more well known migration of rural farm families to mill towns in the 1890s and 1900s. In this sense, late-antebellum migration seems to have set an important social precedent for postbellum developments.[35]

In other male-headed households with millworking daughters, fathers often engaged in artisan occupations such as harness making, brick making, iron molding, and carpentry. In one instance, the father of the Hayes sisters—Becky, fifteen, Eliza, seventeen, and Cynthia, nineteen, all factory workers—was a schoolteacher (and was probably employed by one of the mills to educate their workers in evening classes, a not-infrequent practice at this time). Susan Saunders, twenty-two, worked in the factory with two of her seven siblings, while her father worked as a factory guard. With the exception of Mr. Saunders and Mr. Hayes, however, each of whose factory work was highly specialized, none of the fathers of daughters who worked in the factory were factory employees themselves.[36]

Herein lay the crux of the matter for many families. Men were reluctant to give up the independence that life on the farm or life as an artisan represented. As one critic stated about the impact of the textile industry, the arrival of the mills and the new economic order it represented undermined men's power and autonomy. "Labor-saving machines . . . employ more women and children . . . and with them must go a spirited and manly brother, husband, or father to cringe beneath the power of capital."[37] To perform wage work for capitalists was emasculating in a southern culture where men's social and political status was rooted in their independence—a legacy of Jeffersonian republicanism.

If antebellum men believed their identity was at stake if they succumbed to millwork, it helps explain why over half of the households (58 percent) containing female factory workers were headed by women. What is equally interesting in these female-headed households is how infrequently the female heads worked in the mills. Sarah and Eliza Giles, adult daughters of Mrs. Giles, worked in the factory, while their mother claimed the occupation of "house business."

Anne and Martha Brazzleton, eighteen and sixteen, respectively, worked in the mills while their younger sister and their mother, the latter listing her occupation as "housework," apparently stayed home. It is certainly likely that a number of female household heads could not work in the factory because they had young children; factories generally would not hire any one under the age of ten. But in many instances, this was not the case; instead, adult women appeared to be choosing "house business" while their children labored in the mills.

In other instances, single women factory workers in their teens and twenties, and in a few cases thirties, either lived with siblings, some of whom were factory workers as well, and no parents, or in a very few instances boarded with local families. The Pinterfield siblings, five daughters, ranging in age from thirteen to twenty, and one brother, eleven, lived without parents; all six children worked in the factory. Margaret and Nancy Williams lived with their three brothers, all brick masons, and no parents; in an unusual twist, their household included a male boarder named Ghee who also worked in the factory.[38]

These family structures suggest that widows and abandoned wives brought their children to these new factory towns in order to support themselves and their families—support that more often than not fell on the children rather than their mothers. It also suggests orphaned siblings looked to the mills for work. The prevalence of female-headed households corroborates the fact that Georgia industrialists, like southern industrialists in general, deliberately sought female workers and their children, as suggested by the following advertisement from the Eatonton Manufacturing Company: "White women, girls, and boys are such as will be wanted, aged ten years or upwards. Entire families may find it to their interest to engage in our service."[39]

The census records make it exceedingly apparent that the vast majority of female factory workers were young and single. Virtually all lived with family members and most in female-headed households. Without further evidence from other kinds of sources, it is dangerous to speculate further about the nature of these women's lives, except to conclude that for certain families in the piedmont, it was not unknown for young single women to work in the factory, mostly with sisters, sometimes with brothers. Their male family members were more likely to pursue agricultural and artisanal occupations than factory work; their female family members either worked in the factory, engaged in "housework," as was the case for many mothers, or employed themselves independently as milliners and seamstresses (114 Clarke County women listed their occupations as seamstresses or milliners in this same census). One final conclusion can be drawn from these records. Few of these households listed real estate holdings, and very few claimed personal property of any value, indicating that for most theirs was a marginal existence. Millwork attracted poor whites.[40]

The fact that in many of these families men continued to seek independent work outside the mills and mothers stayed in the home suggests the broader power of southern culture to determine proper social roles for men and women regardless of class. These cultural dictates allowed poor men to retain their masculinity and independence and poor married women to retain their femininity and "ladyhood" despite their reduced circumstances. It would seem that these gendered expectations were such critical markers of social respect and status in the Old South that men and women were willing to forego earning wages, since they intimated weakness, vulnerability, and perhaps even unseemliness, and to have their empty purses filled by their children rather than themselves. Poor single women's identities, however, seem to have been more malleable and hence single women's lives viewed as more expendable.

Unlike the mill girls of Lowell, who lived without their families in boardinghouses and had some control over their social lives and wages, the young women in Athens who worked in the mills lived with their families. While this situation offered them some measure of support and protection, it also signaled family reliance on their wages and real limitations on their personal freedom. Given the financial woes these families faced, it seems unlikely that these women could secure much autonomy despite their role as a breadwinner, adding yet another significant contrast to female textile workers' experiences in the antebellum North, or even in the North Carolina piedmont. At the same time, the situation also has implications for understanding the connections between the antebellum and postbellum South. Historians have stressed that in the late-nineteenth- and early-twentieth-century southern textile industry, employers justified paying male hands relatively low wages because working women and children were contributing to the household economy as well. The origins of this family wage system, however, seem more likely to have been forged in the antebellum period when adult males avoided engagement in factory work and factory owners explicitly sought the cheaper labor of women and children.[41]

While the evidence indicates that adult men and adult women skirted wage work in mills despite their straitened circumstances, sending their daughters to work in the mills in their stead—highlighting a significant degree of agency among parents in poor households, as well as their authority over their children—another interpretation remains equally plausible and even complementary. There is little question that mill owners preferred hiring white women and children over white males and slaves because they represented the cheapest labor source available. Cultural expectations about gender, age, and wage work, which compelled many white adults to avoid the factory, despite bad times, may in fact have aided industrialists in their search for bargain-basement laborers. Thus, familial roles and expectations worked in tandem with new economic developments to relegate white women, especially single white women, to subordinate status. As Bess Beatty has effectively argued in this volume, individual women millworkers did find ways to resist that subordination, but that resistance occurred at the intersection of southern family culture and economic change, and as a product of racialized and gendered beliefs.

By the 1840s, promoters of industry in Georgia and across the South argued rather vociferously that factory work saved poor whites from destitution. Preferring to overlook the economic exigencies that compelled industrialists to seek out white labor, factory owners insisted upon the benefits of factory employment for Georgia's growing class of landless white families. The industrialists also stressed their own unique role as benefactors in this situation. In the wake of the panic of 1837, the depressions in the 1840s, and the spread of the plantation economy, with its skyrocketing land and slave prices in the 1850s, leaders throughout the South expressed concern about the dangers of a burgeoning population of poor whites. Industrialists told worried citizens that more manufactories were the best solution. Stated Hezekiah Niles, editor of the *Niles' Weekly Register*, "We have regarded every cotton mill established in the South as a *machine* for the conversion of many to favor the domestic industry of the country—by seeing the good effects of such mills . . . in affording employment to the labouring poor."[42] Throughout Georgia, industrialists contended that employing poor whites prevented their impoverishment and ruin. In a sense, some state and regional leaders were coming to recognize that Jeffersonian republicanism was no longer applicable when growing numbers of whites were destitute. The power of a racialized herrenvolk sensibility that had bound whites together across significant class differences for so long in the South no longer proved operable when poorer whites lacked even the vestiges of independence—a decent crop and arable land.

"[With] the factories built," wrote a Georgia editorialist in 1847, "there is at once an increased demand for labor, which will give profitable employment to hundreds and thousands of our own citizens who are now struggling for a meager subsistence by the cultivation of an almost barren soil."[43] The editor of the Columbus *Enquirer* celebrated the success of the Columbus mills that same year. "We love to contemplate the present improvement and future prosperity of our beautiful city. . . . Manufactories give employment and good wages, to a large number of the industrious women and children of the country, and add immensely to the independence and self-reliance of the people; hence we rejoice to see them sprung up in our midst."[44] Another writer urged planters to invest their capital not in land and slaves "but in the more profitable as well as more philanthropic business of manufacturing."[45]

Yet the actual use of textile mills as the solution to these growing numbers of impoverished whites had not been a foregone conclusion. Since the inception of the textile industry, politicians and promoters alike had debated whether to rely on white or black labor. In 1827, the Georgia legislature entertained a memorial to investigate the merits of supporting textile manufactures and, in particular, to evaluate "the practicability" of using slave labor in the mills.[46] J. S. Buckingham, a little more than a decade later, noted that three mills in Athens employed slave laborers alongside white laborers. One mill owned its own slave hands, while the other two hired their unfree workers from local planters on a monthly basis. Buckingham observed that slave laborers were as capable as free laborers of handling the looms and spindles but proved more expensive. Mill owners paid their hands, both free and slave, $7.00 per month, but they had to feed their slave laborers in addition to giving their owners their wages, making hired slaves too costly.[47]

Not surprisingly, as more and more mills established largely white labor forces, mill owners publicly intimated that all-white labor forces prevented poor white peoples' collusion with slaves. Although racism was certainly endemic in this society and the color line represented significant social hierarchies that some whites were loath to cross, blacks and whites had always worked together in a number of settings, whether on small farms, in artisans' shops, or on the waterfront, and the possibilities for challenging the power and authority of the planter class had always concerned many elites.[48] Blacks and whites could also work together in factories. Buckingham had found black and white factory hands working harmoniously in the Athens Manufacturing Company, the only Athens factory to own its slave hands. "There is no difficulty among them on account of Color, the white girls working in the same room and at the same loom with black girls; and boys of each color, as well as men and women, working together without repugnance or objection," he reported. Few textile companies could afford to own slaves despite Buckingham's findings, however. More telling than the biracial workforce and these harmonious relations was the decision of the Athens Manufacturing Company to sell its handful of slaves in 1843. Although the reason for the sale is not explicit in the records, times were tight in the wake of the 1842 panic. Owning slaves had required an initial outlay of cash to purchase them; it had also necessitated payment for ongoing expenses incurred in providing room, board, clothes, shoes, and health care. Selling these slaves not only eliminated those expenses but brought the company new capital at a rough time for the industry.[49]

The Athens mills notwithstanding, the Georgia textile industry as a whole relied far more on white than slave labor. Certainly a number of industry boosters penned editorials on the suitability of slave labor in Georgia manufactories, but these arguments did not sway general practice.[50] More frequently, newspapers of the period were filled with invective detailing how black competition with free labor undermined white men's independence, arguments that industrialists used to explain their preference for white labor. Of course, the reality was far simpler. In the Georgia piedmont, where these mills predominated, white women and children were cheaper to employ, more readily available, and more tractable than white men, who were reluctant to engage in factory work and were presumed more likely to protest and perhaps even strike like their northern brethren. Moreover, white women and children were cheaper than slaves, who were more expensive overall, tied to the agricultural calendar, and ultimately controlled by their owners if industrialists elected to hire rather than own slaves outright.[51]

The textile industry in Georgia was a difficult one in many respects. It lacked the extensive capital and economies of scale that made ventures in New England successful over long periods of time. Most Georgia mills manufactured similar products and competed for the same local and regional markets. About two-thirds of the goods were sold to merchants in the state; the remaining third were shipped to merchants in the Mississippi Valley, the North, and in some cases, China.[52] Moreover, the railroad had flooded cheap imports into local markets, which created added competition for homegrown goods. Frederick Law Olmsted was surprised to see the number of New England–made coarse and fine textiles sold alongside Georgia-made cotton during his trip through the state in the 1850s.[53] Many of these antebellum mills lacked adequate capital and after constructing their buildings found their enterprise stalled until they could find enough investors to allow them to buy the required machinery. Once in operation, mills had to contend with roller-coaster cotton prices and a series of panics and depressions, which often meant they could not sell enough goods to satisfy their investors. In some cases they were forced to close, in others to limp along undercapitalized, reducing the profitability of the textile industry throughout the state.[54]

The structural realities of the textile mill industry in Georgia forced owners and investors to cut corners wherever they could. Hiring the cheapest labor possible made good economic sense. Not surprisingly, although mill promoters argued to the contrary, factory wages in the Southeast in 1860 were lower than anywhere else in the nation, with the exception of Florida.[55] Textile mills in antebellum Georgia relied on a workforce of predominately white women and children because they were the cheapest available labor source.[56] Twenty years ago, Claudia Goldin and Kenneth Sokoloff showed that women and children comprised a significant portion of the antebellum manufacturing labor force in the Northeast. They also demonstrated that the wages of these laborers in-creased relative to that of men with industrial development.[57] Although women and children were the majority workforce in the manufacturing sector of the economy in the South, their wages did not rise relative to men's wages over the course of the antebellum era. Because poor white women and children had few options for alternative employment, and could not easily migrate elsewhere, they were forced to accept employers' terms.

The mill industry justified this system by stressing the value of an all-white labor force both for poor whites and, by implication, for the citizens of the state as a whole who would not be required to support them if employed.[58] These editorials skated around the fact that women and children were the bulk of their employees, however, rather than poor white men, whose growing presence was the stated cause for concern in the first place. They also ignored the hypocrisy of their rhetoric, labeling millworkers as worthy citizens and voters when in fact women and children, the bulk of these employees, were not entitled to the same privileges of citizenship as men. Although southern culture turned on the no-tion that male household heads secured citizenship and authority through their independence, and wore that badge of independence symbolically by boasting a house full of dependents (if not slaves, at least women and children), millwork profoundly altered the nature of that relationship, in some cases actually making the male household head dependent on women and children for support. Nei-ther industrialists nor politicians could adapt this altered set of social relation-ships into their larger arguments about the value of mills for the Georgia econ-omy and the laboring poor. Thus, the editor of the *Augusta Chronicle* could write in 1852 that employing white labor in factories was "for the benefit of society and the promotion of its great interests, by giving employment to the people, and affording them the facilities for rearing and educating their children, so as to fit them for the active and responsible duties of life, as citizens of this great and free Republic."[59]

Moreover, despite the rhetoric painting millwork as poor white people's panacea, gender notwithstanding, the operatives' experience appears to have been a mixed bag at best. Certainly some mill owners attempted to build a sense of community and create general goodwill by encouraging their workers to pursue their own advancement (and yet again setting precedents for structuring mill life in postbellum factory towns some decades later). The Princeton Manufacturing Company offered religious services to factory workers twice a month. It also created a library for use by its employees.[60] In nearby Graniteville, South Carolina, William Gregg, who embraced a decidedly paternalistic vision of owner-worker relations and whose opinions on wage labor are well-documented, peopled his mills with white families from the South Carolina and Georgia up-country, the majority of whom were women. He also built a school with night classes, as well as a church to encourage moral virtue among his employees.[61] The Howard Manufactory in Columbus furnished churches and schools, too.[62] The *Augusta Chronicle* boasted that all Augusta mills offered "Sunday schools and evening schools, libraries, public lectures and public journals [as] no mean advantages for developing . . . intellectual and moral faculties."[63]

However successful these sporadic efforts to create camaraderie, promote education, and encourage piety were, and however committed employers' writings appeared on these issues, few owners showed much respect for the actual workers themselves and largely ignored the gendered realities of their workforce. Henry Merrell, who supervised several textile operations, including the successful Roswell Mills, reflected about his management days. "I have worried through. I had to 'make out' . . . with hands who looked upon their employer as their natural enemy."[64] He described these employees as "banditti."[65] In an 1847 article on Georgia manufacturing for the *New York Journal of Commerce*, Merrell publicly showed his disdain for his employees, as well as his belief in the value of millwork for their rehabilitation, by stating:

> [The mills] have forced into active employment, and into something like discipline, a very unruly and unproductive class of white population, who, when idle, are, to say the least, no friends of the planter. There are now no paupers, to speak of, in any county of Georgia where a cotton factory exists. By employing the children of such, factories preserve their parents from want. It may be estimated that during the

late scarcity of food which has run through two years, the factories in
Georgia have saved the state from a poor tax which would otherwise
have exceeded all other taxes out together.[66]

For Merrell, industrialists proved philanthropists, saving the state from costly
taxes and debt relief, all for a class of people he viewed as undeserving. Frederick Law Olmsted was equally unimpressed by the textile workers he encountered in Augusta, labeling them "a motley crew." His attitude may have stemmed
from the stories he heard from local residents. A hotel manager, for example,
warned him, "If you ride past the factory . . . you will see them loafing about, and
I reckon you never saw such a meaner set of people anywhere. If they were
niggers they would not sell for five hundred dollars."[67] The manager's comparison of these white workers with slaves is telling. So is his omission of the sex
composition of the group, for it is not clear whether it is all male, all female, or
mixed. His warning to Olmsted does suggest the making of a class identity
based on a kind of resistance to their work, along with the public display of that
resistance before the community, as suggested by the phrase "loafing about."

It is exceedingly difficult to present a true profile of these working people
since it is largely their employers and an occasional traveler or local resident who
has left us with these descriptions. Moreover, a literal social distance and a hefty
measure of disdain clearly emanates from these writings, and personal ones in
particular, in sharp contrast to these observers' public writings, which were
more inclined to extol the virtues of the poor, or at the very least the potential
for their salvation through factory work. Hence Daniel de Bruce Hack, charged
by Augusta industrialist and politician William Schley with overseeing the construction and management of Schley's new textile factory on Spirit Creek outside the city, made fun of the rough "cotton crackers" who came thirty or forty
at a time to watch the installation of the new machinery. He mocked the very
language of these plain folk in letters to his Virginia friends that reported they
called the mill equipment "fixments." Of the young mill women, he stated
bluntly, "The girls are not very pretty," and in the same sentence added, "I am
very pleased with the prospects of business." His employer, Schley, did not
evince much respect for his Augusta workers either. Writing Hack in 1843 about
his visit to textile factories in Richmond, he concluded that in sharp contrast to
his idle Augusta workers, the Richmond operatives "move like lamplighters, and
you never see any two or more talking. Nor do you ever see one at a window—or
otherwise idle."[68] One can only conclude that Augusta workers, whatever their
sex, resisted their circumstances through their attitude.

Although what factory workers made of their employers and their situations is a shadowy subject at best, there are strong indications that wage work brought them as many troubles as they hoped to leave behind, and perhaps explains the bad behavior that managers and other observers complained about. J. S. Buckingham was appalled by the filthy log huts Athens factory workers resided in during the early 1840s. Locals reported that many factory workers were sickly and died prematurely. The Spirit Creek workers near Augusta dealt with successive bouts of influenza that left them weak and debilitated.[69] Even when living and working conditions did not encourage the spread of disease, operatives had to contend with the simple fact that wage work could not be guaranteed year-round. Many small factories failed within a few years, and in some cases within months, of their establishment. Many others slowed down production or stopped altogether in the summer because they either lacked the money to continue or payment for goods they had already produced remained outstanding.[70] Even the trustees of the Roswell Mill, a profitable enterprise in the 1850s, were less than sympathetic to their workers' welfare despite their success. When new state legislation required operatives' working hours be limited to from sunup to sundown, the board members voted that all Roswell employees, the majority of whom were women and children, could either work under the new laws but suffer reduced wages or work the old, longer hours for the same pay.[71]

Frederick Law Olmsted reported that Georgia factory owners had hired New England girls to run the looms but that they had left in haste after encountering sordid working conditions and rampant disrespect.[72] Millwork was a last resort for many poor white women in the piedmont, and not an opportunity for advancement. Chief Justice Henry Collier, in his bid to make textile labor respectable, stressed that factory labor did not "harden a lady's hand." The young white women (and children) who dominated the textile industry in antebellum Georgia may not have acquired calluses during their toil at the looms but little else about their experiences or circumstances was reminiscent of southern ladyhood. These factory laborers were generally poor white girls and women who helped support their families during periods of economic hardship. They were paid low wages, well below those of men, and were subject to the vagaries of the textile industry and the company that employed them. Industrialists stressed their own critical role as providers for poor white Georgians and advocates for their advancement. But the story is more complicated than that. The industry used economic concerns about labor and race, social expectations about gender, and political fears about class not only to create a new workforce that was cheap and relatively tractable but to justify it as well. Poor white families supported these developments and in many cases relied on these new working women to sustain them. Although the end of the Civil War would halt the industrialization movement in the South, it would pick up steam again. By the late nineteenth century, southern industrialists would rely once more on a predominantly white female labor force, dredging up the same sets of arguments and assumptions about gender and class employed a half century earlier to construct this working class, and in doing so, confirming the power of paternalism to prevail across time and place in the South.[73]

## NOTES

1. *Monitor* (Tuscaloosa), 25 February 1846, cited in Richard W. Griffin, "Poor White Laborers in Southern Cotton Factories, 1789–1865," *The South Carolina Historical Magazine* 61, no. 1 (January 1940): 36. On the myth of the southern lady see the now classic book by Anne Firor Scott, *The Southern Lady: From Pedestal to Politics, 1830–1930* (Chicago: University of Chicago Press, 1970).

2. J. S. Buckingham, *The Slave States of America*, vol. 2 (London: Fisher, Son and Co., 1842), 111–14.

3. James L. Skinner III, ed., *The Autobiography of Henry Merrell: Industrial Missionary to the South* (Athens: University of Georgia Press, 1991), 406.

4. Although Bess Beatty does not make this point explicitly in her essay in this volume, her review essay on the influence of women's history on the subject of gender and the southern textile industry does. All the secondary sources she cites in the review essay, however, deal exclusively with the late nineteenth and early twentieth centuries. See Bess Beatty, "Gender Relations in Southern Textiles: A Historiographical Overview," in *Race, Class, and Community in Southern Labor History*, ed. Gary M. Fink and Merl E. Reed (Tuscaloosa: University of Alabama Press, 1994), 9–16.

5. Victoria E. Bynum, *Unruly Women: The Politics of Social and Sexual Control in the Old South* (Chapel Hill: University of North Carolina Press, 1992); LeeAnn Whites, *The Civil War as a Crisis in Gender: Augusta, Georgia, 1860–1890* (Athens: University of Georgia Press, 1995).

6. For a wonderful descriptive examination of women's work in the South see Julia Cherry Spruill, *Women's Life and Work in the Southern Colonies* (Chapel Hill: University of North Carolina Press, 1938). The classic account of women's work in early modern Europe remains Joan Scott and Louise Tilley, *Women, Work, and Family* (New York: Holt, Rinehart, and Winston, 1978).

7. Jacqueline Jones, *Labor of Love, Labor of Sorrow: Black Women, Work, and the Family from Slavery to the Present* (N.Y.: Basic Books, 1985); Deborah Gray White, *Ar'n't I a Woman?: Female Slaves in the Plantation South* (New York: W. W. Norton, 1985); Betty Wood, *Women's Work, Men's Work: The Informal Slave Economies of Lowcountry Georgia, 1750–1830* (Athens: University of Georgia Press, 1995).

8. Rich descriptions of the working lives of black and white women in the plantation world can be found in Scott, *Southern Lady*; Catherine Clinton, *The Plantation Mistress: Woman's World in the Old South* (New York: Pantheon Books, 1982); Elizabeth Fox-Genovese, *Within the Plantation Household: Black and White Women of the Old South* (Chapel Hill: University of North Carolina Press, 1988); and Marli F. Wiener, *Mistresses and Slaves: Plantation Women in South Carolina, 1830–1880* (Urbana: University of Illinois Press, 1998).

9. Jacqueline Dowd Hall, James Leloudis, Robert Korstad, Mary Murphy, Lu Ann Jones, and Christopher Daly, *Like a Family: The Making of a Cotton Mill World* (Chapel Hill: University of North Carolina Press, 1987); Cathy L. McHugh, *Mill Family: The Labor System in the Southern Cotton Textile Industry, 1880–1915* (New York: Oxford University Press, 1988); Linda Jean Frankel, "Women, Paternalism, and Protest in a Southern Textile Community: Henderson, North Carolina, 1900–1960" (Ph.D. diss., 1986, Harvard University).

10. Bess Beatty, *Alamance: The Holt Family and Industrialization in a North Carolina County, 1837–1900* (Baton Rouge: Louisiana State University Press, 1999), 53–57.

11. The literature on southern labor and the textile mill industry in this latter period has been a growing one. Three important studies remain Allen Tullos, *Habits of Industry: White Culture and the Transformation of the Carolina Piedmont* (Chapel Hill: University of North Carolina Press, 1989); David L. Carlton, *Mill and Town in South Carolina, 1880–1920* (Baton Rouge: Louisiana State University Press, 1982); and Melton Alonza McLaurin, *Paternalism and Protest: Southern Cotton Mill Workers and Organized Labor, 1875–1905* (Westport, Conn.: Greenwood Publishing Corp., 1971).

12. Gavin Wright, *The Political Economy of the Cotton South: Households, Markets, and Wealth in the Nineteenth Century* (New York: W. W. Norton, 1978); Eugene D. Genovese, *The Political Economy of Slavery: Studies in the Economy and Society of the Slave South* (New York: Vintage Books, 1967).

13. Thomas Dublin, *Women at Work: The Transformation of Work and Community in Lowell, Massachusetts, 1826–1860* (New York: Columbia University Press, 1979).

14. Kenneth Coleman, ed. *A History of Georgia* (Athens: University of Georgia Press, 1977), 153, 413.

15. Coleman, *Georgia*, 153–54.

16. Ibid., 153–57.

17. Reported in "Industry and Commerce" manuscript, Georgia Writers Project, WPA, Box 57, File 7, Hargrett Library, University of Georgia, Athens, Georgia (hereafter HL).

18. On the backward nature of antebellum southern industrialization see Genovese, *Political Economy of Slavery*, and Norris W. Preyer, "Why Did Industrialization Lag in the Old South?" *Georgia Historical Quarterly* 55, no. 3 (Fall 1971): 378–96. On the developing nature of antebellum southern industrialization see Fred Bateman, James D. Foust, and Thomas J. Weiss, "Large-Scale Manufacturing in the South and West, 1850–1860," *Business History Review* 45 (1971): 1–17.

19. Editorial, *Augusta Chronicle*, 5 November 1846.

20. Michele Gillespie, *Free Labor in an Unfree World: White Artisans in Slaveholding Georgia, 1789–1860* (Athens: University of Georgia Press, 2000), ch. 3.

21. Daniel de Bruce Hack to an unnamed "Dear Friend," December 1834, in Daniel de Bruce Hack Letters, HL.

22. *Athenian* (Athens, Ga.), 24 March 1829; *Niles' Weekly Register*, 31 August 1833, 4; 4 October 1834, 65.

23. Richard W. Griffin, "The Origins of the Industrial Revolution in Georgia Cotton Textile, 1810–1865," *Georgia Historical Quarterly* 42 (1958): 361.

24. J. D. B. DeBow, comp., *Statistical View of the U.S., Being a Compendium of the Seventh Census* (Washington, D.C.: Beverly Tucker, 1854); *Manufactures of the U.S. in 1860, Compiled from the Original Returns of the Eighth Census* (Washington, D.C.: Government Printing Office, 1865).

25. *Southern Recorder* (Milledgeville, Ga.), 13 March 1860, p. 2 c. 5.

26. George White, *Historical Collections of Georgia* (New York: Pudney and Russell, 1854), 570.

27. George White, *Statistics of the State of Georgia* (Savannah: W. Thorne and Williams, 1849), 446.

28. Eleanor Miot Boatwright, *Status of Women in Georgia, 1783–1860* (Brooklyn, N.Y.: Carlson Publishing Inc., 1994), 105.

29. Ibid., citing Augusta *Evening Dispatch*, 4 March 1859.

30. Ernest C. Hynds, *Antebellum Athens and Clarke County* (Athens: University of Georgia Press, 1974), 54–55.

31. George White, *Statistics*, 182–83.

32. Ibid.

33. Manuscript returns, U.S. Census Bureau, Eighth Census, 1860, Clarke County. The census defined male operatives as those fifteen years of age and older and female operatives as sixteen and older.

34. Skinner, ed., *Henry Merrell*, 406.

35. Manuscript returns, 1860, Clarke County.

36. Ibid.

37. Editorial, *Augusta Chronicle*, 27 November 1847.

38. Manuscript returns, 1860, Clarke County.

39. *Federal Union* (Milledgeville), 3 September 1834.

40. Michael John Gagnon confirms my conclusions about Athens women millworkers in his dissertation, "Transition to an Industrial South: Athens, Georgia, 1830–1870" (Ph.D. diss., Emory University, 1999), 88–109. Gagnon's research stretches across the Civil War and reveals that many antebellum patterns regarding workers, their ages, their sex, and their household compositions held true into the New South, once again underlining the importance of antebellum cultural belief systems and economic practices in shaping southern conventions over time.

David C. Ward found similar evidence in his study of industrial workers in the Graniteville Textile Mill in South Carolina, although his intent was to delineate the nature of working-class experience in one factory town rather than explore how and why southern mill owners constructed a largely female workforce in the antebellum era. Female laborers comprised 60 percent of the workforce there; workers lived in family units, many of which were female-headed; many adult men assumed artisan jobs outside the factory; and adult women preferred housework over millwork until 1880. See David C. Ward, "Industrial Workers in the Mid-Nineteenth Century South: Family and Labor in the Graniteville (S.C.) Textile Mill, 1845–1880," *Labor History* 28, no. 3 (Summer 1987): 328–48.

41. For a discussion of the family wage system and its larger implications in this later period see the monumental Hall et al., *Like a Family*.

42. Quoted in Griffin, "Industrial Revolution in Georgia," 361.

43. *Augusta Chronicle*, 7 December 1847

44. Columbus *Enquirer*, 9 October 1847.

45. Editorial, *Augusta Chronicle*, 6 September 1845.

46. *Niles' Weekly Register*, 4 April 1825, 275, quoted in J. G. Johnson, "Notes on Manufacturing in Ante-bellum Georgia," *Georgia Historical Quarterly* 16, no. 3 (September 1932): 219, 225.

47. Ulrich B. Phillips, ed., *Plantation and Frontier*, vol. 2 of *A Documentary History of American Industrial Society*, ed. John R. Commons, Ulrich B. Phillips, Eugene A. Gilmore, Helen L. Sumner, and John B. Andrews (1910; reprint, New York: Russell and Russell, 1958), 357.

48. Timothy J. Lockley, *Lines in the Sand: Race and Class in Lowcountry Georgia, 1750–1860* (Athens: University of Georgia Press, 2001).

49. Board Meeting Resolution, 16 February 1843, Chicopee Manufacturing Company Records, Box 27, HL.

50. See, for example, *Augusta Chronicle*, 24 April 1848.

51. In *The Cotton Mill Movement in Antebellum Alabama* (New York: Arno Press, 1978), 113–73, Randall Martin Miller makes a convincing argument for the economic advisability of using slave labor owned by the mills in textile factories (as opposed to hiring slaves, which was more expensive). He also points out that social opinion discouraged slave labor, despite debates by some southern industrialists to the contrary. He would agree, however, that buying slaves for mill labor was a significant drain on factories with limited capital, which explains in part the reluctance of most Georgia manufactories to buy slave laborers.

52. Pamela Vadman Ulrich, "'Plain Goods': Textile Production in Georgia, the Carolinas and Alabama, 1880 to 1920" (Ph.D. diss., University of Oregon, 1991), 38.

53. Cited in ibid., 40.

54. Skinner, ed., *Henry Merrell*, 133.

55. Fred Bateman and Thomas Weiss, *A Deplorable Scarcity: The Failure of Industrialization in the Slave Economy* (Chapel Hill: University of North Carolina Press, 1981), 74. The annual wage of factory workers in the South Atlantic was $227 in 1860 compared to $268 in New England and $278 in the Mid-Atlantic. The average annual wage throughout the nation was $289.

56. But it is important to note that context is everything. In contrast to the textile industry in Georgia, the iron industry relied heavily on a largely all-male workforce (although women were always present in this industry as well, as Susanna Delfino argues in

this volume). When white male ironworkers struck in 1847 at the Tredegar Iron Works in Richmond, Virginia, the owner systematically replaced them with slaves because they were cheaper and more tractable. See Patricia Schecter, "Free and Slave Labor in the Old South: The Tredegar Ironworkers' Strike of 1847," *Labor History* 35, no. 2 (1994), 165–86.

57. Claudia Goldin and Kenneth Sokoloff, "Women, Children, and Industrialization in the Early Republic: Evidence from the Manufacturing Censuses," *Journal of Economic History* 42, no. 4 (December 1982): 741–74.

58. For example, see the editorial in the *Augusta Chronicle*, 22 January 1848. Also see Whites, *Civil War as a Crisis in Gender*, 43.

59. *Augusta Chronicle*, 28 January 1852.

60. George White, *Statistics*, 182.

61. Ward, "Industrial Workers," 330–33; Johnson, "Notes on Manufacturing," 228.

62. Griffin, "Industrial Revolution in Georgia," 372.

63. *Augusta Chronicle*, 9 February 1849.

64. Skinner, ed., *Henry Merrell*, 133, 170.

65. Ibid., 152

66. Ibid., 413.

67. Frederick Law Olmsted, *A Journey in the Back Country*, vol. 2 (1860; reprint, New York: G. P. Putnam's Sons, 1907), 126–27.

68. Daniel de Bruce Hack to Miss Mary Fairfax, Dunfret, Virginia, [n.d.] December 1834; Hack to Michael Cleary, Richmond Factory, 18 April 1834; Wm. Schley to Hack, Richmond, Virginia, 26 November 1843, Daniel de Bruce Hack Letters, HL.

69. William Schley to Hack, Saratoga, New York, 5 August 1846, ibid.

70. Skinner, ed., *Henry Merrell*, 411, describes these difficulties in detail. Also see *Augusta Chronicle*, 4 June 1840, on the impact of a freshet in Athens on the plight of millworkers.

71. Minutes of the Stockholders, Roswell Manufacturing Company, 30 October 1854, 44–45, DeKalb Historical Society, Decatur, Georgia.

72. Olmsted, *Journey in the Back Country*, 543.

73. The persistence of paternalism is a theme explored most recently in Edward J. Cashin and Glenn T. Eskew, eds., *Paternalism in a Southern City: Augusta, Georgia, 1790–1900* (Athens: University of Georgia Press, 2001).

*Chapter Thirteen*

. . . . . . . . . . . . . . . . . . . . . . . . . . . . . . . . . . .

# Invisible Woman:
# Female Labor in the Upper South's
# Iron and Mining Industries

. . . . . . . . . . . . . . . . . . . . . . . . . . . . . . . . . . .

SUSANNA DELFINO

Many aspects of southern white women's involvement in antebellum wage work still await investigation, but the iron and mining industries constitute an especially interesting field of inquiry on this subject, notably in the Upper South. There, these two traditional sectors of the economy experienced remarkable expansion in the antebellum era, employing thousands of people in Kentucky, Tennessee, Virginia, and North Carolina. Moreover, iron manufacturing was among the most racially integrated of all southern industries, one in which blacks and whites often worked side by side in the same capacity. Through a judicious combination of black and white, owned and hired, skilled and un-skilled, *and* male and female labor—this latter a reality frequently overlooked—iron manufacturers sought to enhance their competitiveness and profitability.

In comparison with the free labor states of the North, the American South was much more rigid in regard to social standards of acceptability of antebellum female occupations. Yet, in other important ways, not much difference seems to have existed between the two regions. This was especially true in the agricultural sector, where, owing to prevailing views about gender roles and the attendant division of labor within farming households, white women's field work, however intensely and steadily performed, was not officially acknowledged either North or South. It was considered but one of the many tasks women were to dispatch, as they constantly adapted themselves to the multiple demands of farm life.[1] In the South, however, scores of nonwhite free women were listed as "farm laborers" in the 1860 population census. This close identification of field work with slavery made white women's farm work even more invisible. In addition, much more than in the North, the general stigma attached to manual labor—which by no means meant that women abstained from performing even the most menial of jobs—further restricted the range of occupations permitted them, and hence they were often left out of official records. To confound the issue, even the customary division between white and black females is often undiscernible in both public and private sources, for the slave women's involvement in the most physically demanding industrial activities (from sugar refining, to lumbering, to brick making) was not much publicized or recorded in the antebellum South. Nor did historians pay attention to these realities until the publication of Robert S. Starobin's pathbreaking work, *Industrial Slavery in the Old South*, some thirty years ago.[2]

Understanding the nature and organization of iron production and its labor requirements in the antebellum Upper South is crucial to an appreciation of the modalities of women's participation in this branch of industry and related mining operations. Thus, this essay begins by detailing the composite and complex world of iron making, traditionally presumed to be a male preserve, and then offers a more careful and nuanced reading of available sources to highlight the surprising presence of women laborers, in all their diversity, in this unique industry.

## THE IRON INDUSTRY IN THE UPPER SOUTH

The following passage, so amazingly reminiscent of the opening lines of Rebecca Harding Davis's vivid portrait of Wheeling, an important iron-making center in late antebellum Virginia, describes the Tennessee Rolling Mills, founded in 1846 by Daniel Hillman Jr., in Lyon County, Kentucky: "The narrow, winding road . . . carried a stream of light-running buggies, rattling wagons and jolting ox carts from the outside world to the giant heart of an iron industry which flamed and roared for nearly a whole booming century. Here, with furnaces flaming and sending dense smoke boiling out of stacks into the sky, as many as 1,000 slaves and about 500 or 600 freemen refined and rolled into sheets the pig iron from a dozen of more tremendous blast furnaces scattered over the wooded hills."[3]

The numerous iron mills clustered in the counties of Lyon, Trigg, Calloway, Crittenden, and Livingston, of which the Tennessee Rolling Mills was one, were part of a larger iron-making district comprising an area around the Tennessee and Cumberland Rivers and across the Kentucky/Tennessee line, including the

Tennessee counties of Dickson, Montgomery, and Stewart, the so-called Land between the Lakes.[4] Together with Virginia, Maryland, and Missouri, Kentucky and Tennessee made up a formidable group of geographically contiguous, iron-producing slave states whose industrial achievements were more than respectable.[5]

Contrary to the traditional image of the Old South as uniformly agricultural, the region's economy was fairly diversified. More particularly, iron making was one of the oldest and more widely pursued activities in vast areas of the Upper South. The beginnings of the industry, which in the seaboard slave states dated back to the colonial age, in the trans-Appalachian regions of Tennessee and Kentucky coincided with the first settlements in the last quarter of the eighteenth century. Due to little if any change in production technology, ironworks nationwide were pretty much uniform for most of the antebellum era; the majority were located in remote areas of the interior where mineral ores, streams, and timberland were plentiful. Except for the increasingly extensive use of steam in place of water power, no appreciable advance in iron manufacturing occurred until the 1840s, when anthracite began to be used as a fuel in Pennsylvania, where it was found in abundance. This development resulted in dramatic reductions in production costs, making anthracite far more desirable than charcoal for use in iron production. However, despite the growing use of mineral coal, the general opinion that charcoal-smelted iron was of a better quality fostered a boom in traditional charcoal-using furnaces, which lasted until almost the end of the 1840s. In many parts of the South endowed with wealth in natural resources, iron manufacturers favored the use of charcoal over mineral coals, especially when considering the heavy costs entailed in plant conversion. Not that interest in technological improvement was lacking in the slave states. In fact, in 1847, Kentuckian William Kelly invented and started experimenting with a new technique—the so-called air boiling process—for making higher-quality iron (steel) at his Suwannee Iron Works, in Lyon County, Kentucky.[6]

Up until the Civil War, the typical ironworks consisted of a complex of installations and buildings. Some were solely engaged in smelting, and some included forges and a rolling mill as well. At its very heart lay the blast furnace, a stacklike brick structure that could be over forty feet high, built against an embankment or on a hillside, for it was from the top that ore, flux, and charcoal were dumped in to be turned into pig iron. At least two founders working alternate twelve-hour shifts directed its operation. Standing in front of the base of the stack, where the hearth was located, the founder checked the air blast pressure, regulated the charge of the furnace, and supervised proper removal of slag and the tapping-off of the molten metal. The latter operation was performed at each shift by a keeper, who was assisted by one or more helpers and five or six laborers. The chief filler, working under the direction of the founder and assisted by five to seven fellers—who carried or wheeled the heavy baskets of charcoal, limestone, and ore to the furnace top—determined the proper mixture of ingredients to feed into the furnace.

At each tapping, the liquid metal was allowed to flow into the sand bed on the floor of the casting house, usually a wooden shed located in front of the furnace. Here, the gutterman prepared the pig beds and the runners to receive the molten metal with the help of four or five laborers who poured the metal into the moulds previously prepared by the moulder, hauled the slag to the dump, removed the pig iron and castings, and carried them to the warehouse. The moulder was usually assisted by a couple of extra laborers, provided on the spot, to supply sand and clay for the moulds and to clean the casting house. The forge, which refined the iron into blooms or bars through the pounding action of either water- or steam-powered hammers, was another important feature of an ironworks. Its workforce, which constituted a true aristocracy among iron-workers, was composed of highly skilled technicians such as finers, knoblers, hammermen, and chafermen, each of whom worked with the help of several apprentices and manual laborers. The last stage of ironworking was rolling, a process through which, under the action of intense heat, iron was made malleable and flattened into thin sheets by passing it between rollers, to be subsequently used for a variety of purposes such as making nails, railroad tracks, and machinery parts. In this phase of ironworking, the heater, the turner, the roller, and the catcher provided the indispensable skills, supplemented by the work of a number of helpers and common laborers or, when railroad iron was produced, straighteners. Furthermore, each ironworks needed a resident pool of carpenters, wheelwrights, and blacksmiths, whose shops were scattered all around the iron-making plants proper, to do general repair work. A sawmill and a gristmill, at a little remove, were also often present, with their attendant sets of laborers. Other skilled workers—like colliers and engineers—in addition to clerks, managers, superintendents, watchmen, cooks, and house servants, completed the full-time labor force of a typical ironworks, bringing the number of its permanent employees to an average of between 75 and 130.[7]

Usually, the master's mansion overlooked the furnace and other installations and workshops. Not infrequently, the manager, clerk, and some skilled workers boarded with him. In 1850, at Peytona Furnace, in Stewart County, Tennessee, H. Milton Atkins, a manager, James Shields, a founder, James McCermit, a collier, and Robert Coleman, a clerk, boarded with Thomas Kirkman, the iron-master. Other employees were accommodated either in boardinghouses or in family dwellings erected in rows near the works. Ironworking communities often featured a school for the benefit of the workers' children. In 1860, William Shaw was the schoolteacher at Peytona Furnace; at the Cumberland Iron Works in Tennessee, William Parker was one of the two teachers listed in the population schedules. Another important facility available at most ironworks was the company store, where employees could buy goods; sometimes, as at Bear Spring Furnace (which was part of the Cumberland Iron Works industrial complex), workers exchanged metal tokens for merchandise against future wages. In the 1850s, both Peytona and Dover Furnaces, located in Stewart County, boasted a post office as well. Sometimes, a church or religious mission was present. One was reported to be at Louisa Furnace by the mid-1850s. At Cumberland Furnace, in Dickson County, a St. James Mission had existed for a long time, while at the Cumberland Iron Works a small church was erected around 1835 by the Stackers, one of the region's most prominent families of ironmasters, after Episcopal minister Dr. Muller had preached at their residence.[8]

However, the property of an ironworks was by no means confined to the plants and buildings just described. In fact, it extended over thousands and thousands of acres of woodland and mineral deposits,[9] giving rise to a unique relationship between the factory and the surrounding countryside. The labor organization for each phase of the iron-making process succeeded remarkably in integrating industry-related activities with farming cycles. The operation of typical antebellum ironworks was largely based on a contract and subcontract system of labor recruitment. Skilled workers as well as teamsters contracted with an iron-making company for a certain minimum amount of work to be done; then, they were to find their own labor supply. This system ensured not only increases in efficiency and productivity but also a measure of control over the labor force, which was largely drawn from the surrounding countryside. In certain operations demanding the labor of vast numbers of hands, such as those related to making charcoal and digging ore, and transporting these materials to the furnace, subcontract arrangements were quite common. This system of labor organization well suited the tastes and needs of the farming populations living in nearby areas, making them more willing to take up contract or part-time work to supplement their families' incomes.

Once "in blast," a furnace operated uninterruptedly, day and night, for several months, usually four to seven. But before this could occur, the long and delicate procedure of preparing charcoal had to be performed. The collection of wood increasingly became a seasonal task for farmers and their sons during the idle periods in agricultural work. Wood choppers cut the wood in four-foot lengths to make cords four feet wide, four feet high, and eight feet long. Then, coal pits (sometimes as many as fifty), which held between twenty-five and sixty cords, were built and the colliers, whose occupation was among the most highly skilled in iron making, fired them, aided by four or five helpers and a couple of part-time laborers. Charring, the process of making charcoal, which usually took eight to ten days, was a very difficult and dangerous job, requiring constant, twenty-four-hour attention. To produce the fuel necessary to run a furnace for several months as well as to dig and wash the ore and collect the limestone required the work of dozens, and sometimes hundreds, of individuals, depending on both the size of the plant and the expected length of operation. Then, teamsters, who normally had contracted to deliver a specific amount of fuel to the furnace, supervised its loading on wagons and its transport along often impassable roads.[10] After many months of operation, the furnace was cooled and, at this time, workers made general repairs and cultivated the company lands. Thus, running an ironworks involved at least twice as many laborers as those employed permanently.[11]

The profitability of the iron business ensured great fortunes to the manufacturers. Daniel Hillman estimated his cost of production at no more than $14.30 per ton, plus $2.00 for shipment to Louisville, while the price of iron ranged between $30.00 and $50.00 a ton during the last two decades of the antebellum period. The price of Kentucky and Tennessee iron was competitive with Pittsburgh's, and some was also sold there. Another measure of the profitability of iron manufacturing can be inferred from the growing value of individual ironworks over time. For example, the property of the Cumberland Iron Works, which was valued at $101,178 in 1841, was worth $504,875 by the mid-1850s. Markets that extended as far north as Louisville, St. Louis, and Cincinnati and as far south as Vicksburg and New Orleans sustained the industry as it steadily expanded. From the 1830s, Louisa Furnace entertained profitable business relations in Missouri and Illinois, too. Not surprisingly, iron manufacturers were among the highest taxpayers in the counties where they resided.[12]

LABOR IN THE IRON INDUSTRY IN THE UPPER SOUTH

If iron meant affluence to the manufacturers, it also meant labor and income for entire communities. In 1840, in Montgomery County, Tennessee, 361 heads of families were listed as engaged in manufacturing and trade, while only 198 worked in agriculture. Most certainly, many of them found employment in the iron industry.[13] No doubt Rebecca Harding Davis's description of the "masses of men, with dull, besotted faces, bent to the ground . . . skin and muscle and flesh begrimed with smoke and ashes" is appropriate here, given all those who labored at and for the ironworks, be they permanent employees, contract, or part-time hands from the neighboring countryside.[14]

Except in areas like East Tennessee, western North Carolina, and western Virginia, where, due to a very low slave population, the manufacture of iron virtually relied on a white manpower, most ironworks of the Upper South used slave labor to varying degrees, making the industry perhaps the most racially integrated in the slave states. By hiring slave labor, which was cheaper than hiring white workers, manufacturers were able to obtain a notable edge over their competitors.[15] Between 1805 and 1809 Ridwell Furnace, located near New Market, Virginia, was using a racially mixed labor force that relied in part on slave hirelings. In June 1805 the company hired two negroes "for serving as gutterman and bankerman." Six months later, the company paid "sundry negroes" for extra labor, following a common practice with hired slaves. In 1808 the company hired twenty-four negroes and contemplated hiring more. At the same time, the white workforce of about thirty people remained stable throughout the period, roughly two-thirds retaining their positions throughout the five-year span.[16] Captain Mockbee, the nephew of managers and owners of ironworks who spent his childhood at Cumberland Furnace in Dickson County, Tennessee, later recalled: "Many of the slaves were hired from their master. After Christmas each year the managers of the furnace would visit the slave owners to secure labor to work at the iron works. . . . Weekly ration was allowed each slave. . . . They would often barter part of their rations to shiftless white folks." Mockbee thus exposed the routine nature of the informal exchange economy in which, as in many other settings, both blacks and whites participated.[17]

However, to the firms that could afford it, slaveownership was even more economical. During the 1850s, the Oxford Iron Works in Virginia owned 220 slaves. Richmond's Tredegar owned over 100, and by 1860 that number had soared to some 450. Yet, the highest concentration of slaves owned either by individual ironmasters or by companies was in the Kentucky/Tennessee district of the "Land between the Lakes."[18]

While the total number of slaves—both owned and hired by the iron companies—working in the Kentucky/Tennessee district is difficult to ascertain, the reports are tantalizing. According to an 1852 source, about 2,000 slaves labored at the iron mills on the Cumberland River alone. Four years later, during the slave insurrection panic that stirred the iron district, forcing many ironworks to shut down, an Evansville, Indiana, newspaper reported: "Through what is called the Iron District, on the Cumberland and Tennessee Rivers, there are from 8,000 to 10,000 slaves employed at the iron works . . . congregated in large numbers, working in the various labors of making charcoal, digging ore, and tending the furnaces."[19]

Ambiguities in the censuses of manufactures, which recorded numbers of employees per firm without further specifying their status, color, and work arrangement with the employer, add to discrepancies between the newspaper figures and those recorded in the few extant company books to suggest an upward revision of the above estimate. The 1860 census reported, for example, that 81 employees worked at Louisa Furnace, in Montgomery County, Tennessee, whereas, according to the company account books, 281 slave workers were employed between 1854 and 1860.[20]

Neither the slave nor the manufactures schedules of the manuscript census indicates the bondmen's actual occupations. However, contrary to the belief long held by historians that slaves were rarely used in industrial activities and, when they were, only in menial jobs, a variety of sources suggest that they not infrequently acquired highly skilled trades in the iron industry.[21] Occasionally, an oral source or a newspaper obituary rescues such slave ironworkers from general anonymity. A story told by one Sherman Gentry in the late 1880s indicates, for instance, that a slave named Brunson, belonging to the Brigham family of Stewart County, Tennessee, was a woodcutter for the Peytona and Lagrange Furnaces for years. According to an obituary for Anderson Gray published in 1892 in the Stewart *Courier*, in the pre–Civil War era he had been a slave forgeman and foreman belonging to Woods, Yeatman & Company, the owners of the Cumberland Iron Works.[22]

Wills and inventories also provide detailed information about industrial slaves. In his last will and testament of 1848, for instance, Elias W. Napier, of the prominent family of iron manufacturers of Dickson County, arranged for the emancipation of about twenty of his seventy slaves, many of whom were engaged in his White Bluff, Turnbull, Mt. Aetna, and Piney forges. Among the freedmen were Amanuel, a forgeman, Tom, a wagoner, Daniel and "Ephragin [*sic*]," both teamsters, and Perry, a coaling ground hand.[23]

The labor force of an ironworks also included many whites. In Kentucky, Laura Furnace employed 130 and Center Furnace, about 200; in Missouri, the

Maramec Iron Works employed about 300. Captain Mockbee noted that at Cumberland Furnace, "There were thousands of men employed at the iron works, most of them slaves, but many white men were also given employment at remunerative wages." According to one contemporary estimate, the ironworks located on the Tennessee section of the Cumberland River alone employed a white labor force of 1,395.[24] This figure appears far too low, considering that an 1855 State Report counted as many as twenty-seven furnaces in that area, a number large enough to suggest that, at the very least, this estimate did not take into account the hundreds of local farmers, their family members, and their farm laborers who did part-time or contract work for the iron companies.

Owing to the highly articulated and flexible nature of white employment in the iron industry, accurate figures and specific occupations for workers are almost as difficult to gather as those regarding the slave labor force. Furthermore, the fact that white workers apparently often engaged in multiple occupations beyond the ones they reported to the census takers is a major obstacle in determining the nature of many people's primary jobs. For instance, William R. Edes, of Lyon County, Kentucky, was a machinist in the employ of the Kelly Company but also a licensed preacher with the Methodist Episcopal Church South. Samuel Williams, a farm owner, was also a master refiner at Union Forge in Lyon County. Gilbert Taylor Abernathy, who is said to have been the one responsible for preserving the account books of Louisa Furnace after it shut down at the outbreak of the Civil War, had been a schoolteacher, civil engineer, iron furnace operator, and large landholder who, in 1860, owned nineteen slaves.[25]

The system of recruiting contract and part-time labor from the countryside generally preserved the anonymity of many whites who performed wood chopping, coaling, ore digging, and hauling operations. Such is the case, for instance, with the Rumfelt family, known to be connected with the iron industry at Peytona Furnace. William "Nick" Rumfelt was engaged in wood chopping for the furnace throughout the 1850s. Toward the end of that decade, he was also the spokesman for his fellow wood choppers in a protest to obtain more prompt payment by their contractor, "Oldman Brown." The 1850 census reported Rumfelt as a family-dependent teenager, and the one for 1860 listed him as the unemployed offspring of Ely, a farmer.[26]

Many people hired in the industry led an "invisible" existence as factory workers. The census, in fact, generally describes them as "day laborers." Rufus and Uriah Pulley, who worked at the Cumberland Iron Works, and the three households of the Parrots were all listed as "day laborers" living a few dwellings away from that of iron manufacturer Henry Hollister, who was the owner of Ashland Furnace and Byron Forge.[27] Rural populations not only depended on the factory for their incomes; they also relied on the company store for supplies on credit, thus increasing their dependency. Rejoicing at the closing of a furnace, one Kentuckian commented: "A god Send for the People it has Ben Runing for the years past on Orders to its Store for goods." Nevertheless, he was happy to hear that a "furnace Some Ten miles from here I see has advertise for two hundred chopers [*sic*] . . . this will help that Class that Lives by woork [*sic*] at Such places." However, evidence would suggest that the farming population derived substantial benefits from such work relations, both in pecuniary terms and in advancement of status. Again in Stewart County, Jefferson Gentry, a native Tennessean who was listed as a farmer in 1850, became a furnace manager ten years later. In the same span of time, both William Boyd, the son of a local farmer, and Allen Townsend had became "coaling ground managers," a highly remunerative position.[28]

## WOMEN IN THE IRON INDUSTRY

Such sketchy documentation of males (whether white or black, slave or free) involved in activities related to iron making makes it understandable how female labor has been even more "invisible," although women must have played a significant role in this industry as well. Their relative absence in the historical record is no surprise given the existence of a strong cultural bias against documenting their contributions, which were widespread during the latter part of the antebellum period and which, strikingly enough, made American women officially "absent" even from engagement in the economic pursuit par excellence of the majority of antebellum families: agriculture. Far from being an absolute novelty, however, this reality stemmed from an ongoing process of "ideological separation of non-market-based labor from 'productive' labor" that, as early as 1792, had made political economist Tench Coxe conclude that women played no part in rural economic life.[29]

The mid-nineteenth century redefinition of income-earning occupations not only placed growing stress on the man's role as family breadwinner but also defined the canons of female "respectability" and "appropriateness" in relation to her involvement in the market economy. This redefinition, however, by no means meant that women did not perform even the most menial jobs, but simply that observers did not want or were unwilling to state for the official record that certain occupations were performed by women. This was generally not true for nonwhite women, whose engagement in farming occupations was punctually recorded by the 1860 census. But even in the South, where standards of acceptability for certain kinds of female labor ran along a subtle line of racial distinction, and where customary divisions between white and black women held up to a certain point, the involvement of slave women in demanding industrial activities went frequently unrecorded as well.[30]

For all their importance as invaluable sources of cultural rather than social history, the manuscript census schedules thus pose even greater difficulties in the reconstruction of female participation in the iron-making industry, which was traditionally considered the preserve of men. Yet figures reported by the censuses of manufactures reveal the presence of scores of women among the permanent labor force of many ironworks in the Upper South. And, in some instances, we can even glean from other sources their color and status, but their actual occupations remain largely the object of conjecture and speculation.

Conventional wisdom has never questioned that, given the physical nature of the work in and special skills required by iron-making operations, whatever services women might have performed at ironworks must have been in the capacity of house servants and cooks. Of course, many women did work in these capacities. Moreover, such chores have usually been associated with slave or free black women. Yet, the records of Hopewell Furnace, in southern Berks County, Pennsylvania, for 1850–53 reveal four white women working as domestics alongside four free black women. In the South in general this type of job does not seem to have been confined to black women exclusively, whether slave or free. For instance, in 1860, A. D. Covey, a forty-nine-year-old white woman from North Carolina, was "house keeping at the mill," most probably the Marion Ironworks owned by J. J. H. & J. K. Walker in Hardin County, Tennessee.[31]

The large number of slave women owned by the Oxford Iron Works, in Virginia, during the 1850s (out of 117 slaves, 35 were women), however, suggests that at least some of them were employed at tasks other than domestic ones. A hint as to their possible occupations is offered by sources related to other ironworks. For instance, among some twenty of the slaves iron manufacturer Elias W. Napier emancipated was "a negro woman named Peggy late wife of Bob dec'd whose occupation at present is to caves in the Coaling."[32] Evidently, slave Peggy was not working in the kitchen at Napier's mills but at the coaling grounds, as many of her sex, color, and condition had been doing for perhaps over a century. Instances of female slaves' engagement in tasks directly related to iron making can be found as early as 1777 in Chatham County, North Carolina, when the Chatham Furnace and Bloomary Forge, which was purchased and managed by the state government during the Revolutionary War, had to resort to slave manpower to cope with the sudden absence of the white laborers previously employed at the works. In a detailed list of the bondpeople and their occupations, five women and three children are included anonymously and described simply as "some of whom to help the collier, some stay at the furnace or forge."[33]

But just as the occupations of house servant or cook were not the sole preserve of black women at ironworks, white women also appear to have performed some of the tasks that a hypocritical tradition has bequeathed to us as worthy only of slaves. Among these, the hardest and most physically demanding were indeed those connected with tending furnaces and forges. However, supposedly less-taxing jobs, like those related to the preparation and hauling of charcoal and ore, could definitely be performed by women, including the collection of wood and leaves to build and cover the coal pits and the loading of charcoal on wagons and its transportation to the furnace.[34] The quarrying of limestone and the digging of ore from surface deposits could be done by women as well. In addition, the slugs of iron had to be picked out by hand, washed in the creek, and either stored or transported to the furnace, and perhaps this operation was relegated to women as well. The recollections of the Starnes family of Washington County, in East Tennessee confirm these conjectures. Before the Civil War, the whole family worked at the iron business in the Bumpass Cove area. Mr. Starnes was a collier, a highly skilled and rewarded occupation; other relatives worked as ore diggers, forgemen, or woodcutters. According to the testimony of Ben Starnes and his sister, Mrs. McNabb, who where children during the 1850s, ore was hauled on tram bins to the mouth of a creek; there, it was washed by George Davenport and Ruth Ralston and floated down the river in boats to the furnace.[35]

Determining the precise roles white women played in the iron-making business presents many difficulties, partly because most of them worked on a task-by-task basis, a fact that prevented them from identifying themselves with a specific job and the skills required for it. Defining women's roles is further complicated by a cultural attitude shown by both census takers and employers, or paymasters, who did not consider it important to record more than the most general information concerning women's work. An example is the case of Ann Popham, who appeared on the payrolls of Pine Forge, Virginia, for the years 1808–12 but whose occupation/s cannot be ascertained. Sometimes, company records are more eloquent in this regard, as are those of Ridwell Furnace, in Virginia, which described Beverly Wharton's occupations as "hauling cord wood coaling and hauling the same."[36] As these examples suggest, women, both black and white, appear to have been employed in mostly unskilled or semiskilled occupations related to the preparation of charcoal and the collection of iron ore and limestone and their transportation to storage places, a fact that strongly contributed to their invisibility as workers.

Generally speaking, the story of women living in the vicinity of iron-making establishments is one of hard and unacknowledged toil from early childhood. Mrs. Heath, born in 1846 in Dickson County, near White Bluff Furnace and Forge, recalled: "I generally worked. I worked out in the fields when I was six or seven years old." Mrs. Mary Frances Tidwell, who was born near Cumberland Furnace, remembered: "I lived on a farm and did a little bit of everything there was to do. They let me do spinning when I was so little I couldn't reach up to turn the wheel. . . . I worked in the fields, too, as well as helping with the cooking and housework."[37] Early on, Heath and Tidwell, like the Parrot girls, who lived a few houses away from that of a prominent iron manufacturer of Stewart County, or Sallie Allen and Jane Bayard, who lived on the premises of the Cumberland Iron Works, would join the list of anonymous "day laborers" who fill pages and pages of the population schedules of the 1850 and 1860 censuses in iron-making districts. These women worked for wages in a variety of capacities and had no reason to be identified or designated as having worked in a single one.

Population schedules provide scant but meaningful evidence of female involvement in specific occupations more directly related to iron-making and the mechanical industries. In 1860, a seventeen-year-old female of French parentage, Marcellen Fulch, was listed as a wood chopper in Stewart County, Tennessee. In Washington County, Mary E. Clouse, a twenty-four-year-old native Tennessean, was reported to be a "keeper at furnace." Was this designation another way to define housekeeping on the furnace premises, or, did it really mean that she performed the work of a furnace keeper, the person who watched the fire and determined when to dump the charges? In 1860, Isabela Ferguson and Martha Smith, from Tennessee and North Carolina, respectively, appear to have been "mechanics" in Blount County, while Ellen South was enumerated as a "nail carrier" in Carter County. In Atlanta, Georgia, forty-four-year-old Nancy Spencer, from England, was listed as a machinist, while a female "pattern maker" from New Jersey and a "moulder" from Georgia (both skilled occupations in the iron industry) were found in Columbus.[38]

While these sporadic glimpses of female engagement in "manly" occupations may be less than accurate due to enumerators' frequent errors in reporting data, they perhaps acquire more weight when viewed from the perspective of the national trend of women's employment from 1850, which was investigated in the early 1900s. The *Report on the Condition of Woman and Child Wage-Earners in the United States*, published in 1910, was the product of this investigation.[39] The study found that "a large increase in the proportion of women employees has occurred since 1850 in the manufacture of metals and metal products." According to the report, by that early date women already constituted 3 percent of the labor force in that industrial branch and were mainly employed in the tinplate departments, in the polishing and finishing operations of metalworking, in the manufactory of nails and chains, as well as in the preparation of sand cores for the molds into which metal is poured. The report's findings about women's presence in the latter three occupations bring us back to our earlier conjectures about possible roles of women in the iron industry: numerous women toiled in furnaces, where sand cores were needed to receive the molten iron, and rolling mills where nails were often produced too.[40]

The report also exposed the general stigma attached to this type of female occupation and thus the widespread reluctance to publicize it. In fact, in 1867, a New York gas manufacturer, after admitting that he used female labor in brass filing, refused to give his own name, because "his male operatives would desert him were it known that a part of their work is now done by women." It is not hard to infer cost-saving considerations from the hiring decisions of this entrepreneur. Soon after the Civil War, manufacturers who were convinced that "in soldering of tubes for steam engines . . . there is a great scope for female labor" employed female machinists for filing, tending light machines, or grinding drills.[41] Many of the occupations in which women were employed immediately following the Civil War required skills that could only have developed over time, suggesting that manufacturers were tapping a pre-existing pool of women experienced in iron making and metalworking. Edith Abbott's study supports this supposition. Utilizing the *Digest of the Manufacturing Establishments in the United States*, issued in 1823 as an additional volume to the Fourth Census, Abbott found women employed in the manufacture of anchors, brass nails, molds, machinery, and many other metal items as early as 1820.[42]

Though certainly not wholly reliable, the figures provided in the *Report of the Superintendent of the Census for December 1, 1852* are at least able to set female work in the iron industry in a more detailed framework. According to this report, 147 women were employed in the production of pig iron in 1850: 9 in Pennsylvania,

14 in Virginia, 5 in North Carolina, 109 in Tennessee, and 10 in Kentucky. In the production of castings, only 1 woman was engaged in Maine and in Pennsylvania, respectively, and 7 in Connecticut, while 9 were engaged in Virginia, 2 in South Carolina, 8 in Tennessee, and 20 in Kentucky, making a total of 48. Finally, wrought-iron making involved 79 women, 7 of whom worked in Pennsylvania, 14 in North Carolina, 1 in Georgia, 55 in Tennessee, and 2 in Indiana.[43]

Another statistical elaboration of the census of manufactures, compiled by Superintendent Joseph C. G. Kennedy of the Bureau of the Census, shows somewhat higher numbers of women engaged in the iron industry: 315 compared to the 274 of the report discussed above. The higher figures involved the heaviest branch of the iron industry, pig iron production, as well as one of its most highly skilled sectors, iron rolling. Furthermore, women appear to have been employed in greater numbers in these two areas in the state of Kentucky. This data corroborates Abbott's conclusions as well as the findings of the 1910 *Report on the Condition of Woman and Child Wage-Earners* for the 1820–60 period.[44]

The official reports of the 1850s illustrate not only that employing women in the iron industry was an already established and growing practice but also that it took place in both the South and the free states. They dispel the notion that this kind of female occupation was typically southern and exclusively connected with slavery. The low numbers of women reported for the free states, where the iron industry had reached gigantic proportions, may be ascribed to the well-known incompleteness of the data compiled by the manufacturing census and, perhaps, to the "cultural" factor exposed in the *Report on the Condition of Woman and Child Wage-Earners*.

Tennessee showed the most impressive presence of women in the iron industry, but here again census figures appear utterly incomplete, for, while 166 females were listed as engaged in that branch of manufacturing in the whole state by 1850, ten years later 156 were listed for the two counties of Montgomery and Stewart alone. Even assuming that most of these women were slaves, their number makes it improbable that they performed exclusively cooking and housekeeping chores at the iron establishments, especially where the percentage of women in the workforce was quite high. At W. C. Napier's Furnace and Forge, in Dickson County, for example, women made up 23 percent of the total labor force. And, according to the 1860 manuscript census, Cumberland Iron Works employed 123 women, making up 18.5 percent of its labor force.[45] Moreover, while it seems reasonable to suppose that many of these women performed tasks strictly related to iron making, especially at rolling mills, where the ratio of male to female workers was between 3 to 1 and 4 to 1, the integrated character of the industry makes it equally hard to believe that all white women were confined only to "external" operations such as digging and washing ore, cording, coaling, and hauling. On the other hand, these activities were certainly part of a female work tradition that had mining at its core.

### WOMEN IN THE MINING INDUSTRY

Mining was another traditional industry of the Upper South. The similarity of its operations with some of those connected with iron making makes women's participation in this branch of industry worth exploring. In North Carolina, for instance, gold mining had engaged no small part of the population from the early 1800s, especially in the central piedmont and mountain counties, where it often was a supplemental activity for farmers and, in the process, allowed them to the develop specific skills. In the last two decades of the antebellum era, plummeting levels of subsistence due to an increasingly negative balance between agricultural output and population growth often led North Carolina farmers and miners to migrate periodically to areas where the mining business was brisk: Georgia, northern Alabama, and, during the 1850s, southeast Tennessee.[46] In the Tennessee counties of Marion, Polk, and Hamilton, copper, coal, and to a lesser extent lead, began to be mined in large quantities around the middle of the decade, attracting North Carolinians in large numbers. In 1860, an impressive 29.5 percent of unskilled and almost 23 percent of skilled miners came from North Carolina—second only to the number of workers coming from England and Wales.[47]

Back in North Carolina, however, smaller-scale mining concerns made family income integration possible in a fashion that did not disrupt established patterns of rural life and allowed for the participation of women and children, too. Among the faded names of the employees listed in the time book of the Ore Knob Mines, owned by the Lillards in Ashe County, North Carolina, it is possible to read that Hametta Lile received from the company $1.00 and board in July 1855, a time of the year when seasonal work dramatically increased the number of boarders at the mine site. Cain Stringer and Missouria, possibly his wife, were instead permanent employees, for their names appear throughout the two-year period covered by the time book, unlike Lile's, which appears for only a season.[48]

At Gaston County's High Shoals Gold Mine, owned by William Alexander Hoke, the scion of a well-known North Carolina family of industrialists descending from iron manufacturer Alexander Brevard, Allison Viols, probably a relative of Welcher Viols, was paid in early March 1849 for hauling one load of ore at $1.00 and one of timber at the same wage. Later in the month, Viols received more substantial sums of money: $10.45 plus $18.00 in two install-ments for work done.[49]

Coal mining was extensively practiced in East Tennessee, where, like in other parts of the Upper South, it commanded the efforts of entire families. Such was the case with the Butters, who worked for the Coal Creek Mining Company, on Poplar Creek, in Anderson County, which was owned by H. H. Wiley & Com-pany. Besides father William, who was regularly engaged in digging and hauling operations, daughter Nancy Ann performed some hauling tasks too. On 6 December 1846, for instance, she was paid $1.00 for hauling two loads of coal of fifty bushels each. Mother Martha, meanwhile, handled relations with the com-pany store. In July 1846 she exchanged corn valued at $1.50 for goods. Other families in the community were equally involved in the coal mining business, and its contributors were not necessarily adults. For example, on 14 October 1847, "Roberts boy Dick" received 2 cents "directly at the banks" for hauling some coal.[50]

Against the backdrop of a rural-industrial society in which working women were still mostly playing walk-on roles, strong, self-assertive females who were not afraid to challenge current notions of female-appropriate "place" and "con-duct" also occasionally appear in the historical record, like Susan Conner and Ellen Brady, two railroad laborers, or Mary Carr, a forty-five-year-old railroad fireman in Hamilton County, Tennessee. Such women provide contrasting im-ages of a slowly but steadily changing Southern economic reality that was in one way or another trying to come to grips with its immanent contradictions.[51]

CONCLUSION

Through a critical overview of sample sources, this essay has illustrated the impact of male-dominated language and work culture on the visibility of labor-ing women in general, and wage-earning ones in particular, in two antebellum industries in the Upper South. The iron and mining industries, long considered the domain of male workers, offer fresh perspectives on the still-limited his-tory of female labor in the antebellum South. Around the mid-nineteenth cen-tury, while the industrial transformation under way was increasingly attract-ing women into the orbit of the market economy as wage earners, and not infrequently skilled wage earners, other forces ultimately obscured their long-standing contributions to national economic development. In fact, the rise of a new culture of "separate spheres" concealed women's past roles in vast areas of the productive economy and dramatically restricted their present "visibility" to a limited range of socially accepted occupations. The above changes did not occur, however, without conflict, contradiction, and confusion. In the South, this process was also accompanied by the upheaval of long-held notions of occupational race distinctions between black and white women in areas ranging from domestic service to millwork. Yet, at the same time that gender was increasingly occupying the very center of the stage in labor relations, overwhelmingly male-bequeathed historical documentation silenced scores of women whose life and labor experiences did not conform to accepted middle-class standards. Consequently, only fragments of untold stories of female workers, who were denied a public voice, are available to us today.

NOTES

1. See, for instance, Nancy Grey Osterud, *Bonds of Community: The Lives of Farm Women in Nineteenth-Century New York* (Ithaca, N.Y.: Cornell University Press, 1991), and Stephanie McCurry, *Masters of Small Worlds: Yeoman Households, Gender Relations, and the Political Culture of the Antebellum South Carolina Low Country* (New York: Oxford University Press, 1995).

2. Robert S. Starobin, *Industrial Slavery in the Old South* (New York: Oxford University Press, 1970).

3. Reminiscences of Robert Wesley Hall, Land Between the Lakes Project (hereafter LBL), J. Milton Henry Collection, b. 7, f. 4, Tennessee State Library and Archives, Nashville, Tenn. (hereafter TSLA). See Rebecca Harding Davis, *Life in the Iron Mills; or The Korl Woman* (New York: Feminist Press, 1972). First published in *Atlantic Monthly*, April 1861, 11–12.

4. "Daniel Hillman" and "Iron Ore, Trigg County," b. 7, f. 4, LBL-TSLA; "Middle Tennessee Iron Furnaces," Jill K. Garrett Collection, b. 21, f. 3, TSLA.

5. A census report of 1852 listed the states of Maryland, Tennessee, Kentucky, and Virginia as, respectively, the third, fourth, fifth, and eighth largest pig iron producers. In the manufacture of castings, Maryland, Kentucky, and Virginia were, respectively, the sixth, seventh, and eighth largest producers, producing about the same amount of iron as New Hampshire and Illinois, and more than Michigan and Indiana. In the production of wrought iron, Virginia was the second largest after Pennsylvania; Maryland and Tennessee were fourth, with the same number of tons produced (10,000) (U.S. Bureau of the Census, *Report of the Superintendent of the Census for December 1, 1852* [Washington, D.C.: Government Printing Office, 1852], 156–58).

6. While these developments did not lead to any substantial technological transformation in American pig iron production, less dependence on timber and water power allowed northeastern iron-making plants to locate closer to urban areas, with obvious advantages in transportation costs (Paul F. Paskoff, *Industrial Evolution: Organization, Structure, and Growth of the Pennsylvania Iron Industry, 1750–1860* [Baltimore: Johns Hopkins University Press, 1983], 17–22; Peter Temin, *Iron and Steel in Nineteenth-Century America* [Cambridge, Mass.: Cambridge University Press, 1964], 20). In 1857, William Kelly contested the claim of Henry Bessemer, an Englishman, for patent rights to the converter process of making steel. The U.S. Patent Office, satisfied with the evidence presented by Kelly, awarded him the U.S. patent ("Iron Manufacture: The Discovery of Kelly Process in Iron Manufacture," "Testimonies of Kelly's employees before the U.S. Commissioner of Patents," b. 7, f. 4, LBL-TSLA).

7. The position of moulder was highly skilled and very well paid and not infrequently occupied by itinerant workers who moved from one ironworks to another. Overall, the around-the-clock operation of a furnace required the labor of about twenty skilled and semiskilled workers and at least twice as many common hands. A forge might require the work of fifteen to twenty men, depending on the number of refining fires and the types of operations involved, while a rolling mill, depending on the number of rolling machines in operation, necessitated an average of ten or more skilled and semiskilled workers, plus several manual laborers (Hurricane Iron & Mining Co., Hickman County, Tennessee, Account Book, 1840, Special Collections Library of the University of Tennessee, Knoxville [hereafter SCL-UTK]; James D. Norris, *Frontier Iron: The Maramec Iron Works* [Madison: State Historical Society of Wisconsin, 1964]; Paskoff, *Industrial Evolution*, 7–8). For the average size of ironworks, see manuscript census returns (hereafter MCR), Seventh and Eighth Censuses, 1850, 1860, Manufactures, Tennessee: Dickson, Montgomery, and Stewart Counties, microfilm edition (originals in Duke University Library, Durham, N.C.).

8. Don F. Adams, "Report on the Peytona Furnace," b. 7, f. 6; "Center Furnace," b. 7, f. 4, LBL-TSLA; Cumberland Iron Works, Papers, Small Collections, TSLA; J. Winston Coleman Jr., "Old Kentucky Iron Furnaces," *The Filson Club Historical Quarterly* 31 (1957): 227.

9. Charcoal-burning iron companies' incessant purchase of wooded lands testifies to their need to secure a steady supply of fuel. Thomas Kirkman, the owner of Peytona and Selina Furnaces, bought almost 7,000 acres from different proprietors between 1845 and 1849 (Stewart County, Deed Books, 15: 468, 527; 16: 426; 17: 320–22; 20: 290–91, TSLA).

10. Toward the end of the antebellum era, many furnaces ran uninterruptedly for nine to twelve months. The amount of charcoal necessary to run a furnace was impressive. One cord of wood produced about 33 bushels of charcoal, and at least 165 bushels were required to produce 1 ton of iron. Lagrange Furnace, in Stewart County, used 35,000 cords of wood annually (Hattie Hall Burnam, "An 18th Century Skill"; "Center Furnace"; Adams, "Report on the Peytona Furnace," all LBL-TSLA; Iris Hopkins McClain, *A History of Stewart County, Tennessee* [Columbia, Tenn.: by the author, 1965], 22; Tennessee General Assembly, Supplement to the Appendix to Senate and House Journals, 1855–56: "A Geological Reconnoissance of Tennessee" [Nashville: The State, 1856], 33–35).

11. Center Furnace, in Trigg County, Kentucky, employed some 250 to 300 individuals,

many of whom were contract laborers ("Cumberland Furnace: The First Iron Works in Middle Tennessee," b. 7, f. 4, LBL-TSLA; William L. Cook, "Furnaces and Forges," *Tennessee Historical Magazine* 9 [1925]).

12. Anthony W. Vanleer, the owner of Cumberland Furnace, was the highest taxpayer in Dickson County in the 1840s and the 1850s. During the 1850s, the Woods, the Stackers, and the Kirkmans were the highest taxpayers in the county of Stewart, while the Hillmans were reputed to be the wealthiest family in Tennessee by the time of the Civil War. See Coleman, "Old Kentucky Iron Furnaces," 255; Thomas Senior Berry, *Western Prices before 1861* (Cambridge, Mass.: Harvard University Press, 1943), 262–76; James Woods to John Bell, 4 September 1852, Polk-Yeatman Papers, TSLA; Cumberland Iron Works, Papers, Small Collections, V-K-2, f. 4, TSLA; McClain, *History of Stewart County*, 22, 26; Ursula Smith Beach, *Along the Warioto. A History of Montgomery County, Tennessee* (Clarksville, Tenn.: Clarksville Kiwanis Club and the Tennessee Historical Commission, 1964), 59; Starobin, *Industrial Slavery*, 148–67; Louisa Furnace, Account Books, vol. 1, 1831–60, Southern Historical Collection, University of North Carolina, Chapel Hill (hereafter SHC); Dickson County Records, Tax Lists, 1847–51, and Stewart County Records, Tax Lists, 1850–60, TSLA; "Cumberland Furnace, Dickson County, Tennessee," clippings, miscellaneous subjects, LBL-TSLA; and "Geological Reconnoissance of Tennessee," 37–38. Large establishments like the Cumberland Iron Works made about 8,000 tons of pig iron and other iron products in 1855.

13. As a measure of the importance of the industry in upper middle Tennessee, the Nashville *Business Directory* for 1855–56 reported at least sixty people in the state capital alone—located not far from the iron district—engaged in ironworking, among whom were moulders, finishers, machinists, pattern makers, stampers, turners, and sheet iron workers ( J. P. Campbell's *Nashville Business Directory, 1855–1856* [Nashville: Smith, Camp & Co., 1856], 13–128; Beach, *Along the Warioto*, 349).

14. Davis, *Life in the Iron Mills*, 12.

15. Starobin, *Industrial Slavery*, ch. 4. Starobin calculated that the annual cost of hired slaves was between 25 and 40 percent cheaper than that cost of free manpower.

16. Ridwell Furnace, Record Book, 1805–9, SHC. See entries for June 1805 and January 1809.

17. "Cumberland Furnace, Dickson County, Tennessee," LBL-TSLA; Cook, "Furnaces and Forges," 87; Norris, *Frontier Iron*, 40; Joseph E. Walker, "A Comparison of Negro and White Labor in a Charcoal Iron Community," *Labor History* 10, no. 3 (1969): 487–97. Both the Maramec Iron Works in Missouri and the Northampton Furnace in Maryland resorted to slave hirelings to increase their labor force.

18. "Cumberland Furnace, Dickson County, Tennessee," and "Cumberland Iron Works," LBL-TSLA; McClain, "History of Stewart County, Tennessee," Jill K. Garrett Collection, TSLA; MCR, Seventh Census, 1850, Slave Schedules, Tennessee: Stewart, Montgomery, and Dickson Counties; Starobin, *Industrial Slavery*, 14–15. The slave schedules indicate that in 1850 Ellis & Oliphant, Phillips & Welsh, and Newell & Newton—all iron firms in Montgomery County—owned, respectively, 48, 40, and 63 slaves. In Stewart

County, Cobb, Bradley & Co. owned 52 bondpeople employed at the Rough and Ready Furnace; Thomas Kirkman employed 117 between the Peytona and Selina furnaces; Maximus Stacker had used 72 at Lagrange Furnace; the Cumberland Iron Works, owned by Woods, Stacker & Co., owned 350; while the giant, Kentucky-based Tennessee Iron Works used about 1,000.

19. "Manufacture of Iron on Cumberland River," *Hunt's Merchants' Magazine and Commercial Review* 27 (1853): 644–65 (hereafter *HMM*); *Evansville [Indiana] Journal*, 6 December 1856, quoted in Charles B. Dew, "Black Ironworkers and the Slave Insurrection Panic of 1856," *Journal of Southern History* 41 (August 1975): 324.

20. Louisa Furnace, Account Books, vol. 2, 1854–60, SHC.

21. As early as 1767, the Virginia *Gazette* reported "finers, hammermen, and colliers" among slave occupations. The iron industry's growing reliance on slave labor made for bondpeople's increasing specialization in skilled positions during the following century. In the early 1850s, toward the end of his life, Montgomery Bell, a prominent Tennessee iron manufacturer, resolved to emancipate all his slaves and send them to Liberia, where, he trusted, they would survive and prosper by applying themselves to the only pursuit they knew well: iron making. The Journal of the Executive Committee of the American Colonization Society for 30 December 1853, reads: "His [Bell's] slaves have been his only workmen; they have among them miners, colliers, moulders" (Virginia *Gazette*, 6 August 1767; American Colonization Society, Journals of the Executive Committee, 30 December 1853 and 25 June 1854, Montgomery Bell Papers, b. 1, f. 8, TSLA). See also Starobin, *Industrial Slavery*; Charles B. Dew, *Ironmaker to the Confederacy* (New Haven: Yale University Press, 1960) and *Bond of Iron: Master and Slave at Buffalo Forge* (New York: W. W. Norton, 1994); and Ronald L. Lewis, *Coal, Iron, and Slaves: Industrial Slavery in Maryland and Virginia, 1715–1865* (Westport, Conn.: Greenwood Press, 1979).

22. "Sherman Gentry Story," Black History, 1886–92, b. 7, f. 1, and obituary of Anderson Gray, Stewart *Courier*, 13 May 1892, b. 6, f. 1, LBL-TSLA.

23. Dickson County, Tennessee, Records, Deed Book A, 1804–56, esp. 101–26 and 102–3, TSLA.

24. "Cumberland Furnace: The First Iron Works in Middle Tennessee," LBL-TSLA; Cook, "Furnaces and Forges"; "Center Furnace," LBL-TSLA; J. Milton Henry, *Land between the Rivers* ([Clarksville?]: Taylor Pub. Co., 1970), ch. 3; Norris, *Frontier Iron*, 39–56; "Manufacture of Iron on the Cumberland River," 644–45; "Geological Reconnoissance of Tennessee," 34–35.

25. "Testimonies of William Kelly's employees," LBL-TSLA; Louisa Furnace, Account Books, SHC.

26. There may have been other reasons behind factory workers' "invisibility." For instance, the fluctuating fortunes of individual ironworks during the decade between the two successive censuses of 1850 and 1860 might have demanded reduction of the labor force, or even temporary discontinuation of operation (Testimony of Therese Rumfelt in "Report on the Peytona Furnace," LBL-TSLA; MCR, Seventh and Eighth Censuses, 1850 and 1860, Population Schedules, Tennessee: Stewart County).

27. MCR, Seventh and Eighth Censuses, 1850, 1860, Population Schedules, Tennessee: Stewart County.

28. Robert Love to Jesse Love, 18 February 1875, LBL-TSLA; MCR, Seventh and Eighth Censuses, 1850 and 1860, Population Schedules, Tennessee: Stewart County.

29. Stanley Lebergott, "Labor Force and Employment, 1800–1960," *Output, Employment and Productivity in the United States after 1800*, Studies in Income and Wealth, vol. 30 (New York: National Bureau of Economic Research, distributed by Columbia University Press, 1966), 130; Jeanne Boydston, *Home and Work: Housework, Wages, and the Ideology of Labor in the Early Republic* (New York: Oxford University Press, 1990), 47.

30. Starobin, *Industrial Slavery*, 164–66.

31. Walker, "Comparison of Negro and White Labor"; MCR, Eighth Census, 1860, Population Schedules, Tennessee: Hardin County.

32. Dickson County, Tennessee, Records, Deed Book A, 102–3; Starobin, *Industrial Slavery*, 166.

33. James Milles to Archibald Maclaine, 25 March 1777, Chatham Furnace Papers, SHC. The reason offered by Mr. Milles, manager and superintendent of the furnace, to Maclaine, state commissioner, for this mass flight of white laborers was their need to return home to tend their own crops. However, more "political" considerations seem to have been at the root of this turnout, for, apparently, they would not work if Mr. England, one of the co-owners of the furnace, "was at the Works" (Milles to Maclaine, 31 March 1777, ibid.).

34. Charcoal weighs only twenty pounds to the bushel (Burnam, "18th Century Skill," and "Cumberland Furnace: The First Ironworks in Middle Tennessee," LBL-TSLA).

35. Embreeville history, "Embreeville," b. 3, f. 11, Boschen-Fink Papers, SCL-UTK.

36. Pine Forge, Shenandoah County, Virginia, Ledger, 1808–12, SHC; Ridwell Furnace, Record Book, SHC. For general attitudes regarding the recording of women workers' occupations see Sara Horrell and Jane Humphries, "Women's Labor Force Participation and the Transition to the Male-Breadwinner Family, 1790–1865," in *Women's Work: The English Experience, 1650–1914*, ed. Pamela Sharpe (London: Arnold, 1998), 172–79.

37. Dickson County *Herald*, 8 October 1937 and 14 April 1939, cited in Jill K. Garrett "Historical Sketches of Dickson County, Tennessee," typescript, 1971, SCL-UTK.

38. MCR, Eighth Census, 1860, Population Schedules, Tennessee: Blount, Carter, and Stewart Counties; Georgia: Fulton and Clarke Counties.

39. Charles P. Neill and Helen L. Sumner, eds., *Report on the Condition of Woman and Child Wage-Earners in the United States, in History of Women in Industry in the United States*, 19 vols. (Washington, D.C.: Government Printing Office, 1910), ix.

40. According to a letter written by H. Denison, merchant at Natchez, dated 30 October 1800, nails were extensively manufactured in Tennessee and Kentucky. See also "Early Manufactures in Tennessee and the Western Country," Tennessee Historical Society miscellaneous files, TSLA. In 1858, the Tennessee Iron Works of Kentucky had eight nail machines ("Daniel Hillman," LBL-TSLA).

41. Neill and Sumner, eds., *Report*, 222–23.

42. Edith Abbott, *Women in Industry: A Study in American Economic History* (New York: D. Appleton and Company, 1926), 68–81.

43. U.S. Bureau of the Census, *Report of the Superintendent*, 156–58.

44. Joseph C. G. Kennedy, *Abstract of the Statistics of Manufactures According to the Returns of the Seventh Census* (Washington, D.C.: Government Printing Office, 1859), 63–68. This report gave the following women's employment figures: furnaces: Georgia (29), Indiana (2), Kentucky (18), North Carolina (1), Pennsylvania (20), South Carolina (6), Tennessee (117), Virginia (14); iron forges: Georgia (1), North Carolina (18), Pennsylvania (7), Tennessee (51); foundries: Connecticut (8), Maine (1), New Jersey (4), North Carolina (9), Ohio (1), South Carolina (6), Virginia (1); and iron rolling: Kentucky (20).

45. While it is not at all clear whether iron manufacturers stated only the number of their wage-earning employees—that is, free workers—or included the slaves as well, in this calculation I have assumed that the figures related to the "hands employed" that appear in the census schedules refer to the permanent, or full-time, labor force. Napier's furnace and forge provided work for fifty men and fifteen women. The Cumberland Iron Works, for 664 men and 123 women. See U.S. Bureau of the Census, *Manufactures of the United States in 1860. Compiled from the Original Returns of the Eighth Census* (Washington, D.C.: Government Printing Office, 1865), clxxxv–xxxviii; MCR, Eighth Census, 1860, Manufactures, Tennessee: Dickson and Stewart Counties.

46. Paul Salstrom, *Appalachia's Path to Dependency: Rethinking a Region's Economic History, 1730–1940* (Lexington: University Press of Kentucky, 1994), ch. 1; Charles C. Bolton, *Poor Whites of the Antebellum South: Tenants and Laborers in Central North Carolina and Northeast Mississippi* (Durham, N.C.: Duke University Press, 1994), 1–16.

47. Susanna Delfino, *Sviluppo economico e trasformazioni sociali nel Sud degli Stati Uniti, 1790–1860* (Milan: Franco Angeli, 1987), 152–54 and 198, table.

48. Ore Knob Mine, Ashe County, North Carolina, Time Book, 1855–56, Lillard Collection, TSLA. "Missouria" or "Missoura" was a common name for females born between the 1830s and the 1850s.

49. High Shoals Gold Mine, Account Book, 1848–49, William Alexander Hoke Papers, SHC.

50. Coal Creek Mining Company, Records, 1846–49, Wiley-McAdoo Papers, McClung Historical Collection, Lawson McGhee Library, Knoxville, Tennessee.

51. MCR, Eighth Census, 1860, Population Schedules, Tennessee: Hamilton County.

# Contributors

. . . . . . . . . . . . . . . . . . . . . . . . . . . . . . . . . . . . . . . . . . .

E. SUSAN BARBER completed her Ph.D. at the University of Maryland, College Park. She teaches at the College of Notre Dame of Maryland, where she is assistant professor of history and coordinates the women's studies program. She has published several articles on social life in Confederate Richmond.

BESS BEATTY is an associate professor of history at Oregon State University. She has published *A Revolution Gone Backward: The Black Response to National Politics, 1876–1896* (1987) and *Alamance: The Holt Family and Industralization in a North Carolina County, 1837–1900* (1999). Her new project has the working title "Traveling Beyond Her Sphere: American Women Tour Europe, 1814–1914."

EMILY BINGHAM is an independent scholar in Louisville, Kentucky, where she has taught at the University of Louisville and Bellarmine College. She co-edited with Thomas A. Underwood *The Southern Agrarians and the New Deal: Essays After I'll Take My Stand* (2001). She is currently completing a book about three generations of an assimilating Jewish family in the nineteenth-century United States.

JAMES TAYLOR CARSON is the author of *Searching for the Bright Path: The Mississippi Choctaws from Prehistory to Removal* (1999) and a number of articles and essays on gender and the Mississippi Choctaws. His essay in this volume is part of an initial endeavor to explore more broadly relations between gender and production across the native South. He teaches history at Queen's University in Kingston, Ontario, Canada.

EMILY CLARK is assistant professor of history at the University of Southern Mississippi. She holds a Ph.D. in history from Tulane University and is the author of the forthcoming *Masterless Mistresses: The New Orleans Ursulines and the Development of a New World Society, 1727–1834*. Her articles have appeared in the *William and Mary Quarterly* and the *Historical Journal*.

STEPHANIE COLE is assistant professor of history at the University of Texas at Arlington. Her book, *Servants and Slaves: Domestic Service in Antebellum North / South Border Cities*, is forthcoming from the University of Illinois Press. She is currently working on a study of the construction of race in the U.S. Southwest during the Jim Crow era.

SUSANNA DELFINO teaches American history at the University of Genoa, Italy. She has written on the U.S. South, the early Southwest, and the West. Among her major publications (all titles have been translated from the Italian) are: *Yankees of the South: Economic Development and Social Transformations in the Southern States, 1790–1860* (1987), *Land and Happiness* (1990), and *Frontiers of Democracy: The American West between Myth and History* (1996).

MICHELE GILLESPIE is an associate professor of history at Wake Forest University. She is the author of *Free Labor in an Unfree World: White Artisans in Slaveholding Georgia, 1790–1860* (2000). She is currently working on a biography of Katharine Reynolds, progressive social reformer and wife of R. J. Reynolds.

SARAH HILL is an independent scholar in Atlanta who received her doctorate in American Studies from Emory University in 1991. Author of *Weaving New Worlds: Southeastern Cherokee Women and Their Basketry* (1997), she recently curated *Native Lands: Indians and Georgia*, a major exhibition at the Atlanta History Center. Her current research is on Cherokee removal and relocation.

BARBARA J. HOWE received her Ph.D. in American and English history from Temple University. She is the director of women's studies and an associate professor of history at West Virginia University, where she teaches the history of American women and writes about the history of West Virginia women. She also has been involved in numerous public programs related to West Virginia women's history and the history of women at West Virginia University.

TIMOTHY J. LOCKLEY lectures in American history at the University of Warwick, England. The author of *Lines in the Sand: Race and Class in Lowcountry Georgia, 1750–1860* (2001), he is currently engaged in a project exploring charity in the antebellum South.

STEPHANIE MCCURRY teaches history at Northwestern University in Evanston, Illinois. She is author of *Masters of Small Worlds: Yeoman Households, Gender Relations and the Political Culture of the South Carolina Low Country* (1995). She is currently writing a book on the body politic in the Civil War South.

DIANE BATTS MORROW is assistant professor of history and African American studies at the University of Georgia. She has published three other essays on her current research interest, the Oblate Sisters of Providence. Her book on the antebellum experience of this first black Roman Catholic sisterhood, *Persons of Color and Religious at the Same Time: The Oblate Sisters of Providence, 1828–1860*, is forthcoming from the University of North Carolina Press. She is continuing her research on the Oblate Sisters into the twentieth century.

PENNY L. RICHARDS is a research scholar with UCLA's Center for the Study of Women. She holds a Ph.D. in education from the University of North Carolina at Chapel Hill and did postdoctoral work in the history of special education at the University of California at Santa Barbara. Her current research interests include the history of developmental disability, nineteenth-century family caregiving, and antebellum geographic education for girls.

# Index